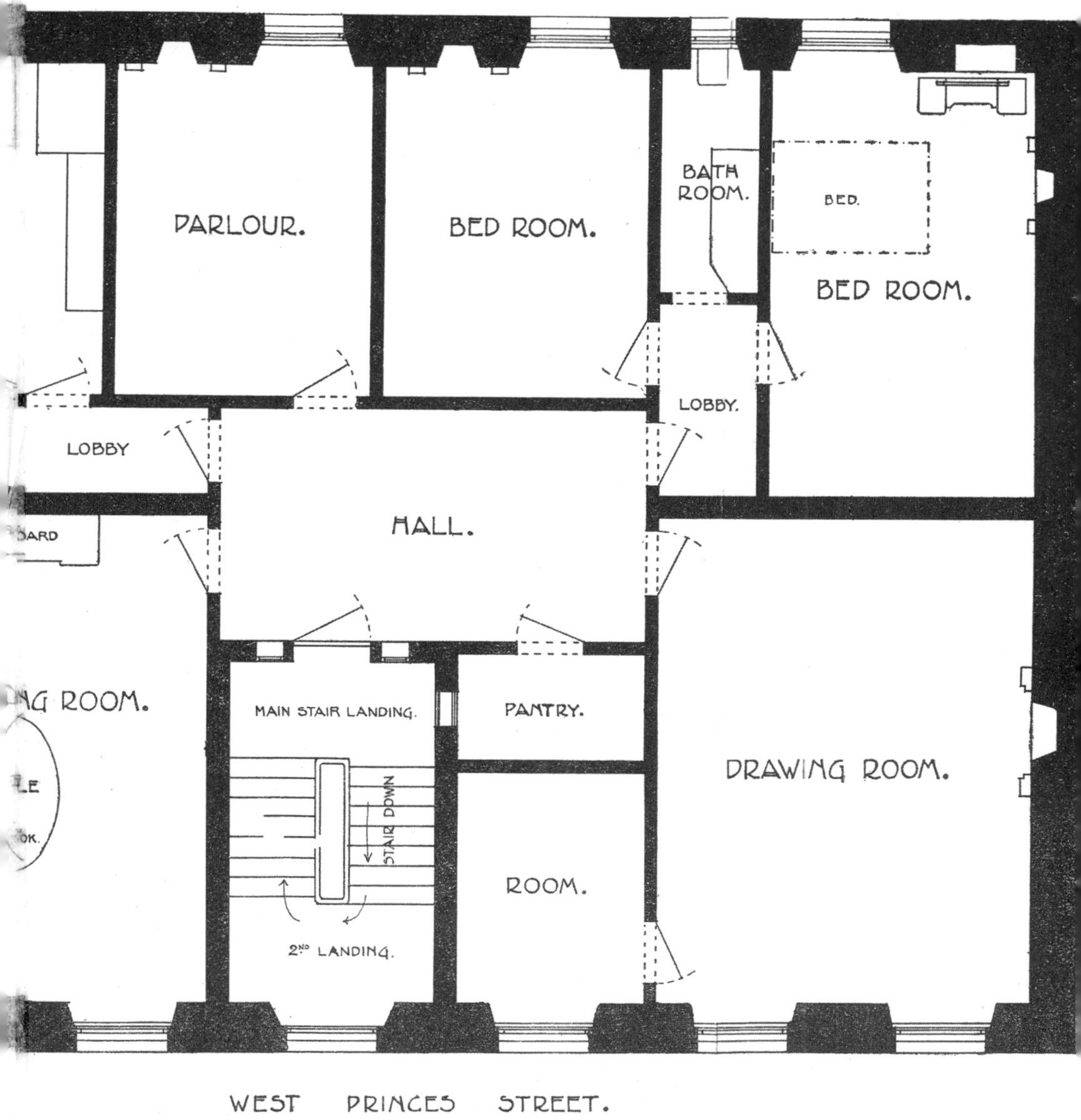

PARLOUR.

BED ROOM.

BATH ROOM.

BED.

BED ROOM.

LOBBY

LOBBY.

⌐ARD

HALL.

⌐G ROOM.

⌐LE

⌐OK.

MAIN STAIR LANDING.

PANTRY.

DRAWING ROOM.

STAIR DOWN

ROOM.

2ND LANDING.

WEST PRINCES STREET.

PLAN OF HOUSE

10 11 12 13 14 15 16 17 18 19 20   30.   FEET

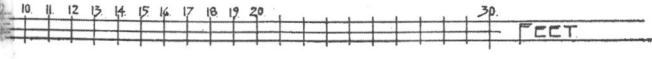

produced in Court

THE OSCAR SLATER MURDER STORY

**NEW LIGHT ON
A CLASSIC MISCARRIAGE
OF JUSTICE**

Richard Whittington-Egan

NEIL WILSON PUBLISHING• GLASGOW

For my beloved Rooney
who 'elped.

Neil Wilson Publishing Ltd
303a The Pentagon Centre
36 Washington Street
GLASGOW
G3 8AZ

Tel: 0141-221-1117
Fax: 0141-221-5363
E-mail: info@nwp.sol.co.uk
http://www.nwp.co.uk

A catalogue record for this book is available
from the British Library.

ISBN 1-897784-88-0
Typeset in Novarese
Designed by Mark Blackadder
Printed by ColourBooks Ltd, Dublin.

CONTENTS

Preface   vii
Acknowledgements   xi
Prologue: Time Machine with a Trolley   1
1   All the Days of Her Death   5
2   Nightmare on West Princes Street   21
3   Pantomime Noir   37
4   Looking for Mr. Oscar   48
5   Discovering Miss Gilchrist   61
6   The Return of the Alien   75
7   The Granite Man of Peterhead   89
8   The Libelling of Dr. Charteris   101
9   Trench Warfare   113
10 Resetting the Record   127
11 The Fourth Guardian Angel   145
12 The Order of Release   166
13 The Day of Judgment   182
14 Codicil and Coda   193
15 If Not Slater – Who?   200
16 The Ladies of Lanark   222
17 The House that Jack Built   230
18 The Secrets of Lot 631   243
19 Retrenchment   253
20 Eighty Years On   267
21 The Mystery Solved?   280
22 In the Eye of Time   299
23 Odds and Endings   313
Bibliography   320
Index   325

Other titles written by Richard Whittington-Egan:

Liverpool Colonnade
Liverpool Roundabout
Liverpool Soundings
Liverpool – This Is My City
Tales of Liverpool, Murder, Mayhem and Mystery
Liverpool Characters and Eccentrics
Liverpool Ghosts and Ghouls
Liverpool Oddities
Liverpool Log Book
The Great LIverpool Blitz
Pocket Money Guide
Churchill Centenary
The Ordeal of Philip Yale Drew
The Riddle of Birdhurst Rise
The Identity of Jack The Ripper
A Casebook on Jack The Ripper
William Roughead's Chronicles of Murder
The Quest for Jack The Ripper: A Literary History, 1888-2000

Edited by the same author:

Weekend Book of Ghosts
Weekend Second Book of Ghosts
Weekend Book of Ghosts and Horrors
Weekend Book of Ghosts and Horrors No 2
Weekend Book of Ghosts No 5

Written with Molly Whittington-Egan:

The Story of Mr George Edalji
The Bedside Book of Murder
The Murder Almanac

Written with Geoffrey Smerdon:

The Quest of the Golden Boy: The Life and Letters of Richard Le Gallienne

PREFACE

I am only too well aware that this book will raise strife and cause contention. You cannot blow away the dust of getting on for a hundred years' accepted error and prejudice without provoking argument, refutation, accusation and violent dissension. People strongly resent their well-embedded beliefs and received opinions being challenged, let alone uprooted.

Particularly emotive will be my revelations as to the newly-canonised Detective Lieutenant Trench. Strictly, the fact of his multiple dishonesties is irrelevant to the fact of his seemingly-selfless delayed action in support of what I am entirely happy to accept as his genuine belief in the blamelessness of Oscar Slater in the murder of Miss Gilchrist; but it is important because, as they say in court, it goes to show character.

Far more important, though, is the recognition that, as I am able to show here, whatever his morality, Trench got a number of crucial facts wrong. Never in any way deeply involved in the official investigation of the murder, in no sense on the inside track, he was a pretender with an inflated notion of his acquaintance with the facts. He had no right, and no apparent reason, to assume Dr Charteris' guilt as a corollary to Slater's innocence. Lieutenant Trench not only suspected the wrong man, but also attached to him a spurious motive. He was 'fitting up' Charteris, even if perhaps in a perfectly well-intentioned way. And, following Trench's martyrdom, the faithful have been continuing the good work, taking a leaf – ironically – from the book of the Mr Ure whose methods they profess to despise.

It has been something of a convention with the pro-Slaterian faction to make scapegoats of the Glasgow police, to accuse them of grasping at straws and proclaiming them sturdy evidential twigs, of railroading Slater to the execution shed. I am in no way in accord with this point of view. It is, indeed, manifestly unfair.

To take just one example. In the matter of forensic investigation the accusation has been wrongly levelled against the police that they totally neglected fingerprinting. Untrue. I put into evidence for the first time the following extract from a letter addressed, on 24 February 1909, to the Chief Constable of Glasgow by Melville L. Macnaghten of Scotland Yard, to whom specimens of Slater's fingerprints, together with the box of papers found broken open in the spare bedroom, had been despatched. Macnaghten wrote: 'The work box, which is being returned today, has been examined, but finger prints – sufficiently clear for purposes of comparison – cannot be found.'

All previous accounts of the Slater case have, quite properly as I think, accepted the innocence of the panel, but it is in the transference of the conviction of his innocence to a conviction of murder to an innocent man – Dr Francis Charteris or, perhaps, Wingate Birrell – that, I contend and facts confirm, so many writers have been in serious error. In breach of truth, too, for the authors of book after book, eschewing the burdensome business of original thought and research, of finding out things for themselves, have simply followed uncritically in the narrative footprints of their predecessors. Sadly, few have felt the need to conduct any sort of wide-ranging personal investigation.

Facts have been lost sight of and falsehoods, learned by repetition and rote, have become accepted truths. And yet, with the exception of a handful of new disclosures, some significant, some – such as the much-vaunted anonymous letters wildly and without any demonstrable evidence accusing Wingate Birrell of the murder – providing mere misleading hearsay, all of the facts have been there all of the time awaiting discovery and recognition.

Make no mistake, very considerable archival sources exist out there. In Edinburgh there are the official papers lodged at West Register House; there are birth, marriage and death certificates at New Register House; there are the papers preserved at the Crown Office; there is the very considerable William Roughead Collection in the Signet Library. There are also to be found, by those who take the trouble to look for them, certain scattered police papers and the documentings of various legal personages. There are records preserved now in Austin, Texas. There are the newspapers relating to the transatlantic life of Helen Lambie or Gillon which are to be seen in the Peoria Public Library. There was, until a few years ago, Oscar Slater's widow, Mrs Lina Leschziner, living in Glasgow. And there were still a number – admittedly steadily waning over the years – of surviving actors who had played parts in the tragedy, to be contacted and interviewed, as, indeed, I contacted and interviewed them.

There were new discoveries waiting to be made. I was fortunately able to make them. And every new fact presented here can be sourced for the sceptic.

Beyond a tendency to accept the entire blamelessness of Oscar Slater in the matter of the death of Marion Gilchrist, I came to the subject *tabula rasa*, with no preconceived notions. At one stage, later, I began to suspect Wingate Birrell of having killed his aunt, but more closely focused investigation failed to dredge up a single piece of what I felt I could regard as real evidence remotely supportive of such a conclusion.

I cannot and do not for one moment believe that Dr Francis Charteris or Archibald Hamilton Charteris, or Mrs Elizabeth Charteris, their mother, was in any way involved. These persons were all comfortably situated financially. They had no expectation of benefiting from Miss Gilchrist's will to any significant extent – if at all. Even if the motivation had been, as has been suggested *ad nauseam*, to get their hands on Miss Gilchrist's revised will, what would have been the point of that? To destroy it? Ridiculous. All that she would have retained in her possession would have been a copy of the original document, lodged, as Archibald, a solicitor, would well know, safely beyond the grasp of marauding hands with her law agent. To have a sight of the new provisions of the altered will? What practical good would that have done the Charterises? No, there is absolutely no good reason to postulate any Charteris – or Birrell – involvement.

I do offer an alternative to the somewhat curling-at-the-edges familiar familial solution, but, I emphasise, it is only a suggested possible scenario.

I lay absolutely no claim to having 'solved' the Oscar Slater mystery. What I *have* done is to find sound reasons for the exoneration of people unsoundly suspected, even accused.

Richard Whittington-Egan

ACKNOWLEDGEMENTS

I am primarily indebted to the former Lord President, Lord Emslie, for his permission to examine the Slater papers and productions lodged at the Justiciary Office in Edinburgh, and to Mr A H Hutson of that office, who made their proper display to me his especial concern.

I am grateful, too, for willing help extended to me by the Faculty of Advocates, and also by Mr George H. Ballantyne, former Librarian of the Signet Library.

The late Lord Cameron was a good friend and a continual source of inspiration to me throughout the many years of research involved in the writing of this book.

Most helpful also were Mr Craigie Aitchison, son of the late Lord Justice-Clerk, Lord Craigie Aitchison, who so ably argued, and won, Slater's case before the Court of Appeal; Mr Norman Crombie Macpherson, son of the late Norman Macpherson, of Messrs Norman Macpherson & Dunlop, SSC, Edinburgh, Slater's agents in the matter of that appeal; and Mr Colin Shaughnessy, of Shaughnessy, Quigley & McColl, the successors of Messrs. Joseph Shaughnessy & Sons, the firm of Glasgow solicitors with whom Oscar Slater's agent, the late Ewing Speirs, and subsequent to his untimely death, Alex Shaughnessy, were associated.

An especial debt of affection as well as gratitude is owed to Oscar Slater's widow, the late Mrs Lina Leschziner, who became to me not only a valued informant, but a dear and sadly missed friend.

To the late William Ratcliffe, former Assistant Chief Constable of Glasgow, my gratitude for sundry cross-illuminations in relation to the official career of the late Lieutenant John Thomson Trench.

The United States State Department kindly supplied me with full details regarding the Oscar Slater extradition proceedings of 1909.

The late Dame Jean Conan Doyle was of considerable

assistance in matters concerning her father's dealings with Slater and his manifold problems in that context.

Mrs Margaret Land – the daughter of Maggie Galbraith Ferguson's daughter, Margaret – threw a great deal of light upon the relationship between her aunt, Marion Gilchrist Ferguson, and old Miss Gilchrist.

On a less direct line, the late Jack House, when solicited, never failed to do his level best to provide help and guidelines, for which I was, and am, sincerely grateful. Mr Jonathan Goodman was, as ever, vigilant on my behalf.

Miss Irene Bell, of Edinburgh, and the late Andrew Melbourne, of Glasgow, were towers of strength, and the distinguished Scottish journalist and commentator, Mr John Linklater, proved a kind and helpful friend, most generously sharing with me important new information of his own discovering.

For many aids and favours I am in the debt of Mr David Byram-Wigfield, of Cappella Archive, Great Malvern.

Finally, there is Mr Lewis MacDonald, whose contribution has been not only enormous, but crucial. While eschewing the cliché, I must also employ it in saying, in all sincerity, that without him this book could not, certainly in its present form, have been written.

Richard Whittington-Egan

Prologue:

TIME
MACHINE
WITH A
TROLLEY

The scent of Christmas is in the air – aroma of oranges and silver-bedded tangerines, turkey and roast chestnuts; sparkle, ice-sharp, of sugar-frosted mince pies.

The short December afternoon has died early into winter darkness. Glasgow's Sauchiehall Street is vibrantly alive, a sound and fury of clash and colour.

Four shopping days to Christmas. Hogmanay looming.

Great waves of shoppers surge and eddy through gaudily hollied and tinselled stores. Jostling crowds spill into the roadway. Jingle of harness and clatter of hooves. Clang of tram-cars – 'high-built glittering galleons of the street', AE[1] called them – ablaze with light, grinding up and down, shuttling back and forth, between the front lines of prosperously embattled shops.

Lost trams of Glasgow. Dead and vanished as clumsy, rumblesome dinosaurs. Skeletal in tramway museums. Sepia photographs in chichi shops, preserved, maple-framed, for kitsch

1 George William Russell (1867-1935), Irish poet and artist.

remembrance, mounted on modish walls.

Ghost trams of Glasgow, clanking now only through the ever-thinning avenues of old folk's memories. And that is where we can still – but only just – hail them. We can stay the clock. We have a purpose – a destination.

Hold tight. Ding-ding. 'Fares, please.'

We are on a time machine with a trolley, travelling back along the fixed iron rails of time.

Back 93 years . . . until the iron rail dwindles to a slender organic thread, stretching from a limbo-lost Glasgow. It is the vanished world of Oscar Slater and Miss Marion Gilchrist; a place of tall hats, frock-coats and button boots, of beehive toques and parasols and pavement-sweeping skirts. A city of purse-proud merchants and masters, of copperplate clerks stranded on high, counting-house stools, and of nights of a thousand and one muttering, sputtering gas-lamps.

Materially, much of that old world survives. The houses wherein the once-upon-a-time joys and sorrows, splendours and miseries, set the air dancing, or sinking with heavy melancholy, still stand. But they shelter now a tenantry that knows nothing of the dreams and dramas for which their homes were once the stage.

In some respects the view from the plate-glass window of our time tram is little changed. The thin blue line of the City of Glasgow Police was drawn then. The same old war between law and disorder was – and is – being engaged.

We see our fellow-passengers, the witnesses we need to question, clamber aboard – Lieutenant Trench, Sir Arthur Conan Doyle, William Roughead, Ewing Speirs, Alex Shaughnessy, David Cook, William Park, Craigie Aitchison. Each plays out his allotted part in the grand Slater drama. We see each alight at his appointed stop, turn . . . and walk off into the great silence.

Ding-ding.

We who remain are carried inexorably on to the all-change-please terminus.

Arrived, we, too, will, in our turn, disappear from the well-worn track; but we shall have travelled on through new scenes, new vistas, denied to those who were forced to descend before us.

'Fares, please.'

Away at the upper reaches of Sauchiehall Street, by Charing Cross, with screech and groan of metal, our tram sways and curves to the right, heads down sparse-lit St George's Road. A little way along on the left-hand side, the crude yellow radiance of another passing tram brightens for one yielding moment the gloomy corners of West Princes Street.

The rude, festive spirit of the city centre seems left far behind.

Here, we are into the territory of the Edwardianly genteel. Here, Christmas will be celebrated sedately, in sober Calvinistic style, with decent Scots enjoyment; douce and decorous. Here, are dark streets of tall, well-kept, stone-built tenements, foursquare behind stout railings; clean-limbed, oblong windows, lace-curtained; the chaste frivolity of an occasional adventurous fanlight. Here, in old-fashioned thoroughfares – long rows and short terraces and gentle crescents – is respectability regimented, good taste made richly manifest.

The gleam of rain, drowned out in Sauchiehall Street by the opulence of golden light, is here reflected on empty pavement; solitary pools in the nimbuses of spaced street-lamps.

And here, in that early part of West Princes Street which is known also as Queen's Terrace, up there behind the first-floor set of blank-eyed windows, alone except for a maid-servant, Helen or Nellie Lambie, aged 21, old Miss Gilchrist has her being.

We have reached our destination.

We are in the Gilchristean presence.

This is where the Slater case begins.

For this is the rainy Edwardian evening of 21 December 1908. With an oblatory bow in the direction of the late Sacheverell Sitwell, one might, adjusting his words from another Scottish criminous context, dub it the night when blood fell on the antimacassar.

Chapter One

ALL THE DAYS OF HER DEATH

The shape of Monday, 21 December 1908, seemed no more sinister than that of any of the precedent Mondays, some 4,326 of them, in the 82-year life of Miss Marion Gilchrist. No sign, no portent of disaster arose to mar the smooth features of the showery day that lay ahead.

At 8am as the soft Glasgow rain beaded and dropleted the bedroom window of her comfortable, middle-class flat on the first floor of the solid, dark stone house on comfortable, middle-class West Princes Street, Miss Gilchrist stirred in her best quality sheeted, blanketed and eiderdowned cocoon as her maid, little Nellie Lambie, tapped on her chamber door, bearing a fine bone china cup of fragrantly steaming tea to add a refined taste of pleasure to her mistress' matutinal greeting of the new day – her 30,288th, and last, on earth.

At 82 years of age – and eleven months, to be exact – you do not tumble out of bed in any splendid frenzy to salute another dawn filched from the eternal dark: you compose and comport yourself with staid and steady gravura. Miss Gilchrist accordingly tarried abed until rising midday. Pacing herself, she attended to her toilette, dressed – slightly creakily – with her customary meticulousness, then, not forgetting the three finger rings she always liked to wear – the mourning-ring in memory of her mother, the gold ring that had belonged to her father, and her own favourite gold ring with the two diamonds, three rubies, and her name inscribed on it – selected a trinket or two for discreet embellishment, and crossed the hall, stately, to the dining-room for luncheon.

Thereafter, between half past one and two o'clock, having carefully apparelled herself in her outdoor clothes, and telling Nellie that she was going to pay a couple of small outstanding accounts, Miss Gilchrist sallied in dignity forth from her house.

Some two and a half hours later, the First-Day-of-Winter's darkness closing about her heels, Miss Gilchrist returned home. Less than three hours' measure of sand now remained in the upturned glass of her life. Time ticked her dwindling minutes sonorously away on the heavy-breathing grandfather's clock in the hall.

Shortly before the chimes of seven, Miss Gilchrist sent Nellie out to fetch her her usual copy of the Glasgow *Evening Citizen*. Actually there were some other errands also to be run. For one thing, more milk was needed. Miss Gilchrist handed Nellie a half-sovereign and a single penny. Deciding that she would go for the paper first, Nellie put the milk jug and the half-sovereign down on the dining-room table. She left her mistress sitting there in the dining-room looking at a magazine. Carefully locking the flat door and shutting the downstairs close-door behind her, clutching the penny that she had been given, Nellie trudged off through the rain. Macready's, the newsagent's at 190a St George's Road, was barely a hundred yards away. The errand would take less than ten minutes.

Let us leave Miss Gilchrist peaceably there, as Nellie left her, an old lady, cosy beside the orange glow of the sea-coal fire, spectacles on the tip of her nose, mercifully all oblivious of the import of the approaching footsteps on the stone stairs, placidly reading on the edge of eternity.

The ground-floor flat, immediately below Miss Gilchrist's, was what is described in Scotland as a 'maindoor house', that is to say it had its own private entrance – a separate front-door giving access to the street. This door, numbered both 51 West Princes Street and 14 Queen's Terrace – Queen's Terrace being the name given to a section forming the south side of the east end of West Princes Street – shared a pediment, at the top of five wide, shallow steps leading up from the pavement, with another door set on its left. This second street-door – numbered 49 West Princes Street and 15 Queen's Terrace – opened into a small passage, lobby, or (Scots) close, apart from, and running behind which, the maindoor house occupied the whole ground floor. From this close, three short flights of common stair led up to the first-floor flat, where Miss Gilchrist had lived for the past 30-odd years.

The tenants of the ground-floor flat were the seven members of the Adams family. Although her neighbours for the better part of 27 years, Miss Gilchrist's relationship with them had not progressed beyond amiable, weather-chatting acquaintance. The Adams household was virtually a matriarchy, its titular head, Mrs Rowena Sophia Adams, a venerable 76-year-old widow.

On this December evening, her 40-year-old bachelor son, Arthur Montague Adams, a professional musician, and five of his sisters – Selina Lucy Jane, Laura Emma, Adela Florence, Octavia Emily and Alice Maud – all of them music teachers, were in the house. The music of time had arranged that this tranquil and melodious ensemble were, all unknowingly, about to give ear to one of the most terrible and discordant, not to say *misterioso*, criminous passages ever played out in their city.

There was another apartment above Miss Gilchrist's on the top – third – storey. It was unoccupied. The old lady was severally reported as being unhappy about the empty flat upstairs, as it meant that there was no one other than herself in occupancy of the building: too much of an invitation to undesirable visitors. And the advent of undesirable visitors was precisely her most disturbing recurrent nightmare. Miss Gilchrist, it must be explained, suffered from a positively morbid dread of burglars, which manifested itself right down to the extreme man-under-the-bed syndrome.

To be fair, this was no idle, irrational phobia, for Miss Gilchrist nurtured a passion for precious stones and a keen appetite for gold. Over the years, she had amassed a large quantity of valuable jewellery. Her collection may have been her pride, but her joy was heavily alloyed by her continual worry about it; an eminently reasonable fear that intruders might relieve her of the £3000's worth of choice pieces, some of which it was one of her little foibles to hide away in a hanging pocket among the folds of dresses at the back of her wardrobe, and to conceal about her bed, as well as, it is said, in a number of other carefully selected secret places.

To foil these would-be robbers, whose imagined depredations were the disproportionate tax which the poor old lady paid on her harmless, jackdawish fascination with the golden and glittery, she generally kept her back windows claustrophobically tight-locked, and had the door of her apartment fitted with, in addition to a normal heavy-duty lock and chain, a stout bolt and two patent locks, one a Chubb, opened from within by two separate catches complicatedly requiring turning in opposite directions, and from without by two different keys, similarly requiring to be turned clockwise and anti-clockwise, respectively.

The close-door downstairs was usually kept shut on an ordinary check-lock, and was opened from the outside with a latch-key. It could also be opened from both of the flats above by means of a long chain attached to the latching mechanism and operated by a hand-lever – not unlike that activated by a hangman – one of which was situated, large and conspicuous, *inside* the entrance doors of both of the upstairs apartments. Bear in mind, therefore, that any caller would have to negotiate two barriers. He would ring at the street-door. If this were opened for him from aloft, he would still have to pass muster upstairs at the heavily barricaded entrance door of Miss Gilchrist's apartment. He would be likely, too, to be the subject of intermediate covert scrutiny, for it was her frequent habit, having manipulated the hand-lever to unlatch the main street-door, to creep quietly out to take a peep over the banisters to see who was coming up. And if for any reason she did not like the look of the visitor, she would dart lizard-swift back to remain incommunicado behind the vast ironmongery of locks and bolts.

The territory beyond that formidable brace of barriers was one of good, sound, middle-class comfort rather than luxury; comfort trimmed at the edges by the deckled scissors of parsimony, for of her domestic economy it was said that Miss Gilchrist was one who would share a kipper – best quality, of course – between two. The apartment door opened on to a fair-sized hall, about 18 ft long by 10 ft wide. Immediately on your left as you entered this hallway, just beyond the hand-lever for opening the close-door, was the door to the dining-room, a large room, 21 ft 6 in long by 15 ft 9 in wide, illumined by two tall windows, fitted with Venetian blinds, and looking out on to West Princes Street. Over to the right-hand side of the hall was the drawing-room, equally spacious and high-ceilinged in the best Edinburgh–Glasgow tradition. Its twin windows also overlooked West Princes Street, and a door situated on the right, down at the windows' end, led into a much smaller apartment, opening off the drawing-room. It, too, had a tall window on to West Princes Street. Both of the main rooms were in atmosphere and décor adamantly Victorian; walls hung with many oil-paintings in heavy ornate frames, furniture ponderous and well-polished, a towering folding screen to protect against ubiquitous Glasgow draughts in the cluttered drawing-room, large and ugly ornaments distributed in legions over mantelshelves and all exposed and vulnerable surfaces.

Past the dining-room door, past a narrow stretch of wall where a grandfather's clock ticked stolidly away, was another door; the last on the left-hand side. This led into what might be called the servants' quarters. It opened on to a small lobby, the furthest portion of which, partitioned off, constituted the 'bed alcove' – an institution shared by Scotland and France. Here, with its own separate door giving direct access from this stifling, windowless cubby-hole to the kitchen, the maid-servant slept. No nonsense about equality or the common humanity of slaveys and suchlike inferiors in those halcyon days.

Unlike the bed alcove, the kitchen was roomy and had a window with a pleasing enough view on to the back green. Here was the sink (jaw-box in Glaswegian parlance), the range, and the pulleys, for indoor drying of the washing.

Across on the right-hand side of the hall, exactly opposite the lobby door to the servants' quarters, was an identical lobby door leading to what may be termed the bedroom complex; for, opening off the lobby on to which it gave, were the main bedroom, a second, smaller bedroom, and the bathroom, together with, as the house-agents euphemise, the usual offices. Presumably the maid-servant was permitted to trespass into this 'western wing' for hygienic purposes, as these were seemingly unprovided for in any other discriminatory out-of-the-way corner.

Rather confusingly, Miss Gilchrist generally slept in the so-called spare bedroom. This was in fact the larger of the two rooms and was furnished with a suite of the finest figured walnut. It was here that her jewels were kept. Both bedrooms had a back-garden outlook, as did the bathroom.

The demesne was completed by two further rooms – or, rather, one and a 'roomlet'. The parlour, in which was located Miss Gilchrist's small, but sturdy and surprisingly heavy, safe – used not for the safe-keeping of jewels, but the stowing away of her private papers – also had a view over the back court. It was entered by a door situated towards the left-hand corner of the rear wall of the entrance hall – the fifth of the six doors therein. The sixth, that of a roomlet described as a pantry, was set on the right of, adjacent to, and on the same wall as, the front entrance to the apartment.

Such then, was the extent of the Gilchristean estate and messuage. Here, in this fortress-like stronghold, this carefully reinforced terrain, the timorous Miss Gilchrist felt reasonably secure, but like the pessimist – he of the belt *and* braces – she had arranged as long-stop, additional insurance in case of emergency, with the Adams family that if at any time she should require urgent assistance, she would knock three times on the floor.

Now, at a few minutes after seven o'clock on this Monday evening, the summons was to come.

Down in the Adams' dining-room, which was directly below that of Miss Gilchrist, Christmas preparations were rustling the air. Arthur

Adams was, in fact, struggling with paper and string, wrapping up a parcel of seasonable groceries for 'a young lady friend who is very delicate'. With Arthur and the innominate delicate one, was his sister, Laura, who was expecting pupils that evening, one of whom, due for a music lesson at seven, had been unable to come. Laura was standing by the fireside, flicking through the evening paper.

Suddenly, the quiet of this innocent domestic vignette was brutally shattered by a tremendous thud on the ceiling, exactly above where Laura stood.

The time was between seven o'clock and three minutes past.

'That sounds as if Miss Gilchrist has fallen,' said Laura Adams in some alarm. As she spoke, the door opened and her sister Rowena[1] came in. 'There was a very funny noise upstairs like a heavy fall,' Laura told her. 'Don't you think Arthur should go up and see?'

Before Rowena had a chance to reply, they all heard what Arthur Adams was later to describe as 'three distinct knocks on the floor'.

Laura's first thought was that Miss Gilchrist must have had a fit and fallen down. Then, remembering how they had some time previously told the old lady upstairs that if she ever wanted anything she was to knock on the floor and they would go up to her, Laura turned to her brother and said: 'Miss Gilchrist evidently wants something. You'd better go up and see.'

Adams found the close-door of No. 49 ajar. Strange, it should have been on the check-lock. He ran directly up the three flights to Miss Gilchrist's landing. He saw that the front-door of the apartment was safely closed and apparently locked. Let into the wall on either side of the big wooden door were panels of frosted glass, and through these he could see that the gas was lit in the hall. He pulled the brass knob of the door-bell. Waited. No response. He rang twice more. Still no response. He listened for any sounds inside the flat. Heard nothing.

He had been standing, poised irresolutely, ear cocked, for, he calculated, about half a minute, when an odd noise started up inside the flat. 'It seemed to me to be the sound as if it was

1 Mrs Rowena Eliza Margaret Adams or Liddell, aged 48, Arthur Adams' eldest sister, was married to George Liddell, a teacher, and resided at 63 Elmbank Street, Glasgow.

someone chopping sticks – not heavy blows.' Perplexed, he lingered on for fully a further minute, or perhaps a minute and a half, hearing the noise of stick-cracking once, or it might be twice, more. It must, he thought, be the maid chopping sticks for the morning fires. 'I formed the opinion that the girl was doing up her kitchen and that she was not going to open the door.' Pretty well satisfied in his own mind, he retreated down the stairs and, leaving the close-door ajar as he had found it, returned to his sisters. He had been absent about three minutes in all.

But during her brother's absence Laura had heard more puzzling sounds coming from above, sounds as of 'something going on'. She could not, she said, describe it. 'It might have been the moving of furniture, or of some person moving about in the dining-room.'

'I'll go up again, if you like,' offered brother Arthur. Both trepidant sisters said that they liked . . . so, immediately, up he went again.

It was about six or seven minutes after seven.

The seventh and last chime of a nearby clock was just fading on the damp air as Nellie Lambie set off through the rain and darkness to Macready's, the newsagent's. It was less than three minutes' walk away. As she reached the corner, she met a policeman whom she knew, Constable John Harrison. He was off duty, in plain clothes, and they had a little chat 'for about five minutes'. Then, across the street, she spotted P.C. William Neill, whom she also knew. She did not, however, have any conversation with him. She bought a copy of the *Evening Citizen*, pocketed the halfpenny change, and made her way straight back to No. 49. There, she found the close-door, which she had carefully shut when she went out, open, and, sharp-eyed, noticed a wet footmark on the first step of the stone stairs. On the second, there was another. She had been out for ten minutes at the most.

Arriving at the first floor, she was astonished to see Mr Adams standing outside Miss Gilchrist's door. He was never a visitor at their house.

Arthur Adams had, in fact, been standing there for only a minute or two, for this was his second visit. This time there had been no sound of any kind coming from the flat. He had given the bell a good strong pull and was just about to tug again when he heard the distinct tapping of footsteps in the close . . .then coming up the stair . . .and Nellie Lambie appeared, holding the evening paper in her hand.

Without polite preliminaries, Adams, now knowing for the first time that the old lady had been left alone in the house, greeted her immediately with his anxieties. 'There must be something wrong in your house.' No beating about the bush with him. 'Perhaps,' he suggested, 'your mistress has fallen down. There was a terrible crash on the ceiling below.' He emphasised it: 'Our ceiling was like to crack.'

But Nellie did not seem particularly perturbed. She did not think that Miss Gilchrist had fallen down. She looked at him askance, a bit old-fashioned, as they say. 'Oh, no. It must be the pulleys,' she said. She explained that the kitchen pulleys, the clothes' poles on which the washing was hung up to dry suspended from the ceiling and raised and lowered by an arrangement of ropes and wheels, had been giving trouble, and had recently fallen clattering to the kitchen floor. The rope had since been repaired, but, as a portion of it had frayed, she thought it might well have given way again.

Mr Adams heard. But, commendably cautious, characteristically conscientious, he told her: 'I'll wait and see that everything's all right.'

Nellie unlocked the door with her brace of keys. The hall lamp, a single jet caged in an open-ended cylinder of thick blue glass set within a wrought-iron frame, was lit, but not really bright, the gas being only half on. She stepped into the hall and started to walk to the lobby door leading to the kitchen. She was going to check the pulleys. Adams remained hovering uneasily at the threshold, half in, half out, one foot on the door-mat on the landing.

It was then that something very strange – totally unexpected and to this day totally unexplained – happened. From the direction of a bedroom a well-dressed man appeared. He walked calmly and coolly as if the house belonged to him. But instead of coming directly across the hall to the front-door, he kept in close to the wall until he came up to where Adams was standing. The man did not seem excited in any way, his demeanour was more that of a visitor who was thoroughly familiar with the place. It never occurred to Adams to stop him.

> I did not suspect him – and the girl Lambie said nothing. I just imagined him to be a friend of Miss Gilchrist or of the servant. A rather gentlemanly-looking fellow, he certainly did not look like a burglar. He came up to me quite pleasantly. Our eyes met. I thought he was going to speak, but he passed without a word, almost brushing clothes with me. Directly he passed me, he ran downstairs like greased lightning and banged the door at the foot of the close. I knew he was a thief then.

What exactly Lambie did immediately after opening the door of the apartment is a crucial question. Adams consistently stated that she stepped into the hall and began to walk towards the kitchen. She had been, he said, eight or ten steps – perhaps a little more – into the hall when the man appeared. She stood and stared. She turned round and looked after him – and never said a word.

Nellie, on the other hand, said in her first statement: 'I stepped into the hall and at once saw a man about the middle of the hall. He seemed coming towards the door from the direction of the spare bedroom.' In her final statement she said:

> When I opened the door I was standing on the mat. As soon as I had opened the door, I saw a man in the lobby. The man was a few paces from me in the hall, walking as if he had come out of the spare bedroom. He walked quite slowly and passed me on the mat.

The discrepancies between Adams' and Lambie's statements are important because of their bearing upon the question of how good an opportunity Lambie was afforded to see, and therefore afterwards reliably to identify, the man in the blue gaslight.

Adams went on to say that, without a word or glance in his direction, Nellie proceeded, first, into the kitchen. She found there the pulleys sound and *in situ* and called out to Adams: 'All's right!' She went next across the hall and into the spare bedroom, thinking that, as the gas in the room was alight, which it had not been when she went out, Miss Gilchrist might be in there. But the room was empty. Finally, and only after Mr Adams had shouted to her, in tone both vexed and anxious, 'Where is your mistress?', she made her way to the dining-room. She went only as far as the door of the room, expecting to see Miss Gilchrist sitting as she had left her. 'I looked about but couldn't see her in her chair.' She moved further into the room. Stood rooted . . . horrified. She saw not Miss Gilchrist, but a pair of legs and what looked like Miss Gilchrist's clothing bundled on the floor. For a second or two she could not believe her senses. She could not see the face of the alien thing huddled on the familiar dining-room hearth-rug, for, most eerily, its head, torso, and the greater part of the lower limbs were covered by a hairy skin rug, glistening with blood drops. Surely those stiff marionette legs and that crumpled heap of clothes were not her spry, imperious mistress. Lambie's mind could not comprehend this sudden indignity conferred by brutish death. She reacted in the only way she knew how. She screamed, once, piercingly, then raced out of the room, across the blue-shadowed hall to the outer door and the protective presence of the attendant and transfixed Mr Adams.

'Oh, come and see . . . my mistress . . . she's lying on the floor. There's something wrong. That man has done something to Miss Gilchrist.' It came jerking out in a sort of breathless staccato. She began to weep. Gently. Then bitterly, her thin shoulders shaking.

Adams bounded across the hall and peered into the dining-room. He saw Miss Gilchrist lying on her back, diagonally, head towards the left end of the fender, feet towards the table and the door. 'A horrible spectacle,' was how he described it. He did his best to blot out the blood, the brain tissue on mat and mantel; the horrid dark bundle humped slackly on the rug, atavistically reminiscent of the shapeless shadow bundle of nameless dreads on the nursery floor. He felt sick. He realised that unwittingly, witlessly, he had allowed Miss Gilchrist's assailant to escape. That made him feel stupid – guilty. 'I thought my best plan was to make after the man as quickly as possible. I wasn't in the house more than half a minute after the man passed me at the door and I started after him.'

Shouting a warning to the girl – 'Go to the close-mouth and stand there till I get back' – whey-faced and battling the surges and spasms of his own stomach, Adams flung himself down the stairs with such horror-spurred alacrity that 'I nearly fell down.' He found the close-door tight-shut. He feverishly pulled back the snib and ran out into West Princes Street.

He looked to the right, east, towards St George's Road, but could see no one. The empty stretch of wet road and pavement shone static as the untroubled surface of a reflectionless mirror. He looked to the left, west, towards Park Road. In the middle distance were several people. He dashed up the street like a baffled beagle, looking into Queen's Crescent on his right as he went. But of the running man there was no sign. Puffing now, Adams reached the end of the block; a matter of 140 yards. He could see no one in the least resembling the man in the blue gaslight. The Glasgow night had enfolded him. So there, at the corner of West Princes Street and West Cumberland Street,[2] the hot pursuit ended.

Meanwhile, Nellie, near to the tether's end of her nerves, had slipped over the road to the house of the doctor at No. 1 Queen's Crescent. Her friend, 19-year-old Lizzie McIntosh, was a servant there. She went to pluck at her sleeve for moral support as much as anything, but unfortunately Lizzie was not able to get away to accompany her back to No. 49. Returning forlorn, Nellie gratefully espied the figure of her beat-trudging acquaintance whom she had seen from over the street earlier that evening, Constable William Neill. She was about to rush across and pour into his startled ear the whole ghastly story of the terrible thing that had happened since they last waved cheery greetings to each other barely ten minutes before, when a breathless Adams appeared; so, instead, she and Adams together gasped out to Neill their joint tale of horror.

As Adams and Neill headed up the stair to Miss Gilchrist's flat, Nellie, whose jangling nerves and liberal adrenalin release would not let her stay still, sped off to break the news of the tragedy to Miss Gilchrist's 44-year-old spinster niece, Margaret Dawson Birrell, who lived at 19 Blythswood Drive,[3] about a quarter of a mile away. What Helen Lambie then said – or did not say – to Miss Birrell is, as we shall later see, a matter of supreme importance.

Thus at approximately 7.15pm did the law, in the modest person of
P.C. William Neill, make its official entry into the case of the wanton
and felonious killing of Marion Gilchrist.

A manifestly agitated Arthur Adams tremulously led the way
into the oppressively still dining-room. The fire crackled. The
gasolier blazed. Constable Neill crossed over to the fireplace, lifted
the rug from Miss Gilchrist's head, and was appalled. Her face had
been beaten in. There was a deep hole on the left side between the
eye socket and the left ear, the lobe of which had been completely
torn away from the cheek. The left eye-ball was entirely missing; it
had been burst and driven into the brain. The right eye was partially
torn from its socket. There was a gaping, ragged wound on the right
cheek, extending from the mouth, together with a kind of bloody
maze of red gaps and pink bone splinterings across the right
forehead and right-hand side of the head. The grey hair was darkly
matted with blood. Parts of the brain were escaping. Yet, incredibly,
and most horrible of all, the mercilessly battered Miss Gilchrist was
still alive, still faintly breathing. Neill had difficulty in accepting the
horrid tenacity of life. He saw the pathetic, barely perceptible
flutterings of breath, but a kindly censor in his mind brought the
shutter down. 'I thought she just breathed her last at that moment.'
But, just in case, 'I sent Mr. Adams for a doctor'.

Not sorry to have an excuse to flee the deathly
claustrophobia of that room, Adams went swiftly across West Princes
Street to No. 1 Queen's Crescent to summon Lizzie's employer, Dr
John Adams, a namesake but no relative.

P.C. Neill, also glad to breathe an air less fraught than that of
the Gilchrist dining-room, descended for a brief break to the close-
door, about which a crowd, somehow getting wind that something
was interestingly amiss, had begun to gather. He saw, too, a
welcome sight: marching measuredly towards him was his fellow-
constable on the West Princes Street beat, Frank Brien.

Next to arrive was Dr Adams. He examined the battered
remnants of his elderly neighbour. The last flutterings of the life
force had by now been eternally extinguished. He was careful, in the
circumstances, not to interfere with the body, but that did not
prevent him from darting a number of very shrewd glances about

the room, and making certain observations which led him to form a definite opinion as to how the injuries had been inflicted. Silently, he picked up his bag. Silently, he left the house. That he, the first medical man on the scene, was never subsequently called to give evidence, nor even precognosced, is so remarkable as to impart a most disagreeable feeling of unease.

As Dr Adams was departing, Nellie Lambie arrived back from Blythswood Drive, closely followed by Miss Margaret Birrell, and it was at this point that a second medical man made his appearance. This was Dr Robert Perry, who, now 81, had been Miss Gilchrist's doctor since 1892. One of his servants had told him that there was a crowd outside Miss Gilchrist's house and that they were saying that she had been murdered. Concerned, Dr Perry called to see if the rumour was true, was shown the body of his patient, but did not touch it.

The third medic to arrive at No. 49 was Dr John Wright, casualty surgeon to the Western District, Glasgow police. He reported: 'I found that nearly every bone in the skull was fractured . . . the head was practically smashed to a pulp.'

There was a fourth doctor who came to join the throng inside the second-storey flat at 15 Queen's Terrace that night. His name was Francis James Charteris, and he has, quite unjustifiably, been cast by posterity to play a very sinister rôle in the death of Miss Gilchrist.

Born in 1875, Francis James Charteris was the son of Dr Mathew Charteris, who was to become Professor of Materia Medica and Therapeutics at the University of Glasgow. His mother, *née* Elizabeth Greer, had in fact been previously married to Marion Gilchrist's younger brother, James. She had borne him a daughter, Mary Greer Gilchrist, before, after only five years of marriage, he had died. It was in April 1873, that his widow remarried.

Apart from his half-sister, Mary, Frank, as he was generally called, had two brothers: Archibald Hamilton, one year his senior, and John, who, born in 1877, was two years his junior.

Thus did Miss Marion Gilchrist acquire, in addition to her legitimate niece, Mary, three 'honorary' nephews.

The Charteris brothers all did well in their chosen careers – Archibald ending up as Professor of International Law at Sydney University, Frank as Professor of Materia Medica at the University of St Andrews, and John as a brigadier-general.

In 1907, Frank Charteris, who had duly qualified after studying medicine at the universities of Glasgow and Leipzig, married. His bride, 28-year-old Annie Fraser Kedie, was not only an MA, but also a rich young woman. Her father, Robert Kedie, having arrived in Glasgow from Hawick in the early 1860s, had entered the employment of Messrs Stewart & M'Donald, and risen to become a partner in that flourishing firm of warehousemen and manufacturers.

Young Dr Charteris had settled into private practice at 400 Great Western Road – only a short distance from where 'Aunt' Marion lived – where, somewhat unusually, he had a private laboratory. All available photographs of him seem to have been taken in later years, but, whatever the age, they show the austere, patrician features of the old Scottish law-giver or the old-style professor of medicine. There is no criminality in the face: it is the visage that looks down from the bench on the shivering miscreant ready to be sentenced.

These Charterises were of the upper echelons of the professional classes of Glasgow. There was, it is true, a touch of trade in the forebears, but no matter; especially as this was Glasgow and not Edinburgh.

Frank Charteris was a man of strong professional ambition, and a life of marked achievement lay ahead of him. It is typical of the moral tone of the man that he should adopt an attitude of discreet guardianship of his eccentric honorary aunt, whom he knew to be in a perilously unprotected position, but who was too stubborn to accept direct advice. That was why he pressed upon her the gift of a handy-sized watch or guard dog, an Irish terrier named Barney, to protect her person and her store of jewellery. Although he was far from being a regular caller, and she was not of the inner circle of his family, only a person who felt a real concern for his kinswoman would have bothered to select and supply the dog.

There was, to be sure, the odd social encounter. Miss Gilchrist had been invited, with her maid in attendance, to Frank Charteris' fashionable wedding, at which his uncle, the Very Reverend Archibald Hamilton Charteris, DD, LLD, former Professor of Biblical Criticism at Edinburgh University, and one of His Majesty's chaplains in Scotland, officiated.

Let there be no doubt about it: Dr Francis James Charteris was a man of duty as well as ambition.

Chapter Two

NIGHTMARE ON WEST PRINCES STREET

As the night wore on, more people, official and unofficial, started to arrive at the quiet house in usually sedate West Princes Street.

The Procurator-fiscal, James Neil Hart, bustled up the steps of No. 49 and vanished into its dark maw.

The bulky, imperial wax-mustachioed and impressive person of another arrival, Superintendent Ord, most adequately embodied the full majesty and dignity of the law. Tall, corpulent, round face, shrewd, darkly undershadowed eyes, well-groomed, glossy black hair, and exuding a sub-militaristic air of invincible authority, he looked, and was, a top-brass policeman to the tips of his pudgy fingers. Smartly tailored and crisply linened – clerical-grey suit, well-brushed and boated bowler, black tie discreetly asserted by a simple gold ring – he seemed the rubber-stamped epitome of sober, middle-class success. Actually, nothing, certainly not rank and station, had come easily to John Ord. The son of an Aberdeenshire stableman, he had only reached one of the pinnacles of his profession – Detective Chief Superintendent in charge of the whole of Glasgow's Detective Department – after a long and tortuous climb through every grade of the service.

Ord, accompanied by Detective Lieutenant William Gordon of Central District, had arrived at West Princes Street at about 8.45pm, and had been greeted at the door of No. 49 by Superintendent William Miller Douglas, Detective Inspector John Pyper and Detective Constable Duncan MacVicar, all of the Western District.

Pyper, tallish, on the spare side, usually puffing away at an outsize pipe, was made unforgettable by the fierce black beard, which lent him the aspect of an old-fashioned, fire-and-brimstone preacher. Now, with practised eye – more than 30 years since he, a crofter's son, left New Deer, Aberdeenshire, to don the blue tunic – he was astutely observing, calculating, deducing.

First, the murder room. Well furnished. Good, solid stuff. Walls hung with fine big pictures. Obviously originals. Everything of excellent quality. Money and taste. Then . . . all else receded . . . the corpse became the focus of his every strained attention. In his intensity of concentration it ceased to be the sad and broken remains of a fellow human being; it became for him, just as a cadaver does for a medical student, nothing more than a subject of exquisite fascination and challenge. Coldly, clinically, his mind registered the details. He would repeat them meticulously, like a student doing a *viva*, first to Superintendent Ord, and many, many times thereafter.

Pyper's superior, Superintendent Douglas – described as tall, slim, small beady eyes, small clipped moustache, somewhat pimpled about the chin, eye-catchingly smart in his heavily-braided dress uniform – had, on his arrival at about five minutes past eight, after viewing the body made his way to the so-called spare bedroom and there saw the only other signs anywhere in the flat of the terrible visitant's incursion. Three boxes, all broken open, were lying on the floor. One of them was a lady's wooden work-box. It had contained private papers, chiefly letters and receipted accounts. Its lid had been wrenched off. The papers were scattered about the floor. Another was a brush box, containing a brush and comb. The third was a lady's glove box. In it were one or two pairs of gloves.

Nellie Lambie told him that these boxes were normally kept on the dressing-table, beside another brush box which still lay, seemingly untouched, *in situ*.

What Douglas did find that was of interest, was a box of matches and a spent match, which had obviously come from that box and had been used by the intruder to light the gas. With an uncanny appropriateness, the matchbox was labelled 'The Runaway Match'. Manufactured by Bryant and May, this was a brand which was not in wide general use; it had never been used in Miss Gilchrist's household. Not only were the matches of a large, old-fashioned kind, but they were generally sold, not in single boxes, but in packages of a dozen or a half-dozen boxes, and were usually purchased from grocers' shops rather than tobacconists'. Douglas was quick to note that there was no blood on either the matchbox or the matchstick.

Indeed, and this is perhaps remarkable, outside the confines of the sanguineous dining-room, not a drop or smudge of blood was found anywhere in Miss Gilchrist's neat and clean apartment.

Ord's henchman, Lieutenant Gordon, was the next to apply his expertise to the riddle. Having noted 'two or three round spots of blood' on the tongs inside the dining-room fender, his attention was particularly attracted by the coal-scuttle –

> It was lying outside the fender on the same end as the tongs, and it
> occurred to me, as there was no blood on the scuttle, the lid of which was
> broken, that the deceased's head had struck the coal-scuttle and probably
> spurted blood on the tongs.

Lambie was asked to search the house to see if anything was missing. She declared that a brooch, which was usually kept with a diamond ring and two others in a little open dish on the spare bedroom dressing-table, had vanished. It was a gold brooch, crescent-shaped, about the size of a half-crown, and set with diamonds. She had seen it lying in the dish on the Sunday, the day before the murder. Nothing else appeared to be missing.

Ord, viewing the body, had noticed that Miss Gilchrist's dress was open at the neck. This was an important observation, and may provide the answer to the riddle of the missing brooch. Ord suggested that Miss Gilchrist had actually been wearing the brooch, to fasten the neck of her dress, and that when her assailant seized hold of her, the brooch came away in his hand and he unthinkingly pocketed it and bore it away with him. Unfortunately, Ord failed to examine the broken work-box in the spare bedroom sufficiently carefully, and did not therefore spot what appeared to be a finger-mark on it.

The time had now come to question the two vital witnesses as to precisely what they had seen.

Helen Lambie first.

> The man held his head down and I didn't get a look at his face. I think he might be five feet eight or nine inches in height. I couldn't say whether he had a beard, moustache or whiskers, or was bare-faced. He had a light-coloured overcoat, like fawn-coloured, about three-quarter length. He wore a cloth cap, I think. I can't tell whether it had a scoop [peak] or brim or not. I don't remember having seen anyone in the house who in the least resembled the man I saw coming out of the house.

Mark well the terms of this, the first description that Lambie gave. She was later to improve, or improvise, upon it most startlingly – and worryingly. He would become a *dark* man with a *dark-coloured* cap, wearing a fawn-coloured *waterproof* coat; not, she would insist, a rainproof cloth coat. She did not get a view of his full face, but did see the side of it. She noticed nothing peculiar about it. The peculiarity that she did notice was that when he walked he shook his shoulders a little and carried his head forward. Later still, she would add such refinements as that his coat was open, he had carried nothing in his hands, and the 'cap' was 'something of the shape of a Donegal hat'. She would also reduce his height to 5 ft 7 or 8 in. So much for Nellie's vision – and revision.

Arthur Montague Adams' description of the stranger in the hall corresponded in some respects with Nellie's, but in other ways differed substantially. He maintained that, from where he was standing, on the threshold of the flat door, he had had a better opportunity of seeing the man than had Lambie, who, he insisted, was well into the hall when the man appeared. According to Adams:

> The man wore a light-grey overcoat – it might be fawn-coloured – coming

down to his knees. I cannot say what kind of cap he wore, but I think it was a felt hat. He was clean-shaven and very dark. He was like the type of a clerk or commercial traveller. I thought from appearance that he might be a man of twenty-five to thirty years old.

Adams, too, indulged in subsequent amplification:

He was a sharp-featured man. He wore dark trousers and a light-coloured overcoat reaching down past his knees. I do not think it was a macintosh. I cannot say whether he had brown boots or black boots. I am not certain whether the man wore a hard bowler hat or a cap.

And later:

Just an ordinary face . . . nothing special about him. Not a well-built man, but well-featured. I cannot exactly swear to his moustache, but if he had any it was very little. I saw nothing special about his nose. I did not notice anything about his way of walking at all. He had nothing in his hand as far as I could tell.

Neither Lambie nor Adams had seen any bloodstains on the stranger. Would they know the man again? Lambie did not think that she would be able to identify him. Adams said that he had seen the man's face quite distinctly, and thought that he would know it again. Adding, characteristically, honestly, 'But I could not be sure'.

Putting their heads together, Ord and Gordon, Douglas and Pyper, cobbled up a description of sorts of the wanted man, and, at 9.40pm, the following notice was issued to the Glasgow Police:

An old lady was murdered in her home at 15 Queen's Terrace between 7 and 7.10pm today by a man from 25 to 30, 5 feet 7 or 8, think clean-shaven. Wore a long grey overcoat and dark cap. Robbery appears to have been the object of the murder, as a number of boxes in a bedroom were opened and left lying on the floor. A large-sized, crescent-shaped gold brooch, set with diamonds, large diamonds in centre, graduating towards the points, is missing and may be in the possession of the murderer. The diamonds are set in silver. No trace of the murderer has been got. Constables will please warn booking-clerks and railway stations, as the murderer will have bloodstains on his clothing. Also warn pawns on opening regarding brooch, and keep a sharp look-out.

It was after 11pm when, at last, Adams returned to his own house. Nellie Lambie had gone off to stay the night with her aunt, Mrs Helen Robertson, at 15 South Kinning Place.

One by one, those who had business in, or came in grief to, the house in West Princes Street slipped quietly away. Ord stayed on longer, later, than most, listening to what his officers had to tell him. They had searched the flat carefully for any implement or weapon. They had found nothing. Conclusion: either the murderer took the weapon away with him, or he had used something that came to hand in the house, something they had as yet failed to identify. Except for a box of Runaway Matches, not a single clue, nothing, had emerged to throw any light on this singular affair. There was no trace of house-breaking. Pyper had examined the windows. Apart from the kitchen window, unsnibbed and open two or three inches at the top – which is how Lambie said that she had left it – and presenting no signs of having been tampered with, all the windows had been firmly closed, and none of them seemed to have been interfered with in any way. Gordon had paid particular attention to the front-door and its various locks. They were all untouched.

What kind of burglar was it anyway who took a solitary brooch (*if* it had been taken – even that was not certain in this extraordinary case) and left lying around untouched gold and diamond rings, gold watches and chains, and even ready cash?

The more he thought about it, the more certain Ord felt that whoever it was who had come to the flat that evening had been let in by Miss Gilchrist herself. The murderer had gained admission by ringing the bell and having the door opened to him. There was no sign of any struggle. Surely that meant that the killer was someone known to Miss Gilchrist. A friend? A relative? Someone whom she knew and trusted and would not be afraid to let into the house when she was there on her own. Well, that should narrow the field a bit.

Issuing a last instruction that the body was to be left lying untouched where it was until the next day, Chief Superintendent Ord departed, leaving alone in that dark and now empty and silent house, the luckless Constable Brien, to keep, spike-haired and bolt-eyed, the lonely watches of the night with the hideously mangled dead.

When the good burghers of Glasgow, stout and otherwise, opened their morning papers on Tuesday, 22 December, they received a severe matutinal shock over their salt porridge and marmaladed baps. 'Brutal Crime in Glasgow' ran the headlines. And the second and third deckers: 'Defenceless Old Lady Murdered. Girl's Ghastly Discovery. A Mysterious Visitor. Supposed Assailant Met on Stair'. Then, in finer print and finer detail . . . 'Particulars of one of the most revolting tragedies of which the city has ever been the scene.' Readers were told that 'throughout the night the detective force maintained a vigilant search. All the likely haunts of the criminal classes were visited. The inmates of all lodging-houses and most of the hotels were systematically examined'.

The first tentative theories were advanced. From the fact that only a brooch of no great value was taken away, it was thought that jewellery might not have been the quest of the man. The circumstance that a number of papers had been removed from a box and thrown upon the floor seemed to suggest the possibility that he might have been looking for some particular document. There was also, in the police view, the likelihood that the man had been foiled in getting the jewellery, or whatever it was that he was after, owing to want of time.

Adams was quoted as thinking that robbery was clearly the motive, and that the intruder had probably climbed the rone pipe at the back of the house and found the bedroom window unfastened. While he was ransacking the room, the old lady, hearing the noise, had risen from her chair, but before she could reach the hall the man had rushed upon her.

There was also the story of the silent watcher. Dr Perry's wife, who lived at No. 11 Queen's Terrace, said that for four or five evenings previous to the murder she had noticed a man standing at the corner of Queen's Crescent, opposite Miss Gilchrist's house, which he was evidently watching. She described him as young and athletic-looking. He gave the impression of being fairly well-dressed. He was wearing a light overcoat. The presence of this same man on the same spot at the same hour each evening had impressed her so much that she had mentioned it to her maids, who had also observed the young man. In view of what had happened, she had no doubt now that the watcher was someone who had heard about the old lady's jewellery and was simply waiting for a chance to get into the house.

Fleshing out the persona of the victim, the papers said that the deceased lady came of an old Glasgow family. Her father, the late James Taylor Gilchrist, had been a successful supervisory and consulting engineer. Described as 'an attractive, tall, erect person, healthy for her age, and looking more like sixty-five than the four-score years which she had exceeded,' Miss Gilchrist was said to have been well-known in the district in which she resided, and regarded by her friends and neighbours as exceedingly well-off. She owned considerable property throughout the city. She was known to be fond of jewellery, and to possess many valuable pieces. She had long been a member of St John's United Free Church, in George Street, and took a great interest in religious and philanthropic work. She had a wide reputation among the poor for her benevolence.

According to Lambie, Miss Gilchrist received comparatively few visitors, and seldom had male callers. Certainly there had been no man at the house recently. Her mistress was, she said, most timid. She was easily upset by any unusual noise, had a wholesome dread of burglars, and was very loth to be left alone in the house. For the past year she had had apprehensive fears that she was not safe in her flat. So nervous was she on some occasions that Nellie had been obliged to share her bed with her. Arthur Adams confirmed that Miss Gilchrist had harboured a mortal terror of finding a man in the house, and on several occasions had asked him to search her flat to allay her fears. Indeed, it was thus that the arrangement came into being that, by tapping on the floor, she would let him know that his presence was urgently wanted upstairs.

It was the *Daily Record* that opined that: 'A rather significant feature of the tragedy lies in the fact that some time ago the old lady's dog was mysteriously poisoned, and the surmise is that the deed was premeditated.' The circumstances, as related by Lambie, were that when she and her mistress returned from a holiday at Girvan, on the Ayrshire coast, at the end of August 1908, the dog was allowed out from half past one to a quarter past six on the first Sunday in September (6 September).

> I took it out again for a walk that same evening. It could not walk and I had
> to carry it home. It looked peculiar and it got worse. It died that same night.

I carried it down to the washing-house the next day, and it was taken away
by a dustman. Its tongue was hanging out before it died, but it was not
vomiting. Miss Gilchrist told Dr Perry of the affair, and he thought by the
symptoms it had been poisoned. Its hind legs seemed to be useless. Miss
Gilchrist had had it for two years. She got it as a present from Dr Charteris.

Lambie thought that the dog had eaten something disagreeable,
but Miss Gilchrist was convinced that Barney had been deliberately
poisoned.

Following tight on the heels of a long and hectically unproductive
night, the Glasgow police, tired, frustrated, faced the dawn of
Tuesday, 22 December, coming up grey, cold and uninviting over
the Clyde, without exuberance. As soon as the watery – of course it
was still raining – winter morning light creaked down, Inspector
Alexander Rankin, of Western District, found himself poking wetly
about the soaking back greens of No. 15 Queen's Terrace, and
properties adjacent thereto. 'Go', Inspector Pyper had told him,
while the lamps yet burned yellow in the office, 'go and see if you
can't come up with the murder weapon – or at least a footmark.' And
Inspector Rankin had gone, and taken with dedication and a sense
of purpose to the quartering of the greens. By 10am, with the sun
now high though hidden behind suffusing clouds of moisture,
Inspector Rankin's patient fossicking was rewarded. It had yielded,
from almost directly below the kitchen window of Miss Gilchrist's
house, a large iron auger or screw-bit, lifting which, he had seen a
mixture of brown and grey human hairs adhering to its underside.
From their length he judged the hairs to have come from a woman.
There was also what appeared to be rust on the auger, but it might
just as easily be blood. Nor could the auger, he decided, have lain
long where he found it, for the grass beneath it was not etiolated,
but quite green. Rankin bore auger and hair off in triumph to the
Western Police Office. Sadly, it was to prove a damp squib.

Interestingly, the Edinburgh *Evening Dispatch* representative
had elicited some fresh facts in the course of an interview with Miss
Laura Adams. She told him that one of her sisters, who was
somewhat of an invalid, was expecting a parcel on the night of the

murder. She kept looking out of the window for the postman, and saw, walking up and down the pavement outside as if waiting on something, a young man. He was wearing a light overcoat, and she thought that he had answered to the description of the individual wanted. It seemed likely that he was waiting till Lambie left the house.

Sharp and bright on the morning of Wednesday, 23 December, in the balneal, white-tiled, disinfectant-edged mortuary of Glasgow Royal Infirmary, medical jurisprudentialists Professor John Glaister and Dr Hugh Galt set to work to put together an impersonal sort of inventory of the awfulnesses visited upon the living body of the late Marion Gilchrist.

Their report began in the time-honoured low key of such reports: 'The body was that of a well-nourished elderly woman. Death-stiffening had disappeared from the body. The skin was markedly pallid in appearance.'

Then, an end to the mildness, it moved brutally swiftly into its recording of the atrocious. It was indeed an appalling catalogue of savageries. They itemised each of the dreadful injuries to the head and face. Several bones forming the right temple and back of the head were shattered, and pieces driven in upon the brain. Parts of both upper and lower left eyelids had been forced into the brain cavity. On dissecting the chest cavity, the breast-bone was found to be completely fractured, throughout its entire thickness, about the middle. The third, fourth, fifth and sixth ribs on the right side of the chest were badly fractured. Examining the thoracic organs, the pathologists found both lungs healthy, and the heart very healthy for that of a woman of Marion Gilchrist's age. Examination of the abdominal organs revealed a normal stomach, containing some partially digested food, both kidneys were granular as the result of chronic affection, and where were small tumours of the womb and its appendages. The remainder of the organs were normal.

The conclusion. The doctors testified on soul and conscience that they were:

of opinion that the cause of death of the said Marion Gilchrist was extensive wounds and fractures of bones of face and skull, and fractures of breast-bone and ribs, together with shock and bleeding therefrom, that the said injuries were produced by forcible contact with a blunt weapon, and that the violence was applied with considerable force.

A little later that same Wednesday, Superintendent Ord received a letter which had been addressed to the Chief Constable of Glasgow, James Verdier Stevenson, by Captain J Lumsdane, commander of the Anchor Line vessel, S.S. *Furnessia*. Writing, on 22 December, from 46 Park Drive South, Whiteinch, Captain Lumsdane had this to say:

Re. the murder of the old lady in Queen's Terrace. The manner in which it was perpetrated is typically American. Similar deeds are of almost daily occurrence in New York. Burglars kill their victims to prevent the probability of future recognition, and battering their heads in is the usual method.

In consequence of this communication, the official attitude of the Glasgow police underwent a change, and Ord, who was inclined to think it improbable that the murder had been committed by a Scotsman, considered that it might well have been the act of someone acquainted with the theory and practice of violence 'over there', and gave orders that thought and inquiries should be particularly directed to foreigners in Glasgow.

It was neither lack of enthusiasm nor want of energy, but absence of that vital additional ingredient – which the former cannot conjure up or the latter manufacture – luck, which denied the beavering police success. Then, on that Wednesday afternoon, it seemed that the missing ingredient was in sudden and most unexpected manner generously supplied.

Shortly after 4pm the telephone rang in Ord's office. It was a Northern District detective, John McGimpsey. He told the Superintendent that, emerging around four o'clock that afternoon from his flat at 9 Seamore Street, he had been chance hailed by a neighbour, Mrs Barbara Barrowman, who was coming up the stair. She lived with her husband, Robert, an iron moulder, and daughters, Barbara and Mary, on the stair above McGimpsey, in the same tenement. 'Have you got any word of the West Princes Street murderer yet?' she asked him. And when he told her no, she had intimated that her 14-year-old daughter, Mary, could a tale unfold. And she had gone on to explain that the girl had seen a man running away from Miss Gilchrist's house. 'If all's true that our Mary says,' she added, 'you'll know him by a crooked nose.'

Ord lost no time. Detectives were despatched to Seamore Street forthwith. Mary Barrowman told her story. She was employed as a message-girl by Malcolm Maccallum & Son, Boot and Shoe Makers, at 333 Great Western Road.

> About 7pm on Monday, 21 December, or it might be shortly after it, I left my employer's shop with a parcel to be delivered to 36 Cleveland Street, off St Vincent Street. I went from Great Western Road into West Princes Street, and when almost opposite a close there, which I have since learned is No. 15 Queen's Terrace, I saw a man coming hurriedly out of that close and come down the five or six steps therefrom to the pavement. I think he came down two steps at a time. He was running when he came out and he continued to run along West Princes Street to West Cumberland Street. Then I returned and went straight along West Princes Street and delivered my parcel. There is a street-lamp quite near the close and it was lit. The man was tall, about 28 or 30 years old and not broad made. Clean-shaven, he had a slight twist on his nose. He was pale-faced. He wore a fawn overcoat, I think a waterproof. He wore a dark suit, which appeared either blue or black. He had nothing in his hands, which were bare. He had on what I think is known as a Donegal hat[1] – it seemed of light grey tweed.
>
> I did not observe whether he wore a [watch] chain at his breast. He wore brown boots. I thereafter went back to the shop by St George's Road and West Princes Street. I think it would take about half an hour to go from the part of West Princes Street where I saw the man first to Cleveland Street and back, and I imagine it was about a quarter to eight when I reached West Princes Street again, and I saw two or three people standing about near the close. I did not then speak to anyone or hear anything as to the murder. I got back to my employer's shop, and, at about eight o'clock, it was closed. My father has a shop in St Vincent Street,[2] and I think I went there after eight o'clock.
>
> I was again at West Princes Street about nine o'clock on my way home for the night when I saw a crowd near the said close. I spoke to someone in the crowd and asked what was wrong, and she told me there had been a murder of a woman there. When I got home I told my mother. I did not see anyone come out of the close after the man. There was no one at or near the close at the time when the man came running out, and while he was in my sight he did not join, nor was he joined by, anyone. There were one or two persons coming east along West Princes Street while he

1 That is a soft, round cloth hat, with a soft brim all round. It did not have any peak such as an ordinary cloth cap.
2 No 480. This was a newsagent and tobacconist's shop, variously described by Mary Barrowman as her father's and her brother's shop.

was running west, but I did not know any of them.

Although no clue had as yet proved concrete enough to warrant the arrest for which all Glasgow was clamouring, McGimpsey's gift had gone a wondrous way towards lightening the hearts of Superintendents Ord and Douglas, who, as the head man of the Western District, bore the actual executive responsibility of the case.

But there was a snag: no matter what allowances you made for mistakes and malobservations, there was simply no way that you could equate the figure of Mary Barrowman's elaborate description with the man in the hall described, admittedly more sketchily, by Adams and Lambie. Did this, the police began to wonder, mean that there were perhaps two men involved?

In the course of the last couple of days the detectives had lost no time in making careful and widespread inquiries of the late Miss Gilchrist's relatives. They had questioned her niece, Miss Margaret Dawson Birrell, closely, and Superintendent Douglas had had a long consultation with Miss Gilchrist's solicitor, Mr James Macdonald. They had discovered that Miss Gilchrist had three sisters living. Two of them resided in Glasgow – Mrs Jane Gilchrist or Birrell, aged 68, lived with her husband, Dawson Birrell, at 23 Blythswood Drive; and 70-year-old, widowed, Mrs Elizabeth Lawrie lived at 7 Ashton Terrace, Partickhill. Neither of them had any children. Mrs Birrell last saw her sister Marion about 1893. Mrs Lawrie had never visited her. The third sister, Mrs Christina Gilchrist or Lee, aged 75, had never visited Marion either. A widow, she was living at Minard Villa, 20 Craigie Road, Ayr. She had four sons and three daughters.

A fourth sister, Mrs Janet Gilchrist or Birrell, married to Walter Birrell (Dawson Birrell's brother), had died aged 67, in 1896. She had three surviving sons and one daughter.

Apart from the Lee and Birrell families, there was of, course, the Charteris family, which was, as we have seen, related more remotely to Miss Gilchrist. Its members included Mrs Elizabeth Charteris (*née* Greer), her daughter Mary by James Gilchrist, and the three children of her second marriage – Archibald, Francis and John Charteris. The whereabouts of all these at the time of the murder were meticulously checked by the police. The legions of the Lees were in Glasgow, Ayr, Liverpool, Maidenhead, and Sydney, New South Wales. Mary Greer Gilchrist, now married to Dr Anthony McCall, lived in Bournemouth. The Charteris 'nephews' were in Glasgow and India. The Birrell offspring, James, George and Margaret, were in Glasgow, except for the third son, Wingate Birrell, who had not been heard of for some years, but the police traced him to Woolwich, London.

The short December afternoon's light was already on the wane when, a little before three o'clock on Thursday, 24 December, small knots of people began to gather near the premises of Messrs Wylie & Lochhead, undertakers, in that gloomy thoroughfare of dark coaches, Berkeley Street. Miss Gilchrist's body had been quietly removed from the Royal Infirmary to the undertakers' premises the previous evening. Everything had been done to keep the occasion as private as possible. Indeed, Mr Adams, who had been invited to join the mourners, knowing that his appearance would be a signal for the curious watchers, waiting for the hearse outside the house in West Princes Street, to follow him, did not dare to leave by his own front-door, but slipped unobtrusively out by the back. And yet, in the strange, inexplicable way of such things, the intelligence had spread from lip to ear, 'They're burying her from Wylie's.'

Before the quarter had struck, the first tentative nodes of the Berkeley Street crowd had accreted about them large numbers of frustrated hearse-watchers, arrived from their speculative stations outside No. 49 and the Royal Infirmary, augmenting the count to some three or four hundred bystanders.

While, at three o'clock, the spectators waited, and the body, encoffined in polished oak, with finest brass mountings, and bowered in white flowers, four wreaths on top – one of white lilies entwined with evergreens, two bouquets of white lilies, and a bouquet of white chrysanthemums – lay, also waiting, in the hearse station in the courtyard, a short service was conducted in a little side-room by the Reverend Dr John Carroll, who had been Miss

Gilchrist's minister at St John's.

Then, at about 20 minutes past three, the hearse, followed by six two-horse carriages and watched by the crowds thronging the pavements and pressing forward now for a glimpse of the coffin behind its glass walls, moved at a snail's pace smoothly out of the undertakers' yard. The horses, strapped by sweating stable-lads to shiny ebony, the black ostrich plumes on their heads nodding to the measured tune of slow-jingling harness, manes and tails exquisitely pulled and brushed and combed, hooves oiled to within the last gleaming inch, the cortège started inexorably forth on Marion Gilchrist's last earthly journey.

Out into Berkeley Street. On to Bath Street, which bore the shrinking mourners gratefully out of the public gaze, into the labyrinthine anonymity of the busier streets. The shops were beginning to light up as the simple funeral procession wound through the city. A brief farewell flirtation with the things of this world in the warm, living flow of Renfield Street, encountering the last rush of present-buying Christmas Eve shoppers, too intent all upon their own absorbing affairs to spare glance or thought for the dark cavalcade wending its way to the eternal shadows. On, out of the perimeter of light, into the quieter streets – Cathedral Street, High Street – unrolling a sombre stone carpet to the gate of the Necropolis, that high hill or mound of Glasgow's long-slumbering dead.

The approach to the gates was thinly lined with a loiter of onlookers. The coaches swung along the outward carriage-way to the Eta section of the graveyard that lies above the picturesque quarter of Ladywell. Prompted by curiosity, attracted by the newly-upturned soil, a group of women, most of them with wreaths for other graves in their arms, had gathered among the tombs on the steeply-rising ground above, so as to look down upon Miss Gilchrist's open grave.

The smell of the earth was strong. The mourners debouched; between 25 and 30 of them; difficult to make an accurate count in the gloom. But quite a respectable turn-out. Mr Adams was there. So were solicitor Macdonald and ex-bailie, Councillor William Sorley, of Partick, the jeweller who had sold to the decedent so many of her treasured pieces. Also present were a number of ladies and a little girl.

The interment took place in the grave belonging to the Gilchrist family; No. 34, marked by a large, grey pedestal tombstone, topped with a carved stone funerary urn, from which fall the petrified drapes of a mourning cloth or veil. After the coffin had been lowered into the ground, the Reverend Dr Carroll offered a final short prayer for the repose of the startled soul of the old lady who had made so hasty and horrendous an exit from a cosily familiar life. The filling up of the grave began. The mourners, leaving Marion Gilchrist in her lair, returned to their coaches and the world of twinkling lights below the hill. There was a scraping and a whickering. The muffled noise of horses' hooves sounded in the deepening dusk. A little night breeze rustled the quilt of dry and withered leaves whispering over the patted-down grave.

Chapter Three

PANTOMIME NOIR

And suddenly it was Christmas.

Miss Gilchrist had been tidied away in the ground yesterday, but it was far from being a case of out of sight, out of mind; she was in the minds of a great many people. As in some pantomime *noir*, the broker's men – Macdonald the lawyer and Dick the auctioneer and valuer, each in his different way charged with the disposal of her worldly goods and chattels – would, this Christmas morning, move into old maid Marion's whilom stronghold in search of her hidden treasure: her jewels.

Meanwhile, unseen but universally hissed, the Demon King, red of hand and free of foot, moved through the enchanted stone forest of the city.

The gallant Douglas and his brave band, watched over by Ord, gave chase – in all directions. That 'all directions' was, in a Christmas nutshell, the trouble; for by now, the clues, such as they had been, were gathered, sifted, and found drastically wanting. It looked for all the world as if the police's Christmas stocking would remain empty. Then, seemingly right out of nowhere, along came the best present that they could ever have hoped for. The unlikely Santa Claus was a 27-year-old bicycle maker and dealer, Allan McLean.

Earlier that day, Ord, in his office at Police Headquarters in St Andrew's Square, had been arranging the distribution of a notice authorised by Chief Constable Stevenson to police forces everywhere. It contained the following descriptions of *two* men: 'The man *first* described, leaving the house, and about the same time another man, *second* described, was seen descending the steps leading to house and running away.' The statement went on to elaborate: first, 'A man from twenty-five to thirty years of age, five feet seven or eight inches in height, thought to be clean-shaven; wore a long grey overcoat and dark cap.' This was clearly an amalgam of Lambie and Adams' descriptions. The 'long grey overcoat' has been adopted from Adams' description. Lambie, it will be recalled, spoke of 'a light-coloured overcoat, like fawn-coloured, about three-quarter length.' The 'clean-shaven' was also Adams' contribution, as Lambie had specifically said that she 'couldn't say whether he had a beard, moustache or whiskers, or was bare-faced'. Second, 'A man from twenty-eight to thirty years of age, tall and thin, clean-shaven, nose slightly turned to one side (thought to be the right side); wore a fawn-coloured overcoat (believed to be a waterproof), dark trousers, tweed cloth hat of the latest make, and believed to be dark in colour, and brown boots.'

Ord had also, having first consulted with Chief Constable Stevenson and obtained his *fiat* in the matter, issued, with the air of a fisherman laying out his lines, for publication in the evening papers, a description of *the* (singular) wanted man; this one being based on Mary Barrowman's testimony.

The early editions of the evening papers were on the streets by about two o'clock in the afternoon. At 6.10pm a bite. Allan McLean arrived at the Central Police Office bearing his Yuletide gift of information. A German Jew, known to him only by the forename of Oscar, had been offering for sale at a gambling club of which they were both members – the Sloper Club, No. 24 India Street – a pawn-ticket for a valuable diamond brooch. It had been pledged, so he had been told, for £60 on the day of the murder. McLean described this man Oscar as being about 30 years of age, standing 5 ft 8 or 9 in, of sallow complexion, clean-shaven, or with a very small growth of moustache, and with a twisted or broken nose, the slight twist being, he thought, to the right. He wore a dark suit and a fawn overcoat – McLean thought that it was a waterproof – and a dark cap. McLean further recounted:

> About a fortnight before December twenty-first, I joined the Sloper Club. I think Mr Oscar was a member before me. For about a fortnight or three weeks after I joined, I had been down every night, and I think I would meet Mr Oscar there every night. I only missed him twice. Either the Saturday night [19 December], or the Sunday night [20 December], or the Monday morning before the twenty-first December [night], was the last time I saw Mr Oscar at the club. We all left the club together. Mr Oscar left us at the corner of St George's Road and walked across the street to his own house.

So, although McLean knew neither Mr Oscar's surname nor his address, he could, he said, point out the place where he lived.

Superintendent Ord was quietly jubilant. Now, with the cycle dealer's tip to add to the message-girl's tale, it was at last starting to look as though they were beginning to get somewhere.

In the wee small hours of what was technically 26 December, the police went a'calling on the Moudie.

In order for that opaque statement to make crystal-clear, and rather exciting, sense, it is necessary to go back to seven o'clock on Christmas night, at which time Superintendent Ord packed Detective Inspector William Powell smartly off with that impresario of the bicycle, Mr Allan McLean, to identify the house wherein the promising-sounding Mr Oscar had his mysterious being.

The Superintendent's final, strict instruction to Powell was that under no circumstances should he talk to, question, or make any contact of any kind with anyone, for fear of alerting and scaring Mr Oscar away. Thus stringently briefed, Powell and McLean padded off into the dark and emptyish streets of Christmas night, up and along Sauchiehall Street to Charing Cross. There they paused. McLean pointed across to a close near the junction of Woodlands Road and St George's Road. The premises which he indicated were No. 69 St George's Road; a mansion block situated less than 400 yards, three minutes' walk, from Miss Gilchrist's.

Powell, having thanked and dismissed McLean, went into the close and up the stair – and proceeded to disregard Ord's strictures. He paid a call at a second-floor flat occupied by a Mrs Bertha Bernstein, whom, by odd coincidence, he happened to know well. From her, or rather from her loquacious maid, Ruby Russell, he learned that she frequently encountered a man answering the description of Mr Oscar coming down the stair from the flat of Mr Adolf Anderson, a dentist, who lived on the floor above.

Extremely pleased with himself, Powell returned hotfoot to St Andrew's Square.

It was getting on for midnight when, accompanied by Detective Sergeant David Lyon and Detective Constable John Millican, Powell paid his second visit that night to St George's Road. The three police officers made their way quietly up the dim-lit stair and rang at Anderson's door. A long wait, then the sound of locks and fastenings being manipulated, and there, rubbing the sleep from her eyes, stood a dressing-gowned Katharina Schmalz. A German, her English was by no means good, but she understood Powell's questions well enough to tell him that no man named Oscar lived there, that she was the maid-servant, and that Madame was away with a gentleman. That the gentleman in question was in fact Oscar Slater sheltering behind the *nom de guerre* of Adolf Anderson, she did not volunteer.

Having been assured that she had no objection to their having a look inside the flat, the trio trooped in and began to poke around. It was Millican who chanced upon the vital clue. In the main bedroom, strewn about the floor, were sheets of paper and pieces of torn newspaper, obvious indications that some packing had been going on. Rooting among this detritus, his eye was caught by a piece of paper with some red sealing-wax on it. It turned out to be a label addressed: 'Oscar Slater, Esq. c/o A. Anderson, Esq. 69, St George's Road Glasgow.'

'What about that man?' Millican asked the German girl.

'A friend of Madame's,' she said. 'He is away for a holiday with Madame.' She did not know where they had gone.

Having searched the entire flat and found no one else there, no dentist's instruments, and nothing of an incriminatory nature, the detectives descended to the flat immediately below Anderson's, that of Mrs Catherine White. The maid-servant there, 17-year-old Kennethina Mackenzie, told them that between eight o'clock and half-past that night, luggage had been carried downstairs, and she had seen Anderson leaving in the company of a tall, dark-haired young woman.

It was at this point that Powell despatched Lyon and Millican to the Sloper Club to enquire after Mr Oscar. The club-master there, George Sabin, informed them that for a period of about four weeks prior to 20 December, a man known to him as Oscar Slater had been frequenting the club. He had been introduced there by Hugh Cameron, a member who lived in Cambridge Street.

Christmas night had by now well shaded into Boxing Day morning as the detectives tramped off to Cambridge Street, where, arriving at No. 140 at approximately 2am they awoke with their insistent knocking a thoroughly bewildered and alarmed Moudie,[1] who had come blinking forth from his bed to join his wife at the front-door.

The Moudie, a 38-year-old bookmaker's clerk and self-described dealer in jewellery, showed his night callers into the kitchen, and the questioning began. Yes, he knew Oscar Slater. Last saw him at about six o'clock on Thursday evening (24 December) in Sauchiehall Street. Slater had given him a pawn-ticket on the Tuesday (22 December), or perhaps it was on the Wednesday, for a diamond brooch, asking him to find a buyer for it. The brooch had been pledged with Mr Liddell, the pawnbroker in Sauchiehall Street. Cameron had returned the unsold ticket to Slater on 24 December. They had met that afternoon and gone to the Cunard Line shipping offices in Jamaica Street. 'I had heard from him a

1 Moudie is Scots dialect for a mole or mole-catcher, but according to Hugh Cameron it meant in Australia a boundary rider, a man who rides round the fences of a sheep-shearing station at night – 'I was in Australia for about six years, and it was sometimes part of my duty to do this.'

fortnight previously that he was going to America. He had received a letter from a friend in San Francisco asking him to come out, as things were going well there.'

The hectic night of 25-26 December had yet space for the prosecution of one last inquiry. At 4.30am a messenger was sent from the Western Police Office to the home, at 1109 Argyle Street, of the manager of Liddell's pawnshop, Peter Crawford McLaren, to root him out of bed and get him to go to his business premises at once. He found two police officers awaiting him there. They wished to take possession of a diamond brooch pawned on 21 December. McLaren refused to open the premises and told the detectives that the brooch in question had been in his continuous possession since 18 November. Inspector Powell was fetched to lend his weight to the confrontation. McLaren still refused, and, faced with such intractability, there was nothing, beyond a display of displeasure, that the thwarted Powell could do about it. Peter McLaren went off, back to his interrupted night's rest. The Inspector, tight-lipped, vanished into the watery light of the official dawn.

At a more civilised hour of Boxing Day morning, Lieutenant William Gordon was sitting in the vanished Mr Anderson's flat at No. 69 St George's Road, attempting, not without sundry linguistic difficulties, to amplify the testimony of Miss Katharina Schmalz – and he was not doing at all badly.

Making his way up the stair, Gordon had passed two women coming down, and had had a sort of intuition that they had emerged from the Anderson house. Having succeeded in eliciting from the now more forthcoming Schmalz that Mr Anderson and Madame had in fact gone to London, and learning that Schmalz herself intended returning to London that night, Gordon asked, 'Are those two ladies who went downstairs living in the house?' 'Yes,' she told him. And at that precise moment the women came back into the flat.

They introduced themselves as Mrs Luise Freedman and Mrs Elsa Hoppe, and explained that they had taken over the tenancy of Mr Anderson's flat. Mrs Freedman said that she had known Mr

Anderson, otherwise Oscar Slater, for some six years, and that she was a half-sister of Madame Andrée Junio Antoine or Keibrow, with whom he was living. She and her step-sister, Mrs Hoppe, in England on a visit from Thale, in Germany, had heard while staying in London that Oscar and Andrée were in Glasgow. They had arrived on *Weihnachten* Eve, only to find Slater and Keibrow packing. He said that he had received a wire and must go to Monte Carlo at once. The sisters intended to stay in Glasgow for a further fortnight.

Somewhere about eleven o'clock that same morning, another police officer of the name of Gordon called, together with his fellow inspector, Allan Campbell, at Liddell's pawnbroking office. Peter McLaren still refused to give up the gold and diamond crescent brooch of Slater's pledging, but agreed to go with Gordon and Campbell to the shop of William Sorley, who had sold Miss Gilchrist's brooch to her, taking the pawned brooch with him for Sorley's inspection. Sorley and his assistant examined it. Both stated categorically that it was not Miss Gilchrist's brooch.

And that is where the case against Oscar Slater should have finished . . . before it began.

But it didn't.

It is all too easy to put up the thought that the way in which the police stayed with Oscar Slater after the clue of the brooch had failed is one of the enduring 'mysteries' of the case. However, it is in fact all too clear. With their minds arranged in his direction, even if the brooch did have to be jettisoned, here was a gift under pressure, a likely suspect. He was a foreigner – hadn't they been told to look out for a foreigner? – out of place in the good or goodish parts of Glasgow, living in the locality of the crime, a man of glaringly bad character, violent, a gambler and a pimp. And hadn't Mary Barrowman's arresting crooked-nose identification provided just about the ultimate detail? Finally, as they saw it, he had precipitately fled from Glasgow on the heels of the murder.

Accordingly, their first priority must be to discover Slater's present whereabouts. Schmalz had said London. Mrs Freedman had said Monte Carlo, via London. The Metropolitan Police had therefore been contacted. Schmalz was being shadowed in the hope that she might lead the detectives to Slater's hideout. Meanwhile, in Mr Asquith's celebrated phrase, they could only 'wait and see'.

And while they were waiting and not seeing, the Glasgow detective force got down to the dull, routine grind of trying to put together a sort of diary-cum-timetable of Slater's last week before his so-sudden disappearance. They succeeded well enough – but it yielded nothing of any real help in their quest for damnatory circumstances. On the contrary, Duncan MacBrayne, a young assistant at John Wilson's, the Sauchiehall Street grocer's, who knew 'Mr Anderson' well, whilst making his way home at 8.15pm on the evening of 21 December – just about an hour after the murder – had met Anderson/Slater in St George's Road, a few yards from No. 69. 'He was dressed in a grey suit of clothes and a grey cap. He had no overcoat on. I noticed nothing peculiar about his manner. He seemed quite cool and unconcerned.'

Shifting and sifting through great bundles of papers – reports, observations, ruminations, statements, precognitions and all the other intimidating ancillary apparatus of ongoing stone-walled investigation – Superintendents Ord and Douglas were to spend months struggling to put at least the framework of a case against Slater together; but even now, at this early stage, blizzards of 'facts' were blowing in, and, like snowflakes, melting away as one tried to grasp and assemble them into a meaningful pattern. But, whatever, burning like a beacon before them, was the utter conviction that Oscar Slater was their man.

To sum up: Slater had been shown to have been in possession of clothes similar to those worn by the unknown suspect. He was known to have had an interest in jewellery and actually to have done some dealing in it. That he happened to have pawned a brooch that was his – or his woman's – was just a red herring. Albeit, a useful one so far as the police were concerned, in that by pure chance, almost an act of God you might say, it had put them on his trail.

One official view was that Slater had quite genuinely decided a good while before the date of the West End Murder to leave

Glasgow, but when he had heard by chance of Miss Gilchrist's treasure-trove, he had made up his mind that the latter would leave with him. He had laid his carefully thought-out plans cunningly, preparing his friends and acquaintances for his sudden departure, telling all and sundry that he would be leaving. Fully three weeks prior to 25 December, Slater was speaking quite freely to the Moudie and various members at the Sloper Club of his going back to the United States shortly, and quite openly giving his address there as c/o Caesar Café, 544 Broadway, San Francisco.

On 26 December, Slater had sent a letter to his friend Max Rattmann, who had handed it over to Inspector Pyper. It had been written from the North Western Hotel, Liverpool.

> Dear Max,
> Surprisingly leaving Glasgow. Forgot
> to say good-bye. Let me hear from you as
> you have my address. Freedman's girl
> took over my flat; keep yourself as well
> as your wife well, and remain –
> Your friend,
> O. Slater.

The vital information provided by the Rattmann letter was that Slater was in Liverpool. Before this there had been every reason to think that Oscar and Andrée had run off to London. The truth was that they had arrived at the North Western Hotel, at Lime Street Station, Liverpool, in the early hours of the morning of 26 December, and left later that afternoon on board the *Lusitania*, bound for New York.

As the days of the voyage wore on, all Glasgow, all Britain for that matter, speculated about the anonymous man – the police had not disclosed Slater's name – now on the high seas. The ongoing cliff-hanger gave an edge to Glaswegian 'halves', and lent spice to the mildest teetotaller's fare. The excitement and tension mounted. From their armchairs in Glasgow, the citizens, with no wirelesses or television to enliven the dull evenings of their lives, were able to follow through their newspapers the thrilling chase across the Atlantic.

The winter weather was not being kind to the *Lusitania*. Her passage, a rough one, had been menaced by a blizzard, and she was delayed. Not until 7p.m. on Friday, 1 January, 1909, did she arrive off Sandy Hook. A revenue cutter, the *Hudson*, slipped away from the New York Battery and headed for the Ambrose Channel lightship. A considerable sea was running outside the bay, but the little cutter stood boldly out to the big Cunarder. The *Hudson* steamed aside, and six United States' lawmen clambered over the side of the great liner.

A cablegram had been despatched on 30 December:
To Detective Bureau, Police, New York. Lady murdered here 21st current. Valuable diamond brooch stolen. Oscar Slater, nose slightly twisted, disappeared suddenly. Accompanied French woman. Sailed Saturday *Lusitania*, second cabin, as Otto Sando. Undesirable. Movements suspicious. Interrogate. Search. Shadow. – Chief Constable, Glasgow.

The passengers had been assembled in the second-class dining-saloon to undergo the normal questioning by immigration officials. A bulkily built, bronzed man with an unmistakably twisted nose was practically the first individual that Detective Lieutenant George T Leeson spotted. A steward told him the bronzed man's name. Sando. 'The tall, black-haired woman beside him is his wife.'

The six hunters thereupon moved in swiftly to surround and isolate the couple, and the interrogation began. Slater said that he was not a US citizen, but had taken out papers under the name of Anderson. 'I am a dentist, having lived in New York and having had a business at 445 Sixth Avenue up till a few years ago,' he explained. He was known in Scotland as Anderson, because a Scottish name was good for business.

Up to this moment Slater did not know about the charge against him and no mention had been made of the murder. Suddenly Leeson asked: 'Do you know a young [*sic*] woman in Glasgow named Gilchrist?' Slater said that he did not. Then called across to his 'wife', 'Hilary, do you recall any Gilchrist?' She replied that she had never heard the name.

'Didn't you read the papers before you left Liverpool?' Leeson persisted.

Well, yes, come to think of it, he did remember the papers

describing Miss Gilchrist's murder, but he didn't read all the particulars. He'd left Glasgow four days after the murder and gone straight to Liverpool.

The interrogators then invited the pair to a cabin below, where they were both searched. Nothing suspicious was found on Andrée. Oscar yielded up a pawn-ticket for a three-row diamond crescent brooch. At no time did he show the slightest nervousness. 'Mrs Sando' gave her maiden name as Andrée Hilary Antoine, and said that she was the daughter of Malone James Antoine, a Parisian merchant, and that she had lived in Paris. She had married Oscar Slater in Glasgow, on 12 July, 1901.

None of Mr Sando's fellow-voyagers had the faintest inkling of the true identity of the glossy, beautifully-tailored and turned-out *Mitteleuropean* gentleman, moving with such well-mannered grace and charm among them, taking his meals in the second dining-room with his pretty young wife, gallantly saluting the ladies as, with expected regularity, he gravitated to the smoking-room – his natural habitat – where, fairly popular with its habitués, he spent a good deal of the trip playing cards.

When the ship docked, Slater was arrested by two United States deputy marshals. Told that he must accompany them as their prisoner to the Federal headquarters building in New York, he went deadly pale and bleakly muttered a refusal to answer any further questions. As he was led off, his 'wife' was firmly escorted away to be detained on Ellis Island, the immigration station in New York harbour.

Things were not looking good.

Chapter Four

LOOKING FOR MR OSCAR

So what manner of man was Oscar Slater – the Great Suspect? Well, to start with, his name was not Slater: it was Oscar Joseph Leschziner . . .

It had been a big decision and it took big courage. More courage, perhaps, than to bend to the will of the Fatherland. But 22-year-old Oscar had decided that rather than, like the rest of the *Junge Männer* of his cohort, allow himself to be conscripted into the army to do a stint of compulsory national soldiering, he would up sticks – such thin bundle of sticks as he possessed – and quit the Homeland. He would be a soldier . . . of fortune.

In a sense, the decision was not a new one. Since his boyhood years Oscar had realised that Beuthen, the small, smoke-circled and coal-dust-begrimed mining town on the right bank of the Oder, in Upper Silesia, was not for him. Indeed, it had not proved a propitious place for the Leschziner family. His memories of it would all be as gritty as the fine coat of soot that had seemed to powder, and smother, everything in Beuthen that your fingers touched.

Adolf Leschziner, his father, a master baker, had not prospered there. It had been a long, hard struggle, selling his daily bread to earn his daily bread. But for a time German-Jewish persistence – industry, attention to detail, reliability in the quality of his goods, politeness to his customers, husbanding of his small resources – had seemed to pay dividends. The faltering business blossomed slowly, and not without pain, into a flourishing concern.

Then . . . disaster. Sadly, Adolf Leschziner's flesh was not as strong as his will. His health broke down. He and his family came to know hard times. Fortunately, Oscar's mother, Paula, was a sterling character. She it was who shouldered the burden, became what so many fine Jewish mothers before and after have had to become, the family's mainstay. With her master baker enfeebled by progressive disease, she took the bread-maker's place as the breadwinner, turning her skill as a midwife into the slender means of eking out a bare, harsh existence for them all.

It was perhaps as a 'perk' of her greatly appreciated status in the service of the community, that her son, Oscar Joseph, was brought into a not overly kind world within the carefully sanitised portals of the Midwives' Institution at Oppeln, then located in the upper Silesian province of Prussia.[1] The day of the birth was Monday, 8 January, in the leap year, 1872.

Oscar's youth was not quite so brave as the retrospective face he put on it. After a local elementary school, and a brief spell at the Beuthen Gymnasium, he was, in 1887, at the age of 15, apprenticed by his mother, at considerable personal sacrifice, to a Beuthen dealer in wood, Herr Schuttenberg.

In 1890, his indentures served, Oscar left the wood merchant's. He was, and always would be, different from his brothers and sisters. They were cast in the mould of orthodoxy, content to remain in and around Beuthen. Although not religious, he was a good Jewish boy in that Hebraic familial essential of being a loving and unforgetful son, but he was shot through with an alien streak of romance. He was dreamy, imaginative and ambitious, made of that pioneering stuff which, despising the safe, quiet,

1 Since 1945 it has been in the Katowice province of southern Poland, and is now known as Opole.

humdrum existence of a little provincial town, ends up on Ellis Island or the fatal shore of Australia. He wanted other things.

His bred-in-the-bone restlessness would take him to New York, San Francisco, St Louis, Berlin, Hamburg, Paris, Nice, Monte Carlo, Brussels, London, Edinburgh and Glasgow: a long way from Beuthen. He was never to return there. All the rest of his life would be lived abroad. He would find himself as an entrepreneur, an exploiter, a Wandering Jew. He would not, he swore, be one of life's victims, like his poor father. He had long ago decided to be one of the takers. Small Quixotic generosities aside, it was not in him to give, save on the basis of cast bread being returned on the waters increased ten-per-cent-fold. He had been all his years thus far closely acquainted with poverty. Now he wished to sever the connection.

Oscar's first step to that wider freedom, which was in the end to teach him that poverty may grind men down, but riches are illusory, took him away to Berlin, where he found work in a timber merchant's office. He did not warm the seat of the high stool long. The soles of his feet beginning again to itch, he moved on a couple of hundred miles north-west to Hamburg, where he was soon financially well installed as a clerk in a bank. Presently espying an opportunity for self-betterment, he took up a position in the cashier's office of Hamburg Municipal Hospital at Eppendorf. It was while there that he reached military age and was called up for medical examination. A healthy, strongly built young man, he was passed A1 by the doctors and drafted into the artillery section of the army. He never arrived at the barracks.

Oscar Joseph Leschziner vanished. Oscar Slater was born.

By his own reckoning, it was about the year 1895, that, at the age of 23 Oscar first set foot on English soil. London was his objective, and it was there that the – relatively – innocent young man from Beuthen underwent a strange metamorphosis. The process had, no doubt, begun shortly after he had cut the umbilical apron-strings of home. He would have become necessarily street-wise in the big cities of

Berlin and Hamburg. Consider his predicament in London: on the run from the military, he arrived on the unknown shore and entered the unknown city which spoke an unknown tongue. He would have saved some small money from his last gainful employment. It would not have gone far, and now things must have taken on a frightening aspect.

> I was handicapped by a lack of knowledge of the language. I could not work in an office. [So] I turned towards the things I could do, and in turn became a clerk for bookmakers, was a bookmaker myself, and in the end conducted several clubs.

He pursued his further education through the academies of billiard halls and card schools, acquiring a winning skill that left little to chance and nothing to luck. Other tempting things beckoned. An uncounted part of the young Oscar's capital available for investment was his youthful good looks and that sturdy, attractive body on which the military authorities had set their sights. Different sights were set upon it now – those of eager young foreign women reaping a reasonable harvest in London from prostitution. They looked with lust, but saw, too, the desirable protection that would be afforded by the young Lothario's physical strength.

Time has washed away the addresses of the cheap rooms in cheap hotels and boarding-houses where Oscar struck early camps, but it is likely to have been within the Kings Cross–Bloomsbury–Fitzrovia–Soho quarter that he found his first shelter, and hereabouts set up with a pliant, or even suppliant, young adventuress, like himself a stranger in a strange land. And it was here that he reached a Priestleyan dangerous corner, destined to alter the direction and shape of the entire remainder of his life. He fell for her . . . and fell from grace.

Many foreign women and their 'bullies' were at that time heading up over the border, and Oscar was one of those who made his way to Edinburgh. The first reliable intelligence as regards his residence in that Athenian city dates from 1897. It emanates from the Edinburgh City Police, under whose eye Oscar had come because of the disreputable life he was by now leading. PC 284 David Valentine recalled: 'I knew Slater well. He used to frequent a brothel in Cheyne Street, occupied by a foreign prostitute.'

Always extremely smartly dressed, quite a dandy in fact, and with a good deal of money passing through his hands, flashing his bundle of fivers in the bars and billiard rooms, he impressed some of his associates as a man of charm, education and culture. Others thought him a mountebank, a liar, and, at cards especially, a cheat. Besides being a great billiards player, Oscar was an acknowledged expert at all manner of card games – and a highly skilled sharper. At a house in Thistle Street which he ran as a club or card saloon, and which was largely frequented by Germans who played faro, he was rumoured to keep one of the most skilfully devised machines for manipulating cards that was ever invented.

He is said to have been a man of very violent temper, and complaints were repeatedly lodged with the police concerning his ill-usage of Annie Hansen, a professional prostitute with whom he lived as man and wife. It was this evil temper of his which was responsible for the sole occasion upon which he found himself in the hands of the Edinburgh police. On 4 November 1899, he appeared in the police court charged with disorderly conduct; to wit fighting with a fellow-German on Waverley Bridge. The prosecution alleged that he had been drunk. He was fined 20 shillings or seven days. The other man was also fined 20 shillings.

Following a run of convictions for prostitution and one for assaulting a police officer, and faced with yet another charge of prostitution, Annie Hansen or Slater, due to come up again at the police court on 26 June 1900, failed to appear. Her bail was forfeited and a warrant granted for her apprehension. But the warrant was never put in force, as she had left the town. Glasgow was now about to be favoured with the presence of Oscar and Annie.

But before he quit Edinburgh, Oscar had his nose broken in a fist-and-foot fight with a compatriot well-named Brash. The fight was promoted by the impossibility of the combatants seeing eye to eye over the proportional division of some tainted money.

As he turned his battered profile to the West, and Edina's fair city slipped away, castle and rock like a fading mirage behind him, Oscar felt a faint stab of regret, embryonic nostalgia.

Glasgow had decided to celebrate the new century with a Great Exhibition. Its buildings spread across the 73 acres of Kelvingrove Park and its immediate neighbourhood, and during the six months of its opening – 2 May to 9 November, 1901 – the Exhibition drew a record of 11,500,000 visitors; and among the many shady moths attracted by its bright flame was Oscar.

The record is, as one might expect in the case of so impetuous a character as Slater, smudged about the edges, but the likelihood is that, between the leaving of Edinburgh and the triumphant entry into the golden fleecing fields of Glasgow, there was a breath-gathering intermezzo back in London, for he was to write:

> And so I came to the time of my life when I met a lady from Norfolk, who was afterwards to become my wife. I first saw her in London. I have not the desire to go deeply or more fully into this part of my career, but will tell you that eventually we were married in Glasgow and were as happy as any pair of lovers could be.

The facts do not quite bear out this idyll. The name of the lady in question was Mary (or Marie or May) Curtis Pryor, and she was an American subject. They married on 12 July, 1901, at Shamrock Street Register Office, and settled in at 33 Kelvinhaugh Street. It did not take the Glasgow police long to divine what was going on at No. 33. It was being used as a brothel, and the police saw Mrs Slater repeatedly taking men to the house. So the brutal truth emerges to shatter the Oscarean idyll. And, the final nail in the coffin of idealised romance, not only was May Slater leading an immoral life, but she was also an incorrigible drunkard.

Oscar's periods of residence in Glasgow between 1901 and 1905 were liberally punctuated by longish away-break spells, mainly back in London. It was there that he met Robert Rogers. He was to become his best metropolitan friend. In his thirties, Rogers, of 36 Albemarle Street, London West, described himself as a financial agent. He had a business interest in jewellery, and it was at Hatton Garden that he first encountered Oscar, where the latter, doubtless in full flower as one of his diamond merchant incarnations, was cannily buying, and equally cannily selling, precious stones. The two of a kind instantly took to each other.

There was a definite away-break in September 1902, when Oscar and May went to Scarborough, in Yorkshire. It was there, on 17 October, 1902, that Mary Slater was convicted on two charges of theft from a house where she and Oscar had taken furnished lodgings. For having taken more than just lodgings, she was sentenced to two terms of imprisonment of three months, to run concurrently.

It was after the Scarborough débâcle and its unfortunate consequences, and a brief period of recovery and rehabilitation in Glasgow, that, in 1903, Oscar and May took off for the south of France – to Nice, and to test his luck at the tables of Monte Carlo. His luck was out. Hoping to combine pleasure with business, hoping to enjoy – and win at – a few friendly poker parties, hoping to cover expenses and realise a healthy profit, not only did he lose his stake money, but also his own and his wife's jewellery. Later in 1903, he was back in London – and back in trouble: fined five shillings for being found in a gambling club, and bound over on his own £10 bail not to go into the club for a year. And more trouble in Glasgow: fined one pound for striking a man named Ferdinand, with whom he had been gambling, and who had, said Oscar, insulted him.

By the following year, 1904, Oscar and May's fairy-tale marriage was over. They had separated. Not uninvolved in the matter of their separation was a personage referred to by May Slater as 'the woman Junio'. This was Andrée Junio Antoine, an attractive, 19-year-old Frenchwoman, whom Slater had, literally, picked up at that redoubtable Victorian and Edwardian flesh-mart, the promenade of the Empire, Leicester Square. In 1905, they began to live together as man and wife. Of his legal spouse, Oscar had only this to say: 'She was a drunken woman and I adopted aliases to prevent her tracing me.' Surprisingly starry-eyed and unbitter about him to the end, May would neither say nor hear anything wrong said about her defecting husband. He had, she said, always treated her with the greatest kindness.

In the early months of 1906, Oscar and Andrée embarked on a trip to Europe, before sailing from Cherbourg, aboard the *Lucania*, for the United States, reaching New York on 5 May 1906. There, in partnership with John Devoto, who, said Oscar, had seven gambling places, he rented from one Peter de Silvestri premises at 114 West Twenty-Sixth Street, in the borough of Manhattan, for $60 a month, and opened up a gambling club. By the following year, 1907, Oscar was the proud manager of another, more impressive, uptown and upmarket club on Sixth Avenue. Business was good. He was making plenty of money. On 9 November 1907, brimful of optimism, he filled in a Declaration of Intention form, which was an application to become a citizen of the United States of America. Whatever his intention, the gods had already decided the disposal of that intention.

For the sake of Andrée's health, the couple returned to Paris in January 1908. They stayed there for a matter of weeks before returning to New York in February. But a mere three months after that they were back again in Paris, where they remained until August. Then, in the last days of that month, they arrived in London.

On 5 September 1908, Oscar, representing himself as Mr O. Junio (or, it has been said, Junior), rented a furnished flat at 45 Newman Street, off Oxford Street, for Andrée, where, as Madame Junio, he set her up, together with the prostitute's *de rigueur* guardian maid, a German girl named Katharina Schmalz. Men run truer to form than racehorses. Andrée had become the latest in Oscar's string – Annie Hansen, May Slater, Andrée Junio Antoine. During those weeks while Andrée was 'working' in Newman Street, Oscar stayed with his friend Robert Rogers at 36 Albemarle Street, and, now wearing his dental hat, brandished a shiny new visiting-card engraved with that address and the legend 'A. Anderson, Dentist.'

Stricken once more *mit der Wanderlust*, on 29 October Oscar packed and took a train, and travelled to Glasgow once again. In his A. Anderson persona, he put up at the Central Station Hotel. It was early in those first days back in Glasgow that, strolling nostalgically down Sauchiehall Street at about five o'clock in the evening, he bumped into an old friend of eight summers before. This was none other than the Moudie. They had originally met over the green baize at the Crown Hall Billiard Rooms, 98-100 Sauchiehall Street, in 1900, and he was destined to become Oscar's closest Glaswegian crony.

The Moudie had not, though, been Oscar's first encounter

with a familiar face. He had barely stepped off the train at Central Station when, next morning, he found himself shaking hands with Max Rattmann, who had himself just stepped off the train from London. Rattmann, a 28-year-old German, had lived in Britain since 1897. He had known Oscar in London, where he had kept a restaurant. They had never been on terms of intimacy, but used to meet frequently at a gambling place, the Travellers' Society Club, No. 12 Denmark Street, off the Charing Cross Road. Police inquiries were subsequently to identify Rattmann as a man otherwise known as George Schmidt, who had four convictions for dishonesty in London, and whose last sentence had been three and a half years' penal servitude in 1902.

By Tuesday, 3 November, the Oscarean finances, dented after five days of mounting hotel bills, patently stood in need of relief, and to that end Oscar betook himself to more modest lodgings in a boarding-house in Renfrew Street. And it was to this signally less expensive domicilement that Andrée and Katharina were summoned. They duly arrived on 4 November.

With the women temporarily ensconced in Renfrew Street, Oscar started to hunt around for more permanent quarters. Wandering about the West End, keeping an eye open, he spotted a flat to let in an imposing sandstone block, St George's Mansions, hard by Charing Cross. It was situated on the third floor of the right-hand wing of the same building as Messrs Stuart & Stuart, house furnishers. Letting no grass grow under his feet, Oscar negotiated an 18-month lease on the flat at No. 69 St. George's Road, furnished it with goods hire-purchased to the tune of £178 16s 6d from Messrs Stuart & Stuart, and had Andrée, Katharina and himself comfortably established therein by 10 November.[2]

During the course of the next five weeks a regular pattern of

---

2 Negotiations for the letting of the flat were conducted with the manager of Messrs Stuart & Stuart's, who rejoiced in the wonderful name of Isaac Paradise. Interestingly, Messrs. Stuart & Stuart, who rented the flat to Slater, were themselves only tenants of the building. The quidditative fact is that the owners of the property and ultimate landlords of Slater's questionably utilised flat were . . . the Glasgow Police.

living evolved, as described by Schmalz:

> Madame received gentlemen there at No. 69, and walked the principal
> streets. Madame usually went out in the afternoon, and visited the Empire[3]
> at night. Mr Slater usually went out in the morning at about eleven, and
> returned to lunch at two o'clock. He would go out again after lunch, and
> returned to dinner at about seven o'clock. After dinner he would go out,
> and usually returned after twelve at night.

It could never be Miltonically said of Oscar that he did 'scorn delights, and live laborious days'. Laborious nights, perhaps; tinkling 'tombwards to the lilt of coins,' through an ambience of pubs and clubs and spirit shops, billiard rooms and music-halls hung thick with eye-stinging, throat-catching, lung-threatening cigar and cigarette smoke, heavy-laden with fumes of beer and reek of whisky, all deceptively ameliorated by the sickly perfume-waftings of what Arthur Symons called the Juliets of the streets.

With Oscar Slater we enter into a whole, novel, Germano-Glaswegian underworld, peopled by strange denizens with Runyonesque monikers – the Moudie, the Soldier, the Acrobat, Willy the Artist, Little Wrestler, the Diamond Merchant – and curious demi-mondaines of the stamp of Max Rattmann, Josef Aumann and Max Brooks. A tricksy world of street-betting, whores and whoring, reset or the harbouring of 'iffy' goods, playing the horses and the cards, and tickling the ivories of billiard-balls for money. In such surroundings, Oscar would never be far to seek. There he would be, rubbing shoulders with thieves and touts, resetters and recidivists, bookmakers and boxing men, wrestlers, prize-fighters and fellow-ponces, in drinking club, billiard hall, gambling den or brothel . . . lurking behind the festoons of secret curtains, flicking down a winner's card, cutting a fine public figure on the green baize, treating crony or victim to a convivial glass. Wherever, at all hours of the day and night, his potential prey might be, there could be found Oscar, spreading a net for the innocent – such as still-wet-behind-the-ears young men, diurnally employed in the offices and warehouses of the district, having a macho night on the town – and not-so-innocent, older and should-be-wiser men hopelessly addicted to gambling and gaming.

At this period Oscar was very much in the company of Hugh

---

3   The Moss Empire Palace Theatre, 35 Sauchiehall Street.

Cameron, the Moudie. They shared the good – and easy – life. Mornings, perhaps a game or two of billiards at James Galbraith's Crown Hall Billiard Rooms, or in Peter Johnston's rooms, one stair up at 126 Renfield Street, opposite the Pavilion Theatre, not to mention the Imperial Billiard Conservatory, at 84 Mitchell Street. In the afternoon, it might be a visit to the roller-skating rink in Victoria Road, or to one, or several, of a host of favourite watering-holes, including Alexander Gall's public-house at 15 Cowcaddens Street, Peat's public-house and Galloway's spirit shop, in Hope Street, or Andrew Miller's, at 92 Cambridge Street, so favourite a haunt of exiled Germans that it was known as 'The Hamburger'. And in the evening, if not a trip to a music-hall, then the city heart was generously encircled by a fine, glittering coronal of clubs – the Mascot, in Renfrew Street, the MOSC or Sloper Club, and the Motor Club, next door to each other in India Street, where gambling delights were to be had into the really wee hours of the morning – like 7am!

It was, as we have already noted, Hugh Cameron who introduced Oscar to the MOSC. The letters of the club's official (registered in Edinburgh), acronymic designation stood for 'Members of the Sloper Club'. Ally Sloper was a popular cartoon character of the period. Oscar was elected a member on 23 December 1908, but he had, as a prospective member, been allowed to use the club since the latter part of November. Although he was to be seen on at least a couple of occasions within the portals of the Sloper's illustrious neighbour, the Motor Club, which occupied the first floor of No. 26 India Street, Oscar was never a member, and had merely been taken there as guest of the ubiquitous Moudie.

Moving about the city in 1908, Oscar became again what he had been in 1901, 1903, 1904 and 1905, a familiar Glasgow figure, and the omens were all indicating that he was digging in, preparing to settle down. What more harmless and respectable presignification than his Saturday visit to the hardware merchants' establishment of Messrs Hepburn & Marshall, at 54 St George's Road, and his purchase of such touching items of premeditated domesticity as a galvanised pail and a bouquet of brushes to go with it? And in further support of the doctrine of good intention, did not the nest-building Oscar return to the hardware merchants' emporium three days later – 10 November – and purchase two dozen coat hooks, one toilet fixture, and a half-crown, pre-packaged 'Card of Household Tools', which included a screwdriver, a brogue, a gimlet, a pair of pincers, and a small, lightweight hammer, all of nine inches long.

Little by little, treading softly, and occasionally on people's corns, Oscar became accepted, or, if not precisely accepted, recognised and tolerated in the milieu of his day to day existence, his somewhat erratic interchange with the shopkeepers, in and around St George's Road.

Throughout that November and December of 1908, the graph of the state of Oscar's financial affairs went up and down as ecrhythmously as the temperature markings on the chart of a patient with blackwater fever!

12 November. Hopeful prognosis. Oscar opens a Post Office Savings Bank account in the name of A. Anderson, and buys Consuls.

14 November. Relapse. Oscar pledges a diamond scarf-pin with Liddell's for £5.

17 November. Decided trough. Oscar pledges purse, studs, and other small bits and pieces for an obviously much-needed £6.

18 November. Trough deepens. Oscar pledges a crescent-shaped diamond brooch at Liddell's, getting £20 on it.

The financial doldrums persisted.

7 December. Oscar pledges a pair of binoculars at Bryce's pawnshop for £2 10s.

9 December. Oscar raises a further £9 from Liddell's on the diamond crescent-brooch pledged on November 18th.

17 December. Slight upcurve in fiscal health graph. Oscar deposits £5 in his Post Office Savings account.

19 December 19. Remission seems to have been only slight and transient. Oscar borrows five shillings from George Sabin, secretary of the Sloper Club, and another modest sum from a gambling friend, Robert Scott Beveridge.

20 December. Financial state of health plunges. Oscar writes to the Post Office Savings Bank asking for all his money *at once*.

Monday, 21 December 1908.

A cross-roads.

And, as so often happens at life's cross-roads, two events provided signposts. Two letters: one from London, one from San Francisco. The London letter, from Robert Rogers, brought the news to Oscar's breakfast-table that his wife, hot on his trail for money, was demanding his address. The San Francisco letter was from John Devcto. Come out, it invited, to San Francisco, where business is good . . .

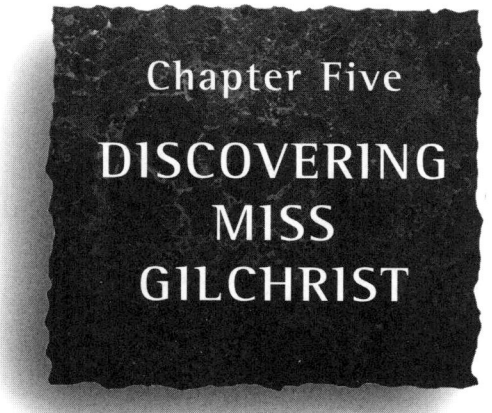

Chapter Five

DISCOVERING MISS GILCHRIST

For the first 47 years of her life Marion Gilchrist was a rôle model of the stereotypic, self-sacrificial, Victorian spinster daughter, who, either by misfortunate circumstance or dutiful design, suffered the season for marriage and its fulfilment in motherhood to pass over her as she devoted herself to the loving care of a widowed father. He, James Taylor Gilchrist, cast in the heroic mould of the founding fathers of the city of Glasgow, was a self-made man. The son of a Glasgow shoemaker, he rose, across the harsh span of 50 industrious years, from apprentice millwright to consulting engineer. On New Year's Day 1821, at the age of 22, he married 20-year-old Christina Finlay, a weaver's daughter, and, in the best tradition of that era, was to father a substantial family of three sons and six daughters.

Wednesday's child, Marion, was born on 18 January 1826. At the age of 12, she had seven siblings. By the time of her violent death, some 70 years later, out of all that jolly company only four sisters – herself, Christina, Elizabeth and Jane – would remain.

By the early 1870s, the heroic mould of James Taylor Gilchrist was beginning to show the cracks of time, a fissure here, another there; starting to break up. This gradual fragmentation broke clean on 10 January 1873, when, at the age of 74, he succumbed to congestive apoplexy, which is to say cerebral haemorrhage.

Now, Marion, a week and a day short of her 47th birthday, was alone. She was to become even more alone, isolated from her kind and kin, when the terms of her father's will became known. He had, with the exception of a legacy of £100 to his then unmarried daughter, Elizabeth, and the sum of £24 per annum to his son, Marshall, left everything of which he died possessed to his daughter, Marion.

This, predictably, caused trouble. Marion's siblings felt that she had somehow done them out of their patrimony. There were family ructions; bad feelings and resentments were expressed, dividing the family as only money can. There ensued the virtual severance of all connections between Marion and her sisters and their offspring. By 1908, only three out of that whilom amplitude of nephews and nieces had, theoretically at any rate, contact or commerce with wickedly rich Aunt Marion. We know that Janet's daughter, Margaret Dawson Birrell, and brother James' daughter, Mary Greer Gilchrist or McCall, visited her. So, too, did her 'courtesy nephew', Francis James Charteris.

It would have been about the middle of the year 1877, that Marion, aged 51, with mother, father, three brothers and a sister lying below that sad stone urn marker of mortality in the Necropolis, and four sisters living – to whom it was as if she were already interred with those others' bones – closed the door of the home where all those years she and her father had lived, 140 West Campbell Street, behind her, and closed it also upon the Gilchrist family life and companionship which she had, prior to the publication of her father's will, all her days known. She moved off now to that flat in West Princes Street, where, 30 years into the future, her fate would come to meet her up the cold stone stair.

The life that prim Miss Gilchrist spinsterishly lived at neat and tidy, spick and span, polished and cosy No. 15 Queen's Terrace was a withdrawn and secluded one, keeping herself most exclusively to herself, owing and being owed by no one. By definition, such a life is difficult to reconstruct. It is only through the sly eyes of servants, the imprudent lips of the occasional visitor or friend, and by keeping a cocked ear for rumour, that it is possible to gain a glimpse here, a hint there, a small insight somewhere else, beyond the carefully erected barriers.

It was shortly after Miss Gilchrist's move to West Princes Street that Maggie Galbraith came into her service as a maid. Maggie believed herself to be only 16. Actually she was 21. Previous writers appear to have experienced difficulty in identifying her. She is clearly recorded at New Register House in Edinburgh as having been born on 11 September 1856, in the hamlet of Borve, near Castlebay, on the Outer Hebridean island of Barra. Her father: John Galbraith, a shoemaker. Her mother: Isabella McKinnon or Galbraith.

The shoemaker's daughter was to stay with Miss Gilchrist for 12 years, until, in 1889, she was married from her mistress' house to David Ferguson, a railway goods' guard from Greenock. Throughout the following 19 years of Marion Gilchrist's life, the Fergusons were to remain on the most intimate terms with her. They frequently visited her, and, after they had moved from Glasgow to Kilmarnock in 1903, were often invited to stay at her flat with her. And she would often go to stay with them in their little house in Kilmarnock.

Each summer it was Miss Gilchrist's habit to take the whole Ferguson family away with her to a house at the coast, which she would rent for a couple of months. They became, in effect, her surrogate family – Maggie, the daughter she never had; David and Maggie's children, her grandchildren. The daughter born to the Fergusons in 1892 was, at Miss Gilchrist's own request, named after her, Marion Gilchrist Ferguson, and was from the beginning the apple of her eye. Subsequently, a son, David, and another daughter, christened Maggie Galbraith, completed the Ferguson family.

A servant lost may have been a friend gained, but filling the domestic gap was far from easy. Between Maggie's departure and the arrival, sixteen years later, of Helen Lambie, Miss Gilchrist endured a succession of young women servants, good, not-so-good and indifferent. Most of them came and as rapidly went, vanishing unmourned into the lumber-room of things past. One of these, Jane or Jeanie Hay Duff, who arrived in 1895 and left in 1900, testified interestingly that Miss Gilchrist was 'generally reputed to be a very wealthy person of means, and as having a lot of jewellery. I found in talking to other maids that this seemed to be well known in the neighbourhood'.

On 13 October 1905 young Nellie Lambie trundled her modest tin trunk to the bed alcove beside the kitchen at No. 15. Despite the fact that Miss Gilchrist kept a tight-ship economy, Nellie liked her mistress – 'She wasn't very liberal in her housekeeping, but she was a kind lady. I don't know of anyone who had any ill-will to her or was likely to have injured or murdered her. I've never heard anyone speak ill of her.'

Nellie was able to fill in a few more names of callers in the, albeit thin, visitors' book for No. 15. There was Miss Gilchrist's niece, Margaret Dawson Birrell, there was Mrs Charteris, that is the former Mrs Elizabeth Greer or Gilchrist, and her daughter, Mrs McCall – 'I have heard Miss Gilchrist speak of Mrs Charteris and her daughter as people who came to the house to watch and see what was going on.' As regards male visitors, they were either 'gentlemen from the church or business gentlemen. She had two nephews named Birrell. I don't know their names. I don't know where they stay. Neither of them was ever in Miss Gilchrist's house to my knowledge'.

It is a well recognised fact of social history that in those days the servants' hall was a regular hotbed of snobbery, tuppence ha'penny looking down on tuppence. Its occupants would boast to, and vie with, each other regarding their master or mistress' wealth and status. This, by some weird mechanism of reflected glory, would decide their own below-stairs standing! Nellie insisted that her sole object in telling folk about Miss Gilchrist's fine jewellery had been 'to show that I was in a good place, and that my mistress was a person of means'.

There have been those who have professed to find in Miss Gilchrist's excessive-seeming concern about her admittedly valuable trinkets, evidence of something alarmingly more than eccentricity. Did all this obsession with those bright baubles, that fixation about men in presses and burglars under beds, transgress the boundary lines of normalcy? Did it add sinister significance to Report No. 759 in the Glasgow Police Information Book, which I discovered held in Strathclyde Regional Archives.[1] The report, dated 22 December 1908, 2.45am, written by Detective Inspector Pyper, contains the following most unexpected, and here for the first time revealed, paragraph:

> Miss Gilchrist was insane for a time a few years ago and was under the guardianship of a Mrs McLelland, wife of the late Mr James McLelland, of Thomson & McLelland, Writers, 180 West George Street, who were her agents.

On 3 August 1892, at the age of 66, Marion Gilchrist had indeed signed what is known in Scotland as a Factory or Commission; that is a deed granted by A empowering B to act for him in one of several transactions, which is the equivalent of a Power of Attorney in English law. Miss Gilchrist's business affairs were to remain in the hands of Messrs McLelland, Thomson & Towers Clerk until 1905, when she removed them into the professional care of James Macdonald.

John Stewart, a senior partner of the Glasgow firm of stockbrokers, Struthers & Stewart, who had known Miss Gilchrist all his life – he was 52 – and had been her stockbroker since 1889, was very upset by the rumours which were being bandied about Glasgow regarding her. It was being said that she was a resetter – the Scottish term for a receiver of stolen goods – and that men frequented her house in connection with this; that she had uncut and unset diamonds and other precious stones; that she was Nellie Lambie's mother; that she had had an illegitimate daughter and that Mrs Ferguson was that daughter. These stories were, of course, all arrant nonsense.

Mr Stewart's last glimpse of Miss Gilchrist was on Friday, 18 December, when she had called at his office.

1 (Reference SR/22/63/10)

At three o'clock on Saturday, 19 December 1908, Miss Margaret Dawson Birrell took afternoon tea with her aunt. She had made it one of her customarily short visits.

> I spent an hour with her. She seemed in particularly good health then, although she was hardly a strong woman. At that visit she pressed me strongly to come back soon and see her, and I promised to come back very soon.

She did. Within 48 hours . . . to find Aunt Marion an unrecognisably battered cadaver.

Two weeks to the day after Miss Gilchrist's murder – Monday, 4 January 1909 – the morning papers revealed the identity of the prime suspect, the man with the twisted nose: Oscar Slater.

On the previous Saturday (2 January), he had been delivered to Room 76, Post Office Building, at the lower end of City Hall Park, the office of Commissioner John A Shields, of the District Court of the United States for the Southern District of New York, before whom he was arraigned. Mr Charles Fox, counsel for the British Government, most oddly ignoring the fact that that ticket, being for a brooch of his own which Slater had pawned, had not the slightest significance as regards Miss Gilchrist's murder and her missing brooch, had asked that the pawn-ticket found on Slater be made part of the record in the case. This was consented to by Mr William A. Goodhart, attorney, who, together with Mr Hugh Gordon Miller, had been retained to represent Slater.

The hearing for the granting of the requested extradition warrant was set for 19 January at 2pm Bail was refused and Slater was committed to the Tombs Prison. If, as he was so often and so passionately to declare, Slater was both innocent of the crime and ignorant of the circumstances surrounding and the people involved in it, then it was a truly Kafka-esque situation in which he found himself blindly entangled.

Back in Scotland, a warm and grateful feeling murmured across Glasgow like an audible sigh, palpable as the breath of the mistral. With Slater under lock and key, everything, it seemed, was neatly parcelled, nicely tied up. But prophetic indeed were the words of that day's Glasgow *Evening Times*: 'The case in reality is only beginning . . .'

All of this American activity had, of course, been taking place beyond the ken of the Glasgow police and public. The first that they knew of it was when they read about it in the newspapers. Knowing now that Miss Gilchrist's killer was safely 'entombed', the police were determined to attend to the permanent closure of the door and make the rock-seal secure.

Like his father before him – William Hart, who had prosecuted Madeleine Smith in 1857 – James Neil Hart was Procurator-fiscal. In Scotland, the police never prosecute. Their responsibility is the investigation of crime, and once a person has been arrested control of the investigation passes to the Fiscal. He is a full-time civil servant, and must be either an advocate or, more usually, a solicitor. Fiscal Hart had for some time now been toiling away in his office at County Buildings, in Ingram Street.

One of the people into whose conduct he had been closely inquiring was a 37-year-old widower named Patrick Nugent, who had, for a time, paid court to Nellie Lambie. And she had stated that she had told Nugent that Miss Gilchrist was very well-off and had jewellery. On 31 December Detective Officer John Trench had been despatched in search of Nugent and had found him residing with his Irish family – including four brothers, all miners – at Carfin, a mining town two miles north-east of Motherwell. A local constable described Nugent to Trench as 'a low-class bookmaker, convicted several times for betting offences, who had the local reputation of being a rake, two women in Carfin having had children by him'.

Nugent told Trench that he had met Nellie Lambie at a dance at New Year 1908, and had walked out, briefly, with her. She had on one occasion admitted him to Miss Gilchrist's while her mistress was from home. He was in the West Princes Street flat for about three hours. He had had tea and she had shown him Miss Gilchrist's room, and played the piano to him. He had given Nellie up because he was a Roman Catholic and she was a Protestant. He had since met and married someone else.

Trench had also visited Nellie Lambie's family at Holytown,

about 11 miles south-east of Glasgow, and reported: 'Her parents and relatives are in poor circumstances, and the local constable describes them as a "rum lot".' But he heard nothing to Nellie's detriment.

On the afternoon of New Year's Day, Fiscal Hart received a telegram informing him that Crown Counsel thought that the Gilchrist murder was a case in which 'two officers should proceed to New York if apprehension effected and demand for surrender granted'. Accordingly, Hart sat himself down at 11pm in the fine, spacious grey stone house at 25 Newark Drive, a leaf-bowered corner of Pollokshields, where he lived a bachelor life, and wrote nominating his Chief Sheriff Criminal Officer, William Warnock, and Detective Inspector John Pyper to undertake the mission. The decision was also subsequently taken that because, judging by previous Home Office experience, the American court would not be satisfied without having oral witness-identification of Slater, Arthur Adams, Helen Lambie and Mary Barrowman should accompany Warnock and Pyper to New York. The company of five embarked from Liverpool aboard the White Star liner *Baltic*, on 13 January.

As the *Baltic* slipped quietly out past the Bar, some determined police legwork was being carried on in Glasgow. Miss Annie Armour, a booking clerk at Kelvinbridge subway station, some half-mile from Miss Gilchrist's, was interviewed. She remembered a man – dark, medium height, clean-shaven, wearing a high collar, light overcoat, waterproof, she thought, collar half turned up, and a darkish hat or cap – who came rushing into the turnstile, threw down a penny without speaking a word, and, before she could give him his ticket, dashed off down the stairs to the platform. Widespread inquiries failed to net this odd bird.

Throughout those January days the taking of statements went relentlessly on, especial attention being accorded to those who stood in close relation to the deceased lady, either by ties of blood or bonds of affection.

Her nephew, George Gilchrist Birrell, said:

My parents are dead. I have one sister alive, Maggie Dawson Birrell. I have two brothers: James Aitken Birrell, 103 Rolland Street, and Wingate Birrell, whose address I don't know, but I have been told he is in London. He was in the Army, but I think deserted. Our family and Miss Gilchrist were not on visiting terms.

Margaret Dawson Birrell, interviewed, said that her mother had died in 1896. Since then she had been seeing her aunt

several times in a year, but not often. My brothers, George and James, occasionally visited me, but they never used to talk of Miss Gilchrist and her house, nor did I to them. I am quite sure they do not know anything about any property which she had.

Statement of James Aitken Birrell:

The deceased was my aunt. I knew whereabouts she lived, but I did not know her house in West Princes Street. It is over forty years since I last saw her and I did not correspond with her. I never heard that my aunt was possessed of a quantity of diamond jewellery until after this investigation began.'

His wife, 40-year-old Mrs Mary Nimmo or Birrell, knew her though – only too well. Listen to this precognition, given at Glasgow on 12 February 1909:

I knew of the deceased Miss Gilchrist as my husband's aunt, but I only saw her once to my knowledge, and that was, so far as I can recollect, about seven years ago.[2]

At that time my husband and I were in rather straitened circumstances, and I was about to be confined. My husband told me that he understood his aunt was a kindly person. I suggested that he should call on her and see whether she would give us any assistance, but he would not do so. I proposed that I should call on her and my husband said I might please myself in that respect.

Accordingly, I did call on her one forenoon at her house in Queen's Terrace. I found Miss Gilchrist and explained to her who I was, and asked if she could give my husband a little assistance. She received me kindly enough, but she said she did not know my husband and she did not want to know him, and she refused to give any assistance, and said he should apply to his friends.

I explain that I was about half an hour sitting in the drawing-room before Miss Gilchrist appeared. I think she had been dressing. I had not more than three or four minutes' conversation with her when she did come.

Miss Gilchrist was dressed with a black satin gown and wore two diamond rings and a gold chain. I think I am right in saying she also wore a diamond crescent brooch in her dress. I told my husband that Miss

2 It will actually have been in 1901. Mary Birrell's daughter, Margaret May, was born on 27 May 1901. Tragically, she died a little over two months later.

Gilchrist wore two diamond rings, and I may have said that Miss Gilchrist was gorgeously or handsomely dressed. I thought she was very handsome. I never saw her again. I only heard of her murder on the Tuesday night (22 December), when my husband came home with a newspaper and told me.

My husband was at that time in the employ of the Income Tax Office in St Vincent Street, and so far as I remember was at work then from about 6.15 till 9 or 9.30pm. He was much shocked when he heard of the murder.

Mrs Maggie Galbraith or Ferguson says:

Miss Gilchrist was very confiding with me and yet she never told me much of her private affairs. Last year she told me that she had left my family and me something, adding – if we got it, as she said she knew she had enemies who might interfere with the disposal of her property after she was dead. I did not think that the enemies she spoke of would do her personal harm. She also told me some time this year that she was getting sour at Mrs McCall, who had been saying that she was to get all her money. I said I thought that Miss Birrell was entitled to something as she had to work hard and was not married like the others. I had never any friends at deceased's house, and I don't think my husband would have any either. He called at Miss Gilchrist's house on Monday, fourteenth December, 1908, and again on Thursday, seventeenth December, 1908, about purchasing a dog for her. Miss Gilchrist was a good friend to me while living, and I would sooner have had her living than as it is now. I have no idea who could have done the deed.

At the request of Fiscal Hart, Mrs Mary Greer Gilchrist or McCall was seen at her home, Boscombe Court, Bossoney, Bournemouth, by an officer of the Hampshire police. She told him:

Miss Gilchrist was my aunt. We were very good friends and devoted to each other. The last time I saw her alive was on Monday, tenth February, 1908, when I left her after nursing her through an illness for three weeks. This was the last occasion I was at her house in Glasgow, until after the murder was discovered. Helen Lambie was then in the employ of my aunt. During the three weeks I was nursing my aunt I saw a good deal of her jewellery. She was in the habit of keeping her jewellery in an old leather bag in the wardrobe in her bedroom. I have known her to have the bag in bed with her. When the maid, Lambie, was out, my aunt, if required would answer the door herself.

Mrs McCall, when further questioned later, added that her aunt was fond of a bargain and might purchase anything at the door.

I know of her having, during the time of the Glasgow Exhibition, bought some pieces of carpet from foreigners who appeared to have found out her address and called on her with carpets. My aunt told me afterwards that they pressed her into buying them.

The *Glasgow News* of 23 January 1909, announced: 'An inventory of the estate of the late Miss Gilchrist has been lodged with the Sheriff-Clerk of Lanarkshire. Her estate has been returned at £15,758 8s 1d'
   High stakes.

Bits and pieces had been filtering across the Atlantic from 'Over There'. The intelligence was that Oscar Slater was maintaining an attitude of cheerfulness and expressing continuing confidence in complete exoneration. He had been brought up again before Commissioner Shields on 19 January, but the proceedings had been of the briefest; a formal adjournment for one week, in order to allow for the party from Liverpool to arrive.

The *Baltic* steamed into New York on 25 January, five days late. The voyagers from Glasgow were whisked off by cab to Smith & McNell's Hotel, corner of Fulton and Washington Streets. Next day the messengers of justice were to keep their postponed appointment with Commissioner Shields.

Tuesday, 26 January 1909.
They were standing – Mr Fox, Inspector Pyper, Mr Adams, Nellie Lambie and Mary Barrowman – in the corridor outside the entrance to the court-room. It was just before three o'clock in the afternoon. Three men came bustling along, passed them, and, after some moments of fumbling hesitation, went into the court. According to Inspector Pyper, Lambie and Barrowman simultaneously touched his arm and simultaneously said: 'Oh, there is the man away into the court.' A chance encounter in the court corridor . . . the first flesh-and-blood glimpse afforded Adams, Lambie and Barrowman of the man Slater. Chance – or design? Circumstance carefully orchestrated to assure that witnesses and Slater should happen to be in the right place at the right time, from the prosecution standpoint, that is.

Whatever, this was an incident of supreme importance, for everything turned upon the question of identity. Slater was putting forward a defence of mistaken identity, and it was consequently a prime requirement that nothing should be permitted to interfere with, or in any way prejudice, the process of fair identification.

Already, we know, for an admitted fact, that photographs of Slater had been shown to Adams and Barrowman. The reason that none was shown to Lambie was that she had plainly stated that she had never seen Miss Gilchrist's visitant's face. If, however, as by interested parties claimed, Lambie's and Barrowman's recognition of the *handcuffed* man in the corridor was – handcuffed hints apart – spontaneous, genuine, effected without guidance, guile, hint or prompt, nod or wink, then the occasion of the *actual* identification was there and then, and their subsequent pantomime of 'identifying' that same man in court was pure farce. Lambie, asked if she could see present in the court the man she had seen on the night of the murder, replied with commendable caution: 'One is very suspicious, if anything', and went on to say that she had identified the man by his walk. He didn't walk straight and was 'sort of shaking himself a little' as he walked. She demonstrated a somewhat stilted specimen walk. Then, amid dead silence, pointed a finger at Slater.

Slater's counsel, Mr Miller, asked her: 'What were you all doing pointing to this man when I saw you standing in the door?' To which, with pert impertinence, she rejoined: 'That was my business and none of yours.'

Young Mary Barrowman acquitted herself well. She answered counsel's questions clearly and unhesitatingly. Asked by Mr Fox: 'Do you see that man here today?' she looked from face to face for fully half a minute amid breathless suspense. Then, after another sweep of the crowded court-room with her keen eyes, she stooped, peered over at Slater's two bulky, lawyers who had been standing partially in front of him, slowly pointed a finger at Slater and said: 'That man here is very like him.'

Then it was the turn of Arthur Montague Adams. He had known Miss Gilchrist since he was a little boy. He was not, alas, the most observant of mortals. He had not noticed Slater passing by in the corridor outside the court. He had not noticed the crookedness or otherwise of the nose of the man in Miss Gilchrist's hall. He had not noticed the man's hat. Asked by the Commissioner, point-blank,

'Is there anybody in the room here that you identify as that man?'
Adams' reply was: 'I couldn't say positively. This man (indicating
Slater) is not at all unlike him. Very much like him.' Questioned as
to whether he had noticed anything remarkable about the man's
way of walking, Adams said, 'No. I thought he walked like a
commercial traveller', which rather cryptic definition he enlarged to:
'Just an ordinary walk.'

Mr Miller: 'You don't swear this is the man you saw?'

Adams: 'No, sir.'

The second day of the hearing turned out to be little more
than an *entr'acte* – the wearisome reading out of deposition after
deposition.

The third and mammoth day of the drama was Friday, 29
January.

Mary Barrowman was recalled. Mr Miller asked her if it was not
so that in her deposition she had described the man whom she had
encountered in West Princes Street as tall and thin? Yes, she said,
she had. Miller asked Slater to stand up. Then, as he stood there,
comfortably sleek, well-covered, not very tall, Miller, glancing over
to the Commissioner, remarked: 'I ask your Honour to take judicial
notice of the prisoner at the bar.' At this, Mr Fox shot out of his seat.
'Wait a moment,' he called out. 'Now, Mary, attend to me. Do you
think this man standing here (indicating Slater) is tall?'

'I do,' answered Barrowman.

'And thin?'

'Yes.' Without another word, Fox resumed his seat. And Mary
went back to hers. Mr Adams (recalled) was the last witness of the
day. Mr Miller asked him: 'Are you prepared to say that this
defendant here, Oscar Slater, is the man whom you saw in the hall?'

'Well, no sir,' said Adams.

As both sides had now finished with the evidence of the
witnesses from Glasgow, they were, the Commissioner told them, at
liberty to sail for home.[3] Further hearing of the case was adjourned
for one week.

However . . . on the afternoon of 3 February, Mr Miller

3 Adams, Lambie and Barrowman sailed for Liverpool aboard the *Baltic* on Saturday, 30
January 1909.

released a bombshell. He informed the Commissioner that his client was willing to waive extradition and return voluntarily to Glasgow to stand his trial.

As Miller presented it, Slater's decision implied the accused's confidence in his ability to clear himself of unjustified suspicion. The truth is that this was not the heroic, self-confident choice of innocence which popular belief has ever since held it to have been. In fact, Slater had been presented with Hobson's choice. His American lawyers had put it to him that although the evidence adduced against him was circumstantial and the fight over his extradition was likely to be a long one, there was little doubt that ultimately international comity would force his reluctant return to Glasgow. How much better for him, then, to go willingly; such a step would assuredly create an infinitely more favourable impression on a Scots jury.

The Court of Mr Commissioner Shields convened for the last time in the matter of Oscar Slater on Saturday morning, 6 February. Mr Fox asked that the defendant be remanded in the custody of the United States Marshal to await the action of the Secretary of State; that was the issue by the proper authorities in Washington of the warrant for his extradition.

In this topsy-turvy case of the exceptional which did not prove the rule, one may perhaps be excused for applying the appropriate topsy-turvy Shakespeareanism that valour was not, for Slater, the better part of discretion.

Chapter Six

THE RETURN OF THE ALIEN

Slater was growing restive. It was going on for six weeks now that he had been in the Tombs. The warrant from Washington for which he, Warnock and Pyper seemed to have been interminably waiting arrived at last on 11 February.

Mr Warnock scuttled frantically – but happily – around New York, finally managing to fix up berths for the three of them on the Anchor Line's *Columbia*, sailing for Glasgow at noon on 13 February: estimated time of arrival in the Clyde, Sunday, 21 February.

A complaining 'Mrs' Slater was booked, third class, aboard the Cunarder *Campania*, under the anagrammatic identity, Salter. She landed at Liverpool on 17 February and proceeded, via London, to her home in Paris.[1]

Oscar and his two guardians were accommodated in one of the *Columbia's* pair of hospital rooms; large, airy and lockfast. Oscar afterwards wrote:

1 *Rue des Trois-Frères, Montmartre.*

I was favoured with the very painstaking attendance of a very nice stewardess or nurse. She asked me every morning how I had slept, and my answer was that I had slept well. She told me that if I had not been in that cabin, she would have had the comfort of the bed. I thereupon asked her if it was her pillow that I was sleeping on, and when she answered in the affirmative I at once informed her, much to her amusement, that therein lay the reason for my customary sweet repose.

There spake the practised lady-charmer, the Beau Brummell of the brothel.

Throughout the voyage, Slater was usually cheery, but there were several occasions when he suffered fits of despondency, and wept bitterly.

There was a lot of snow and the *Columbia* passed through a fair amount of loose ice, but inside the hospitable hospital room all was snug, and the ice-floes went unnoticed. The *Columbia* ploughed on. Oscar leant back in his chair, lit a small cigar, and, with a confident if not contented heart, awaited landfall.

In those faraway, long ago days of the 'Atlantic greyhounds', a popular post-kirk Sunday pastime was to go down to the river-bank and watch the great liners steam in majesty up the Clyde. Generally, weather sufficiently enticing, three or four hundred folk would be out big ship-spotting, but on this hazy, though fine, February Sunday, huge crowds had been gathering since early morning, every eye scanning the horizon for the *Columbia*, with – as their newspapers had told them – Oscar Slater a prisoner aboard.

As twelve noon struck, the huge bulk of the *Columbia* hove into view and came, almost imperceptibly, to a stop at the Tail o' the Bank, off Greenock. 'Here she comes!' the shout went up at Stobcross Quay as the great ship swung round the bend of the river at Yorkhill, a mere couple of miles west of Queen Street Station, right in the centre of Glasgow. The swing-bridge was bedecked, and the ferry steps opposite the Anchor Line berthing shed were buttered thick with neck-craning scrutators.

But . . . no Slater.

Then came the news: he was already safely lodged in the Central Police Office in St Andrew's Square. When the *Columbia* had previously come to a standstill, a tender, the Anchor Line's *Express*, had drawn alongside and taken him and his escort off. Watched by practically all the ship's passengers, they had departed down the gangway from the *Columbia* to the *Express*, Pyper in front, then Slater, handcuffed to him, Warnock behind. About to descend, Slater had just raised his hat in courteous farewell salutation to the crowded rail of spectators, when something most uncalled for happened.

Oscar recalled:

> I had just left the liner and had received the handshake and the good wishes of the captain, the doctor, and the purser. I was handcuffed, and as I got on to the tender one of the members of the crew kicked me. There was not the slightest provocation for it. I did not know the man and I had not spoken to him. I turned round and said that was not a fair thing to do seeing that I had not even been tried on the charge that had been preferred against me. It hurt me more mentally than it did physically.

It was a presignatorily symbolic ending to Oscar's 3,000-mile journey to face the out-of-tune music. He now exchanged his apartment in the Tombs for Cell No. 4, Hall D, of the penitentiary in Duke Street, Glasgow.

Outside the prison walls, February slid into March, and March was moving rapidly towards April. Inside, time dragged and lay heavily. But Oscar had made some progress. He had found himself an excellent and dedicated agent or solicitor in Ewing Speirs, writer, of Messrs Joseph Shaughnessy & Sons. He had found a devoted champion in the Reverend Mr Eleazer Philip Phillips, Minister of the Hebrew Community in Glasgow, who, sternly convinced of Slater's blamelessness, had set himself the task of opening a defence fund on Oscar's behalf. But Glaswegian Jewry was showing scant disposition to come to the aid of a compatriot in distress, responding with neither emotional nor financial generosity to his plight. Indeed, Rabbi Phillips was advised in pikestaff-plain terms that in offering succour to Slater, he was 'acting in his personal capacity and not as a minister of the synagogue'. It seems pretty certain that it was Slater's clear prior involvement in the seamier side of the city's life, his widely advertised status as a pimp and gambler, that went fatally against him.

On Friday, 23 April, Oscar Slater was taken from Duke Street Prison and delivered to the governor of Calton Gaol, in Edinburgh. His trial date was fixed as 3 May, 1909. As April's last snail-paced days wore away, Oscar, like a knight of old preparing for battle, made ready the armour of smart clothing that hung waiting in the wardrobe of his self-esteem. He would enter the lists a martial dandy, to whatever end.

On Saturday, 1 May, Andrée arrived in Edinburgh. She put up at Houston's Temperance Hotel, 31 Lothian Road.

Two days to go.

The *Weekly Mail* of 1 May, 1909 nudged its readers:

> The beginning of the end has come. Oscar Slater appears before Lord Guthrie in Edinburgh on Monday to answer the most serious charge that can be brought against any man – the charge of murder.

In fact, Monday brought only the end of the beginning.

The trial of Oscar Slater was an utter disgrace. Special circumstances so ordained it. For the Lord Advocate, Alexander Ure, KC, MP, it became a personal issue. He had only just been appointed, and this was to be his first big trial. He was to present the prosecution case. It would be his first public performance in his new rôle, and he was ambitiously anxious to do well, to *win*. This boded ill for Oscar, for it implied the possibility at least that the new broom might sweep aside the niceties of the traditionally neutral, which is to say emotionally uncharged, presentation of the evidence by the prosecution in capital cases.

A second misfortune was the character, the unconscious bias, of the judge. Charles John Guthrie was a profoundly good and honest man, but he was a son of the manse, far happier inspecting the morally sanitised ranks of the Boys' Brigade, of which he was to become the National President, than presiding over the distasteful aftermath of the criminal evil that men do. A foreign pimp such as Slater would have been, indeed was, anathema to him. It could, and did, warp his judgment.

The merry month of May was ushered in shivery as a shorn lamb. Winter was lingering in the lap of spring.

Monday, 3 May 1909. Up on the chilly eminence of the high slopes of the High Street of Edinburgh, Parliament House stood bleak and empty. It was vacation time. The Courts were not sitting. All was forlorn. The long corridors – usually a bustle of court officers, policemen, witnesses, agents, and filled with bobbing wigs and fluttering gowns as a heavy traffic of advocates flitted from court to court, and to and from the Advocates' Library – were silent and echoingly sepulchral, the advocates' polished wooden boxes with their brass name-plates ranged along the walls looking like miniature coffins. Broodingly desolate, too, was the great Parliament Hall, normally presenting the lively and awesome spectacle of splendidly apparelled legal gentlemen, in deep thought and even deeper consultation, pacing gravely back and forth before the bright-burning fire and beneath the portraits of dead and gone judges, who gaze down in frozen, marmoreal dignity upon these their lineal successors.

The High Court of Justiciary, the supreme criminal court in Scotland, sat in Edinburgh in a fine late-Georgian court-room – No. 3 – which has been the scene of many of the country's most notable trials. Ure, prosecuting Slater, was assisted by Mr Thomas Brash Morison, KC, Advocate Depute, a constitutionally stern man, later to become a notoriously stern judge, and Mr William Lyon, Advocate Depute, subsequent Sheriff of Ayr. Senior counsel for the defence was Mr Alexander Logan McClure, KC, Sheriff of Argyll, leading Mr John Mair.

Standing in the well of the court, a focus and magnet of attention, was a table on which the productions (anglice: exhibits) were laid out – 69 of them, overflowing on to the floor. They included various articles of wearing apparel, a red skin rug – bloodstained – Miss Gilchrist's false teeth and skeins of her grey hair, a work-box, a jewel-case, an auger and a hammer, looking *en masse* like the contents of a serial killer's car boot.

As the hand of the clock below the gallery touched the twenty-five minute mark, a trap-door in the floor immediately in front of the dock was raised, and, like a pantomime genie, the prisoner materialised from the nether regions and was escorted into the dock between two guardian constables.

Lord Guthrie, the vacation judge, an impressive figure in the robes of the Justiciary – white faced with scarlet crosses – took his seat on the dais. This raised bench where the judge sits is flanked by two fireplaces in which, on chilly days, bright fires burn for his Lordship's comfort.

A jury of fifteen good men and true was empanelled and sworn.

Slater stood to hear the reading of the indictment.

His trial had begun. It was to last four days.

Since the virtually verbatim account of the trial, edited by William Roughead, is available in Hodge's *Notable British Trials* series, it is not proposed to tax the limited space available in this volume by an unnecessary regurgitation in fine detail, but rather to refer the interested reader to the N.B.T. report.

In Scotland there are no opening speeches by counsel, as is the custom in England. The trial of Oscar Slater began with Lord Advocate Ure calling the first of 60 witnesses for the prosecution, as he set about his self-appointed task of painting as damning a picture of Slater and his activities as Crown delving had made possible.

Hungry for victory, he had selected three strongholds of defence denial for out-and-out attack, hopeful annihilation.

First, he would storm the position which asserted that Slater was not the man who had, on a great many occasions in the weeks preceding the murder, been seen by positive clouds of witnesses watching Miss Gilchrist's premises.

His second onslaught would seek to destroy the claim that it was not the accused who had battered Miss Gilchrist with a hammer, and that Slater was not the man seen in the hall by Adams and Lambie.

Thirdly, he would bring his heavy artillery to bear to demolish the proposition that Slater had not fled the country, a fugitive from justice, following the publication of his description in the Glasgow papers on the afternoon of Christmas day.

Ure's initial tactic was to establish in the jury's mind that the accused sometimes dealt in jewellery. This was because he was postulating jewel-theft as the motive of the crime. He therefore called Jacob Jackson, a German warehouseman, to testify that, about the middle of November 1908, Slater had tried, unsuccessfully, to sell him a diamond ring. The abortive transaction had, of course, not the remotest connection with Miss Gilchrist's missing brooch.

Ure's next objective was, with the testimony of 13 assorted witnesses, to convince the jury that the mysterious stranger unquestionably seen repeatedly loitering about West Princes Street for some time before the murder was indeed Slater. But such was the conflict and dubiety of the evidence, that in this he was not successful.

The highlight of the first day came when Helen Lambie stepped up into the witness-box. It was crucial to the prosecution case that she should link the man in the Gilchristean hall with the man in the dock. She did her best, insisting now that she had not actually gone into the flat, but remained beside Mr Adams on the threshold as the man approached and walked out of the front-door. She was also now saying that she *did* see a part of the man's face. 'I got a good look at him.' It was Slater. The Lord Advocate sat down well pleased with her and himself.

McClure was smartly on his feet, reading from the extradition proceedings and asking Lambie why, in America, she had said that she did *not* see the man's face. 'I did see his face,' she replied. 'There has been a bit left out' [of the transcript]. McClure persisted. Lambie wriggled. She did not come out of it too well.

The following day (4 May), Detective Inspector John Pyper gave his evidence, and McClure, cross-examining, succeeded in bringing out the essentially unsatisfactory nature of Lambie and Barrowman's identification evidence.

Arthur Adams, a pleasant-spoken man of rather slight build, with brown hair and a fair moustache, came across as being of a nervous and extremely conscientious temperament. He rendered his account of the discovery of the crime in a quick, nervy way. The vaguely bird-like Adams steadfastly declined to identify the prisoner as the man in the hall. All that he would say was that he closely resembled him.

Mary Barrowman, faced with a barrage of rapid-fire questions from McClure, stuck gamely to her guns, vehemently denying that she had identified Slater in New York because of a conversation she had had with Lambie while crossing the Atlantic, unshaken and unshakable in her belief that Slater was the running man with the twisted nose.

Professor Glaister opened the medical evidence, enunciating his theory that the assailant had knelt on Miss Gilchrist's chest while striking violently at her head with a blunt instrument – most likely, he thought, something on the lines of the claw-hammer produced, which had been found in Slater's trunk. McClure was very effective in cross, driving home the point that wounds so terrible must have given rise to massive bleeding, yet no unequivocal bloodstains could be discovered on anything belonging to his client.

Dr Hugh Galt, while accepting that the hammer exhibited *could* have been used, thought a heavier weapon more likely.

Professor Harvey Littlejohn considered it impossible that the auger from the back green at Queen's Terrace could have inflicted the wounds.

On Day Three – 5 May – with 44 prosecution witnesses already heard, Ure still had 16 more to call. Relentlessly, the Lord Advocate steam-rollered on, flattening the ground for the first footings of his iron-clad case against the frankly bewildered Oscar.

For some time it had been becoming obvious that the fire had gone out of the belly of the prosecution case. The main facts had been told; all that remained was icing – very poor quality icing at that – on the Crown cake, and those spectators who had come hopeful of gladiatorial pyrotechnics were becoming increasingly bored by what savoured of pointless prolongation.

It was nevertheless the turn now of the defence and the 14 witnesses it had managed to scrape together. They did not, to be honest, make a very good showing. They were in the main a fairly dubious collection of characters hardly calculated to inspire confidence in the minds of righteous, upstanding, conventional Scottish jurors. Rather pathetically, it was the absolute best that Oscar could muster.

Hugh Cameron – the redoubtable Moudie – dressed dandiacal for the occasion in frock-coat, high collar with a dark blue scarf, held in position by a broad gold ring, its wink and glitter echoed by the conspicuous gold ring on his left hand, the ensemble completed by dark, striped trousers, white waistcoat with blue stripes and pearl buttons, traversed by a handsome gold watch chain with thick, fat links. He made an excellent impression in the witness-box, leaning with an actor's ease on the ledge in front, speaking unhesitatingly in a natural, unaffected sort of way.

Slater's face twitched and flushed a dull red when Cameron, asked bluntly by the Lord Advocate if it was not the case that the prisoner had been living on the proceeds of prostitution, agreed that that was so. This was the first of a number of instances of disgraceful behaviour on the part of Ure. There was absolutely no justification for his introducing such character assassination, for it had nothing whatever to do with the charge that Slater had murdered Miss Gilchrist. McClure should have protested at once. The judge should have intervened. Neither did anything.

Another of Oscar's decidedly shady friends, Max Rattmann, followed the Moudie into the box. His testimony proved pretty worthless. Likewise that of Josef Aumann, a German gentleman possessed of the very slightest English vocabulary and the very grossest of foreign accents.

Now, at last, with the two final witnesses of the trial, the door of the mysterious household at No. 69 St George's Road was surely about to be opened and the domestic life hidden behind it revealed. The young woman who had been sharing Oscar's life, Mademoiselle Andrée Junio Antoine, was called. Amid a flutter of prurient excitement, she moved elegantly to the witness-box. Tall, pallid, she was quietly but modishly turned out – smart brown tweed costume with fur necklet, a sable fur around her shoulders, fashionable hat trimmed with broad-striped greenish ribbon. Her testimony, apart from her confirmation of Oscar's whereabouts at the time of the murder, was disappointingly devoid of 'revelations'. The Lord Advocate did not cross-examine her.

In Andrée's wake came Katharina Schmalz, unflatteringly described by the press as 'the grim, dwarfish servant in Slater's home'. In fact, no one did better than Katharina in filling in the details of what she succeeded in making sound like an innocuous household. She stuck, throughout a half-hour's fierce-ish cross-examination by Ure, to her simple story, and lost not a feather.

What was the sum of the day's proceedings? Shipping clerks and railway personnel had spoken of the journey of Slater and his lady to Liverpool and New York; all agreed that his had been an ordinary travelling transaction with nothing about the accused's demeanour to suggest that he was a fugitive from justice. And Slater's counsel had shown that his departure from Glasgow had been an open one. McClure had also produced witnesses who could testify to his client's departure from Johnston's Billiard Rooms for home on the night of the murder, so that, ostensibly, he had been accompanied to his very door in St George's Road, and beyond it, by the evidence of his mistress and maid.

The fourth and final day of the trial – Thursday, 6 May 1909.

As the first witness, Samuel Reid, was summoned, sunshine, broad and generous, flooded in through the two large windows over the bench, picking out in bold relief the imperial coat of arms surmounting the canopy above the judge and setting shafts of prismatic spotlights, filtered from the edges of the yellow parchment blinds, in a migrainous, dancing dazzle about the faces of some of the prime actors in the potential tragedy. Reid, a middle-aged man, speaking with a foreign accent, was, like Slater, a Jew, and put on a cap to take the oath in orthodox fashion. A bookmaker, it had been his custom, when resident in Glasgow, to dine every Sunday with Slater and spend the evening at his home. He had come over from Belfast, where he now lived, to testify that from six o'clock to half past ten on Sunday night, 20 December 1908, he and his small son, Percy, had been at Oscar's home with him; clear proof that a mysterious watcher seen by two witnesses – Robert Brown Bryson and Andrew Nairn – hanging about West Princes Street that night was not Slater. The Lord Advocate made no serious challenge to this alibi; he just did his best to tarnish the witness with questions about his and Slater's unwholesome gambling habits.

McClure's last effort on Slater's behalf was to put up two medical witnesses – Drs Robertson and Veitch. Neither considered the hammer belonging to Slater to have caused the decedent's injuries. Their evidence amounted to no more and no less than that of the doctors for the Crown, travelling the same latitudes and longitudes of speculation, and signally failing to reach any terminus of certainty.

And that, said Mr McClure, closed his case.

Time for Mr Ure, newly-minted Lord Advocate, to address the jury.

Starting off rather quiet-voiced, as he warmed to his demolition work he raised his tones, and, becoming impassioned, would strike the rail of the dock with his left hand every now and again, to emphasise the sincerity of whatever point he was seeking to hammer home; in his right hand, his handkerchief, clutched like a snowball. He told the jury that up to the previous afternoon he would have thought it a serious difficulty to conceive of the existence of a human being capable of doing such a dastardly deed as the most vicious slaying of Miss Gilchrist. But, having heard from the lips of one [Hugh Cameron] who knew the prisoner better than anyone else that he had followed a life descending to the ultimate depths of human degradation, with a withering scorn in his tone and expression, he added:

> For by the universal judgment of mankind, the man who lives upon the proceeds of prostitution has sunk to the lowest depths, and all moral sense in him has been destroyed and has ceased to exist, that difficulty has been removed. I say without hesitation that the man in the dock is capable of having committed this dastardly outrage.

The Lord Advocate's behaviour was the dastardly outrage. McClure should have been up on his hind legs *instanter*. Lord Guthrie ought to have silenced Ure. Continuing uninterrupted, Ure said that the motive for the crime was plain as daylight. Robbery. 'We shall see in the sequel how it was that the prisoner came to know that she [Miss Gilchrist] was possessed of these jewels.'

There was no sequel . . . because there was no evidence that Slater ever knew of Miss Gilchrist's valuable hoard.

Unworried by such trivia, preoccupied with his need for victory in his 'maiden' big trial, Ure went on building, with infinite skill and infinite ruthless transgression of the accepted boundaries of legal custom and fairness, his case against Oscar Slater.

The accused, said Ure, had written to his bosom friend, Cameron, that he could prove with five people where he was when the murder was committed. The Lord Advocate proceeded then to examine the evidence of the proprietor of the Renfield Street Billiard Rooms, Peter Johnston, and his billiard marker, Adam Gibb, as to Slater's presence *circa* 6.00 to 6.30pm on 21 December. 'Neither of them would say the prisoner was there.' Nor, in Ure's submission, could Rattmann or Aumann provide acceptable evidence that Slater was in the Renfield Street Billiard Rooms at or near the time of the murder. 'Well, then,' he summed up, well satisfied, 'Out of the five people . . . that is the best that can be done. The prisoner is hopelessly unable to produce a single witness who saw that he was anywhere else than at the scene of the murder that night.'

This was a very cavalier piece of forensic chicanery, a completely unjustified, contemptuous dismissal by exclusion of the evidence of Andrée Antoine and Katharina Schmalz that Oscar was at home having his dinner at the material time.

Ure went on:

> It is said that a fortnight or three weeks, or a month before, he [Slater] spoke of going to America. I dare say he did; I am certain he did. There is no doubt whatever he had made up his mind, as soon as the deed was accomplished that he would not stay in this country one moment longer than was absolutely necessary. I say that this flight was precipitated, and the moment fixed by the publication of his description in the newspapers at two o'clock on the afternoon of 25th December.

Shortly afterwards, the Lord Advocate made the very serious blunder of stating that Slater's *name* and description had at that time appeared in the Glasgow newspapers. In fact, his name was not published until 2 January 1909, when it appeared in the *Glasgow Herald*. Again, McClure should have challenged this statement. Not a word! Slater was not being well served by his counsel.

Ure told the jury that Slater had booked a cabin on the *Lusitania* in the names of Otto and Anna Sando – 'For some reason or another which has not been explained, which cannot be explained consistently with innocence.' This was very unfair. As McClure should have interjected, Miss Antoine *had* explained that she and Oscar had used false names to throw the legal Mrs Slater off their traces.

Lord Advocate Ure's speech was widely hailed as a marvel. He had spoken for an hour and fifty minutes with never a single written note. Discussing this prodigious performance with William Roughead, Sir Edward Marshall Hall drily remarked: 'That may account for its manifold inaccuracies.'

Mr McClure, in his speech for the defence, very properly reminded the jury that it was entirely upon the evidence of Hugh Cameron – 'unless what the girl Antoine said herself, that in the prisoner's absence she received gentlemen,' be accepted – that information concerning whatever depth to which Slater may have sunk depended. But the strongest that McClure seemed able to manage in the way of protest was that that was a subject that 'We are not to go into. It should not have been here referred to, and is not in the case.' Having cited the celebrated and cautionary case of mistaken identity, that of Adolf Beck (1896), and having to the best of his ability put the moral frighteners on the fifteen, good and truly, Mr McClure sat resoundingly down.

It was now 3.35pm Everything stopped for tea.

Then . . . Lord Guthrie's summing-up.

It was a disaster. Unbelievably, his Lordship delivered himself of the following far-from-judicial comment regarding the prisoner: 'He has maintained himself by the ruin of men and on the ruin of women, living for years past in a way that many blackguards would scorn to live.' After which, leaning over at a backwards tilt in a supreme, and supremely distasteful, effort to be fair, to be judicial, Lord Guthrie observed: 'It is nothing remarkable to find a man of that kind taking a wrong name, telling a lie about his destination, going by different names, murder or no murder.'

At this juncture the learned judge made a further unbelievable blunder. Against all the doctrines of criminal law, he told the jury:

> The Lord Advocate founds on the prisoner's admittedly abandoned character as a point in support of the Crown. He is entitled to do so because a man of that kind has not the presumption of innocence in his favour, which is not only the form in the case of every man, but is a reality in the case of the ordinary man. Not only is every man presumed to be innocent, but the ordinary man has a strong presumption in his favour.

His Lordship's summing-up brought about a change in Slater's hitherto optimistic attitude. Now, at last, he was beginning to realise how thin-spun was the web of his fate. Indeed, no one who had listened to Lord Guthrie's charge to the jury could doubt what, however couched and swaddled in the robes of judicial impartiality, the judge's own opinion was.

The jurors filed out. Lord Guthrie left the bench. Counsel and agents melted from the scene. According to legal custom, the prisoner remained seated in the dock between his ramrod guardians, their batons drawn. Around him a torrent of talk surged to fill the panelled court-room's upturned wooden bowl of silence.

At four minutes past six, high above the clamour, the ringing of the jury bell was heard. The Babel was abruptly burked as the straggly crocodile of jurors shuffled back in. Mr John Waldie, warehouseman, foreman, answered the question. 'The jury, by a majority, find the prisoner guilty as libelled.'

An awed hush had fallen on the court, disturbed only by the incongruous flapping of the yellow blinds as the evening breeze swept in through the slits of opened windows. Leaning over the front of the dock, Oscar Slater gave a convulsive sob, and, stretching out his arms to judge and jury in the age-old Jewish gesture of supplication, in a harsh, guttural tone gasped out: 'My Lord, my father and mother are poor old people. I came on my own account to this country. I came over to defend my right. I know nothing about the affair. You are convicting an innocent man.'

Lord Guthrie assumed the black cap and pronounced sentence of death.

The trap-door opened.

The last fragment of the well-cut, well shoulder-padded jacket of Oscar's 'court suit' whisked away, down into the engulfing darkness of the stair.

The trap-door closed with a bang over Slater, who, with his goods and chattels forfeit to the Crown, was, in the eyes of the law, already a dead man.

From a waiting room nearby came the sound of Andrée Antoine, sobbing.

Chapter Seven

THE GRANITE MAN OF PETERHEAD

The year, 1909. The seventh day of May. A gallowsman now, with the eight o'clock walk a mere three clear Sundays distant, Oscar was taken back to Duke Street Prison and housed in Cell No. 1, Hall D. A large, well-lighted place, it was the condemned cell. Here Prisoner No. 942 would await his death – never from this day forward for a single second alone, guarded, nursed, cosseted like a fattening calf, 'lest himself should rob their scaffold of its prey'.

Eighteen days the unhappy man lay under sentence of death. Welcome divisions in the slow drip of hours were the practically daily visits of Rabbi Phillips, with his constantly reiterated message of hope.

While Oscar, lost to the world, was making brave efforts to come to terms with 'the terrible inevitable', within the grim walls of Duke Street, others, without their frowning compass, were making equally brave efforts on his behalf. For there was a strong feeling abroad that the verdict had not been justified by the evidence.

Lord Guthrie felt no such doubt. 'As the judge in the case,' he wrote to the Secretary for Scotland, Lord Pentland, 'there is strictly only one question which falls to me to answer, namely, was the evidence legally sufficient to entitle the jury to convict? I answer this question in the affirmative.' He did, however, have opinions to offer on two other questions. Did he consider the verdict right; would he, sitting without a jury, have held the charge proven? Answer: Yes, he would. Second question: In the whole circumstances, should the sentence be commuted to penal servitude for life? Answer: Yes. 'The question of the propriety of a reprieve . . . is a question of statesmanship rather than of law, and the important element seems to me the fact that, out of 15 jurymen, six were in favour of acquittal.'

The *Evening Citizen* of 14 May purveyed the chilling news that what was discreetly referred to as 'the hangman's paraphernalia' was being taken into Duke Street that Friday.

A Memorial, a most workmanlike document prepared by Ewing Speirs, pointing up all the weaknesses and contradictions in the Crown's case, was forwarded to Lord Pentland, accompanied by petition sheets bearing well over 20,000 signatures.

For some days Oscar had been hearing the echo of the hammers putting together the intended instrument of his doom. Pierrepoint had been engaged. Slater's coffin – a simple deal box – had been knocked up. All was set for 'the law to take its course.' Oscar confided to Warden D. McLeod that he would rather hang than spend 15 years in prison and then come out into the world branded a murderer.

At seven o'clock on the evening of 25 May, Governor William Bedlington Buglass at Duke Street Prison received a telegram from the Secretary for Scotland. Buglass and the prison medical officer, Dr James Devon, went to give the good news to Slater. As they entered the condemned cell its occupant's manner became instantly and intensely anxious and pathetic. Holding forth his hands, he cried: 'Am I to be hanged?' Told that Lord Pentland had instructed that sentence of death should be respited, Oscar turned ashen; he did not know the meaning of the word 'respited'. Hastily, the Governor explained.

And so it came to pass that Oscar saw the sun rise on what was to have been his day of destiny, Thursday, 27 May 1909, and was also alive at the darkening of the day.

May 26 1909 dawned for Oscar Slater at 5.45am.

It was the first day of the rest of his life.

Public reaction to the news of his sparing was mixed. There seems to have been some confusion as to the precise significance of 'respite' – the Scots understanding of the meaning of the word no better than Slater's own, initially.[1] This confusion has, indeed, lingered on to puzzle a recent writer on the case, Thomas Toughill, who observes:

> If he [Slater] was guilty, he should hang; if he was innocent he should be set free. There was no halfway house. The "Conditional Pardon" granted by Edward VII is therefore not easy to comprehend.

Mr Toughill's difficulty seems to arise from his failure to appreciate the entirely formal nature of the standardly expressed official document to which he refers as a 'Conditional Pardon signed by King Edward VII', who, says Toughill, 'pardoned Slater of Miss Gilchrist's murder on condition that he spent the rest of his life in penal servitude'.

Quite so.

But this document was not unique, specially tailored for Slater; it was the usual document issued in any case where a reprieve is granted. It is signed not by the monarch himself, but, at a remove, by Lord Pentland, 'By His Majesty's Command'. Toughill announces in triumph: 'The existence of this pardon has not been revealed until now.' This is a meaningless point. Its existence did not need to be 'revealed'; the *fact* of Slater's reprieve predicated its existence.

Mr Toughill's is, I am afraid, the discovery that never was!

His further point that Slater's subsequent appeal 'seemed to

---

1 *'Respite' just means stopping the execution for a temporary or fixed period. There are two types of pardon: absolute or conditional. 'The ordinary case of a conditional pardon occurs where a person sentenced to death is pardoned on condition that he is detained in penal servitude for life.' (The Late Rt. Honourable Sir JHA MacDonald, Lord Justice-Clerk, A Practical Treatise on the Criminal Law of Scotland 1948, p.353)*

be a nonsense in view of the fact that Slater had already received a Royal Pardon in respect of Miss Gilchrist's murder, a fact of which no mention was made during the entire proceedings' is, I fear, itself 'a nonsense'. Slater's appeal was directed to the establishment of his *innocence* of the murder. This had nothing to do with a pardon for a crime which he utterly denied having committed. He had been dismissed with a large, undeserved, question-mark still suspended about his neck.

Lord Guthrie's comment in a private letter to James Miller Dodds, Under Secretary for Scotland, is of significant interest. 'You remember that at the meeting at the Chancellor's [Lord Loreburn], the view was expressed that if Slater were respited, the case would not be one for release, under the ordinary practice, at the end of 20 years.' Here, surely, is provided a measure of officialdom's genuine belief in Slater's blood-guilt.

Envisage if you will – which fortunately for the preservation of his sanity Oscar Slater did not – a granite block of eighteen years' imprisonment within the penitentiary walls of the drear edifice on the bleak north-east coast of Aberdeenshire, Peterhead Convict Prison.

Thursday morning, 8 July 1909, was the day the call came for Oscar to gather up his thin tally of worldly goods and head north. 'Slater will now have to dree his weird,'[2] commented the *Weekly Mail* pragmatically.

That fate meant working in the quarries. Known henceforth as Convict No. 1992, he was given a big hammer and told to break the massive granite blocks. Thus, in hard labour, did the heavy toll of days drag by: every new dawn importing a false sunrise of hope, each evening seeing its unfulfilled demise.

As the months mounted, the granite entered Oscar's soul. Unpicked at the seams by time's relentless fingers, the moth-ravaged mantle of easy urbanity slipped and fell away. The globe-trotting cosmopolitan's charm and courtesy and ever-ready smile

2 Endure his fate.

gave place to the – always underlying – dour, heavy, Germanic persona; the infra-stratum of enduring despair. A resentful, sullen, unresponsive and rebelliously touchy-tempered loner, isolated not only by language, but also by alien habitude of thought, he loomed and lumbered threateningly in the dank stone passages of the prison, and bulked large and menacing in the fogs and mists of the quarries. He called them the places 'where men's souls have been hammered into the very granite they have broken'.

The raw Scottish winter was to prove a perennial punishment which there was no avoiding. 'One is unable to work in the cell in winter time as it is punishingly cold. At night the only garment a prisoner is allowed to retain is his shirt. In the winter it is terrible in these refrigerators.'

But in the long litany of cruel inflictions administered by nature and by man to man in that harsh penal settlement perched on the iron lip's edge of the German Ocean, most terrible of all was the eternal, enveloping, smothering silence. 'A silence of silences,' wrote Slater. 'So great is it that one might hear a pin dropping on the floor. It is this silence which plays such havoc with a man's mind.'

It was this silence which was about to be riven by the trumpet calls of a certain great 'paladin of lost causes' who had decided to take up that of the forlorn and fretting prisoner of Peterhead.

Brooding in Peterhead on grievances major and minor, real and imagined, Oscar wrote – on 25 February 1910 – to Alexander Shaughnessy, the solicitor who had replaced Ewing Speirs, who had most unexpectedly died at the unhappily early age of some 35 years while attending a political meeting the previous December, 'Everything is going against me, and I can see myself lost and buried in prison.'

Although it is nowhere survivingly recorded as a matter of historic fact, it is nonetheless virtually certain that it was Alexander Shaughnessy who brought 'the great paladin', Sir Arthur Conan Doyle, into the Slater affair.

In April 1910, William Hodge & Company, the Edinburgh and

Glasgow publishers, issued in their *Notable Scottish Trials* series a volume on the *Trial of Oscar Slater*, edited by William Roughead. With Doyle's triumph in the rehabilitation of the young Parsee solicitor, George Edalji, the convicted horse-maimer of Great Wyrley, fresh in his mind, and Roughead's masterly volume fresh from the press, Shaughnessy made a diffident approach to Doyle, sending him a copy of Roughead's book. Doyle found it an atrocious story, 'realised the wickedness of it all' and was 'moved to do all I could for the man'.

In truth, Oscar had already been doing everything he could for himself. The first quaintly expressed, and equally quaintly spelt, appeal, painstakingly scribed on blue prison notepaper, had gone out to the Scottish Secretary on 19 July 1909. Others followed on 13 October and 31 December. On that last day of 1909, he had petitioned the Secretary for Scotland –

> Please help me . . . I lay helpless here in prison, my dear old parents, whose days are only counted, praying that light shall come in my Affair. Your servants have taken me, like a sheep is taken to the slaughterhouse, and knowing all the time I had nothing to do with the crime. My Lord, I am an innocent man, I swear by God the Almighty that I never heard the name of the murdered woman . . .

Throughout 1910, Oscar continued to bombard the Scottish Secretary with petitions for justice denied. There was a blue paper petition from Convict No. 1992 on 8 July and another on 20 August. In this last, Oscar wrote:

> My Lord – Only 14 days ago, I received from my Glasgow agent a copy of my trial [with Roughead's Introduction carefully excised], and by reading it I have found some points which not have been cleared up at my trial because the chance to be examined as a witness was taken away from me by my counsel.

Oscar's final communication to the Secretary for Scotland in 1910 was dated 14 November. In it he confesses to Lord Pentland that he has lived an 'unsteady life', but asks, 'Why shall I *for this reason* only be made to be a murderer? Fifteen years I am in Great Britain, and never have been in prison for any crime.'

Nor did Oscar cease from strife in 1911. Twice he wrote to Pentland. On 7 March: 'I, as an innocent, broken-down man, crave to you to inform me if anything regarding my liberty has been done by you My Lordship.' And on 23 September:

My Lord I pray you to help me, I am an innocent man and know nothing
about the murder, I never (to my belief) have even been in the street
where the lady Miss Gilchrist was murdered. Never I will cease to trust in
you my Lord, and I alwise [sic] will live in hope to get my justice of you.

But his Lordship's servant, 'most humble and most obidient [sic]',
cried out in vain into the unanswering void. The silence around
Peterhead remained heart-breakingly unbroken.

However . . . on 1 December 1911 there came to Alexander
Shaughnessy from Windlesham, Crowborough, Conan Doyle's
Sussex home, a letter from Sir Arthur. 'I must wait a short time as I
am full of work. Then I will look over the whole question thoroughly.'

Nearly two months went by. On 29 January 1912, Doyle wrote
apologetically to Shaughnessy: 'If I have done nothing in the Slater
matter it is not that I have lost interest, but that I have been
somewhat overworked and unable to do much.'

Then . . . five months on . . . triumph.

On 12 July 1912 Sir Arthur sent a letter to Shaughnessy
bearing the eagerly-awaited grand news. 'I have been long delayed
but now I have come back to Slater and hope to have the article
finished by this weekend. My plan is to publish it in one of the
prominent monthlies, as this will ensure considerable comment on
the case.'

It was on that same 12 July that Shaughnessy wrote to the
Crown Agent in Edinburgh, telling him that he had learned lately of
the existence of a certain statement made by Helen Lambie which
did not emerge at the trial. Apparently, immediately after the
murder Lambie had 'proceeded to a dwelling-house within a short
distance of the murdered lady's house and informed the occupant
of that house that Miss Gilchrist had been murdered and that she
knew the person who did it, as she had identified him when he
passed her. She mentioned the person's name and it certainly was
not Oscar Slater'.

In his letter to the Crown Agent, Shaughnessy requested a
copy of that statement. He also asked for the name and address of
the person to whom Lambie had made this statement.

I have myself searched the extant official archives thoroughly
for evidence behind the explosion of this delayed-action bomb and
found nothing. There is absolutely no trace of any such statement.

What I *have*, however, discovered is a sufficiency of dispersed data with which one may, like Professor Owen building up D*inornis* from a single fragment of femur, assemble a satisfactory reconstruction of the course of events.

The key document was a letter, written on 16 July 1912, by Shaughnessy to Roughead. In it, he tells him that the informant referred to in his [Shaughnessy's] letter to the Crown Agent was a detective, and that this informant had said that

> the Detective Department were [sic] very much surprised at the verdict
> and practically every one of them are [sic] convinced that Slater is
> innocent. Over and above, my brother[3] had a talk with a prominent official
> in the CID here, who gave him the same information. Of course, this latter
> individual did not wish his name disclosed.

I also found among the Crown Office papers a letter, dated 24 July 1912, to the Crown Agent from Fiscal Hart, who wrote: 'I feel certain that no such statement was made by her [Lambie] either to the police or to me. I never heard a suggestion of such a statement having been made by her at any time.' He then reveals the identity of the person to whom Lambie's alleged statement was made. 'The witness Miss Birrell[4] was not examined by the police . . . I find she was not asked with regard to Lambie having called at her house that night and she certainly made no statement on the subject.'

Shaughnessy's comment, written to Roughead, was: 'The inevitable conclusion . . . is that by some means the statement was allowed to slip out of sight in its transmission from the Detective Department, Glasgow, to Edinburgh.'

Mr Shaughnessy's 'inevitable conclusion' depended, of course, upon the reliability of his informant, the unnamed detective. This proposition we shall presently examine.

Doyle, to whom all this had been confided, wrote to Shaughnessy (July 16th, 1912):

> If Lambie knew the murderer – and her conduct at first was so
> extraordinary that one could almost imagine that she was in connivance
> with him – then she had some strong reason for shielding him and putting
> the guilt elsewhere. What reason could it be save love? Have you any idea
> who it was that she eventually married? I would like also to have Miss

3   John Shaughnessy, his partner in the firm.
4   Margaret Dawson Birrell, of 19 Blythswood Drive.

Gilchrist's will looked up and see what were its terms. I wish I felt surer about Nugent *and his pals.*

In a second letter, Doyle writes, exonerating Nugent: 'I am glad about Nugent as it clears a difficulty. On the other hand it can't be said definitely that he could not in all innocence have told others about the jewels.' And Doyle went on to say that he had always felt it possible that the man who killed Miss Gilchrist was not after her jewels. 'He did not take anything but the brooch and that may have been a blind. It was the box of papers which attracted him.'

This was a wild, completely unjustified leap, as was Sir Arthur's subsequent assumption that the intruder had been searching for the old lady's will. He was performing well below the standard of his fictive *alter ego*, Sherlock Holmes. The letter concluded:

Have you any knowledge of whom Miss G's heir was? Or was there any *mauvais sujet* among the young men of the Gilchrist family? I don't suppose Lambie would now stultify herself by telling the truth and if we could only get at the relative whom she saw that evening. Would it be impossible to get in touch with the Gilchrist family and find from them what relative lived near in 1908. If a fiver will open that detective's mouth I'm ready to provide it – or even a tenner if he will really help us. I think it would be wiser to investigate without asking help of the authorities, for if we do they may very well warn Lambie and others to shut their mouths.

Sir Arthur is, it would seem, sketching in the first shadowy lines adumbratory of an official conspiracy theory.

What Shaughnessy believed to be a vitally important meeting took place on Saturday, 20 July 1912, when the anonymous detective came to his office, Ocean Chambers, at 190 West George Street, with his strange, off-the-record tale.

Still, despite his previous avowal to the contrary, bulldogishly toying with the notion of Nugent's guilt, Doyle asked Shaughnessy:

I wonder if you ever collated two separate pieces of evidence got in New York and Edinburgh. The one showed that the last time Lambie saw Nugent was the final week of September before the murder. The other that Miss G's dog was poisoned on September 7th. That is remarkable is it not? I suppose Roughead knows what he is saying when he says Nugent was fully exonerated. But how about Nugent's disreputable friends in the gambling line whom he told of this old lonely rich woman. Nugent through his hold over Lambie could have got duplicate keys which were surely used, poisoned the dog and made all easy for the assassin.

Then came the good news.

I have finished my task. It [the proposed article] has run to such length
that I am inclined to think that a sixpenny pamphlet would be the best
way of ensuring widespread attention.

Sir Arthur Conan Doyle's 99-page pamphlet, *The Case of Oscar Slater*,
was published by Hodder and Stoughton in August 1912, in an
edition of 25,000 copies, grey wrappers, at sixpence.

In it, Doyle wrote:

> It is notorious that nothing is more tricky than evidence of identification.
> The evidence for the prosecution really resolved itself into two sets of
> witnesses for identification. The first set were those who had actually seen
> the murderer, and included Adams, Helen Lambie, and the girl
> Barrowman.

He noted the worrying discrepancies in the original descriptions
provided by this trio. The second set consisted of twelve people
who had, at various dates, seen a man frequenting the street in
which Miss Gilchrist lived, and loitering in a suspicious manner
before the house. These witnesses had, said Sir Arthur, seen
portraits of the accused. They were well aware that he was a
foreigner, 'and then they were asked to pick out his swarthy Jewish
physiognomy from among nine Glasgow policemen and two railway
officials. Naturally they did it without hesitation.

Doyle also pointed out that,

> What the police never could produce, however, was the essential thing,
> and that was the least connecting link between Slater and Miss Gilchrist, or
> any explanation how a foreigner in Glasgow could even know of the
> existence, to say nothing of the wealth, of a retired old lady, who had few
> acquaintances and seldom left her guarded flat.

The challenge presented by the gauntlet thrown down by Sir Arthur,
the White Knight, was taken up by the newspaper reviewers with
markedly varied responses. The Scottish 'heavies' were
preponderantly dour. *The Scotsman* commented, thin-lipped,
regarding the view of 'an outside spectator, even if he is the creator
of the most popular detective fiction of our day. The gist of the
special plea set up is that the evidence of identification was
deficient and that the Crown failed to connect Slater with the
robbery committed at the time of the murder.' The *Glasgow Herald*, no

more enthusiastic, opined: 'It seems improbable that this movement for the review of Slater's sentence will have any result. It is indicative of Sir Arthur's bent for special pleading that he seems ready to accept an alibi supported by Slater's mistress and their servant.'

The point here, though, was that the Lord Advocate stated that the prisoner was hopelessly unable to produce a single witness to say that he was anywhere else than at the scene of the murder that night.

Doyle counters:

The evidence of the mistress that Slater dined in the flat at seven on the night of the murder I pass, but I do not understand why Schmalz's positive corroboration should be treated by the Lord Advocate as non-existent. What evidence could he [Slater] give, save that of everyone who lived with him?

Under Scots law at that time a re-trial would have been impossible, there being no Court of Criminal Appeal such as recently established in England, but it was possible for the Secretary for Scotland to advise the Crown that there might be a reconsideration of the evidence and a re-examination of the witnesses.

How did the Sassenach newspaper pack react?

Pride of place to the old Thunderer. Sitting decorously upon the fence, *The Times*, of 21 August, pronounced:

There is but one answer to all [Sir Arthur's] objections, and that is that they have probably been considered already, and with extreme care. If Sir Arthur's arguments lead the authorities to revise the case, no one will think the labour wasted; but it is by no means certain that such a revision will result in the prisoner's favour.

The *Westminster Gazette*, less bet-hedging, came out firmly for Doyle:

If the evidence against Slater were no stronger than the creator of "Sherlock Holmes" shows it to be, then only an uncommon stupidity and a deliberate plot could have brought about the conviction.

The issuing forth of Doyle's book was almost like an unconscious answer to an appeal wrung from the prisoner of Peterhead back in October 1910, when he wrote in his curious English to Rabbi Phillips:

Is no help for me, Mr Phillips? Is it not possible that a writer could be found who brings the wrong done against me to the light? Surely the people who thinks I am innocent believes it is a mistaken identity; they don't know it is what you call a put-up job.

The fire lit by *The Case of Oscar Slater* began to take hold. It was reported that when Parliament reassembled questions were to be asked regarding the Slater case. And while the controversy smouldered, Doyle despatched – on 7 September – a letter and a copy of his booklet to the Secretary for Scotland. The effect was galvanic. Two copies of Roughead's book were ordered post-haste, and, on the instruction of John Lamb, Assistant Under Secretary, a communication sped off to the Crown Agent, Sir William Haldane, requesting that 'the precognitions and productions in the case of Oscar Slater be sent up to us for perusal'. The Scottish Office was patently girding its loins.

Three months passed. A quietus. Then, the Secretary for Scotland was informed that on 10 December Mr Marshall Hall would ask him in the House whether any further investigations could be made into the propriety of the conviction of Oscar Slater . . . and, 'in view of the uneasiness as to the justice of the verdict which has been expressed both in Scotland and in England, will he state what steps he proposes to take'.

An unmoved and immovable Mr McKinnon Wood, who had that year succeeded Lord Pentland as Secretary for Scotland, duly replied that no new considerations had, in his opinion, emerged, such as would justify his re-opening the case, and he did not consider it to be his duty to enter into public discussion of the case in reply to the honourable and learned gentleman's question.

The curtain fell on hope.

Chapter Eight

THE LIBELLING OF DR CHARTERIS

The year 1912 having been laid in burnt-out ashes to rest, with wreaths of dead nettles in the place of autumn's optimistic bouquets of dahlias, 1913, justifying the endemic pessimism of the triskaidekaphobes, passed in a hiatus of unease, fertilising no new bloomings of hope.

But 1914 was, from the very start, to be different. The harbinger of hope renewed was that same detective who, in July 1912, had brought his confidential information to Alexander Shaughnessy. Now we may discover his name: John Thomson Trench.

The son of a ploughman of Lasswade, in the parish of Liberton, Midlothian, Trench had joined the Glasgow police in 1893, aged 24. Prior to that, he had served seven years in the 1st Battalion Royal Highlanders – the Black Watch. His career in the force had been one of steady progression, from constable 3rd class to his commissioning as a lieutenant of police on 5 November 1912. A highly successful organisation man, it remains to this day a puzzlement as to who – or what – it was that had, back in 1912, steered his steps to Mr Shaughnessy's door. And now, two years on, one January day in 1914, he was telling his disquieting tale again, to another Glasgow solicitor, David Cook.

Cook, practising at 59 Bath Street, was 41 in 1914. He was attractive neither as to appearance nor personality. Peter Hunt, doubtless via Roughead's advising, describes him as 'heavy-jowled, with a large head and sparse grey hair. There were pouches under his eyes. His mouth was large, his lips thin, his complexion grey. His voice was rasping.'[1]

But he was an astute lawyer and an able pleader, with a lifetime's experience in defending people charged with criminal offences. He was also an old and intimate friend of Trench's.

On 27 January 1914, Dr James Devon, Medical Officer of Duke Street Prison and one of His Majesty's Prison Commissioners, to whom Cook had the previous day shown Trench's statement, addressed a letter to McKinnon Wood. Naming no names, referring to Trench merely as 'a member of the Glasgow police force', Devon said that he had had put before him a statement which had surprised and shocked him. 'I have assured the officer and the lawyer in question that you can be absolutely relied upon to act fairly.'

On 13 February McKinnon Wood replied: 'If the constable mentioned in your letter will send me a written statement with the evidence in his possession . . . I will give the matter my best consideration.'

Ten days later, Cook provided McKinnon Wood with Trench's name, adding in his letter that that officer was

> naturally apprehensive that his disclosures regarding the conduct of the police may ultimately come to the ears of his superiors . . . he fears that he will be a marked man should he be for a moment suspected as the person revealing the inside information. Had the information now supplied by Trench been laid before the jury, I venture to say there would have been no possibility of a conviction.

Wood's reply – on 10 March – threw Cook and Trench into a real flurry.

1 *Oscar Slater: The Great Suspect*, page 158

> You speak of treating the matter as confidential. I fear this is impossible . . .
> I propose to send the papers to the Procurator-fiscal at Glasgow . . . this
> seems to be the appropriate and inevitable course to adopt.

Appropriate? Anything but. Inevitable? Cook and Trench prayed not. Off to McKinnon Wood by the first available post went Cook's somewhat anguished response.

> If Mr Hart conducts the enquiry he does so with the knowledge that his
> office in the event of Slater's ultimate liberation will be more or less under
> the lash of public opinion. I fail to see how Mr Hart can be expected to do
> justice to himself and to Slater.

And the following day Cook wrote again to Wood:

> In the event of your deciding that Mr Hart shall conduct the investigation, I
> will be compelled to have recourse to the columns of the press, if for no
> other reason than to put the parties connected with the investigation on
> their guard. I may add that from the outset Hart believed that Slater was
> the murderer. Surely a neutral person ought to be entrusted with the
> inquiry?

McKinnon Wood 'heard'.

On 8 April 1914, a package was delivered to James Gardner Millar, KC, Sheriff of Lanarkshire, wherein were parcelled copies of the correspondence with David Cook, together with certain precognitions, and an invitation from Mr McKinnon Wood to inquire into and report on these matters.

What has since become scathingly known as the Secret Inquiry opened on the morning of 23 April 1914, in Sheriff Millar's room at the County Buildings, Ingram Street, Glasgow. This apartment, behind the closed doors of which the not-so-grand inquisition was to take place, was a large one, almost as large, in fact, as any of the court-rooms in the building. At the top end was the sheriff's desk, where he sat with, on his right, his clerk, Andrew Sandilands, who was to take down in longhand the evidence of witnesses, who would be seated at the other side of the desk facing the sheriff. These witnesses, while waiting their turn to be called, were accommodated in charge of an officer in a court-room on the opposite side of the corridor. Each witness was seen alone, and as each in turn crossed to Sheriff Millar's private chamber, the door was meticulously locked behind them.

Millar's terms of reference were, to say the least – or, indeed, the most – of them, limited. The inquiry was to be confined to questions of fact; it should in no way relate to the conduct of the trial; it was to take place not in public, but in strict privacy; no witness was to be put on oath, but should be merely admonished to speak truly. In view of this stultifying, toothless brief, Cook, Roughead and Doyle shared the opinion that the inquiry would be 'more or less a farce'.

This is the point at which the libelling of the blameless Dr Charteris begins. In short, Trench had claimed that Lambie had told Miss Birrell that the man she had seen in Miss Gilchrist's hall was Dr Charteris.

Trench stated:

> On December 23rd, I was instructed by Chief Superintendent Orr to visit and take a statement from Miss Birrell, 19 Blythswood Drive. I had particular instructions to question her with regard to Dr Charteris, and as to what Lambie said when she visited her house on the night of the murder.

What Trench alleges that Miss Birrell had to say is based upon his claimed 'word for word' recollection. The document gets off to a dubious start, describing Miss Birrell as 'now residing at 6 Kelvinside Terrace, or 275 Wilton Street, Glasgow'. To begin with, the address in question should have been 6 Kelvinside Terrace North, anyway – another directional straw! – but the unfortunate truth is that the Miss Margaret Birrell who had indeed lived at that address was not Miss Gilchrist's niece. A further disqualification is that the lady had died in October 1912, at the age of 66.

Here is what, according to Trench, Miss Birrell had had to say in the statement which he insisted that he had taken from her.

> I know that Marion [sic] Gilchrist or McColl [sic)] a daughter of Miss Gilchrist's brother, was the supposed heir to Miss Gilchrist's wealth. I am aware that Miss Gilchrist visited the McColl [sic] family at Bournemouth. That was some time previous to the murder. On her return, she time and again declared her determination to alter her will. It was believed by some of her relatives that she had done so. She made no secret of her intention. She was positively nasty with any relative who might call. Miss Gilchrist stated to me that none of the Charteris family would finger a penny of her money.

If one accepts this Trench-transcribed statement, Nellie Lambie had, on the night of the murder, told her:

> 'Oh, Miss Birrell, Miss Birrell, Miss Gilchrist has been murdered, she is lying dead in the dining-room, and Oh, Miss Birrell, I saw the man who did it.' I replied, 'My God, Nellie, this is awful. Who was it, do you know him?' Nellie replied, 'Oh, Miss Birrell, I think it was Dr Charteris. I am sure it was Dr Charteris.' I said to her, 'My God, Nellie, don't say that. A murder in the family is bad enough, but a murderer is a thousand times worse. Unless you are very sure of it, Nellie, don't say that.' She again repeated to me that she was sure it was Dr Charteris. The same evening Detectives Pyper and Dornan visited me, and I learned from them that she had told them it was Dr Charteris. I told a number of my friends about it, including a member of the Glasgow Corporation, who communicated with Chief Superintendent Orr. On Wednesday afternoon, 23rd December, 1908, Detective Trench visited me, and I told him exactly what Lambie had told me.

Trench said that on receiving this statement he returned immediately to the Central Police Office and told Superintendents Orr and Ord what Miss Birrell had said.

> Chief Superintendent Orr seemed impressed with the statement, and remarked, 'This is the first real clue which we have got.' I was instructed to write out the statement. I did so. In handing that statement to Superintendent Ord, he said, 'I have been ringing up Douglas (that is Superintendent Douglas of the Western) and he is convinced that Dr Charteris had nothing to do with it.'.

Trench further asserted that, with Detective Keith, he visited, on 3 January 1909, Nellie Lambie, then staying with her aunt at 15 South Kinning Place. He showed her a sketch of Oscar Slater which he had received from Superintendent Ord. She did not recognise the man.

> I touched on Dr Charteris, asking her if she really thought he was the man she saw. Her answer was, 'It's gey funny if it wasn't him I saw.' It will be noted that some time after the murder, but on the same evening, Dr Charteris called at Miss Gilchrist's house. Lambie in addition to saying it was 'gey funny, etc.', made the further remark, 'Fancy him asking me to go and stay with him that night. I would watch it. He might have done the same to me.' She further said, 'Gey funny he appeared so quick back in the house.'

And Trench summed-up:

> My conclusion after meeting Lambie was that, if she had had anyone to support her, she would have sworn to Dr Charteris. If Dr Charteris was the man, the whole mystery (as yet unexplained) of how the murderer obtained access to the house is cleared up. The aunt opened the door to her nephew.

Margaret Dawson Birrell, spinster, aged 49, living now at 61 Rupert Street, where she practised as a masseuse, gave evidence crystal-clear and adamantine. It homed like a guided missile straight to the core of Trench's tale – 'Helen Lambie did not say to me that she knew the man. She did not mention to me the name of Dr Charteris.' Shown the statement said to have been made by her to Trench on 23 December 1908, she said: 'I now solemnly declare that I have never made such a statement, and all that is contained in it is absolutely false.'

Next came Helen Lambie, now Mrs Gillon and the mother of a three-year-old daughter, to deny with equal vehemence the statement alleged by Trench to have been made by her. Not one word of truth in it she said, 'absolutely false'. She had, she told the sheriff,

> seen Dr Charteris in Miss Gilchrist's house on one occasion before, and I was at his wedding along with Miss Gilchrist and Marion Ferguson, the former maid's daughter. The man I saw leaving the house was not at all like, nor did I ever see Dr Charteris dressed like, the man I saw. I saw Dr Charteris that night when he came along to the house. As I could not be left alone in the house, he asked me to come and stay in his house, but I told him I preferred to go to my aunt's.

Lambie recalled Trench and Keith's visit to her at her Aunt Helen's, but not their showing her a sketch of Oscar Slater. Neither of the detectives had mentioned Dr Charteris, and she had not said, 'It's gey funny if it wasn't him I saw'. She had made no such remark as 'Fancy him asking me to go and stay with him that night', or 'It was gey funny he appeared so quickly back in the house'. Then, very earnestly, Lambie said to Millar: 'I wish to make it quite clear that neither to the Procurator-fiscal nor to the police, nor to anyone else, did I make the statement that Dr Charteris was the man I saw leaving the house.'

Charles Frederic Cowan, a 36-year-old analytical chemist, who was Miss Birrell's lodger, assured Sheriff Millar that he had not heard Helen Lambie mention Dr Charteris, either when she arrived at Miss Birrell's or when, later, he escorted her to her aunt's.

In the matter of young Mary Barrowman, Trench had in his statement confessed cynicism.

I am forced to the conclusion that Mary Barrowman was not at or near Miss Gilchrist's close at the time the murderer rushed there from. I have had from her employer and from his sister an emphatic statement that Barrowman did not deliver a message on the night of the 21st at Howitt's house.[2]

Trench points out that in her original statement Barrowman made no mention of having been at a Band of Hope meeting – 'If one compares the statements, it cannot be doubted but that Barrowman either lied in her original statement or lied at the trial.' Nor was there, said Trench, any reference in her original precognition to a man knocking up against her. It had merely said that the man ran past her.

Trench's misgivings regarding the reliability of Mary Barrowman's evidence were now evaluated.

William Roxburgh Barbour, grain merchant, aged 45, voluntary superintendent of the Band of Hope Mission at Lansdowne Mission Hall in Walker Street, spoke well of young Mary and of her honesty, but he could not help on the matter at issue, being unable to say whether or not she had been present at the 21 December meeting.

Then, cheerfully inflexible, in tripped Mary herself, to tell her story to the sheriff. And, yes, she definitely *had* been at that Band of Hope meeting.

Her boss, Colin Maccallum, owner of the boot and shoe shop, confirmed his certainty that Mary had gone with a parcel to Mr Howat's on the night of 21 December, adding for good measure: 'I never said to Lieutenant Trench that I was sure that Barrowman did not go that message on the night of the murder . . . That statement is absolutely false.'

Time and time again that phrase, 'absolutely false', came beating like a recurrent theme through the responses of the witnesses.

Sheriff Millar thought it right to obtain a statement from Agnes Brown, a 37-year-old schoolteacher, whose testimony seemed to have a bearing on the identification by Barrowman. She said that shortly after 7.08pm on the evening of 21 December 1908, she had encountered two men running in a westerly direction along West Princes Street. They had turned down Rupert Street and run on

2   Actually, James Howat, of 36 Cleveland Street.

towards Great Western Road. She had identified one of them as Oscar Slater.

The evidence of Duncan MacBrayne, who knew Slater and had seen him standing a few yards from his own close-mouth at about 8.15pm on December 21st, also struck Millar as reflecting significantly on Barrowman's statement.

Nor was it only lay witnesses who were denying the claims put forward by Trench. His own colleagues in the force were testifying against him. Here are a half-dozen of them. They surely cannot all be out of step.

Chief Superintendent John Orr, now Assistant Chief Constable of Glasgow, did not recall instructing Trench to visit Miss Birrell, or receiving any report from him of his questioning of her. He had, moreover, never remarked, 'This is the first real clue we have got.'

Superintendent John Ord said that the police had satisfied themselves at the time that Dr Charteris had nothing to do with the murder. He was quite certain that Trench had not told Orr and himself that Miss Birrell had said that Lambie had told her that the man she saw leaving the hall was Dr Charteris – 'I am astonished to hear such a statement made, and I say quite solemnly that it is not true.' He added that if, as Trench claimed, a written statement had been handed to him, it should be on the file. It was not – and the numbers on the file were consecutive.

Detective Inspector Andrew Nisbet Keith, who had accompanied Trench on the Lambie interview of 3 January 1909, had 'no clear recollection of what occurred'. But he definitely did not remember any pencil sketch of Slater, or Trench, bringing the conversation round to the question of whether Lambie had known the man who left Miss Gilchrist's house, although he conceded 'it was very likely that was done'. He had heard no talk of anything being 'gey funny' or of Lambie's being invited to stay the night at Dr Charteris' and saying: 'I would watch it. He might have done the same to me.' Having had all the parts of Trench's statement that concerned him read over to him by the sheriff, Keith commented: 'The whole thing is news to me, and I have no recollection of its having occurred.'

Superintendent William Miller Douglas' version of events

contrasted strongly with Lieutenant Trench's. In the matter of an alleged visit by the police to the house of Dr Charteris, the contrast could scarcely have been more stark. Trench's allegation was:

> I am aware that on 22nd December, the day after the murder, Superintendent Douglas, along with Detectives Pyper and Dornan, drove in a taxi-cab to the house of Dr Charteris, at 400 Great Western Road. I am also aware that they did so in view of information supplied by Helen Lambie. I have endeavoured from time to time to elicit what took place in Dr Charteris' house, but I am without information.

Douglas told Sheriff Millar:

> I am perfectly sure it is untrue to say that on 22nd December, accompanied by Detectives Pyper and Dornan, I drove in a taxi-cab to the house of Dr Charteris . . . The statement made by Lieutenant Trench with reference to this supposed visit to Dr Charteris' house has been read over to me and it is absolutely without foundation. The true story with regard to the visit is that on 23rd December Detectives Pyper, Gordon and I went to the house of Mrs Charteris at 4 Queen Margaret Crescent, partly on account of a statement made by Helen Lambie on the 22nd, as to the unfriendly relationship between Miss Gilchrist and Mrs Charteris and partly to exhaust the enquiry as to Miss Gilchrist's relatives.

In this connection, a hitherto undiscovered document is of paramount importance. It is a report of a police interview with Helen Lambie on the day after the murder and it is reposited in the Crown Office's vast archive on the Slater case.

> Lambie is specific.

> During the whole time I was in the deceased's employment I always cleaned the windows and did the washing. We had no charwomen or window cleaners coming about the house, and the only persons whom I ever heard the deceased say anything against was [sic] Mrs Charteris of No. 4 Queen Margaret Crescent, Hillhead . . . and her daughter by James Gilchrist viz. Mary Gilchrist or McColl [sic], who resides in England, Boscombe Court, Boscombe, Bournemouth. She frequently said to me that she disliked them . . . She [Mrs Charteris] had three sons . . . and the only time that I saw any of them at the house was about three years ago when Dr Charteris attended a party in the house and at that time he brought an Irish Terrier to Miss Gilchrist.

Superintendent Douglas also told the sheriff that Dr Charteris had explained how he came to be at Miss Gilchrist's later on the night of the murder. Someone, on hearing of the murder, had telephoned to Mr James Macdonald, who was Charteris' solicitor, under the mistaken impression that he was Miss Gilchrist's law agent, who, by one of the series of incredible coincidences with which the Slater case is positively starred, was *also* a James Macdonald.[3]

On hearing of the murder, Charteris' agent had promptly telephoned him, suggesting that he should break the news to his mother. Charteris determined that, before agitating her, he would go along to Miss Gilchrist's and verify that she really had been killed.

Douglas said that 'full enquiry was made into the movements of Dr Charteris by the police, and I am satisfied that he had nothing whatever to do with the murder'.

Detective Lieutenant William Gordon gave evidence to the effect that when he took a statement from Miss Birrell on 22 December 1908, she had said nothing of Lambie's having told her that the man in the hall was Dr Charteris. Indeed, on the night of the murder he had himself pressed Lambie regarding the man, and 'She told me she was quite unable to identify him'.

Chief Detective Inspector Pyper echoed this – 'She [Lambie] never said anything to me about Dr Charteris being the man.' He had also examined Miss Birrell, who told him in terms that she had no suspicion of any person. 'I have not a shadow of doubt that Dr Charteris had nothing to do with the murder,' concluded Pyper.

Finally, James Dornan, promoted now from sergeant to inspector, came forward to state that although he had been present at a number of interviews with Miss Birrell and Nellie Lambie, he had never heard either of them say anything at all that would throw suspicion on Dr Charteris.

And the odd policeman out, the solitary colleague who seemed, partly anyway, to confirm Trench's story, was Chief Inspector Alexander Cameron. He remembered that

previous to my visit to Mr and Mrs Birrell [Miss Margaret Birrell's Uncle Dawson and Aunt Jane] on January 9th, 1909, he [Trench] told me that Miss Birrell had said to him that the girl Lambie had said to her that the man who had passed her in the lobby was *like* Dr Charteris.

---

3 According to Dr Charteris himself, it was not his but his mother's solicitor who contacted him.

In spite of all these locked-horn refutations, Lieutenant John Thomson Trench, compeared by the sheriff, stood unabashed.

> Notwithstanding I am told that both Miss Birrell and Helen Lambie emphatically deny the whole story and express astonishment at it, I adhere to my statement that that was what Miss Birrell told me . . . I visited Helen Lambie . . . I was so much impressed with her statement that I mentioned the fact to Superintendent Ord next morning, asking if Dr Charteris might not be the man, and his reply was: 'Douglas has cleared all that up, and what can we do?'

Ridiculing – and this time on securer ground – the Crown allegation of a flight from justice, Trench had suggested – in the statement which he had submitted earlier to the Secretary for Scotland – that Slater had made preparations to leave Glasgow well before Allan McLean had gone to the Central Police Office. Nor had the journey out of Glasgow been a secretive one. Slater and Antoine booked tickets to Liverpool. Their luggage was conspicuously labelled 'Liverpool – Lime Street'. In Liverpool, staying in Room No. 139 at the North Western Hotel, where he registered as Oscar Slater, the 'fugitive' made no secret of having come from Glasgow and of intending to depart on the *Lusitania* for America. Nine witnesses – a Glasgow shop assistant, two Glasgow street porters, three Glasgow railway workers, a Liverpool shipping office passenger manager, a Liverpool hotel baggage porter and a Liverpool superintendent of police, who submitted 16 depositions from Liverpool witnesses – all testified to Slater's departure being as cool, calm, collected, and open as daylight. This overt itinerary did not impress one as being that of a guilt-ridden fugitive.

Trench brought his precognition to an end with something of an – albeit rather garbled – explanation:

> I have never seen Dr Charteris. I did not make any statement previous to the trial, either to the Fiscal or the Agent for the defence, as to what I now say Miss Birrell and Helen Lambie had said to me. I said nothing at all after Slater was condemned to death until he was reprieved, and even then not for a considerable period, when I mentioned it to Mr Shaughnessy, the agent for Oscar Slater.

Then comes this most opaque sentence: 'I did not think much of the incident by itself, and it was only when I discovered other facts that I brought this one up.'

A theory has been punted that there was an official police 'conspiracy' to spare Dr Charteris, of whose innocence they stood in no doubt, from what they regarded as the potentially damaging assertions to his good name made by Lambie. Trench might have got wind of this 'cover up' and misinterpreted it, convinced that powerful friends were hushing up the part that the well-connected doctor had played in Miss Gilchrists' death, and made the foreign Jew the scapegoat. His sense of justice and fairplay outraged, he set to work to fix the guilt where he believed it truly lay.

All things are, of course, possible, but this I would frankly have thought ingenious but unlikely.

By Saturday evening, 25 April, 29 witnesses had been questioned by Millar and their answers recorded by Sandilands. The Sabbath having, in solid Scots tradition, been kept holy as a day of rest, the inquiry papers, together with Sheriff Millar's report, were, on Monday, 27 April 1914, posted off to London.

Chapter Nine

TRENCH WARFARE

There can be no denying that 1914 was a pivotal year in the Oscar Slater affair. It was to see – in a sort of preternaturally extended Ides of March, stretching from that year's April right on until the following year's May – the downfall of Good Policeman Trench, and the groundless calumniation of a hardworking GP.

Trench would accuse, be accused, and end up disgraced and dismissed.

On a wider canvas of tragedy, the shooting of an Austrian Archduke by a Serbian student on 28 June 1914, would trigger the explosion of the bloodiest, most terrible war that the world had ever known.

That momentous year began for John Thomson Trench in quiet triumph. On 1 January in the New Year Honours, he was awarded the King's Police Medal, citing the fact that he was 'Conspicuous for gallantry in arresting dangerous criminals on several occasions, and has a distinguished record in the detective service'. His fellow-recipient of that honour was Superintendent

John Ord. They travelled down to Buckingham Palace, where, on 12 February 1914, they were presented with their medals by King George V. Only seven months later, at the age of 45, Trench was out on the hard, unyielding pavement, out of a job, out of pocket – £170 per annum – and with a wife and six children to support.

Although Trench's fate has been described as a self-engineered predicament, the result of deliberate self-sacrifice in the cause of justice, there was actually nothing intentional about what turned out to be self-destruction. He never sought martyrdom. It was thrust upon him. It was a condition which, paradoxically, he had taken every step that he could think of to avoid. The received vision of him as a tragic, stainless figure offered up on the altar of a malevolent, corrupt even, establishment, and pursued thereafter with relentless spite, partakes of wishful fantasy.

Animated by the praiseworthy desire to protect the innocent, the authorities supervising the production of the 1914 White Paper, *Case of Oscar Slater* (the Stationery Office publication presenting the 'Copy of Statements submitted to the Secretary of Scotland, and of the Evidence taken at the Inquiry held by the Sheriff of Lanarkshire, on the 23rd, 24th, and 25th April 1914'), substituted for the name of Dr Francis James Charteris the randomly selected letters 'AB', and wherever in the printed document material occurred which would plainly have indicated the identity of Charteris, showers of asterisks were inserted in its stead.

It was, as is so often in life the case, with the best of intentions that the worst of results was achieved. For, as it transpired, the effect was virtually the direct opposite of what was intended. It raised and perpetuated the suspicions of the press and public mind against the mysterious, innominate AB. Not only that, but it meant that many of the most telling rebuttals of Trench's allegations against Dr Charteris landed on the cutting-room floor. The full, unbowdlerised version of the 1914 evidence did not come into the public domain until 1990.

The device may perhaps have succeeded within a relatively narrow frame, but the alleged implication of Dr Charteris, as proposed by Trench – and he would seem to have been the doctor's sole accuser – appears to have been an open secret in certain quarters. It was known to sundry members of the police and the legal profession. The doctor's name was being bandied back and forth, with winks as good as nods, between Roughead, Doyle, Shaughnessy and Cook. Moreover, the challenge of 'AB' and the teasing of the asterisks were guaranteed to set the guessing-game addicts and the armchair arm-chancers naming names down the years.

The White Paper was published on 26 June 1914. Ten days earlier the Secretary for Scotland had closed the door on hope for Oscar Slater once again, telling the Commons: 'After careful consideration of the information obtained in the course of a full and searching inquiry, I am satisfied that there is no case established to justify my advising interference with the sentence.'

The whistle-blower's reward followed swiftly. On 13 July Chief Constable James Verdier Stevenson wrote to the Town Clerk, John Lindsay:

> I have to report to the Magistrates' Committee that I have suspended Detective Lieutenant John Thomson Trench for the offence of communicating to a person who is not a member of the Glasgow Police Force, viz. to Mr David Cook, Writer, Glasgow, information which he had acquired in the performance of his duty, and copies of documents from the Official records in the case of Oscar Slater, convicted of the murder of Miss Gilchrist on December 21st, 1908 . . .
>
> It is contrary to public policy and to all Police practice for an Officer to communicate to persons outside the Police Force information which he has acquired in the course of duty without the express sanction of the Chief Officer of his Force; and the giving of information is expressly forbidden by the instructions to the Glasgow Police in the following words, 'He should not divulge his instructions nor give information which he may acquire in the performance of his duty to any person outside the Force' (Instruction Book, page 33) . . .
>
> If he was acting with an honest purpose I cannot conceive why he should not have made his communication to his Chief Constable. He cannot say that he would not have received a hearing, as he was always treated with confidence by me . . .
>
> I can no longer consider Detective Lieutenant Trench as a trustworthy officer, or fit to hold a position in the Police Service. I have, accordingly, suspended him from duty, awaiting the decision of the Magistrates' Committee.
>
> I do not make any comment on the statements made by Detective

Lieutenant Trench as given in the Parliamentary White Paper, as they may form the subjects of litigation.

On 21 July Trench addressed a most humble and quasi-apologetic reply to Stevenson:

> Knowing as I do the Oscar Slater case and having a firm belief that he is innocent of the crime for which he was convicted, the matter pressed upon my mind for a considerable period until latterly I could not sleep for thinking of it.
>
> I felt I must do something and not knowing how to act one day in January last I met Mr David Cook, Writer. In the course of conversation with Mr Cook I decided to ask his opinion about the matter. I told him what my belief was and he then informed me that Dr Devon had been consulted by the Secretary for Scotland in regard to the case and that he would speak to him about it.
>
> Some time afterwards I was invited by Mr Cook to meet Dr Devon in Mr Cook's house which I did. I told Dr Devon that I had been worrying myself about Slater's case and explained to him certain things which I knew and which had come to my knowledge through inquiry and otherwise.
>
> Dr Devon wrote to Mr McKinnon Wood about the matter and it was pointed out to me that he was the proper person to receive any information bearing upon the case as he was the only person who could deal with same.
>
> On 13th February, 1914, a letter from Mr McKinnon Wood to Dr Devon was handed to me by Mr Cook. I was assured that it completely protected me against any breach of Police Regulations. Some time afterwards Mr Cook prepared on my behalf the evidence in my possession and I posted same at the General Post Office to Mr McKinnon Wood... From the time that I posted the information to Mr McKinnon Wood I have taken no part in the matter except to give evidence before the Sheriff at the inquiry . . .
>
> I have time and again bitterly regretted that I did not consult my Chief Constable in the matter. Looking back I can only wonder why I did not do so, but having once committed myself I was helpless . . .

This explanation cut little ice with an implacable Stevenson, who forwarded it, on 30 July, to the town clerk:

> In his first explanation Trench attempted to justify his action by the statement 'that the information and copies of documents were handed by him to Mr Cook, for transmission to His Majesty's representative the Secretary for Scotland, in obedience to a written request from that gentleman for same'.
>
> In his statement of 21st instant, he abandons this attitude. He now

admits that his action was wrong, he expresses deep regret, and he pleads in extenuation that having once committed himself he was helpless. I can only take this to mean that having committed himself into Mr Cook's hands, he was compelled to acquiesce in any action which Mr Cook chose to take, such as the publication of the newspaper articles to which by his own showing Trench apparently objected.

He also pleads that he was assured (he does not say by whom) that the letter from Mr McKinnon Wood to Dr Devon, handed to him by Mr Cook, completely protected him against any breach of the Police Regulations.

I believe both of these pleas to be true, and that the information supplied by Trench was used, as he suggests, in a manner that he never anticipated. I cannot, however, regard these pleas as extenuating his offence, and I adhere to the view of his conduct expressed in my letter of 13th inst.

He did not act from any sudden impulse, but in a deliberate and calculated manner well knowing that he was acting improperly, as is fully shown by his statement. If his purpose was honest and if his statements could bear examination, there was no need for the secret and underhand course which he took.

He gives no satisfactory reason for taking this course, and now says he bitterly regrets that he did not consult the Chief Constable in the matter, and looking back one can only wonder that he did not do so.

There remains also the fact that according to the White Paper the witnesses positively and explicitly denied that they did the acts or made the statements attributed to them by Trench.

Trench also despatched – on 1 August, 1914 – a precautionary letter to Mr McKinnon Wood, an appeal to the Secretary for Scotland that, with the risk of dishonourable dismissal now a very real possibility, that august personage should come to his aid.

Right Honourable Sir. – Mr Shaw, SSC, 53 George Street, Edinburgh, has forwarded me copy of communication which you addressed to him on 29th ult. relative to my case . . .

I relied entirely on the invitation contained in your letter [of February 13th] when I forwarded through Mr Cook the information. In the communication which accompanied the information the stipulation was expressly made that 'I was not to be victimised'.

I trust that you will allow me to say that I regarded your invitation to send the information, and your acceptance thereof, as ample protection against any breach of discipline that might be alleged against me. Perhaps on a reconsideration of the terms of your earlier letters you will agree that I had ample grounds for my belief.

Moreover, I was advised that your authority was an ample safeguard and your letter was handed to me as such . . .

My feeling in the matter . . . is that a communication from you to the Magistrates or to me direct so that I might produce it would exercise considerable influence in their deliberations regarding me.

I, therefore, venture to make this appeal to you to intercede with the Magistrates on my behalf. I trust to have a reply before the date of the Magistrates' inquiry, viz., 12 August.

I have the honour to remain, Right Honourable Sir,

Your Obedient Servant,

John T. Trench.'

Honourable Sir remained dishonourably silent.

Prior to his arraignment before the Magistrates' Committee, and in response to the report against him furnished to the magistrates by Chief Constable Stevenson, Trench himself prepared a 'reply' for submission to the Glasgow magistracy:

I must seek to clear your minds of the impression which the Chief Constable seeks to convey to you in his letter . . . that I had all the information regarding Slater's case for a number of years, did nothing with it, and then suddenly revealed it. Such a suggestion casts a sinister aspect over my conduct. No one could avoid drawing the conclusion from such a suggestion that there must have been some strong incentive or motive to reveal the information.

The Chief Constable has also declared in his letter – 'If he was acting with an honest purpose I cannot conceive why he should not have made his communication to his Chief Constable', and regarding which I desire him to state exactly and in definite terms what this charge is in this connection.

These two statements combine, as I have said, to cast a suspicion over my conduct, and which, I regret to say, have been uttered without investigation on his part to justify its utterance.

The first mistake he makes is the allegation that I possessed the information all along. I respectfully deny that . . .

None of the information was known to me except the incident which is now known as the A.B. incident. All that was entrusted to me at the time of the murder, independent of the A.B. incident, was a search of Slater's house in company with other officers, and the rendering of assistance in the identification proceedings in February, 1909.

The inquiries relative to the other matters were conducted either by officers of the Western or Central District. I did not make personal inquiries until December last year . . .

I have always had grave doubts concerning the guilt of Slater.

> My inquiries into the case relative to the A.B. incident did not
> permit me to hold any opinion definitely regarding the charge alleged to
> have been made in that direction. I was, as a matter of fact, assured that
> there was nothing in it, and I accepted that . . .

Trench then related how his success in 1912 in pulling off the rescue of Charles Warner, the suspected killer of Miss Milne in the celebrated Broughty Ferry murder case, stirred up memories of Slater's case.

> I made inquiries. I gained information that made me doubt more still. I
> never intended to probe too deeply at all but the remark of a brother
> officer showed me that there were suspicions elsewhere than in my own
> mind. I then went thoroughly into the case and was shocked to find that
> there was nothing in the case that would stand open investigation . . .
> I found that the thought of an innocent man lying in Peterhead
> proved too much for me. I was worried, could not sleep nor get if off my
> mind.

It was all to no avail. On 14 September the magistrates of Glasgow held a special meeting 'to consider the case of Mr John Trench'. They unanimously pronounced him guilty under Section 78 of the Glasgow Police Act 1866, and dismissed him from the force.

There are in the Slater case a number of satellite mysteries subsidiary to the central – and still unresolved – question of who did kill Marion Gilchrist. One of those minor – or perhaps not so minor – mysteries is why Chief Constable James V. Stevenson, in the lee of the 1914 inquiry, was so implacably determined that Trench should be sacked. It was a decision which, in terms of police discipline, seems, at least on the surface, to have been somewhat harsh; in its effect on public perceptions of the case it may also appear almost crass.

The dismissal of Trench was certainly to have repercussions that can scarcely have been unpredictable. It served further to fuel the indignation behind the vigorous newspaper campaigns then being waged against Slater's conviction and the refusal of the Secretary for Scotland to reopen the case. Furthermore, it was to bestow upon Trench the martyrdom that he strove so carefully to avoid. And with that martyrdom it was to confirm in the minds of the conspiracy theorists that John Trench had most certainly been telling the truth, the whole truth and nothing but the truth – and that there had plainly been a cover-up.

In short, the dismissal of Trench, besides being a personal tragedy for the man himself, may be seen as a public relations disaster for the Glasgow police, which is perhaps to assume that Glasgow's finest would have lost any sleep in 1914 about such an esoteric concept as public relations.

The Chief Constable's action in calling for the dismissal of one of his brightest officers may be interpreted, of course, simply as that of a martinet, smarting under a challenge to his position and determined to reassert his authority. Another explanation – namely revenge – is given by William Roughead in his *Classic Crimes*, first published in 1951:

> Trench's chiefs had never forgiven him for the disloyalty to his caste shown by him in the matter of Warner's waistcoat, whereby he spoilt a fine case of circumstantial evidence. The time had come when, in the vulgar phrase, they could get some of their own back.

Roughead's explanation here may be based, literally speaking, on slightly false premises. The Broughty Ferry case had, after all, been handled by the constabulary in Dundee, on the east coast of Scotland – not those in Glasgow on the west. Nevertheless, the general allegation that Trench's dismissal was a blatant case of revenge and retribution for his whistle-blowing persists strongly to this day.

It has also been suggested by some people with police force connections that there must have been another reason for the dismissal of Trench besides his conduct – right or wrong – in the Slater case. They may have a point. What is clear is that in 1914 there had already been question-marks set against Trench which had nothing to do with the murders of either Miss Jean Milne or Miss Marion Gilchrist. And these reservations may have served to influence Stevenson's decision.

Detective Lieutenant Trench has been sung by every writer on the case as the uncanonised saint of the Slater redemption. He has become an icon, regarded just this side of idolatry. He has been presented over and over again as a character noble and stainless; self-sacrificial in the cause of justice. Doubtless, there is some truth here, but it is only part of the story.

What follows is totally new, and for many who have known only Trench's Sunday-best profile, the exposure of this sinistral – or sinister – aspect will be, as it was for me, a thoroughly disconcerting revelation. I anticipate hands and eyebrows raised in horrified criticism. But I am not making it up. I am providing facts, not offering opinions.

The first disconcerting hint that I received that all was not quite so rosy as I had always believed in the Trenchian garden of remembrance came in a conversation which I had in 1986 with a former Assistant Chief Constable of Glasgow, William A. Ratcliffe, who was by then living in retirement in Kent. Mr Ratcliffe, who died a few years ago, had a number of novel insights to impart on the Slater case. One of these concerned the probity of Detective Trench. He told me that, without a doubt, John Thomson Trench's dealings with the criminal underworld had been far from above board. In fact, he indicated that Trench was corrupt, a 'bent copper', whose behaviour had, indeed, been causing disquiet among a number of his colleagues for several years before the events of 1914 that led to his dismissal.

It must, I think, be at this point emphasised that I was not prepared to rely solely upon Ratcliffe's testimony, however apparently disinterested and sincere-seeming. It would require subsequent research in archives, both official and private, to provide confirmation that Mr Ratcliffe was neither mis-remembering nor, with advancing years, unknowingly inventing.

The rumblings against Trench had, so the evidence indicates, been going on for as long as five years, which takes us back to 1909, the year of Slater's conviction. In 1914, in the weeks between Sheriff Millar's inquiry and Trench's dismissal, a worried John Ord was to gather some rather unexpected background material about Trench. At the age of eleven he had appeared at Edinburgh Sheriff Court and, on 12 April 1880, had been convicted of the theft of wood, and dismissed with an admonition. On the same date, his mother, Margaret Thomson or Trench, had been found guilty of the reset of the stolen wood, and sentenced to 15 days' imprisonment. Revealed, too, was Trench's Army record. During the first four and a half of his seven years with the colours, his conduct was rated 'very bad'. In August 1886 he was sentenced to 21 days' imprisonment with hard labour for absenting himself without leave and losing his uniform. He was five times convicted for being drunk, and on two occasions the charges were aggravated by his creating disturbances in the barracks.

These might seem to be, indeed were, relatively minor infractions – the regrettable excesses of youth – but, in the prevailing climate of growing suspicion, even such remote misdemeanours were obviously regarded as worthy of note.

Considerably more seriously, Ord had, on 22 April 1914, the day before Sheriff Millar's inquiry opened, written, in confidence, to Chief Constable Stevenson, under the heading 'Alleged Report by Detective Trench as to the Statement made by Nellie Lambie concerning Dr Charteris':

The first time I heard of such a report was from Detective Trench himself on Sunday 29 March and the reason I had any conversation with him on that day was as follows:–

In the *Daily Record* of March 24th, 1914, there appeared an article on the Slater case apparently inspired by Mr Cook.

It contained, said Ord, restricted official information, and he [Ord] suspected that someone had been furnishing Cook with excerpts, either from the book containing reports supplied to Mr Hart, or from the Slater case correspondence file.

During the day the name of an officer who had left the service got coupled with the leakage and I accordingly wrote a private note to Detective Trench (whom up to this date I had looked upon as one of the most trustworthy officers in the service) to come and see me . . .

Trench called at Ord's office on Sunday, 29 March. 'I told him of my suspicion, and asked him to have quiet inquiry made regarding the leakage of information.'

Later, adds Ord, their conversation had turned upon the points raised by Mr Cook,

when Trench surprised me by saying that Nellie Lambie had made a statement to Miss Birrell on the night of the murder to the effect that the man she saw leaving Miss Gilchrist's house was like Dr Charteris. I told him that he was altogether wrong and that it was Mr Charteris the Writer, whose name somehow got abroad, but so far as I knew the information did not eminate [sic] from Nellie Lambie.

To this Trench replied 'Mr Ord don't you remember that one night after you had gone off duty, Mr Orr sent for me and told me that he had heard that Nellie Lambie had made some statement regarding Dr Charteris to Miss Birrell on the night of the murder and sent me to Miss Birrell to ascertain if anything of the kind had been said and that I told you the following morning what I had learned and that you at once rang up Mr Douglas by telephone, and that he reported that he had attended to that matter and that it was all right'.

I again told Trench that he was making a mistake and that so far as I was concerned, I never heard Dr Charteris' name mentioned in connection with the murder. To this, he replied 'It does not concern you, you did your part if a mistake has been made'. I resented this and said 'You are entirely wrong, Trench, but I will enquire of Mr Douglas and ascertain whether he ever heard of such a rumour as it was himself and his officers who had precognosced Nellie Lambie, Miss Birrell and the other witnesses on the night of the murder'.

I also told Trench on the same night that some extraordinary reports were eminating [sic] from Mr Cook's office and being circulated throughout the city and that one of them was to the effect that Mr Cook had had the assistance of two New Scotland Yard officers in getting up his case.

Trench then became very uneasy and commenced to make a rambling statement about a Newcastle case where the local authorities were not trusted to make enquiry and that two officers from New Scotland Yard had been sent to make the enquiry which resulted in it being discovered that there was blame attached to certain police officers.

I then and there told Trench that the only thing annoying me was the fact that information intended only for the Chief Constable and the Procurator-fiscal had been taken from books or documents which were at one time under my charge, and had been supplied to Mr Cook and that some one had *sold* the information to him, and at the same time I mentioned the ex-officer's name who was associated with the deed. Trench promised to do what he could to discover the guilty party.

At the Publicans' Annual Licensing Court on 14 April during an interval the law agents present . . . were talking freely about Trench being the person who had given Mr Cook the information in the case, and that he was suffering from remorse of conscience . . .

That night I rang up Trench on the telephone, and informed him of the contemptuous manner in which his name had been mentioned in my hearing by gentlemen of the legal profession, and I said to him 'Have you made any statement to Mr Cook about the Slater case?' and he replied 'I have not'. I then said 'Have you had any idle talk with him in such a way as that he could couple your name with the case?' and he replied 'No. No' . . . I can truthfully say that I have no recollection of Trench ever having made any report to me regarding the alleged statement by Nellie Lambie; and I am quite satisfied that if Mr Orr had sent him to make an enquiry he would have insisted on seeing Trench's report, and would have instructed him what to do there anent. I am sure Mr Orr will bear me out in this statement.

Ord's indictment of Trench continued:

It is only since I have had heard of Trench's assertions that his extraordinary conduct in my office on 29 March has been made clear to me, and I am of opinion that he has been led into making one false step in stealing the contents of privileged documents and is now making false statements in order to justify his position.

I know his weakness for notoriety for example, in getting his name into the newspapers in connection with cases likely to excite public interest, and it is very likely that he may have precognosced witnesses on the week following the murder after they had been precognosced by the detectives of the Western District with a view to learning something missed by them and it is possible that he may have interviewed amongst others, Miss Birrell.

On 29 July 1914, some two weeks after Trench's suspension, Ord submitted another report to Stevenson.

It appears that ever since he [Trench] entered the Detective Department he has been suspected by his brother officers of giving information to bookmakers and thieves. In particular he has been suspected for a number of years by Detective Sergeant [John] McKellar, who, as far back as 1910, warned a uniformed sergeant that if he got any warrants to enter betting houses not to mention that he had such to the members of the Detective Department. McKellar has also some information of Trench's connection with thieves.

Further evidence of Trench's alleged dishonesty had come on 13 July from Detective Sergeant John Montgomery, who – it appears at Ord's instigation – had furnished a confidential report to Ord's successor at the Central, Superintendent Andrew Gow Lindsay:

While on day duty as detective constables in 1904, Detective Trench and I took possession of a large quantity of goods in a broker's shop in

Gallowgate, and took it to the Central Police Office . . . and the same day, or the day after, Trench suggested that we should take a pair or two of stockings each, and as he was going to dinner he took one pair away.

When I went home to my dinner I told my wife what Trench had done, and she told me to go straight back and tell Trench to put the stockings back or she would come down and report him. I returned to the office and told Trench, and he asked me to go to his house and get the stockings back, which I did. The waterproof coats which Trench suggested we should take were never removed.

Montgomery adds with a certain anguish:

I never to the best of my knowledge mentioned the matter to any person, and when Superintendent Lindsay asked me regarding the matter today I could not tell a lie. And now I have broken my promise which I gave to Detective Trench in 1904.

Perhaps the most damning of Trench's accusers was Detective Chief Inspector Andrew Nisbet Keith, of Central District, himself an officer of unblemished record who was subsequently to become Chief Constable of Lanarkshire. In a precognition sworn by him in 1915, he says:

Although I was in the same service as Trench, I had not spoken to him for five and a half years before his dismissal. [That would be about March 1909.] I was convinced in my own mind – from information frequently received – that he was not acting squarely, and I wished to have nothing to do with him and not to be associated with him in any case.

Interestingly, papers in the Crown Office's archive record that Trench had a brother who was dismissed from the Glasgow Police Force for obtaining a reward by a false statement. He was subsequently convicted of theft.

The years 1914 and 1915 were certainly *anni horribiles* for John Trench. Honoured, suspended and then sacked.

In May 1914, in the midst of it all, his widowed mother – he had lost his father at the age of four – had died.

The axe having fallen on his police career, he did the only practical thing that he could – he went back to the Army. He had, as we have seen, previously served in the Black Watch. Now he enlisted in the Royal Scots Fusiliers and, early in 1915, was promoted to Provost Sergeant of Stirling.

In April 1915, the readers of the *Weekly News* were regaled with a 'great new series' – Trench's memoirs of '21 Years at 'The Central''. Over the next months the tales of cloak and dagger derring-do were to include 'How I Tracked Karl Graves, the German Spy'; 'The Chase and Arrest of Paul Jules Martein for the Murder of a Lady in Paris'; 'The Dublin North Wall Mystery – How I Tracked and Arrested the Man Who Slew Mary Carroll'; 'The Fallacy of Honour Amongst Thieves – How I Tracked and Captured a Russian Desperado on Information Received', and much more. There were also to be Trench's accounts of 'the two great mysteries which are marked with a red cross in my life story' – the Oscar Slater case and the Elmgrove affair.

With his Army career under way again and his detective exploits being serialised, life had resumed some sort of equilibrium for ex-Detective Lieutenant Trench. But there were still surprises in store.

On 13 May 1915, a former colleague, Detective Duncan Weir, accompanied by a detective officer of the Stirling police, appeared at the camp, Allan's School, Stirling, where Trench was busy overhauling his field kit preparatory to embarking for the Dardanelles.

'I hold a warrant for your arrest,' Weir told him.

Chapter Ten

RESETTING THE RECORD

Standing, supreme irony, in the same dock in Court No. 3, at the High Court of Justiciary, as that in which Oscar Slater had stood, John Thomson Trench, decked out in smart, spit-and-polished military uniform, heard the reading of the indictment charging him - David Cook, standing, dressed spick and span lawyerly, beside him, and John McArthur, conspicuously *in absentia* - with the criminal offence of reset.

The date was Tuesday, 17 August 1915.

Let us see if, pursuing the matter through the sheaves of official documents, we can discover how this sorry state of affairs came about.

As with Trench's ignominious dismissal from the force, so has the reset case been portrayed down the years as the end-product of a vindictive police establishment bent on extracting the last possible morsel of vengeance from a noble and upright officer who had dared to speak out. But this is to show only one side of the story – a romanticised and superficial simplification of what upon closer examination, viewing in the round, seems to have been in reality a very much more complex and controversial affair.

On the morning of Wednesday, 14 January 1914, staff arriving at nine o'clock to open up the shop of Charles L Reis & Co, jewellers, at 209 Argyle Street, Glasgow, discovered that thieves had opened up the place before them, and departed with a £900 price-tag haul.

The police were hastily summoned, and it was promptly decided that this case called for the shrewd know-how and local knowledge of that champion thief-taker, Detective Lieutenant Trench. Sagely,Messrs Reis had provided themselves with cover for such unwelcome depredations of their stock with the Guardian Assurance Company, whose representative, John Buchanan, lost no time in proposing the offer of a £150 reward for the recovery of both the thieves and the property.

Just over nine months before the Reis job, another Argyle Street jeweller's, David Dow & Son, of No. 68, had been robbed of £3,000 worth of merchandise, and it was thanks to information supplied by a dubious character named McArthur that practically all of the jewellery was restored to its lawful owners. Trench, who had been involved in the arrest of the two thieves responsible, was well aware of the helpful 'singing' of McArthur.

This John McArthur, presenting himself as a Glasgow pawnbroker, was known to be a reset man (fence) in a large way of underworld business. Over the years, Trench had, in the course of his official duties, come to know him extremely well, and it was actually in consequence of this auld acquaintance that, on Sunday afternoon, 18 January 1914, Mr Buchanan, 42-year-old holder of the longiloquent title of Assistant Residential Secretary (Burglary Department),Messrs The Guardian Assurance Company, received a visit at his flat, at 25 Belmont Street, in the Hillhead district of Glasgow.

The lieutenant came bearing a cheering proposal: in consideration of a single payment in the sum of £400, the return of Reis' stolen property, 'absolutely intact'. Trench emphasised that *he had been approached by a man* – he named no names – who was simply a go-between, so that it would be pointless to arrest him, and, anyway, to do so would mean that the goods would be gone for ever.

By arrangement, Buchanan presented himself at ten o'clock the following Monday morning at the Central Police Office, where Trench, after introducing him to his superior, Superintendent Lindsay, conducted him in to an interview with Chief Constable Stevenson. The matter of the restoration of the jewels was discussed at length, and the Chief said frankly that he wished that 'the man' – no whisper of McArthur's name had passed Trench's lips – had gone direct to Buchanan with his proposition and had not involved the police. He did not, however, strike Buchanan as in any way opposing the suggested recovery, merely remarking rather drily that what was being proposed would, in England, be held to be compounding a felony!

According to Trench, his claim backed by John Buchanan in his precognition, it was he who at that meeting brought up the possibility of using an intermediary, a 'buffer' he called it, between Buchanan and the dubitable negotiant, one who could neutrally represent both their interests. It was he, too, who had suggested for that rôle his old friend, the law agent, David Cook. That the idea was mooted in the presence of the Chief Constable, who, incidentally, denied that this was so, is not borne out by the evidence. It was not, in fact, until Cook wrote a letter to the Procurator-fiscal in April 1915 that his part in the transactions became known to the authorities.

Immediately after leaving the Chief's room, Trench trotted off to see Cook and set up the deal. Later, Buchanan, weighted down with the requisite £400 in gold, proceeded in company with Trench to Cook's office at 59 Bath Street.

There was another meeting, at 3pm, at the King's Arms, a public-house on the corner of Bath and Elmbank streets, opposite the King's Theatre. It was attended by Buchanan, Trench, Cook and McArthur. An agreement was hammered out. The gold and 'the stuff' would be exchanged at Cook's home, in Annfield Place, Dennistoun, at seven o'clock that evening.

And that was how it came to pass that, exactly one week after the Reis *heist*, the missing jewellery was returned.

But there were those in Glasgow who were not so well satisfied as Mr John Buchanan and his masters. Long memories were reaching back.

The dust had settled on the Reis robbery and its resolution. Glasgow's criminal practitioners were moving on to other people's pastures new, but a fat cloud of suspicion, growing plumper daily, sat suspended over Lieutenant Trench's oblivious head. Daily, too, whispers were waxing ever louder in the tiled corridors of police power. Now, and in the course of many months to come, it would be not just whispers, but plain statements from present and former brother officers, who had worked for years beside Trench, proclaiming aloud, written down in black and white precognitions, strange allegations about him and his funny little ways.

In a precognition given on 16 February 1915, Chief Detective Inspector Keith told of a conversation which he had had with McArthur about the Reis job. He had remarked to McArthur that he had heard on the grape-vine that one of those involved had not been pleased with his share. 'Is that the insurance man?' McArthur had asked. And on being told that it wasn't, McArthur said: 'Oh, is it the other bugger? It doesn't matter, he's never pleased with what he gets for his share anyhow.'

McArthur did not mention any name. Neither did Keith. But the Inspector said in his precognition that 'The dissatisfied person I was referring to was Trench. My reason was that I knew from previous experience that Trench would be involved.'

Detective Sergeant McKellar, precognosced on the same day, said that it had been known almost at once that five hard men, members of the notorious Caulfield gang – Robert Caulfield himself, Richard Craig, Alexander McDonald, James Chapman, and a man named Bell – had committed the crime: 'Chapman has since admitted this to me personally, and he stated that the thieves got £25 each, the balance going to McArthur and the detectives. I took this to refer to Trench and Chief Detective Inspector Murray.'

McKellar was absolutely convinced that Trench, who was in

charge of the Reis investigation, must, like everyone else, have known who the culprits were, but 'his attitude was quite unusual. I have all along known that any information the police had was at once communicated to the thieves interested, and any prospective move on the part of the police was conveyed to this particular gang at once'.

Detective Sergeant Montgomery testified that a day or two before the break-in at the Reis shop, he had received private information that a robbery was to be committed there. 'I told Inspector Murray. Nothing, however, was done. Trench was in charge of the case, but no apprehensions were made. Since he was dismissed I have not known of any information to get out of the police office.'

And yet another detective sergeant, Charles Melvin, of the Northern District Office, went on record saying: 'I do suspect Chief Detective Inspectors Trench and Murray as having given information to thieves . . . those two inspectors were always on the most friendly terms with each other.' Melvin said that he knew, a fortnight or three weeks before it took place, that Reis' was going to be turned over by Caulfield, Craig, McDonald and Bell.

> I did not personally report this to Inspectors Murray or Trench, but it was well known among the detective staff. No special watch was put on, and in my opinion that should have been done, and notwithstanding the police having the information stated, no apprehensions were made.

All this seemed to me to lend a credence, which I had at first withheld, to Ratcliffe's account to me of the alleged scam carried out by Trench. He had told me:

> John McArthur was Trench's prime contact in the illicit business of levying money from insurance companies. Matters proceeded thus: either McArthur, or Trench himself, through McArthur, would suggest a place where a thief might carry out a robbery. The thief would proceed to do so. Trench would then approach an insurance agent and tell him that he thought he could contact a man (i.e. McArthur) who knew a man who had the stolen property in his possession, and that, for the reward money, it could be recovered. And that would duly happen, possibly with the involvement of a crooked solicitor who was a friend of Trench's, David Cook. The thief, McArthur, Trench and, if his services had been used, Cook, would then divide up the reward money.

There is little doubt that this illicit procedure was followed on a number of occasions, but I am by no means convinced of Trench and Cook's involvement – except in the Reis case. McArthur was unquestionably a leading player in every case, but in other instances Trench's rôle in the profitable charade was taken over by other allegedly 'bent' officers, for example Chief Detective Inspectors George Murray and Allan Campbell.

Now, forearmed with all this extra and recondite information, primed with this hitherto secret knowledge – stowed away safely available at the backs of our minds – let us give unprejudiced ear to the remaining police and Fiscal department witnesses as they throw their various and varied lights upon John Thomson Trench and the Brownian movement of bright criminal specks dancing a whirligig about him.

Trench's immediate superior, Superintendent Andrew Gow Lindsay, who had replaced Superintendent Ord, gave a precognition on 20 May 1915.

> On the forenoon of 19 January 1914, Trench and Buchanan called on me.
> One of the first things Trench said was that he had an idea where the
> [Reis] stuff was. My reply was: 'If I knew in whose possession it was I would
> not be long in bringing them here.' He explained this by saying that it
> might be possible to get it back by payment of a certain sum. Trench made
> no reference whatever to McArthur's name. He was very reticent and not
> disposed to say much. As it is not usual to make a detective officer divulge
> the source of his information, I did not press him unduly for particulars. I
> may say that I was strongly adverse to having any dealings regarding this
> stolen property, and that was also the Chief Constable's view. Trench was a
> well trusted officer and I made no attempt to pry into his information.

Lindsay reported what Trench had told him to the Chief Constable. He also instructed Trench to submit a full written report of the whole of the facts to Mr Hart, the Procurator-fiscal. A day or two later he met Trench and asked him if he had done so. He said that he had. 'If Trench states that he informed me of all that had been done regarding the recovery of the jewellery and the part he took in it, that statement,' said Lindsay, 'is untrue.'

Chief Detective Inspector George Murray, of Central, the uprightness of whose character was called into question by so many of his brother officers, uttered a precognition on 13 August 1915. He was at pains to explain his close-seeming relationship with ex-

Detective Trench.

> Trench served in the Black Watch, and at a later period I also served in that regiment. This tended to a certain friendship, which subsisted till about four years ago. At that time Mr Orr, Depute Chief, informed me I should not be unduly friendly with any particular officer in view of possible promotion. I have followed his advice. Trench was dismissed for giving private police information to an unauthorised person. Apart from that, I had no reason to suspect he was giving away police information, and I certainly did not do [so].

Then, flat denial:

> I do not know McArthur and have had no dealings of any kind with him. I know of no association between Cook and Trench, and personally I have always kept Cook at arm's length.

So far as Fiscal Hart – as well as the Crown Agent and Crown Counsel – was concerned, things had been a'brewing for some considerable time in the matter of John McArthur. When, as far back as 8 December 1914, Hart had been instructed by Crown Counsel to have the bold McArthur arrested, the Fiscal's forces – that is, the Glasgow police – had been outpaced and outwitted by that worthy. Missing from his home – 445 Crown Street, Gorbals – he was eventually run to ground in Kilmarnock, and escorted back to Glasgow, by the ubiquitous Inspector Weir, on 27 January 1915.

As well as being charged with reset in the case of the Reis robbery, he was similarly charged as regards the break-in at the premises of David Dow & Son, jewellers, 113 Sauchiehall Street, in May 1914, and at those of Messrs James Smith, jewellers, at 99 Hope Street, in July 1914. To Detective Constable Arthur McIntosh, who had been detailed to fingerprint him, McArthur confidentially observed:

> This is a bad business. The case seems to be pretty black against me. I'm charged with resetting over £2,000 worth of jewellery. I hope to goodness they never prove it.

He continued:

> It'll be a blue look out for some of you fellows. I've heard that Allan Campbell has got a summons. Poor chap, I'm sorry for him after all these years' service. He's not the only one. Oh, but what's the good of me saying anything. There are others – Murray and Trench – and you'll have heard the whole story.

By the end of March things were proceeding apace. On 1 April 1915,

Advocate Depute William Mitchell, indulging in a spot of prophecy, drafted a long memo to the Lord Advocate, Robert Munro. In it, he forecasts that the defence that McArthur will put forward in answer to the charges of reset will be that, in dealing with the stolen property and handing it over to the insurance companies, he was really acting on behalf of the police, and that he might allege that the police were themselves engaged in a criminal conspiracy to defeat the ends of justice and obtain personal profit. Bearing this in mind, Mitchell underlined the very serious character of the charges made against the police and advised that, prior to bringing the charges of reset against McArthur, careful consideration by the Lord Advocate and, probably, by the Secretary for Scotland as well, of the position of the police would, in his view, be required.

The members of the detective force implicated in the charges were Trench, Campbell and Murray. Mitchell spelt it out:

> It is alleged against these three persons, particularly against Trench and
> Murray, that while acting as officers in the detective service . . . they
> deliberately connived at the acts of very clever burglars, and shared in the
> proceeds of the burglaries.

While observing that 'It is significant that a number of members of the Glasgow Detective Force have no doubt in their own minds but that Trench and Murray are implicated in these scandals,' as Mitchell, quite rightly, pointed out regarding the accusations, 'very much of it is hearsay, much the statement of actual criminals'. Even so, 'further investigation either by the Lord Advocate's department or by the Secretary for Scotland seems imperative. It may be, too, that Cook, the writer, and Buchanan, the agent for the Guardian Assurance Company, and even Trench and Murray, may be considered *participes* in the reset.'

On 13 April 1915, David Cook made a very grievous mistake. He addressed what turned out to be so vitally important a letter to Procurator-fiscal Hart that it must be quoted at some length.

> McArthur's answer to the charges is (1) that what he did was at the express
> request of the police in the Reis and Dow cases; (2) and that in the Smith
> case he received a letter from the Guardian Assurance Company; that in
> response to that letter he saw Mr Buchanan who instructed him to recover
> the jewels. McArthur further contends that even in the Smith case he
> understood that the matter had the approval of the police. Certainly their

conduct after the recovery was intimated to them would appear to support the contention of the accused. In none of the three cases does McArthur admit that he made the approach.

In the Reis case Trench represented to me [Cook] that the police would be glad of my assistance in helping Buchanan to recover the jewels. I asked Trench if he was doing the business off his own bat. I had views as to the advisability of Trench as a police official from a disciplinary point of view connecting himself with the matter. He replied: 'Oh, it is all right, the Chief knows all about it. I have seen him along with Buchanan and told him the whole story,' and added, 'I told him that McArthur was the man who helped the police to recover the stuff and arrest the men in the Argyle Street job.'[1]

Buchanan corroborated Trench as to what had passed at the meeting with the Chief Constable and added that the Chief had asked him to report formally if he was successful in recovering the goods.
I [Cook] said: 'Well, if I can help you, gentlemen, good and well. It is no offence so far as I know to recover stolen property in order that it may be returned to its lawful owner. I have no hesitation in touching this matter seeing that the Chief knows all about it.'

In presence of Trench, McArthur said he believed he could get the stuff. I said to McArthur: 'If you get the stuff, will you come to my office with it. I will have Buchanan there to receive it.' He said: 'No. Suppose I were caught with the stuff in my possession, would Trench or any of them clear me?' I said in reply: 'But the Chief knows all about it.' But on no account would McArthur entertain the idea of carrying the jewels in a central part of the city. Ultimately the jewels were handed over to Buchanan in my house, and the money paid.

That night, and within an hour of the recovery of the jewels, I reported all that had taken place to Trench, who said he would call for Buchanan and see if he had got the stuff, and would report to the Chief Constable in the morning.

Trench in his precognition says he went to Buchanan's house, saw the jewellery and reported to the Chief next day. The Chief in his precognition admits the meeting with Buchanan and Trench, admits that Trench reported the recovery, and that he told Trench to report to you. You say you do not remember, although Mr Giles, your Depute, says Trench told him of the recovery in the corridor, and that he told Trench to go in and tell you.

The Chief admits that he received a letter on the day following the recovery intimating that the jewels had been recovered, apparently intact, and requesting his permission to reward Trench for whose services the

1   This was the robbery carried out in April 1913, at the premises of David Dow & Son, 68 Argyle Street.

letter acknowledged thanks.

It must be apparent that had there been any intention to deal with McArthur as an accused person, the jewels ought to have been taken possession of by the police.

A handwritten note with the blue embossed seal of the Lord Advocate's Chambers, Dover House, Whitehall, London, bearing the date 15 April 1915, and initialled by the Lord Advocate, Robert Munro, conveyed his decision in the following terms:

In this case McArthur will be tried in the High Court on a charge of reset. The gravity of the charge and the serious circumstances seem to me to abundantly justify this mode of trial. The trial will be in Edinburgh. I think it highly undesirable to have a case of this type, involving charges against the Glasgow police force, held in Glasgow. It does not appear to me that *in hoc statu* the evidence warrants a criminal charge against anyone other than McArthur. I refrain from dealing with the very serious and shocking charges made against the police. But I think that at this stage the papers with this minute should be submitted to the Secretary for Scotland, in order that he may take such action as he thinks fit.

Meanwhile – on 19 April – Fiscal Hart wrote off to the Crown Agent, enclosing Cook's letter of the 13th for onward passing to Crown Counsel. He had this to say:

Mr. Cook's letter, if it does anything, appears to strongly support the suggestion of the Crown precognition that a conspiracy existed to obtain money from the insurance companies. In this, so far as the Reis case is concerned, the main movers seem to have been Trench and McArthur, who were assisted in the matter by Mr Cook, as he himself acknowledges. Mr Cook throughout refers to what Trench did and said as having the authority of 'the Police'. Indeed, he regards the terms as synonymous. He is quite wrong on the assumption he makes that all the stolen property was recovered in the Reis case. There was a very considerable shortage in this and the other two cases. The fact of Mr Cook reporting to Trench all that had taken place at the handing over of the stolen property seems absurd looking to their relationship.

There seems little doubt that Trench was endeavouring throughout to work with the semblance of the Chief Constable's authority to safeguard himself, but according to the Chief Constable he only made such representations to him as he found necessary to achieve that end. In my view, the Chief Constable was never made aware of the full facts of the case.

The same thing is true of Trench's dealings with my office. No written report was made to me. Trench merely mentioned such facts as he found convenient in a casual way to my Depute, Mr Giles, whom he met in a corridor. I have no recollection of Trench ever having seen me on the subject, and I am quite certain that he never reported to me any of the material facts. Mr Cook terms this 'reporting to me.'

When, at length, Cook's letter reached the desk of the Lord Advocate, sparks flew; it wrought havoc, produced a totally unintended and unexpected effect. Witness the following handwritten card:

> Saturday, 8 May 1915.
> It appears to me that Cook's letter materially alters
> the situation. I think that his guilt and that of Trench
> are indistinguishable from the guilt of McArthur.
> Accordingly the indictment will run against McArthur,
> Trench and Cook.
> Robert Munro.

On the reverse side of the card an Advocate Depute, George Morton, wrote: '12th inst. Procurator-fiscal will apply for a warrant to arrest Trench and Cook on the same charges of reset as McArthur.'

The die was cast.

The warrants were put into execution by – who else? – Chief Detective Inspector Duncan Weir. He formally arrested, cautioned and charged Trench on 13 May.

Trench's reply was:

> This is a cruel charge. It will kill my poor wife. I might as well be killed
> stone-dead. This will ruin me. I cannot come back to the Regiment among
> the men after this. As regards the second and third charges, I had nothing
> to do with them; and so far as the first is concerned, all I did was done with
> the knowledge of the Chief Constable and the Sheriff's Procurator-fiscal.

Weir stated:

> About 11am the following day, 14 May, I apprehended Cook in the County
> Buildings . . . He then said: 'As sure as I have my God to meet, I know
> nothing of the second and third charges. I never heard of them. It is a
> wicked, shameful charge.'

Both the accused emitted declarations. Cook's was practically a repetition of his 13 April letter to Hart. He ended it: 'I am degraded and placed in the dock. If I am guilty, then my co-accused ought to be J.V. Stevenson, Chief Constable of Glasgow.'

Trench insisted that he knew nothing whatever about the Dow

and Smith robberies. As regards the Reis break-in, he simply told again his many times told tale, but this time, wittingly or unwittingly, admitting that it was he who sought McArthur out and not, as he had always previously and adamantly maintained, McArthur who had sought him out. He claimed that he had anyway 'explained the whole thing' to Superintendent Lindsay, that he had 'explained the whole thing' to the Chief Constable, and had also 'explained the whole thing' to Mr Giles and to Mr Hart. The only trouble was that one and all issued their declarations that he had done no such thing.

The two accused were admitted to bail, in Cook's case of £500, in Trench's £250.

Towards the end of June – the 26th, actually – Advocate Depute George Morton wrote to tell the Lord Advocate that he did not intend to make any charge against Trench or Cook of resetting the proceeds of the Dow and Smith burglaries. And on 30 July , a little over two weeks before the date fixed for the opening of the trial, Hart informed the Crown Agent:

> So far as I can gather the defence in this case is that the facts disclosed do not amount to reset, there being no intention to feloniously acquire or retain the property and to deprive the true owner of its use. On the contrary, it is contended, what was done was done wholly with a view to restoring the property to the owner, and this too with the concurrence of the police or in the *bona fide* belief that the Chief Constable concurred.
>
> It will be contended that, however ill-advised and indiscreet were accuseds' actions, criminal intent was altogether absent from what they did. That contention of course leaves out of sight entirely the imposition of the very substantial money payment as a condition precedent to the return of the property. This appears to me to seriously prejudice the argument of the defence, as holding up stolen property to ransom against the true owner is in itself criminal.
>
> Perhaps Crown Counsel will consider the observations of Lord Justice-Clerk in the case H.M. *Advocate* v. *Browne, Burns & Williams*, 22nd Octr. 1903, S.L.R. p.136.

It has become the custom in books about the Slater case to claim a triumphant vindication of Trench and Cook as the outcome of the 'put up job' that landed them in the dock in the so-called reset case. It has been said, and I quote – page 185 of Peter Hunt's *Oscar Slater: The Great Suspect* – that the Lord Justice-Clerk, Charles Scott Dickson, 'In his judicial manner . . . laughed the case out of court.'

I don't think so. Let us see precisely what he did say about a charge which he agreed was serious – no laughing matter. His Lordship began his charge to the jury by pointing out that, according to the indictment, the panels had received the jewellery which had been dishonestly appropriated by theft.

> That means that they are charged with having received goods, knowing them to be stolen, and for the purpose of keeping them from their owner . . . I don't think it is the law at all that you should find the prisoners guilty of a serious crime unless you are satisfied that there is really criminal intent. You cannot make a man a criminal on a charge of reset by merely fine-spun theories of legal propositions; you have got to be satisfied that these two men were criminals to the extent of knowingly receiving and retaining goods that were stolen.
>
> It falls to me now to direct you in law . . . I confess, on these facts, to my mind, it would be exceedingly difficult to find that these two panels are criminals . . . I would think it would be out of the question, either as law or as common sense, to say that every man who received stolen goods, whatever purpose he received them for, was a resetter.
>
> If a man received stolen goods for the purpose of handing them back to the owner, accepted a fee, and carried it out for that purpose, you could not call that man a resetter. Accordingly, to my mind, there is in this case absent one of the main elements necessary to constitute the crime of reset. I think nothing has been put that would justify you in bringing in a conviction against these two accused persons.
>
> In England, I understand, they have a common law offence of compounding a felony. That means to say if you go to a thief and say, 'I will give you £5 if you return me my watch which is stolen, and I won't prosecute you', it is a crime in the law of England.
>
> But then we are different in Scotland, because if your watch is stolen, you cannot prosecute the thief; the only person is the Lord Advocate or his representatives, and accordingly you might make all the bargains in the world with the thief and say you would not prosecute him, that would not interfere in the least with the prosecution by the Procurator-fiscal or the law officers of the Crown.
>
> Accordingly, there is not the same need for such an offence in Scotland . . . even if there were, it would import that you would need not only to pay money to get back your stolen property, but you must make a

bargain with the thief that he won't be prosecuted. There is no suggestion of that kind here. On the contrary, the insurance company were with the police from the very beginning, doing their best to see if they could catch the thief and get him prosecuted, and therefore that kind of suggestion does not come into this case at all.

But that is not the crime that is charged – nothing like it. The crime you are asked to convict the panels on is 'Did you receive these various articles of jewellery knowing them to be stolen? Did you receive them for the purpose of keeping them back from their owner?'

They did not receive them for any such purpose; they got them for the purpose of restoring them to the owner as far as they could, and therefore on the law I direct you that there is no justification at all which would enable you to return a verdict of guilty against the two panels.

I say nothing about the man McArthur, who has disappeared . . . but even as against him, I don't think there is evidence to show that he was a resetter in the sense of the law. But that does not concern us here just now.

Have the two panels, John Thomson Trench and David Cook, been proved guilty of the reset of theft? I think on the facts they have not, but I direct you on the law that you cannot, and ought not to return a verdict of guilty on them, but on the contrary, that you should acquit both prisoners of the charge laid against them.

What the Lord Justice-Clerk seems to have been saying was not that Trench and Cook were innocent of a crime, but that that crime was not the crime of reset, with which they had been charged. Had the case been brought in England, and the charge been criminal conspiracy or, less seriously, compounding a felony, the outcome might have been different. It is instructive to see, as we shall later, what happened to McArthur when he was eventually brought before the Court.

The jury announced a unanimous not guilty. The accused were dismissed from the bar.

Assoilzied,[2] Trench was at liberty to pick up his rifle. Returning to his regiment, he was made up to quartermaster-sergeant and saw service in Egypt from January 1916 to the December of the same year, when he was invalided home.

Conan Doyle, in a letter which appeared in the Weekly News of 28 August wrote that he had always thought that the Oscar Slater

2 Scots law: assoilzie – to absolve or decide finally in favour of a defendant; to free of a charge.

conviction was a scandal, since the conduct of the police, which was the very point at issue, was excluded from the investigation. 'Finally, I think this prosecution, or rather, persecution, of Mr Cook and Mr Trench upon a pretext so flimsy that it was instantly set aside by the judge, is the crowning scandal of the series. I am glad there is talk of a public inquiry.' But the Great War was in progress. People's minds were absorbed, and the inquiry never materialised.

There is a distinct probability that, for all David Cook's protestations to the contrary, John McArthur's flight into outlawry was engineered – and paid for – by him. It all depends upon whether or not you believe McArthur's wife, Maggie. She suddenly appeared at the Central Police Office on the Tuesday afternoon of 7 September 1915, with a tale to tell. She said that when the reset case first came up, her husband had gone round to see Cook, who was at the time ill at home and confined to bed. Cook had told McArthur: 'This is a bad case and will involve us all', to which her husband had retorted: 'Well, you know I have a wife and nine children of a family.' Whereupon Cook, saying that he was sorry for McArthur's children and his wife, added that if McArthur did as he wanted him to do, 'your children will never want, and twelve hours after the case is quashed I will pay £400 in your wife's hands'.

McArthur's part in the bargain was to disappear, leave the country, fail to show up at the trial. The point was that Cook had worked it out that if he, Trench and McArthur were all tried together certain detrimental evidence and productions would have been brought which could not be brought in the absence of McArthur.

Continuing her story, Mrs McArthur said that later, still lying in bed, Cook had told her that he had not long to live, and the anxiety of the trial to come was shortening his days. He handed her a cheque for £200.

Hoping to receive the balance of the promised £400, Maggie McArthur paid another visit to Cook. He was by then back at work at his office. When the question of paying a further £200, the remainder of the sum agreed, was broached, Cook had, she said, turned furiously on her, shouting, 'Damn John McArthur. If he thinks he is going to blackmail me he is damned far mistaken.' She said it was not her husband who had sent her. She had come of her own accord – and only for the sake of her children. But Cook angrily told her he was not giving her one penny-piece more until the day after the trial. She duly presented herself on 18 August only to be told that Cook was away. When she returned two days later he was back.

> I congratulated him on getting out of the case, and he said, 'Damn you and your congratulations. Do you know what you are? You are nothing but a little bitch of a blackmailer.' I said, 'I don't understand what you mean, Mr Cook. I am here for you to fulfil what you promised to John.' He then said, 'Damn the little bugger, he is nothing but a coward at the best, and if I had the little bugger here I would put a stiletto through his back.'

Mrs. McArthur further said that Cook had received £50 from McArthur for his part in the transaction of the Reis restoral at his house, and Trench received £24 out of the £400. McArthur provided corroboration – of a sort – in a letter which he sent to Chief Constable Stevenson on 27 October 1915, verifying the statements made by his wife.

He wrote:

> I would like them to be made public, as the public would know what kind of a scoundrel Mr David Cook and his cats paw Ex L. Trench is, and for Trench's part, what I know of him he ought to go and bury his face in shame, in place of writing to the *Weekly News*, that is saying the least of it, but Trench is not much worse of than some of the officers under your charge but they have done me no harm and why should I try to do them harm but by the way I mearly pointed out that to you, but Mr David Cook as they call him a dirtyer wretch never dawned shoes . . .
>
> If I turned up at the trial and told the right way of the story, that he got £50 and also helped his self to the jewellery and even kept the bag that was taken out of the place, for his own personal use it would not do him any good at the trial and it would also spoil his Slater case that him and his confederate – Ex L. Trench is making a rich harvest of, which he admitted to me, and Trench was also getting well paid through him, the said Mr D. Cook and if he managed to prove the Slater case he would do his best for you to get your discharge from the Chief Constableship as he called you all the Irish names, your Honour, which a common Street boy would not come out with. Yet he is looked upon as an upright gentleman by all who does not know him . . .
>
> I consider I am no more a resetter than Cook and Trench and the rest in this particular case.

John McArthur surfaced again in Glasgow in December 1916. He had, it seemed, been hiding himself away in Canada. He was promptly arrested by the long-thwarted Chief Detective Inspector Weir. He was put up at the High Court in Glasgow in February 1917, before Lord Hunter and a jury, charged with reset in connection with three burglaries – Reis, Dow, and Smith – in Glasgow in 1914.

Cook, cited as a witness for the defence, addressed, on 20 February 1917, a letter to the new incumbent in the office of Procurator-fiscal, Mr P Fraser MacKenna. In it, he wrote:

> In my opinion it is not unreasonable to ask in the event of the defence calling me as a witness that Crown Counsel should have the following points in view, viz:- (1) McArthur says that I promised to pay him £400. If his story be true, he stood to lose £100, and also have a decree of outlawry passed against him. The bail (his own money) was £500; (2) Before a warrant was issued for McArthur's apprehension, and in consequence of information conveyed to him by Mr John Buchanan, auctioneer, he fled.[3]
>
> At this time there was no suggestion of proceedings against me. I regret to say McArthur persistently attempted to blackmail me while I was in a very low condition of health . . . Reflection can only lead one to believe that McArthur fled because of his connection with the Dow and Smith cases, the Crown authorities know that I had nothing to do with either.

Trench, called as a witness, told the Court that he regarded McArthur as a go-between in the Reis affair. When he learned that the jewellery had been recovered, he had informed Mr Hart, who was then Procurator-fiscal. Mr Hart had told him that he must not take possession of jewellery unless there was to be a case against some person. There was no suggestion at the time of any proceedings being instituted against McArthur. Cross-examined, Trench admitted that he had been told by the Chief Constable not to touch the thing further. Everything he did to assist Mr Buchanan was unofficial.

The *Glasgow Herald*, of 24 February 1917, provided a hitherto neglected perspective on the matter.

---

3   There were, by awkward coincidence, two John Buchanans. There was John Buchanan who worked for the Guardian Assurance Company, and there was John Buchanan who was a partner in the firm of Messrs Robert McTear & Co, auctioneers and valuators. He assessed the loss in the Dow case on behalf of Lloyds and in the James Smith case on behalf of the Guardian Life Assurance Company.

Lord Hunter, in summing up, said he could not help expressing surprise at the policy of the insurance company in paying for the recovery of the jewellery. He could not imagine that the head office knew of the circuitous methods that were to be adopted, or they would not have sanctioned the procedure. On the assumption that nothing was done contrary to the law of Scotland, it could not but be obvious to most people that such a policy as that adopted of encouraging 'go-betweens' would in the long run have led to the insurance company having to meet bigger claims, and amounted also to a direct encouragement of crime.

The jury returned a verdict of Guilty. McArthur was borne off to serve three years' penal servitude.

From April 1918 until his discharge in October 1918, Quartermaster-Sergeant Trench was on active service in France. About March 1919, he was taken seriously ill and removed for treatment to a home in Moffat. His condition worsening, he was transferred in May to the Shakespeare Red Cross Military Hospital, Maryhill, Glasgow. And there, on 13 May 1919 – four years to the day since his arrest – he died. Cause of death: pernicious anaemia, debility and cardiac condition, two months. He left a wife, who survived him for 60 years, dying in her one-hundred-and-first year, six children and an estate of £549 5s. 10d.

David Cook lasted a couple of years longer. He died on 21 October 1921, at his home, 4 Princes Gardens, Dowanhill, Partick, Glasgow. Cause of death: acute bronchitis and cardiac failure. At age 49, he was a year younger than Trench. He left a wife, two sons and an estate of £10,732 14s. 1d.

In Peterhead, Oscar Slater was reported to be in excellent health.

Chapter Eleven

THE FOURTH GUARDIAN ANGEL

You could call it, literally, word of mouth. A friendly fellow-convict coming up for release from Peterhead smuggles a stub of indelible pencil to Oscar, who, in turn, contrives to obtain a little strip of transparent glazed paper from the prison's book-binding shop. Tongue tip pressed to teeth, eyes screwed into tight focus, Oscar traces minusculely upon a scrap of tissue-paper a message. He covers the microscopically inscribed fragment with glazed paper, rolls it into a solid ball, coats it with glue filched from the joiner's shop, then binds it with a second layer of glazed paper to make it into a saliva-proof pellet. This pellet is duly passed to the ticket-of-leave man. He carefully secretes it under his tongue, where it will remain undetected by warders who scrutinise everything before, finally, the great gates swing open for him.

True to his whispered promise, that nameless convict delivered the little ball of writing to Conan Doyle. It bore no fresh evidence, only a humble and desperate appeal for help. This was

Oscar's sixteenth year of imprisonment.[1]

Sir Arthur was not the man to allow so abject and ingeniously delivered a cry to go unanswered. The knightly sword flashed forth once more from its well-oiled scabbard, as it had done fully nine or ten years before, and with the mightier pen the old warrior addressed a frank missive to the Secretary for Scotland, no longer the implacable McKinnon Wood, but Sir John Gilmour.

> The man has now served 15 years, which is, as I understand, the usual limit of a life sentence in Scotland when the prisoner behaves well. I would earnestly entreat your kind personal attention to this case, which is likely to live in the annals of criminology.

And in the following day's *Evening Standard* (3 February 1925), as though by sympathetic magic, another knight, Sir Herbert Stephen, a distinguished jurist, rallied to Sir Arthur's new-broken pennant:

> He [Slater] was sentenced to death and has been punished ever since . . . upon evidence on which I suppose no bench of magistrates in England would make an order for the destruction of a terrier which was alleged to have bitten somebody.

There was, too, a third, and most important, lance-bearer hastening to the colours: William Park, a Glasgow journalist, than whose description by Peter Hunt[2] as that 'strange, self-tortured fanatic, whose avowed intent it was to disembowel the Glasgow police' cannot be bettered. Never through all the long years had Park – Trench and Cook's friend and co-agitator – abandoned the fray; but for lack of success hope had atrophied, and he had grown grizzled and bitter. Now he wrote to Conan Doyle.

Doyle had actually been acquainted with the fiery Mr Park since as long ago as 1918, and his respect for Park's tenacity of purpose is unquestionable – although his description of Park as possessed of 'tact and discretion' is unquestionably questionable!

Park was a warm-hearted hothead. It was, however, because of Doyle's faith in him and his unflagging encouragement that Park persisted, against all the odds, with the writing of his projected book on the case of Oscar Slater. Sadly, those odds included, as well as the bottle, his marriage. The latter, if not the former, he managed

---

1 Daniel Stashower in his *Teller of Tales: The Life of Arthur Conan Doyle*, pp 409-10, names the pellet-carrier as William Gordon.

2 In *Oscar Slater: The Great Suspect.*p190

without too much difficulty to relinquish; the parting did not upset the equilibrium of Park's obsession. The book, into which he poured all the very essence of himself, the fruit of laborious thought, heroic concentration, infinite and infinitesimal research, was to be the one solid achievement of his life; the beaverishly putting-together of *the* definitive querulous volume.

The great work was long in gestation, but by the end of 1926, with the help of his sister, Helen, with whom he was living at Mains House, Ballantrae, in a remote and beautiful sea-washed corner of Ayrshire, he had finished it. The book was to be lovingly accouched by Conan Doyle, who had vetted the manuscript carefully throughout the period of its composition. After a spell of acting as unpaid, unsuccessful literary agent, Doyle determined to publish the book himself, from the Psychic Bookshop which he had established at No. 2 Victoria Street, within the shadow of Westminster Abbey. Entitled *The Truth About Oscar Slater*, the book appeared on 27 July 1927.

One indisputable claim may be made on behalf of Mr Park: that he never permitted moderation to disfigure his prejudices. His book was one elongated polemic. But there can be no gainsaying that he delivered a series of masterstrokes in Slater's defence, punching home point after unanswerable point in support of his innocence, and exposing foul ploy after foul ploy on the parts of those seeking to make obvious his guilt. Absolutely fearless. Absolutely – blinkeredly – honest. Indeed, part of the power of Park's book stems from the very fact that it is prejudiced; just as the power of Ure's speech came from the biased construction he put on matters *vis-à-vis* Slater. It is when Park abandons the defence side of the table and makes his way over to prosecute his unnamed – for reasons of defamation – suspect-elect that, in his determined placing of the blame elsewhere, soul and conscience betray him into a piece of very special pleading – persuasive, clever, but blind to the fact that it is, in its entirely different direction, every bit as prejudicially dishonest as Ure's presentation. Park ends up doing to another – Dr Charteris – precisely what he is dedicated to condemning in those who attacked and abused Slater.

Soapbox orators must make sure that their soapboxes are

sound. Several of Park's planks were worm-eaten. The book contains sundry infelicities, repetitions, and such minor errors as calling Miss Birrell instead Miss Burrell, and stating that Lambie went out for a newspaper *every* evening. But there are also major blunders not to be easily excused in one so blastingly critical of the motes of others. Blithely he ignores – or is it fails to recognise? – that Lambie's statement on the night of the murder that she would be unable to identify the man who passed so briskly out of the lobby chimes ill with his contention that she recognised him as Dr Charteris. Futilely, he alleges police subterfuge over the brooch clue and Allan McLean, ignoring the fact that McLean's precognition, sworn on 31 December 1908, plainly says that 'Mr Oscar' fitted the description of the man in the newspapers. Gamely he persists in his denunciations, some justified, others without a shred of proof to sustain them, of all who seem in thought, word or deed to oppose what he believes, no, *knows*, to be right.

And the extraordinary thing is that the cumulative effect provides the illusion of being overwhelming, total truth. But start to break it down and, like a conjurer's trick explained, the magic vanishes; which is not to detract from the overall importance of what Park had to say, and the way that he said it, but merely to underline that the gospel according to Park is not, nor should be, invested with the authority of holy writ.

Writing in the shadow of the coming event, the *Glasgow Evening News* of 25 July 1927, alerted its readers:

> Controversy over the trial and conviction will be revived with the publication by Mr William Park of *The Truth About Oscar Slater*. Sir Arthur Conan Doyle has written a gripping introduction . . . Now, after nineteen years, Mr Park makes known the evidence of a party hitherto unknown in the case. She makes the claim that she was an eye-witness in West Princes Street at the precise moment when the assailant rushed from the stairway. The man, she is prepared to swear, was not Oscar Slater.
>
> In the course of a trenchant appeal for a public inquiry Sir Arthur makes startling allegations against persons in high authority. Says Sir Arthur: Judge Guthrie is to blame because he did not bring out the points which would have thrown light on the truth. The Lord Advocate is to blame because his speech was a heated and unmeasured one, containing statements which were errors in fact. Witnesses were to blame who allowed their testimony to vary at different times and stages of the

The lamp-post outside Miss Gilchrist's house in West Princes Street.
Did Mary Barrowman collide with the murderer here?

Arthur Montague Adams.
Slight, bespectacled, vaguely bird-like:
he walked upstairs and into a murder.

Helen (Nellie) Lambie.
Miss Gilchrist's young maid-servant:
she saw the stranger in the hall.

Mary Barrowman.
She said that she encountered the
Running Man underneath the lamp post.

Minnie not Nellie: The Silent Witness.
In a case riddled with 'mistaken identity'
this picture of Minnie Hayburn or Hamilton
or Brown has been consistently and
wrongly labelled as that of Helen Lambie.

Miss Gilchrist's 'family' line-up on holiday at Ayr.
Left to right: David Ferguson, Miss Gilchrist, Maggie Galbraith Ferguson,
Marion Gilchrist Ferguson, Nellie Lambie.

On holiday on the Isle of Man.
Glasgow master-criminal, John McArthur (top-right, under parasol, with moustache).
Standing beside him, far-right, gang leader Richard Craig.

**The many faces of
Miss Gilchrist.**
Opposite: austere.
Below, left: formal.
Below, right: *spirituelle*.

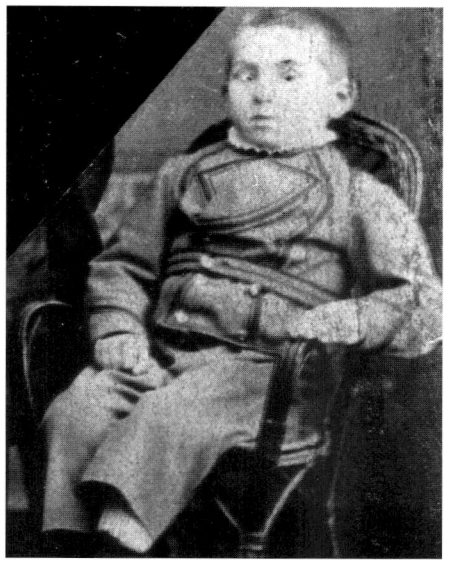

The three ages of Oscar.
Above, left: the infant Oscar – aged 3.
Above, right: the adolescent Oscar – aged 17.
Below: the middle-aged Oscar.

Oscar's parents in Silesia. Paula and Adolf.

Andrée Hilary Junio Antoine or Keibrow.
Oscar's 19-year-old French mistress.

The happy couple at Ayr.
Oscar with his new wife, Lina.

GLASGOW CITY POLICE.

£200 REWARD.

MURDER.

WHEREAS on Monday night, 21st December, 1908, Miss Marion Gilchrist, an old lady, was foully murdered in her house at 15 Queen's Terrace, West Princes Street, Glasgow, by some person or persons unknown,

NOTICE is hereby given that the above reward will be paid by the Chief Constable of Glasgow to anyone giving such information as shall lead to the apprehension and conviction of the person or persons who committed the crime.

Such information may be given at any Police Office in the City, or to the Subscriber.

J. V. STEVENSON,
Chief Constable.

CENTRAL POLICE OFFICE,
GLASGOW, 31st December, 1908.

A tempting offer. It brought in some strange offerings.

Detective Lieutenant William Gordon.
One of the first detectives to arrive on
the murder scene.

Detective Lieutenant John Thomson Trench.
Top row, centre: the 'enigma'.

Superintendent John Ord.
He remained convinced to the end
that Slater was the killer.

The late Miss Gilchrist's Jewels
Which are being sold this week by Auction

A collection of electro-plate, a great many pieces of which were collected by Miss Gilchrist during her lifetime. She also had a hobby of buying out-of-the-way articles, such as lengths of silks, embroidered cloths, children's toys, all of which accumulated in her house in West Princes Street.

Miss Gilchrist's treasure trove.

Dr Francis James Charteris.
He was 'A.B.'

Archibald Hamilton Charteris.
Brother and lawyer.

The Charteris Brothers.
A contemporary cartoon:
Frank (left), Archie (right).

Dr F. J. Charteris telling a funny story to Mr A. H. Charteris.
A brave deed.

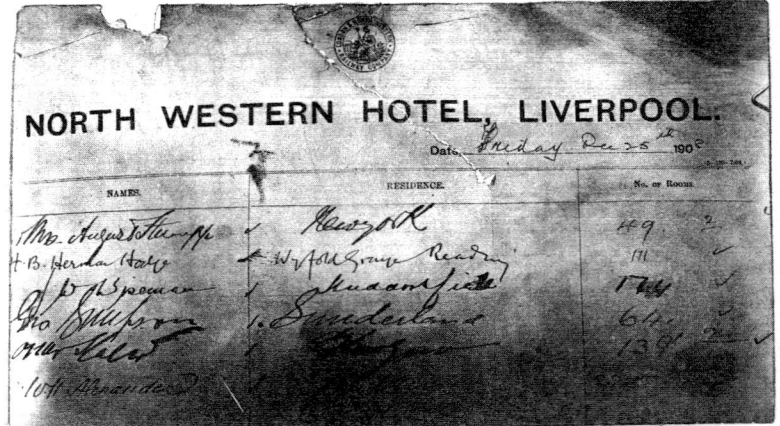

The Liverpool Hotel Register. 'The fugitive from justice' signed it in his own name.

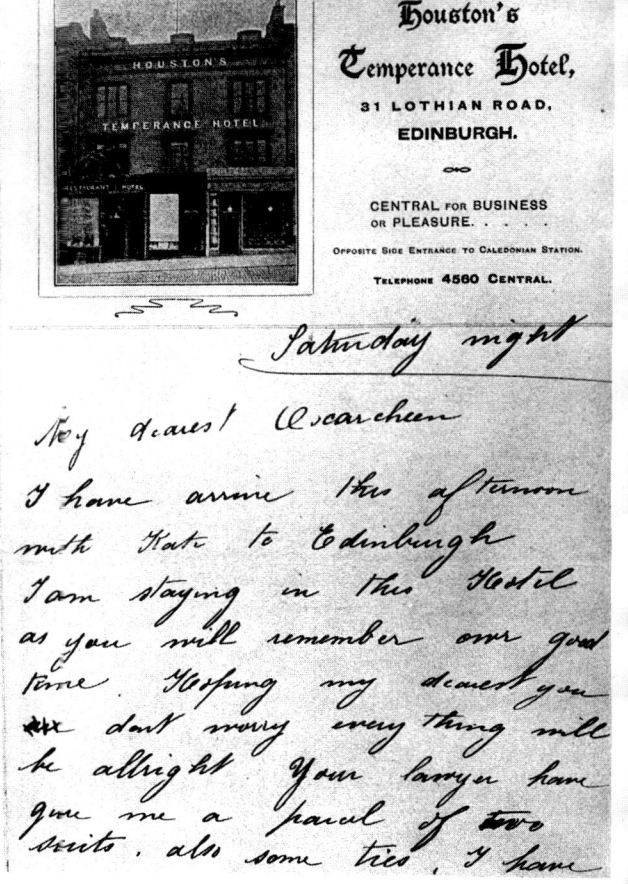

Houston's
Temperance Hotel,

31 LOTHIAN ROAD,
EDINBURGH.

CENTRAL FOR BUSINESS
OR PLEASURE. . . . .

OPPOSITE SIDE ENTRANCE TO CALEDONIAN STATION.

TELEPHONE 4560 CENTRAL.

Saturday night

My dearest Oscarcheen

I have arrive this afternoon with Kate to Edinburgh I am staying in this Hostel as you will remember our good time. Hoping my dearest you dont worry every thing will be allright. Your larvyer have give me a parcel of two suits. also some ties. I have

A small hotel in Lothian Road.
Where Andrée stayed in Edinburgh.

At the Bar. Oscar Slater in the dock.

Members of the Bar. The Lord Advocate, Alexander Ure (second from left), T.B. Mcrison (third from left), the trial judge, Lord Guthrie (upper centre).

At Trial's End. The crowd leaving the High Court, Edinburgh.

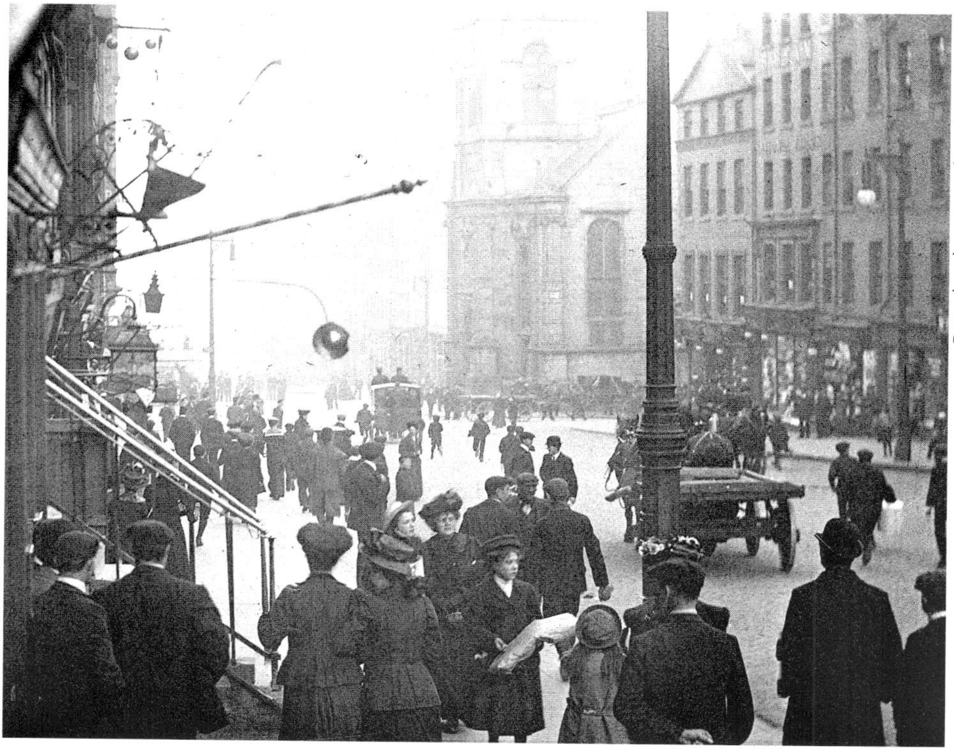

Reproduced courtesy of Lewis Macdonald.

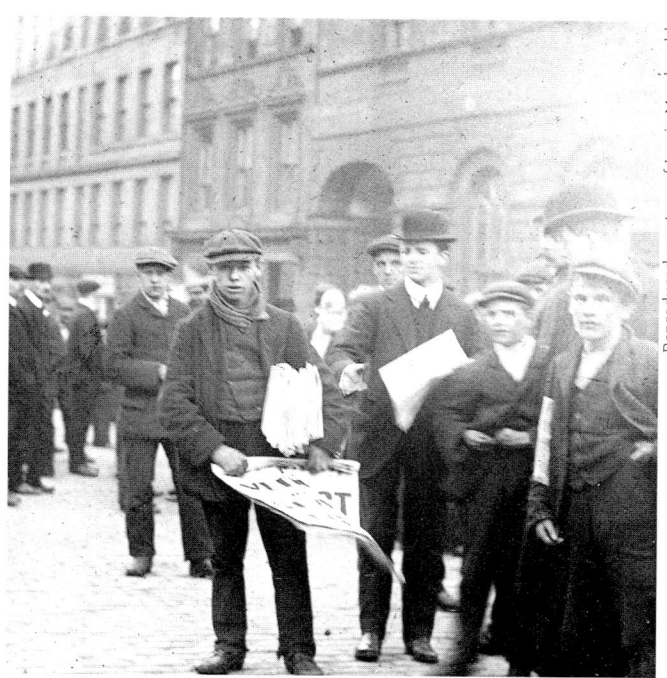

Down at the end of the High Street. Prison van conveying Slater from court to Calton Jail after being sentenced to death.

Reproduced courtesy of Lewis Macdonald.

Read all about it!
A newsboy shouting the verdict immediately after the sentence.

Peterhead revisited.
Oscar enjoying a crack
outside the prison walls.

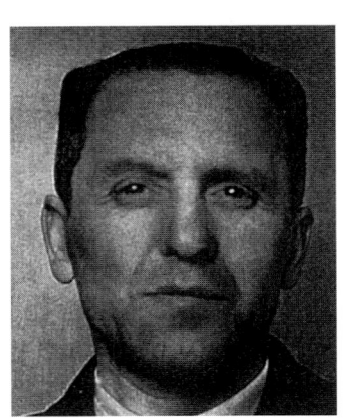

**James Inglis, Glasgow
burglar.** Did he know the man
who killed Miss Gilchrist?

Free at last. Oscar takes his slippered ease.

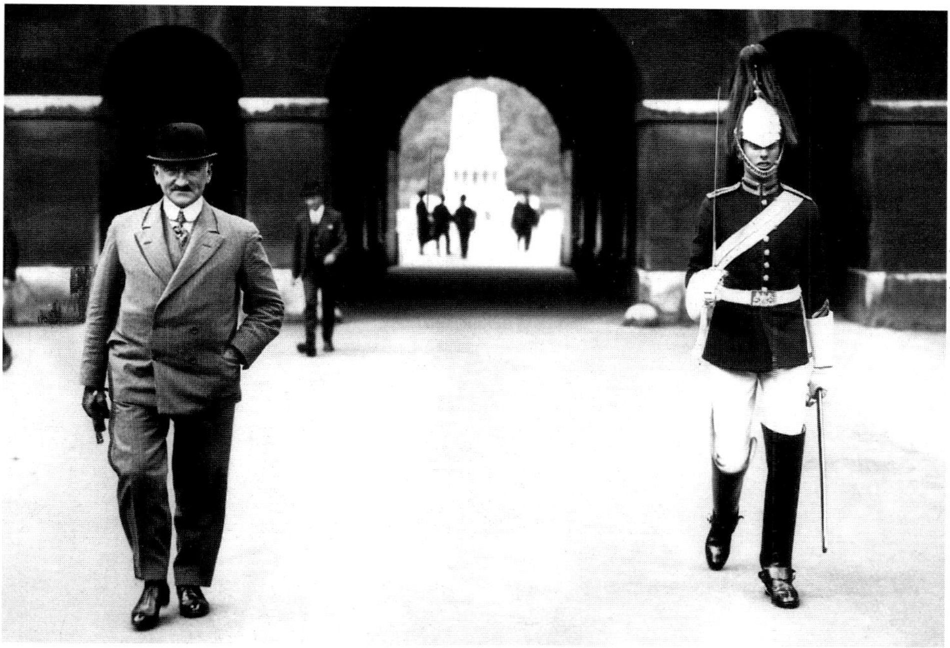

Reproduced courtesy of SMG Newspapers.

Oscar in London. On Horse Guards Parade.

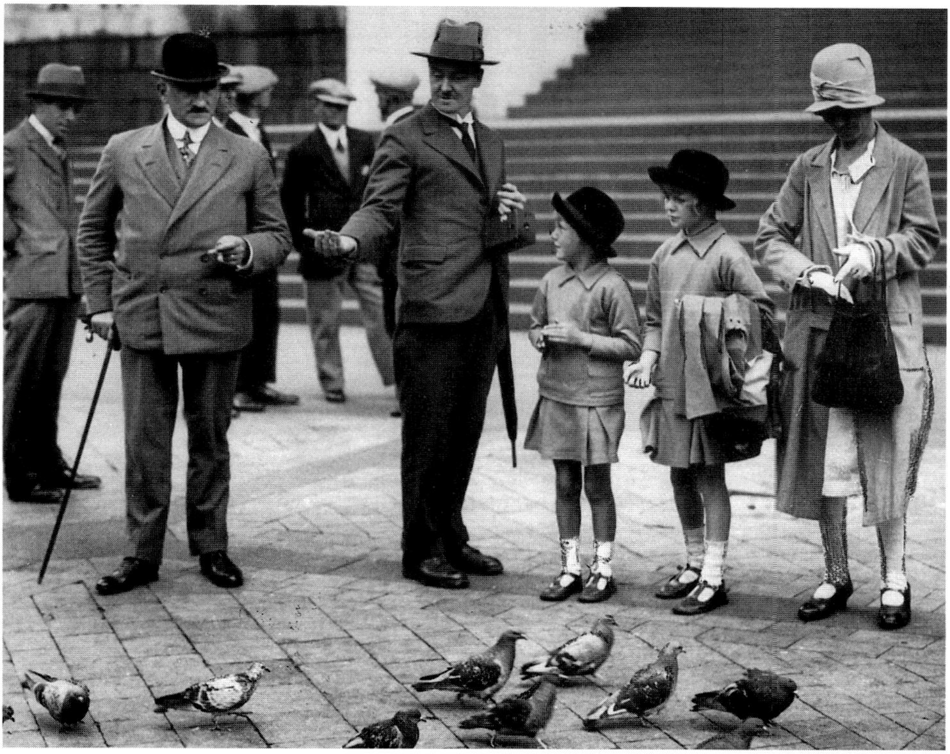

Reproduced courtesy of SMG Newspapers.

Feeding the pigeons.

Here lies Marion Gilchrist. The sad stone urn that marks the mortality cf the Gilchrists in the Glasgow Necropolis.

proceedings. Each successive Secretary of State for Scotland is to blame because he did not use his own independent mind to find out an obvious truth. Sheriff Millar is to blame for the conduct of the white-washing committee of 1914; but above all the Procurator-fiscal and the police, who had the conduct of the case, are those who bear the heaviest load.

It was the Glasgow force which was to receive the first fierce burst from Park's unspiked guns – a commentary without inhibition upon the poor work done in preliminary investigation, their going off after the brooch and a burglar, their omitting to give sufficient attention to such important questions as mode of entrance, the nature of the fatal weapon and the significance of the searching of the private papers.

One must tread carefully, though, in Park's enthusiastic footprints, for he takes certain imaginative liberties. For instance, in describing the stranger in the hall he writes of his 'affecting a courteous and pleasant smile'. There is no evidence for this in either Adams' or Lambie's statements. But it goes to implant the vision of a suave and gentlemanly rather than a Bill Sikes-ish intruder, which coincides with Park's private view as to the identity of the assailant. Dr *Charteris*.

Consider Lambie's behaviour when she saw the man in the hall . . . and Park is off banging his personal drum again. Her 'attitude of apathy and unconcern was incomprehensible, unless we assume that the appearance or knowledge of the man suggested to her mind the absence of sinister motive or evil design on his part'. Dr *Charteris*.

Park draws attention to a question asked of Lambie by Slater's attorney in New York: 'Who opened the door?' Her answer: 'Miss Gilchrist must have opened the door.' Implication: the visitor was someone whom she knew. Dr *Charteris*.

Park is besotted with his suspicion of Dr Charteris.

Having dismissed the validity of the police's so-called brooch clue, and the consequently unjustifiable cable to New York requesting that Slater be held on the evidence of the pawn-ticket, and having disposed of the rationality of the charging of Slater as a murderer on the demonstrably ludicrous grounds of his having absconded, Park moves on to what he stigmatises as the third and worst blunder; that of the alleged recognition of Slater as 'the man' by a heterogeny of eye-witnesses. He then proceeds to produce an eye-witness of his own.

He says:

One of the purposes of this publication is to make known the evidence of a party hitherto unheard of in the case who makes the claim that she was an eye-witness in West Princes Street on the night of the murder at the precise moment when the assailant rushed from the stairway at Miss Gilchrist's flat and reached the street, a party covering in her observation the time and place claimed by the girl Barrowman. This witness, a woman who at the time in question was engaged as a Restaurateur in Glasgow . . . was prevented . . . from giving her evidence at the trial . . . It is her statement . . . that Oscar Slater positively was not that man.

Park goes on to say that the woman paid a visit to Mr Shaughnessy and made a statement.

At a later date Mr Shaughnessy handed the writer, in journalistic capacity, a copy of the statement . . . The writer has recently traced the witness and obtained from her confirmation of her original statement and repeated also an expression of her willingness to give evidence before any tribunal that may be set up.

It is, asserts Park, an assumption by the public that the evidence which emerges during the hearing of a great murder trial constitutes the sum total that has been ascertained. In the Slater case, however, we are sharply confronted with the displeasing fact that the evidence submitted to the Court covered *only part* of the actually known circumstances of the crime and the relation to it of the accused. There was much of material importance to the ascertainment of the truth that was rejected, while much in the hands of the police that was material to the safety of the prisoner was unknown to the defence.

Observes Park:

Considering the long distance we have travelled through a jungle of confusions and blunders, one would expect when one arrives at the trial in the highest criminal tribunal in Scotland there should at last be only firm, sure ground of fact undisturbed by the admission of error.

He proceeds then to a positively scarifying analysis and enumeration of the appalling catalogue of errors and misfortunate utterances perpetrated and emitted by both the Lord Advocate and the trial judge, concluding 'We do not find in the case a single incident or circumstance in which the prisoner's position was justly presented to the Court.'

The book caused an immediate sensation. The reception accorded by the reviewers was more or less uniformly favourable, indeed laudatory, and posterity would seem to have echoed that general acclamation. Nearly fifty years ago, Peter Hunt thought it

> admirably lucid, clear enough for the most befuddled mind to follow. Page by page the Slater case is torn to bits until the reader is left with his hair standing on end in bewilderment that such an injustice could be possible in twentieth-century Britain. Park missed nothing; he did not stretch any statement beyond its meaning.

This is not a judgment with which, in the light of further and fuller research, a light powered by the examination of previously confidential papers and hidden-away archives, I find it possible to concur. By this new light one cannot help but perceive grievous flaws in the arguments of Park's unshakable prejudices. He is a terrier with a rat in his mouth, and, even if it happens to be the wrong rat, he will not let go.

A shock wave registering high on the Slaterian Richter scale was generated by the *Empire News* of 7 August 1927.

'Discovery of a "Dead" Witness' ran the headline. Then . . . the announcement. An *Empire News* Special Commissioner had filed 'surprising information to the effect that Helen Lambie, reported to have died some years ago, is alive under her marriage name in America'.

The *Empire News* had, it said, the name and address of the man who had given them the information that Lambie was definitely alive less than a month ago, and added, 'in the interests of justice that name will be handed over if it is calculated to be of any assistance and official application is made for it'.

As far back as February 1925 it had been stated – in an article by Lovat Fraser in the *Sunday Pictorial* – that Lambie had died since the trial. Now, in the *Daily Express* of 16 September 1927 came further confirmation that Nellie was 'alive and well' and living with her husband, Mr Ronald Gillon, a Scottish miner, working near Pittsburgh, in the United States.

'Mrs Gillon would be quite willing to return to this country for any inquiry into the case ordered by the Government. She is in weekly touch by letter with her mother and sisters, who live in the little Lanarkshire village of Holytown.'

The *Daily News* of 30 September reported that they had sent a cable to the editor of the *Pittsburgh Press,* and that

throughout last week [he] used every method of publicity American newspapers know how to adopt in order to trace Mrs Gillan [*sic*]. Broadcast appeals were made by radio, and announcements displayed in the morning and evening newspapers, but without success.

He en, late of Holytown, was lying low.

A telegram to No. 12 Belgrave Crescent, Edinburgh, on 22 October 1927, was how they brought the good news from Doyle to Roughead.

Lambie confesses her error in *Empire News* tomorrow.
This should end case. Doyle.

And, sure enough, Sunday's paper contained a long article, 'Why I Believe I Blundered Over Slater!' by Helen Lambie.

She was alleged to have written:

It has been said and denied that when first questioned by the police . . . I mentioned the name of a man who was in the habit of visiting [my mistress]. It is quite true that I did so because the strange man coming from the house . . . did not seem strange to me. Otherwise, I should have wanted to know more about his presence there, and certainly would have examined his features more closely.

When I told the police the name of the man I thought I recognised they replied 'Nonsense! You don't think he could have murdered and robbed your mistress!' They scoffed so much at the notion of this man being the one I had seen that I allowed myself to be persuaded that I had been mistaken. The persistence of the police that I was mistaken so shook my own faith in my own judgment that it was easy for me to be convinced against my will that I was mistaken and that it was really Slater I had seen.

The man I thought I saw coming out of the flat had been visiting Miss Gilchrist on another occasion, and I happened to mention his name to my mistress afterwards. She flew into a temper with me and told me if I ever displayed the slightest curiosity about any of her visitors she would discharge me without a character.

Lambie was even more specific:

I am convinced that the man I saw was better dressed and of a better station in life than Slater.

She also said:

I have thought over the case a good deal, and before leaving Scotland I

expressed my willingness to give any assistance necessary to a new
inquiry that I was told had been ordered. I was told that my evidence
would not be wanted.

Conan Doyle immediately, and ill-advisedly, went right over the
top.

On being shown the amazing document published here, Sir Arthur
declared that it was of 'enormous importance'. On reading it through, he
commented, 'It completely knocks the bottom out of the case against
Slater.'

Then, 'for exclusive publication in the Empire News', he solemnly
penned the following:

I have read the document, which, I understand, comes direct from Helen
Lambie, and can be certified by an affidavit from the interviewer . . . it is
not too much to say that it must mark the end of the Oscar Slater case. I
may say that there is nothing which Lambie says here which I did not see,
and describe, in my book, published in 1912.

That very Sunday, Doyle wrote off to Sir John Gilmour – Secretary of
State for Scotland – enclosing a copy of the Empire News:

In this she [Helen Lambie], the chief witness against Slater, tells us that at
the time she recognised the murderer, that it was not Slater, and that she
was bullied and cajoled by the police into making statements against her
own convictions. I find that the journalist who saw her is a man of repute,
and as to the truth of the statement it is not likely that the woman would
invent what is so prejudicial to herself.

I have, I may say, failed to find any evidence that Doyle ever
discovered who the journalist who claimed to have interviewed Mrs
Gillon was.

A letter from Ramsay MacDonald, a former Prime Minister and
now Leader of the Opposition, arrived at the Scottish Office on 25
October. Addressed to Sir John Gilmour, it opened with the words,
'You will now have seen that to all intents and purposes the Slater
case has ended.'

This did not at all accord with the Scottish Office view and a
letter was sent off post-haste to the Lord Advocate, the Rt Hon
William Watson, KC, MP. 'I enclose a copy of a letter from Mr Ramsay
MacDonald . . . The opening sentence is presumably based upon
the authenticity and the conclusiveness of the statements
attributed to Helen Lambie in the Empire News . . . '

Writing to the Lord Advocate again the following day, Mr P J

Rose, of the Scottish Office in Whitehall, observed: 'The *Empire News* article contains passages which cast doubt on its genuineness.' He referred in particular to the part in which Lambie speaks of having, before she left Scotland, indicated her willingness to give any assistance that she could to a new inquiry which had, she was informed, been ordered. 'I was told that my evidence would not be wanted,' she had apparently written.

Rose pointed out that

Helen Lambie made a statement before Mr Gardner Millar in 1914 and must be aware of that fact. It does not appear that the author of the statement in the *Empire News* is aware of that fact. There is no reference in the rest of the article to her appearance before Mr Gardner Millar.

This is powerfully indicative of the dubious validity of the *Empire News* piece.

Away in Ballantrae, happily oblivious of any dubieties as to the genuineness of the *Empire News'* scoop, Lambie and her confession, William Park, positively beside himself, dashed off, on 27 October, a letter of great joy to Roughead. 'It is all very wonderful . . . I think that the statement is perfectly genuine.' Then the Park paranoia raises its multi-tentacled head: 'The only fear I have is that Charteris and Birrell may send out someone to get her to contradict – that it was a journalistic stunt, etc. I have written the Editor to get an affidavit on its accuracy. Gilmour's silence is contemptible.'

By this time, certain other sections of the press were veering towards cynicism. 'It would be interesting to know,' commented the *Glasgow Weekly Herald* of 29 October , 'who was the interviewer and how much of the article is Lambie's own, and how much of it was put into her mouth.' The same day's *Evening Times* announced that Helen Lambie had not responded to an appeal to come forward, and that steps taken by the *Daily News* to trace her in America had failed.

Undeniably, things were beginning to look a bit fishy.

By the beginning of November, Gilmour and the Lord Advocate, who had bumped into one another in the New Club in Edinburgh, had agreed that it would be of advantage to 'try to verify the statement that Miss Lambie is alive', and were wondering if they might ask Scotland Yard to investigate the matter for them; or, tact posed the question, would it be necessary to work through Glasgow?

'I fancy,' wrote Gilmour to Lamb, on 2 November, 'Scotland Yard could get to the root of affairs more rapidly.'

In a handwritten letter to Lord Advocate Watson, a clearly sceptical Lamb opines:

> I think we ought to write to the Empire News asking them to give us any evidence in their possession bearing on the authenticity of the statement and, if they have it, the address of Lambie.

He then, significantly, adds:

> On the face of it, the statement does not appear to be genuine. There is no mention of Lambie's appearance before Gardiner [sic] Millar . . . Now Lambie could not possibly have forgotten that she gave evidence in the Millar inquiry. The whole thing looks like a fake.

In the heel of it, it was, for whatever reason, decided that they would not write to the Empire News.

That newspaper's Special Commissioner, returning to the fray, demanded in its issue of 6 November:

> What is the attitude of the Government regarding the claims put forward by the Empire News for a reinvestigation of the Oscar Slater case now? Helen Lambie told the world through the Empire News that she had reason to revise the evidence she gave at the trial condemning Slater. She raised the doubt as to identity, and Slater must be given the benefit of this doubt, according to British law. This evidence, seeing that the British Consul in Pittsburg [sic] has been in touch with Helen Lambie and has told her to be prepared for a journey to England when called upon, could already have been taken on oath.
>
> Now that Helen Lambie has broken silence, why is it that the authorities, as represented by the British Consul in Pittsburg [sic], should go out of their way to apply 'hush hush' principles regarding what she may have felt disposed further to say to the Press? How can the interests of Slater, imprisoned all these years while the authorities could have found Helen Lambie and Mary Barrowman whenever they wished, be served by asking Helen Lambie not to make any further public statements to the newspapers. Who is this caution and muzzle exercised on behalf of if not Slater?

On 7 November, Conan Doyle, picking up on the Empire News' revelation that Lambie had been called upon by the British Consul or his representative at Pittsburgh, begged to remark upon the fact that he had 'either persuaded or intimidated Lambie into saying no more concerning her false identification of Slater. I would wish to know on whose authority this impediment was placed in the way of truth.'

And, also on 7 November, a draft of a letter of reply to be sent from Sir John Gilmour to Doyle was put together.

> I have read the article in the *Empire News* of 23 October which you forwarded with your letter of 23 October regarding a statement alleged to have been made by Helen Lambie in America on the case of Oscar Slater. I observe that you accept this article as an accurate version of a statement which has actually been made by Helen Lambie who figured as a witness in the Slater case.
>
> I am anxious to receive and to consider any fresh evidence bearing on the case and I need scarcely say that it is incumbent on anyone who has such evidence to supply it to me. I should be glad, therefore, if you could cause me to be furnished with the document which purports to be a statement by Helen Lambie and with any evidence that exists that the document was written by her. I should also be glad to be furnished with information as to her present address and circumstances and as to her history and movements since the Slater trial, giving in particular the date on which she left this country for America.
>
> In this connection I note that on page 13 of your preface to Mr Park's book you imply that the witness Helen Lambie has died since the trial.[3]

That same Monday – 7 November 1927 – Doyle despatched to the Scottish Office 'another document which bears directly upon this matter. The lady in question, a former employer of Helen Lambie, desires that her name should for the time be kept private'.

What had happened was that, pursuant to a letter received from a Mrs Agnes M. Guthrie, William Park and his sister had travelled to Giffnock, Renfrewshire – some five and a half miles south of Glasgow – to see her.

Mrs Guthrie told them that from 1903-5 she had employed Helen Lambie as a maid. 'I found her a very good domestic worker, but most illiterate, of rather a low mentality, very cunning and not at all trustworthy in her standards.' In the summer of 1905 Lambie left and went to work for Miss Gilchrist. Then, suddenly, one Sunday evening in 1908, a week or a fortnight before the murder, Lambie

---

3 In his Introduction to *The Truth About Oscar Slater*, Doyle had indeed written, pp. 12-13, 'It is certainly a most remarkable fact that, in 1909, Slater should have been within twenty-four hours of being hanged and that he should now be alive, while Guthrie the judge, Hart the Procurator Fiscal, Lambie, the chief witness, Millar, the Chairman of the Committee, Trench and Cook, the two men who stood out for justice, and several other protagonists have passed away.'

appeared at Mrs Guthrie's house.

I was informed by her that she had some remarkable experiences at the house of Miss Gilchrist. She gave me a very long story about her peculiarities. Miss Gilchrist had a lot of jewellery and had taken unusual ways to secrete it in the house, under carpets, etc., and had told her that she felt sure there was a man coming to murder her, and that the dog had been poisoned.

I asked her, 'When you are out, would Miss Gilchrist open the door if anyone came to it?' Her reply was, 'Miss Gilchrist would never open the door. She never opens the door. To me she only opens when I give her a signal we have pre-arranged.' I asked her if she had any gentleman visitors. Her answer was, 'Only two – the Elder and the lawyer'

On a subsequent visit to Mrs Guthrie's, a day or two after the murder, Lambie, in reply to a question, told Mrs Guthrie that she would *not* recognise the man who passed her in the hall.

She went on to say that the man held his head down (she acted the attitude to me) and that she had not seen his face. On this point she was most emphatic, leaving no room for doubt as to her inability to identify. I reminded her that she had previously informed me that Miss Gilchrist would on no account open the door without receiving the signal. She instantly burst into a fury and denied absolutely that she had ever told me anything of the kind. I was staggered at what was nothing else than a deliberate falsehood. Lambie did not wish to carry on the conversation further. Almost at once she got up and left the house. The impression I felt was that she knew all about it and knew the man.

Lambie never returned to see Mrs Guthrie again.

Official feeling with regard to Doyle's two letters of 7 November was that a bare acknowledgment of receipt by the Private Secretary might be the best course. 'The suggestion that the British Consul or his representative at Pittsburgh has been intimidating Helen Lambie is almost too grotesque to call for a denial.'

Doyle wrote to 'Dear Sir John' on 8 November, replying to your note marked 'Urgent' . . . I was glad to read the 'Urgent'. Three months have elapsed since the book⁴ was sent in, and that extra time has been added to this innocent man's sufferings. In regard to your questions the report of Helen Lambie's death was universally accepted in Scotland. It would be interesting to know who spread it. It certainly had the effect of heading off those who might wish to question her. It was only by chance

4 *The Truth About Oscar Slater.*

that we found out that she was alive . . . The internal evidence of her
confession is quite conclusive to me . . . but when applied to to take an
affidavit she said she had been called upon by the British Consul, or his
representative, and warned to say no more. If this be so the Government
must have her address – but I could no doubt get it from the Editor of the
Empire News. Steps are being taken to get an affidavit from the journalist,
who is, I am told, a man of some standing.

He may well have been, but it has proved impossible to discover
any record of his having stood up to be counted in this rather weird
transaction. His identity remains to this day another 'Slater case
mystery'. All in all, there seems small doubt that the *Empire News'*
Lambie 'confession' was bogus.[5]

The last flickerings of the dying-down flames of this heated
controversy illumine the pages of a draft reply to Doyle's latest,
prepared for Sir John Gilmour.

You remark upon the fact that Helen Lambie had been called upon by the
British Consul . . . who has either persuaded or intimidated Lambie . . .
and you wish to know on whose authority this impediment was placed in
the way of truth. In your further letter of the 8th inst. you repeat this
suggestion by saying that when applied to to take an affidavit she said that
she had been called upon by the British Consul . . . and warned to say no
more.

I say emphatically that I know of no foundation whatever for these
allegations. I am unaware of Lambie's address, or of anything that has
happened to her since her appearance as a witness in the 1914 inquiry.

No later than the 7th inst. I wrote to you asking for information as
to Lambie's address, for other particulars about her which would enable
me to secure and consider any fresh evidence bearing on the case. I felt
that I was entitled to expect that you would be in possession of facts to
justify your acceptance of the authenticity of a statement made by a
person hitherto generally believed to be dead, and that you would be
willing to assist me by producing these facts. In this respect I must confess
that I find your letter of the 8th inst. disappointing.

The foregoing shows the content of the official mind and surely
underlines how far short of the standard set by Sherlock Holmes his
creator fell. Doyle *knew* nothing. He had been accepting
uncorroborated 'facts' for the truth – as which they were being
presented to him.

But that draft reply from Gilmour was never posted. The reply

5 See further: pp 299-302

that was sent to Doyle on 16 November was briefer and blander.

> Sir,
> I am directed by the Secretary of State to acknowledge your two letters of
> the 7th instant...and your further letter of the 8th instant.
>
> As you are no doubt aware from the answers given in Parliament on
> the 15th instant, it is contemplated that the case will be referred to the
> Court of Criminal Appeal in Scotland and that being so the Secretary of
> State does not feel that he can properly make any further observations in
> regard to the various statements and representations which you have
> advanced in the above mentioned, and in previous, letters.
> I am, Sir,
> Your obedient servant
> John Lamb

Acutely aware of Slater's racial background and antecedents, Sir
Arthur Conan Doyle had addressed the Jewish community in a letter
published on 9 September 1927, in the *Jewish Chronicle*.

> There was an official promise that the book [*The Truth About Oscar Slater*]
> would be read, but nearly two months have passed, and we get no definite
> answer from the Scottish Office. If an inquiry should be refused in the face
> of the unanimous public demand, it would mean that those officials were
> not our servants and delegates, but our masters, who are prepared to
> sacrifice justice in order to cover their own scandalous errors.

In the first weeks of September, Doyle had approached Ramsay
MacDonald, sending him a copy of Park's book, and by 15
September he had heard from MacDonald, who had looked through
the book and written to his late Lord Advocate, Hugh Patison
Macmillan, seeking his opinion and advice. 'I expect any day to hear
from him,' he told Doyle. 'As soon as I do so I intend to get in touch
with the Secretary of State for Scotland, but I wanted to be quite
sure of my ground before doing so.'

Macmillan, who, interestingly enough, had in the earliest days
of his career at the Scottish Bar devilled for Lord Guthrie, must have
replied both swiftly and decisively, for on 26 September MacDonald
wrote again to Doyle: 'I have been going further into the case and
am quite convinced that this man has received a most horrible
injustice and that the matter must be wound up, not only by

releasing him, but by clearing him.' Sagacious politician that he was, MacDonald could not resist adding the cautionary rider: 'What further steps can be taken to indemnify him and to carry the charge into other channels, is another matter.'

There can be no question about it, public disquiet was increasing, approaching steadily that volume where something had to be done. And, in acknowledging this, one should acknowledge also the trinity whose work and efforts over the years had brought it about: Sir Arthur Conan Doyle, who, in 1912, wrote the first pamphleteering defence of Slater; William Park, who, 15 years on, and backed by Conan Doyle, produced a second stinging attack on those who had made Slater the Great Scapegoat; and William Roughead, whose 1910 volume in the series *Notable Scottish Trials* series set the critical tone and provided the ammunition for both the works of conscientious agitation which followed it.

Now a fourth, and very much latter-day, guardian angel was about to spread protective wings about Oscar.

In his wisdom – and it was a wise choice – the editor of the *Daily News* had appointed as his Special Commissioner (as they used to designate special correspondents in those days) one Ernest Charles Clephan Palmer. Rejoicing in the *nom de plume* 'The Pilgrim', charged to go forthwith that breath-holding September of 1927 to Scotland in order to discover – and place before the sometimes vacillating public – the true and whole facts of the enigmatic Slater case, Palmer, at that time in his early forties, was later to become widely known and respected as the Parliamentary Correspondent of the *News Chronicle*.

The Pilgrim's dispatches from the Caledonian front began on Friday, 16 September 1927.[6] Arrived in Glasgow, he quartered himself in a private house in the street where the murder was committed: 'The room in which I write is within a few yards of the

6 In fact, the first three pieces were written from the paper's Bouverie Street office in London.

fatal street lamp under which this child [Barrowman] claimed to identify the supposed murderer.' (Palmer does not take her evidence at all seriously.) And from this lodging he despatched a series of 24 articles, covering pretty well every aspect of the case.

Very early, he tartly observed that Lord Strathclyde, the *ci-devant* Mr Alexander Ure, KC, 'in spite of knowing, as presumably he must know, that the unintentional errors of fact in his final address may have had a decisive effect on the minds of the jury, has kept silent ever since the trial.'

The Pilgrim also felt constrained to write:

> It is clear from further inquiries I have made that at the moment the authorities have not the slightest intention of sanctioning a public investigation. They do not take Sir Arthur Conan Doyle seriously, largely because of his association with spiritualism. They are hoping finally to hush up the whole affair by releasing Slater as soon as it is considered possible to do so without risk.

In his sixth article The Pilgrim abandons all pretences:

> In Glasgow the inquirer finds himself confronted by a plain blank wall of non-committal courtesy. Anyone who goes at all deeply into the case will, I think, have great difficulty in resisting the impression that the authorities having once got Slater into their hands through an entirely false clue, the pawned brooch, manipulated the evidence without any regard for justice or common fairness to the prisoner.

Strong words.

Quite exceptionally, The Pilgrim strikes a false note in his thirteenth article of September 30th. Having recounted the tale told by Trench, he says,

> I propose to make no comment myself, but to quote William Roughead: 'We may note the unexplained fact spoken to by three of the police witnesses that "A.B."'s' movements were strictly inquired into after the murder. Why this was done when neither Trench, Miss Birrell, nor Helen Lambie had mentioned his name is not disclosed.'

The answer, plain and simple, to Roughead and The Pilgrim's question is that it is a matter of police recorded fact that *all* the relations of Miss Gilchrist were the subject of careful – i.e. strict – inquiry as to their motives and movements, Dr Charteris taking his expected place among the ranks of those being formally investigated.

The twenty-seventh, and final, article in the series appeared on 18 October 1927. In it, The Pilgrim wrote:

I have now come to the end of this inquiry. When I set out about a month ago I had an open mind on the question of his guilt or innocence, and it was entirely the pressure of facts that made me after a few days doubtful of his guilt, and in the end as persuaded as one can be of his innocence.

Watching all this from the wings was a pair of severely jaundiced eyes belonging to whilom Detective Sergeant James Dornan. Retired now, with the rank of Lieutenant of Police, he was living at Torhouse, in his native Wigtownshire, whence, exceedingly hot in the area which was once under his official collar, he so climaxed with indignation that, overcoming a professional lifetime's training in keeping to his humble station, on 29 October 1927 he took up his pen to address himself to the Right Honourable His Majesty's Lord Advocate.

Pardon me if I do anything wrong in addressing to you a few brief remarks on the Oscar Slater case . . . In doing this I am not in any way prompted by any feelings about Slater . . . But I do feel at the moment that the comments are unfair to the Crown Authorities and those persons particularly who were specifically engaged on the case endeavouring conscientiously to do justice, to the living and the dead, connected with this horrible murder. I would like confidently to speak my mind, freely to you on this matter at this stage and endeavour to defend my Brethren who are gone and ex-Det. Pyper with myself who are left.

While being aware that there are considerable influential means behind this case, I have always put down a great deal of the trouble which has arisen to what is known as 'Professional Jealousy' in the Police Force, and for a start I would like to name those who were connected with the case. The then Lord Advocate (Mr Ure) who knew Miss Gilchrist well and took an active interest himself . . . Mr Hart and I knew the case from 'A to Z', and Mr Douglas and Mr Pyper nearly as much. I would here refer to the personal jealousy I have mentioned.

The then Detective Superintendent was Mr Ord, who kept a few pet children who could not do wrong, one of whom was ex-Det. Trench (deceased) who has been responsible for a great deal of the trouble. Mr Ord and his pet family felt annoyed because they did not get charge of this enquiry from Mr Hart, who deputed Mr Pyper of the Western District to carry out the enquiry, and in turn he requested my assistance. One part was deputed to Mr Ord, he being at Headquarters, and that was the correspondence with Germany re. Slater's antecedents and character, and in connection with this Det. Trench may have carried over to the County Buildings a dozen-and-a-half reports or so to Mr Hart. And practically any other work he did in the matter we termed as 'poaching', he in no way made reports to Mr Hart. What he did, was this. I have told you how Mr Ord felt slighted, and he would phone Mr Pyper in the Western enquiring what was going on, and on being told might sometimes ask Trench or other pet child to see what they could learn. This did not so bad till Mr Pyper was sent with Mr Warnock and witnesses to America, when Mr Hart placed me in full charge of the enquiry. Mr Ord then phoned me on the matter, but owing to my instructions from Mr Hart I consulted my own Supt. Mr Douglas, and decided not [to] tell him anything about the case. Mr Hart told me to tell no person anything of the case but himself and that if I required assistance I was to get Mr Douglas to assist me and not a neighbour officer.

From what I have said you will see that Trench was not making enquiry here for the Crown . . . but to satisfy the curiosity of slighted Mr Ord, who has often sat outside Mr Hart's door for a very long time waiting to see me when I came out to see if he could learn anything.

Your Lordship will see from what I have written what a straight honest man has to suffer often and say nothing. The late Det. Trench paid back Mr Ord in a nice way, for all that was done for him at the expense of others. I have kept quiet and watched it all. I have read the flowing articles of the late Det. Trench in the press years ago about what he did in the Slater case, and suffered it. But I really feel now that the thing is going too far. It is making a big impression among the 'Public', that those who worked this case were unworthy men, I feel it very much.

Why if Slater was wronged is it not worked from the true facts, copy of which is in Your Lordship's office. Pardon me when I say that I feel that Sir Arthur Conan Doyle & Coy. [sic] are going too far with side issues, and in my opinion does not say much for a literary man. He surely has a large opinion of himself, and a very poor opinion of other people.

Some important statements by witnesses were never lead [sic] in this case, one in particular was the statement by Gordon Henderson. When Mr Pyper and I called on this man, who was then in charge of a club in India Street enquiring for any trace of the murderer who was then unknown, he said: 'Come in, gentlemen, there was a man named Anderson (Slater's name) came here nightly and I have not seen since the night of the murder. After I had missed him some nights I said to his friend (here he gave his name) "What has become of your friend Anderson, I have not seen him for some time," and he replied putting up his hands, "Wheesht, wheesht, he has murdered that woman and is away to America".'

Mr Pyper and I got this German who made this statement, but he denied it. It however was the means of tracing Slater. Although note he had been traced earlier by Central officers, and their actions hunted him, I admit that Slater if that information had been right handled, would never have got clear of the country. The Lord Advocate did not use Henderson at the trial, as he pled for mercy, and that the gang would kill him.

Now Your Lordship, I plead for your tolerance in this matter. My sole object in writing Your Lordships [sic] is to show you my feelings for the case. I am the one that knows it all. Officially and rightly. And I think it is time this bunkum by Trench was put an end to.

That 5 November 1927 brought some Guy Fawkes Day fireworks. They exploded in the *Daily News*. The Pilgrim, back in Glasgow, had made contact with Mary Barrowman, now a married woman of 34. Mr Palmer wrote: 'I found her anxious to make her position clear and to correct any wrong impression that may unwittingly have been given at the trial.'

Barrowman had signed a statement for him. In it she said that on being confronted with the prisoner for the first time in New York, she did not feel able to say anything more than that Slater was *very like* the running man in West Princes Street. On her return to Glasgow the question of Slater's being *positively* the man was raised by Fiscal Hart.

This gentleman was most severe in his treatment of me as a witness. He made me appear at his office day after day. I was in attendance at his office for the purpose of going over my evidence on at least 15 occasions. He went over my evidence, himself doing all the talking and I for the most part listening. He was so much the director of the things that were to be said that I had no opportunity, or very little, to have my say. It was Mr Hart who got me to change my statement from being 'very like the man' to the emphatic declaration that Slater was the man. I want to state most definitely that I thought Mr Hart's demeanour was not what it should be. He was the party who was laying down what was to be said. I was just a girl of 15 years of age then, and I did not fully appreciate the difference between saying that Slater was the man instead of very like the man.

Barrowman also said that Hart was not the only one who 'adopted a strong attitude towards me. Superintendent Douglas was another. This officer I also blame for putting things into my head.'[7]

7 The *Weekly Record*, 12 November 1927

Barrowman, the most deadly witness against Oscar, had recanted. After eighteen years the prison gates must surely open now.

Chapter Twelve

THE ORDER OF RELEASE

The tomorrow of Freedom dawned on 10 November 1927.

Sir John Gilmour announced:

> I have felt justified in deciding to authorise his [Slater's] release on licence as soon as suitable arrangements can be made.'

Not good enough.

Justice demanded more than the minimal restoration of his freedom. The *Daily News* put it exactly and succinctly. 'This unfortunate creature is to be made a ticket-of-leave man in order to get the Secretary of State for Scotland out of an embarrassing dilemma.' If Sir John Gilmour and the department over which he presided imagined that it was possible thus cunningly to close the controversy, without turning a hair, without admitting a wrong conviction, without putting so much as a finger within its compensation-money pocket, they were reckoning without a vociferous press and public's notions regarding the subject of wrong-righting.

William Park telegraphed the *Daily News*: 'The release is only a makeshift to side-track the real issues. Investigation and compensation are still imperative.'

Monday, 14 November 1927.

Dawn crept up from the east, a slow, grey ice-floe, drowning out the darkness, smothering the sparse shimmer of pinpoint yellow lights speckling the land that ran down to the sea. Outside Peterhead Prison, murky figures, huddled in the lee of the high wall for illusory protection from the bone-scraping cold, watched and waited. Inside, within his cage of stone, Slater lay, hypnopompic, listening to the muffled wingbeats of freedom rippling the still air in the chilled granite passages.

Tomorrow had come.

Time: 3pm A closed car hummed swiftly up to the main entrance of the prison. A minute's parley with the serge Cerberus. The gate swung open. The car disappeared into the stony maw.

3.08pm Several warders appeared. Took up positions outside the big gate, came smartly to attention and saluted as the same dark car nosed smoothly out. A small group of convicts sweeping the drive in front of the Governor's house attempted to muster a thin parting cheer, but it was rapidly burked by their vigilant keepers. At high speed, the motorcade – for by now, pursued by a swarm of pressmen in their cars and taxi-cabs, the procession had swelled to such considerable a proportion – moved off. Inside the lead car, Oscar, dressed in his prison 'demob suit' of rough grey tweed, a small brown paper parcel of all his worldly goods on his knee, sat, a mixture of elation and dazedness, beside his guardian *ad litem*, as it were, the Reverend Eleazer Philip Phillips, gulping in the first grateful lungfuls of the fresh air of freedom. Purring through the duskening November afternoon, Oscar and escort were being borne to Peterhead railway station, where they were to catch the 3.35pm to Aberdeen: the first lap of the journey back to Glasgow.

It was 9.25pm when the North Express steamed slowly into the bay flanked by Platforms 4 and 5 at Glasgow's Buchanan Street Station. Waiting there to greet Oscar and the Reverend Phillips was the Rabbi's daughter, Amy. All three clambered into a hired car and were driven off to the Rabbi's house – No. 40 Kelvingrove Street.

The Pilgrim was among the few members of the press permitted to talk with Oscar that night. He recalled:

> Slater struck me as a remarkable man. At the trial his manner was described as 'dominating'. It still is. Though nothing remained in outward appearance of the dapper, well-dressed gambler of 1908, there was the same shrewdness, the same occasional geniality, and the same tendency to dominate. In addition there were clear signs of smouldering indignation.

Present, too, was William Park, whose first meeting with Slater this was to be, and there was a caller, anxious that Oscar should know that he had come. His name was Sam Reid.

And that first night in Slater's own words:

> I had supper with the Rabbi, his good wife, and other friends. What an experience it was to find a spotless white linen cloth on a table that carried the silver that I had almost forgotten existed! When I sat down to that meal in such surroundings and company I felt that I had suddenly been transported to fairyland.

It was long past midnight when Oscar left the house of the Rabbi. He slipped away unseen. Exactly where he spent that first night of freedom was kept – and has remained – a secret. According to Oscar, it was in the house of

> a friend not very far away . . . I had my first night's sleep in a real bed for nearly twenty years. The feeling of getting into a proper bed spread with delightful bedding and pillows into which I sank I am totally unable to describe, and I will never be able to forget.

One of the first, most satisfying draughts of the wine of freedom was shopping; entering a chemist's shop to buy a toothbrush, a newsagent's to buy a paper, various shops to stock up with new collars, shirts, boots, kid gloves, a bowler hat and a walking stick.

Then he took himself off for a holiday, to Ayr, where he stayed in a comfortable boarding-house, Mount Olive, in Blackburn Road, and where he took a daily stroll on the sea-front and went to a cinema for the first time in his life.

What may be called the politics of the Oscar Slater release were now moving forward at a fairly steady pace. All the political parties were, it would seem, in concert as to the desirability of opening up the case to further investigation, but the great obstacle to doing so was that the Criminal Appeal (Scotland) Act 1926 dated only from October 1926. It would require the enactment of special legislation, therefore, if the case of Oscar Slater, dating from 1909, were to be brought before the Scottish Court of Criminal Appeal. That would necessitate a single-clause special Bill to bring Slater's case within an enlarged scope of the Act. If that special Bill were to be passed, the Court could then treat the case as if it were an ordinary appeal. It would have before it the complete record, in the form of shorthand notes of the original trial, and would hear, if need be, any new evidence that might be brought, examine witnesses on oath, and call for the production of documents. The Court's decision would be final. There would be no question of a re-trial.

On 15 November, just one day after Slater's release, the House of Commons had been taken completely by surprise by the Secretary of State for Scotland's reply to a question put by Colonel Harry Day, Socialist Member for Central Southwark, as to whether in releasing Oscar Slater he proposed to set up an inquiry into the evidence produced at the trial. And Sir John Gilmour had intimated that,

> Had the conviction in this case taken place after 31st October, 1926, I should have had the power to remit questions regarding it to the Court of Criminal Appeal, under the provisions of Section 16 of the Criminal Appeal (Scotland) Act 1926. If I could obtain from Parliament the legislation necessary to extend the Act, so as to enable me to refer this case under the provisions mentioned, I am prepared to take that course.

At the end of question time on 16 November 1927, the necessary special Bill was introduced into the House, Sir John Gilmour, of all people, presenting it. This announcement was such a total capitulation to popular demand that MPs paused to take breath after hearing it. Then a murmur of approval passed round the chamber, followed by approbatory cheers. Having passed through all the necessary stages and received Royal Assent, the Bill duly became law.

As a matter of mandatory procedure, Slater had now to present a petition to the Secretary of State for Scotland praying for a free pardon from the King. The Scottish Secretary would then refer the case to the Court of Criminal Appeal in Scotland.

With optimism riding high, there came tidings of the possibility that the well-known Scottish KC, Mr Craigie M. Aitchison, an advocate widely experienced in the matter of murder, would be asked to state Slater's case before the Appeal Court. Things now came down to the common level of pounds, shillings and pence. Roughead told Park: 'Sir Arthur is offering to pay Craigie's fees! We must all get up public funds to stop that. It is magnificent on his part. This act makes him bigger than ever.' But Roughead felt that to permit such generosity would not be fair.

For his part, Doyle was apparently worried that the cost of the legal proceedings might turn out to be bigger than ever he had supposed. He wrote to Roughead:

> [Park] said among other things that the coming proceedings are going to cost 'thousands of pounds' . . . I will make myself responsible as far as I can, and I will find a way of raising money for the trial, but I have no idea of such a sum as that. I agree with you that we should have nothing but the best, but I would like some limitation in advance. Would you give me a word of advice about that.

Roughead passed on Doyle's bursal misgivings to the chosen solicitors, Messrs Norman Macpherson & Dunlop, SSC, of 2a Hill Street, Edinburgh, who wrote promptly and reassuringly to Sir Arthur: 'You may depend upon it that we shall throughout keep the costs moderate.'

A fund was opened to meet the expenses of the appeal. There were – not very successful – door-to-door collections. The Jewish communities in Glasgow, Manchester, and various other cities throughout the country, contributed. But prising money from the public generally proved like drawing back teeth. By the end of June, the fund's final not-so-grand total stood at only £630 7s 3d.

As the year 1927 drew to a close, Conan Doyle sat quietly down in the writing room of the Athenaeum and put his thoughts on paper for Park.

Heading the sheet 'What we are for', he proceeded to enumerate their objectives.

> (1) Safeguarding public against Police. That has already been done for 50 years ahead by the row already made.
> (2) Punishing offender.
> Useless.

(3) To see Slater's honour cleared with attendant compensation. That is the vital thing.

(4) The misstatements of Ure and Guthrie should alone quash the verdict.

(5) But that won't clear Slater's honour.

    To do that we rely on:

    A. Lambie (Can we get her?)

    B. Barrowman (We must guarantee her against perjury proceedings.)

    C. The new witness.[1]

    D. Adams, if still alive.[2]

These seem the essential things – all else is subsidiary.

A.C.D.

The petition setting out the grounds on which Slater's appeal was based had been completed by 2 March 1928, and despatched to the Right Honourable the Secretary of State for Scotland. The petitioner was meanwhile residing quietly in Ayr.

> I await the result of the coming re-trial of my case with the confidence in British justice which kept me alive for 18 years, and saved me, though often driven to despair, from seeking by my own hand the death to which I, an innocent man, had been condemned long years before for a crime I never committed.

So spoke Oscar Slater, not, one suspects, without a considerable degree of ventriloquous aid and sentimental splinting on the part of 'Our Man in Ayr', author of what the *Daily Express* of 27 March 1928, claimed to be

> the first exclusive statement by Oscar Slater, whose manhood years lie buried in Scotland's Sing Sing . . . He is here in a peaceful Scottish seaside town, in the land of Burns amid the inspiring Lowland grandeur which saw the birth of Scotland's champion of liberty and justice, who in words of poetic fire cried to the world for humanity to the oppressed, and arraigned it for 'Man's inhumanity to man.'

Maintaining his alarmingly high note, this *Daily Express very* Special Correspondent, marches blithely on to, and over, the top.

> No scene could be more in harmony with the cause of a man about to join battle with all the powerful forces of the State . . . which branded him as the foulest criminal known to human law – a murderer. Oscar Slater, still by

1 Minnie Hayburn or Hamilton or Brown. See p. 179

2 Dr. John Adams

prison law a convict, is in appearance the antithesis of a murderer. The keen winds of the western seas which wash this rugged Scottish coast have brought back the glow of health to his cheeks . . . He is tall, brown, erect, and sprucely-dressed, and carries himself with the air of a guardsman.

Extending the portrait, the *Empire News* informed its readers:

He spends his time in walks in the surrounding country. He is a wonderfully vigorous walker, 14 miles at a stretch not being too much for his physical strength. A kindly and genial atmosphere – the people of Ayr have been most kind and sympathetic in their mixings with him – has melted out the real man from that icy figure released in November last. There is a ruddy healthy bloom on his cheeks; there is a sturdy strength in his swinging gait. His mind, too, has freshened up. He laughs and jokes; joins in stories over the fireside; and can 'crack' a good one, too. With keen interest and confidence he awaits the ordeal of the rehearsing of his case.

The Lord Justice-General, Lord Clyde, having received the Scottish Secretary's letter and Slater's petition, and pondered upon them for some four and a half weeks, replied, on 13 April, that he held the said petition as a note of appeal by the said Oscar Slater, and appointed him to lodge a Supplementary Note containing such further specification and particulars with regard to any of the several grounds of appeal set forth in the said petition; and such other grounds of appeal (if any) as he might desire to submit for the consideration of the High Court of Justiciary, and that on or before the nineteenth day of May next.

The second stint of legal beavering began. Meetings were held at 4pm on sundry Edinburgh spring afternoons at Mr Craigie Aitchison's residence – 12 India Street – attended by Slater, Park, Roughead, and the representative of Messrs Norman Macpherson & Dunlop.

The Supplementary Note was hammered out; seven closely-typed pages. Dense as an uncut thicket hedge, it presented amplifications under twelve separate heads.

The appointed time for the preliminary hearing, June 8th, was now drawing near. And still there was no sign of Helen Lambie.

Friday, 8 June 1928. The Parliament House, Edinburgh. Court No. 3. It was as if time had clicked into another gear, ratcheted back

19 years. The setting, the furniture, were identical. Only the individuals – or some of them – supplying the set figures had changed. The dock was different. Empty. The prisoner, the accused, sat in the public bar on one of the richly-coloured benches that was, and always had been, at the back of the court. He had arrived early, accompanied by Rabbi Phillips, Mrs Phillips and Amy.

Another early arriver at the High Court of Justiciary that morning was Sir Arthur Conan Doyle. He and Slater were about to meet for the first time. As Slater sat down, Doyle, seated two rows in front of him, turned round and greeted him with a smile. They were then introduced by Rabbi Phillips and shook hands warmly.

Beneath the same wooden canopy, with the lion and the unicorn, sat an identically-robed, scarlet-and-ermine pride of judges, five of them – Lord Clyde, the Lord Justice-General, presiding, occupying the seat previously occupied by Lord Guthrie; Lord Alness, the Lord Justice-Clerk; Lords Sands, Blackburn and Fleming.

Mr Craigie Aitchison, opening, said that the appeal was based on fact and law. He asked leave to call the appellant himself as a witness. He applied for leave to recall Helen Lambie. He referred also to a deposition by Duncan MacBrayne, and asked that it should be produced.

Lord Alness: Is your assertion that the Crown had knowledge of MacBrayne and what he could have said at the time?

Mr Aitchison (bluntly): We know it.

Counsel went on to contend that there was evidence in the possession of the Crown, which could have assisted the defence case, that there was no question of a flight from justice.

The Lord Justice-General remarked that some day they might come to try the police or other authority for their conduct in this case, but they were not doing so now. To which observation Mr Aitchison rejoined that if they made a serious challenge about the conduct of the police vitiating the identification, inquiry could not and ought not to be excluded, and he went on to say that he required to recover the signed precognition of Inspector Warnock, and to be permitted to call witnesses to support the appellant's averral that the alleged identification at New York was entirely vitiated.

The arguments ground on. Aitchison also wanted to call three witnesses in respect of the pointing out of Slater in the corridor outside the Commissioner's room in New York – Mr Goodhart, Mr Miller, and Deputy United States Marshal, Mr John W. Pinckley. Continuing, Counsel informed the Court that he proposed to call an additional witness on the question of identification, a woman who saw a fugitive figure precipitately leaving Miss Gilchrist's house.[2]

The hearing ran into a second day.

The Lord Advocate, the Right Honourable William Watson, KC, resumed the speech in reply to Mr Aitchison's submissions which he had been unable to complete before the previous day's adjournment. What remained of it did not occupy much time. The hearing came to an end in less than an hour.

After a quarter of an hour's adjournment to see if their Lordships were in agreement, the judges trooped back to give their decision on the points raised.

They were prepared to allow Helen Lambie's evidence on the question of identification, her alleged statement and denial, and the evidence on that subject of Lambie's former mistress, Mrs Guthrie.

The Court was prepared, too, to allow the evidence of Mr Pinckley about Slater's being handcuffed in the presence of witnesses in the New York corridor, but would not permit the examination of Messrs Miller and Goodhart, solicitors to the appellant. The evidence of Mrs Hamilton or Brown they had determined to allow to be received.

As to the topic of medical evidence, the Court was prepared to allow the evidence of Mr Roughead and Dr Adams' widow, in regard to what the late Dr Adams had opined, but did not see its way to allowing the evidence of Sir Bernard Spilsbury.

Lastly, the motion for the examination of the appellant: allowing Slater to speak for himself. The judges felt that he had nothing new to say, and that: 'In these circumstances it would be quite unreasonable to spend time over his examination now, and the Court therefore is not prepared to allow his evidence to be received.'

2 This was Minnie Hayburn or Hamilton or Brown.

And that, Lord Clyde thought, exhausted the whole of the application. All that remained was for the Court to fix the time for the hearing of the appeal.

Monday, July 9th, 1928, was the chosen day.

When the Court rose, Slater hastened out by a side-door without speaking to anyone. He was baffled, furious and bitterly disappointed because he was not to be allowed to go into the witness-box to tell *his* side of the story.

Back in Ayr, brooding, Oscar came to a dramatic decision. Filled with resentment at what he regarded as his muzzling, he resolved to withdraw his appeal. Still seething, he got himself aboard a train and, on Monday, 11 June, presented himself on Conan Doyle's London doorstep and informed the horrified Sir Arthur that he had made up his mind to abandon the appeal. Doyle managed, but only with the greatest difficulty, to persuade him to do no such thing.

Afterwards, hearing a rumour, unfounded as it proved, that Oscar had since gone back on his word and had indeed tried to withdraw his appeal, Doyle wrote to Park: 'Oscar Slater seems to me to be mad.' And on a postcard to Roughead he confessed of his reaction to Slater's threat: 'I was in a mood to sign a petition that the original sentence be carried out.'

Thirty days – less than the normal calendar month – to go, and neither sight nor sound nor even quasi-reliable report of the elusive emigrant Gillons. Then . . . someone talked.

Glasgow, Saturday Night (16 June)

The *Sunday Mail* is now able to disclose the address of Miss Helen Lambie She is now living in comfortable circumstances with her husband, Mr Robert Gillon, formerly a miner in Thankerton Colliery, Holytown.

The Gillons' house is at 1005 Garden Street, Peoria, Illinois, U.S.A. Mr Gillon is employed in a foundry at Peoria.

Claiming the discovery of Lambie's whereabouts as the result of their extensive inquiries, the *Sunday Mail* went on to give away the secret of their actually very simply-achieved success: 'The Peoria address has been Helen Lambie's abode for several years, and only recently one of her daughters wrote from it to a friend in Lanarkshire.'

Doyle dashed off a letter to Park on 19 June 1928: 'I see that Helen Lambie is at last located . . . I have written Edinburgh suggesting that we send reply cable to ask her to come – all paid. She won't come, but it will do good with press and Court.'

None of this grand discovery was news to the Crown Office. They had known all about Mrs Gillon, her location and her views, since January.

The *Peoria Star* made hay, a Page One splash, with the story that dropped out of a clear blue sky for them on 19 June 1928.

SLAYER'S FATE IS IN PEORIAN'S HAND

The fate of Oscar Slater, convicted of murder 19 years ago in Glasgow, Scotland, may hinge on the testimony of one person. She is Mrs Robert M. Gillon, 1005 Garden Street . . .

Mrs Gillon has refused to discuss the case at any great length, but she did talk to a reporter of the *Peoria Star*.

Wiping her suds-covered hands on her apron, Mrs Gillon, a slender, ruddy faced woman, appeared at the door of her humble little home in the rear of a barber shop in answer to the reporter's long knocking. On the floor of the kitchen were heaps of clothing, ready for the electric washer that was at work some feet away.

I'm too excited,' she blurted out when pressed . . . and each question she answered with a ready, 'That's my business.

Wednesday, 20 June's *Peoria Star* contained a follow-up story.

Mrs Robert M Gillon, formerly Helen (Nellie) Lambie, will not return to her native Scotland to testify in the appeal of Oscar Slater. This she emphasized to the *Star* in an exclusive interview, and her husband, guarding the interests of his wife, adds that she will not go back even if served with official summons. 'Sir Conan Doyle should not keep stirring up this affair,' says the husband, who does not now permit his wife to leave the house. 'We have tried to live a good life, why go all over that again, it is not fair to our two children,' he says.

In view of the extremely important part which she played in the Oscar Slater story, it seems appropriate to set on record here something of what we know of the personal history of that indomitable little Scotswoman, Helen Lambie.

Nellie was hewn from a solid seam of coal-mining stock, of pure Scottish and part Irish extraction. Both her grandfathers were miners, as was her father, and she was to marry a miner, who was a miner's son. Born on 22 March 1887, she was brought up in the Lanarkshire mining village of Holytown. She was one of at least ten children.

Nellie's decision to 'go into service' was more or less automatic. Her mother had been a servant before her marriage at the age of 16. It was about February 1901, shortly before her fourteenth birthday, that Nellie took her first job, working for a Mr Levi Newman, at 38 Park Road, Glasgow. In August 1903, she went to work for Mrs Agnes M. Guthrie, in Spring Gardens, Kelvinside. She left there to go to Miss Gilchrist's.

A month after Slater's trial, Nellie, then aged 22, married, on 18 June 1909, at her home, Neilson's Land, Holytown, Robert Miller Gillon, a 27-year-old coal-miner. He was a widower. Robert and Nellie's first child, a daughter, Margaret Balfour – always known as Maisie – was born on 30 March 1911, at Sunnyside Road, Holytown. A second daughter, Marion – named, one wonders, after Miss Gilchrist? – was born on 18 October 1918, at No. 3 Sunnyside Road, Holytown. It was some time after the end of World War 1 – precisely when is not documented – that the Gillons, doubtless seeking wider horizons and less narrow pay scales than Holytown and Thankerton Colliery had on offer, emigrated to the New World. Most likely it was around 1921. Exactly where it was that they settled first is not recorded either. One picks up the trail in Peoria in 1923.

Even today, Peoria is a somewhat less than inspiring place to live. It has, of course, expanded and changed since the Gillons' time. A population of close on 105,000 in 1930 had increased a decade later to just short of 112,000. It is the home of the internationally known Caterpillar Tractor Company; of Bradley University and its nationally-celebrated baseball teams; and of the Corn Stock summer theatre-in-the-round. It is quintessential Middle America. One understands the significance of the anxious question which, it is said, used regularly to be asked by theatricals seeking a yardstick of likely middlebrow reaction to their latest play or film: 'How will it play in Peoria?'

And yet . . . and yet . . . There must be those who view the old place differently; or else, whence the stirring sentiment in song, 'I wish I was back in Peoria'? You or I might find it a bit like Shotts (Lanarkshire) or Wigan (Lancs.) on a wet Sunday afternoon, but other eyes see other things, and the Gillons must have found the place to their taste as they stayed there for nearly ten years.

A copy of Leschnik's – memories of Leschziner! – *Peoria City Directory*, consulted in Peoria Public Library, revealed that in 1923 Robert and Ellen [*sic*] Gillon were roomers at No. 2704 South Adams Street. But by the following year they had moved to No. 1005 Garden Street, which I found to be just a short distance away, and where Robert (entered as 'Miner, Groveland Mine') and Helen Gillon were again described as 'roomers or boarders'. The premises were somewhat cramped and situated at the rear of a barber's shop. But in 1925, Robert is no longer a roomer, but a householder. Moreover, the barber must have moved, for in 1926 Haag Bros., washing machine manufacturers, appear to be occupying the shop premises at the front.

In 1927, Leschnik's became Polk's *Peoria City Directory*, and in it Robert Gillon is shown as a labourer with Haag Bros. In 1929, however, he is a miner again. Then, in 1930, reverts to labourer. On his last directory appearance, in 1931, he is listed as employed – in what capacity it is not stated – by the Commercial Solvent Corporation, which seems to have taken over the front shop from, Messrs Haag Bros. In 1928, Margaret Gillon, who would be 17, had taken a job as a mangle operator at the Kew Laundry Company. She moved the following year to the Ideal Troy Cleaners, where she continued listed as a laundry worker up to the final 1931 directory entry.

The house at which throughout all those years the Gillons lived is now No. 2105 Garden Street, re-numbering having taken place in 1956. Whatever it may have been in the 1920s, the area today is somewhat seedy, not to say downright dangerous after nightfall, when the crack pedlars come out from under their stones, and another kind of crack – that of revolver shots – is to be all too frequently heard.

According to the *Glasgow Herald* of 17 April 1956, the Gillons returned to Holytown in 1933, and remained there until the 1950s, when they moved to the north of England. Nellie's younger daughter, Marion, a nursemaid, married, aged 23, on 23 April 1942, at The Manse, Holytown. Her groom was 22-year-old Jack Cook, a carpenter, of 16 Eric Street, Bramley, Leeds, Yorkshire.

Nellie's mother died at 29 Sunnyside Avenue, Holytown, on 1 June 1951. She was 86 years of age. Robert Miller Gillon, Nellie's husband, 'coal hewer, retired', died, aged 74, on 29 June 1956, at No. 1 Lascelles Mount, Harehills, Leeds. Cause of death: cardiac failure and arteriosclerosis.

Four years later, on 2 May 1960, at St James' Hospital, Burmantofts, Leeds, Helen Lambie or Gillon died of cerebral thrombosis and pernicious anaemia. She was 73.

Still fluttering around in the dark, Messrs Norman Macpherson & Dunlop had written to the Crown Agent on 16 June 1928: 'We shall be obliged if you will let us know the last address of the witness Helen Lambie.' Then . . . sudden illumination. On 18 June they wrote to the Crown Agent again:

> We see from a paragraph in today's *Daily Record* that Helen Lambie's address is given as 1005 Garden Street, Peoria, Illinois. The paragraph also states 'that she may announce her readiness to return to this country in time for the Enquiry at the request of the Crown Authorities.'

The Crown Agent replied on 5 July 1928: 'We beg to intimate to you that Helen Lambie is not to be a witness, she having refused to come.'

Not the only disappointment; behind the urbane face of professional preparation things had been going more than a bit awry as regards the Slater faction's much-vaunted new witness. She was not proving to be at all what she had seemed.

On 4 July a precognition of one George Christie Stirton, Detective Lieutenant, Central Division, Glasgow, had been forwarded by John Drummond Strathern, the Glasgow Procurator-fiscal, to the Crown Agent. It stated:

I have known Mrs Brown for a period longer than ten years and I am of opinion that she is unstable mentally and wholly unreliable. She is an associate of well-known prostitutes. She occupies a five-room and kitchen house with her husband at 3 Robertson Street, and my opinion is that it is, at any rate occasionally, used as a brothel.

Mrs Brown's police record is as follows:-

14 December, 1921. Central Police Court, Glasgow. Brothel-keeping: continued to 22nd December, 1921, when charge found not proven.

13th July, 1923. Sheriff Court, Glasgow. Charged with brothel-keeping in her house at 3 Robertson Street: sentenced to three months' imprisonmment.

I also know Mrs Brown's husband, to a lesser extent. He is a stevedore at the docks. Mr Brown has been at the Police Office repeatedly complaining about his wife's conduct. He has himself been charged several times in the Police Court with assaulting his wife. My recollection is that he has undergone a sentence of imprisonment.'

The precognition of 60-year-old Archibald Brown, also enclosed, stated:

On 4 September 1915, I married the witness Minnie Hayburn or Brown. My wife had not been previously married according to my understanding. She certainly stated in the particulars that she was a spinster. She had then a daughter, whose father, I understood, was a Mr Hamilton, but so far as I know she is illegitimate. My wife is neurotic and is very erratic in her conduct and temperament. She has hallucinations and harbours delusive ideas which she believes to be true. She attributes to me and to other people happenings which never occurred and she also has delusive ideas as to herself. In my opinion, my wife would be a most unsatisfactory witness in any case, and so far as the present case of Slater is concerned, I do not believe what she says. From what I know of her she is inclined to think a thing and after she thinks something for a time she believes it to be true and goes on repeating it. I think my wife should be medically examined. I think my wife is beginning to realise that her foolish talk with regard to this Slater case is bringing about a lot of trouble and might possibly result in landing her in trouble. She is in a state of very great excitement, so much so that it is impossible for me to live in the house with her. I doubt whether she will voluntarily go to the court to give evidence. As far as I can see, her desire at the moment is to get out of the whole business.

So it was that, just four days before the appeal was due to be heard, Slater's legal advisers received the following communication:

I am desired by Crown Counsel to inform you that at the hearing of the Oscar Slater appeal on 9 July 1928, leave of the Court will be asked to produce Extract conviction against Minnie Hayburn or Brown.

That did it – and did for it. The following day Messrs Norman Macpherson & Dunlop informed the Crown Agent that they had resolved not to call Mrs Brown as a witness.

That is what you could call starting with a handicap.

Chapter Thirteen

THE
DAY
OF
JUDGMENT

What was to be the final act in the long drawn-out tragedy, the 20-year ordeal by legal battle, was to commence in the historic Court House in Parliament Square, Edinburgh, on Monday, 9 July 1928.

The full Bench of judges was made up of the same five who had already considered Oscar's petition. Counsel – for Crown and appellant – were also the same. Four full days of session were to pass before the Day of Judgment.

Attired in deep mourning and wearing a long veil, Jane, the widow of Dr John Adams, came to confirm that her late husband had been convinced that Miss Gilchrist's murder had been committed with a chair. And, hard on her heels, William Roughead bustled business-like into the box to tell how in an interview he had had with Dr Adams when preparing his volume on the case for the *Notable Scottish Trials* series, the doctor had likewise confided to him his belief that the chair had been the instrument of death.

John William M. Pinckley gave the evidence he had travelled from New York to give of the curious method of identification of Mr

Slater which he had observed being practised by the Britishers in the Federal Building corridor.

Mr Aitchison, having informed the Bench of Helen Lambie's adamantine refusal to come over from the States, and that, accordingly, evidence which would have depended upon her presence could not be called, embarked upon his argument in support of Slater's appeal.

> It is a Pickwickian figure. His face is as pink as a baby's, and a baby also might have owned those eyes of forget-me-not blue. A little heavy the face, but comely and fresh-complexioned withal, redeemed from weakness by the tight, decided lips.

Thus Conan Doyle describing Craigie Aitchison.

> He had been untangling the difficulties of a most intricate case. Deft – deft to the last degree has been that disentanglement. It is a miracle of analysis. What I recall most clearly are those blue eyes, and the plump, capable hands. He talks and talks with a gentle melodious voice, clearing up the difficulties. Those little plump hands accentuate the points. There comes an objection from the judges. The blue eyes seem pained and surprised. Up fly the little plump hands. Once more the gentle voice takes up the tale. The wrinkle is smoothed out and the story goes on. My friend Marshall Hall was a very great counsel. But he could not have argued a case without a jury and before a Bench of Judges as this man has done. His warm human passion would have carried him away. Aitchison has the warm passion also. If there were a jury there he would show it. But it would be wasted upon these five hard-boiled old gentlemen. And so he never crosses the line which divides reason from emotion. I shall never listen to a more masterly presentment.

It was a truly magnificent performance. Craigie Aitchison was to be on his feet, putting his client's case, for 13 hours. He reviewed the medical evidence. Pointed out that as regards the hammer there were divergent views, and said that he was going to submit that the new evidence, the view held by Dr Adams, was very material. Similarly, it might be that on the matter of what had been called by Lord Advocate Ure 'the flight from justice', there was evidence pointing both ways. But, so far as the appeal rested on fact, the crucial question was, obviously, that of identification. He was going to maintain that the evidence of identification was altogether insufficient as a basis for a jury's verdict in a case of murder. He forthwith proceeded to demolish the clouds – or fog – of witnesses as to the loitering men.[1]

The Lord Justice-Clerk inquired of Counsel if it was his idea that all the witnesses who spoke to seeing a loitering man were mistaken as to what they saw, and as to his suspicious movements? 'Indeed they were mistaken on both counts,' was Aitchison's reply. 'When you come to analyse their evidence, it comes to practically nothing.'

Having on the first day of the appeal caused a sensation by alleging that Lambie was a lying witness, on the second day Craigie Aitchison, playing to a capacity audience, returned to the charge. He contrasted what Lambie had said at the trial as to how she had identified Slater in New York – *viz.* 'By his walk and height, his dark hair, and the side of his face' and her further statement there: 'I could not tell his face; I never saw his face' – with her assertion to counsel at the trial that she *did* see the face of the man in Miss Gilchrist's hall. Mr Aitchison commented that, as a witness, Lambie was 'not only false, but unscrupulous', and he submitted that the proper direction that ought to have been given to the jury was that her testimony was negligible.

Discussing the alleged poisoning of Miss Gilchrist's Irish terrier, Mr Aitchison said that there might be nothing at all in that incident, but had it occurred after Slater had arrived in Glasgow, the Lord Advocate would, no doubt, have founded upon it, with a priceless inference to be drawn.

Turning to the evidence given by Mr Adams, Aitchison did not think that his description of the intruder as 'not a well built man, but well featured and clean-shaven', fitted Slater. Aitchison said:

> I do not think there is much doubt as to what this man was convicted on. It was not on that evidence of identification. It was on an attack made on him by the Crown, on misstatements of fact that were made by the Crown, and on hearsay evidence that went uncorrected to the jury.

After reading out practically the whole of the evidence given by Mary Barrowman at the trial, Counsel, observing that Barrowman had given varying accounts of her movements on the night of the murder, contended that no credence could be attached to her identification.

1 See pp 209-221

Referring to the testimony of Duncan MacBrayne, Aitchison said that a witness of the greatest possible materiality from the point of view of the defence had been withheld. 'I think there can be no doubt that if MacBrayne's evidence had been led, the Crown would never have obtained a conviction here.' If it was not inadvertent, it was, he said, without mincing words, a fraud on the prisoner and a fraud on the jury. He argued that the probabilities were all against Slater's being able to get from the billiard saloon, where he was half an hour before the crime was discovered, to Miss Gilchrist's flat, going home first to fetch the hammer, and then make good his escape.

Moving to fresh woods, Mr Aitchison pointed out that the offering of a pawn-ticket for sale by Slater was the starting of a clue that turned out to be absolutely wrong. It would be 'some marvellous coincidence' if, on a wrong clue, the police had got hold of the right man. 'The police in this case started on a false clue, and they have not had the candour and honesty to admit it.'

At the trial it was put that Slater, although actually travelling to Liverpool, had taken tickets to London as a blind. However, they now knew from further evidence, in the possession of the Crown, but withheld from the jury, that this was not so. It was just one more illustration of what they got in this case from beginning to end – the putting aside of anything that told in the appellant's favour.

Dealing with the medical evidence, Aitchison maintained that the prosecution's theory that a hammer had been used as the instrument of the crime verged on the impossible. It would have required the raining of 50 or 60 blows on the head, and the wood of the hammer would have been saturated with blood that no washing or scraping could have removed. He was going to found on the absence – non-calling – of Dr Adams. For all they knew, the verdict against the prisoner might have been obtained on the evidence regarding the hammer. Since two doctors called for the defence took the opposite view of that taken by the two doctors put up by the Crown, medical opinion was clearly divided.

Quoting from the cross-examination of Hugh Cameron – the Moudie – to the effect that witness knew Slater was a gambler and that he lived on the proceeds of women's prostitution, Aitchison submitted that a question by the Lord Advocate as to Slater's mode of living should have been stopped by the Court. It had nothing whatever to do with the case. He added: 'The Lord Advocate put it to the jury without any foundation in evidence whatsoever, that Slater was either a jewel thief or a resetter.' The prosecution had also, he protested, gone to the length of raking up the whole of Slater's past, when his character was not in issue at the trial.

Craigie Aitchison opened the proceedings of the third day of the appeal hearing , Wednesday, 11 July, by announcing: 'I think it is clear that the crux of the case, so far as it is based on fact, is identification. If that breaks down the whole case breaks down.' Which is to say that, if the evidence of the three crucial witnesses was unsatisfactory, the entire prosecution case crumbled away.

As regards Lambie, Counsel held that a man's life could not be put at hazard on the testimony of a witness who was proved to have sworn completely contradictory identification evidence. Barrowman, for her part, had at best a very limited opportunity for observation. She saw, on a dark night, a man with a twisted nose running past her. Were they, asked Aitchison, going to hang a man on that? Adams was so near-sighted that, although he had seen Slater in New York and in the police station at Glasgow, he could not identify him in court without leaving the witness-box and coming down to close quarters.

Counsel moved on to criticise the misstatements of the Lord Advocate which had been allowed to go uncorrected to the jury; that the prisoner knew Miss Gilchrist to be possessed of jewellery; the implication that he was either a jewel thief or a resetter; that Slater cleared out of Glasgow the day his name appeared in the newspapers; that all the prior witnesses to identification deponed to the prisoner's carefully watching the house, whereas, out of ten, there were only three at most who so deponed.

Interestingly, significantly – one could almost fancy to feel the Bench drawing a shawl around its own – Lord Clyde, Lord Justice-General, spoke up at this point, his mind obviously turning to Lord Strathclyde (the former Mr Alexander Ure) now, and for some time past, lying a sick man at his Helensburgh home, expressing the view that while any inaccuracy was to be very much regretted, nobody could completely avoid inaccuracies in such circumstances. He hoped the speeches he had delivered to juries were not on record. (Laughter). He was sure Counsel would be able to pick inaccuracies in them.

In conclusion, a hammering home of coffin nails, Mr Aitchison read out the long list of misrepresentations and non-directions by the judge in his charge to the jury.

It fell to the current Lord Advocate, the Honourable William Watson, KC, MP, to do his justificatory best for his predecessor when on the following fourth consecutive and final day the Court convened. He spoke for two and a half hours. He said nothing that undermined Craigie Aitchison's superbly marshalled case.

Asked by Lord Clyde whether he would like to say anything further, Mr Aitchison replied that he had nothing to add.

The Lord Justice-General then announced that their Lordships would take the case to *avizandum*, which is a term in Scottish law meaning that the Court will take time to consider its judgment, and deliver that judgment at a later date.

The Court then rose.

Eight days later. Friday 20 July 1928.

Decision Day at the Court of Criminal Appeal.

An air of excitement pervaded Court No. 3. The passages leading to it were crowded. Shortly after ten o'clock, Counsel took their seats. The company in the well of the court included William Roughead. Conan Doyle was not present. Slater, in dark brown suit and carrying a grey Homburg hat, picked his way to an inconspicuous seat on the packed benches in the rear of the court-room. Beside him sat the faithful Rabbi and Mrs Phillips.

The quintet of judges came treading measuredly in at 10.25am. Almost immediately, the Lord Justice-General began, in a quiet, clear voice, to read the 5,000-word judgment. It was to take him 25 minutes.

The evidence of Dr Adams was dismissed as hearsay and of no materiality. The evidence relating to Slater's journey to Liverpool and his open signing of the register at the North Western Hotel there as 'Oscar Slater' was also dismissed, the Court being unable to regard it as materially affecting the case. The evidence of Marshal Pinckley as to the farcical nature of the alleged identification by Lambie and Barrowman in New York fared no better.

Things from the appellant's point of view were not going well.

The last piece of evidence was the deposition made by the late Duncan MacBrayne. The Court considered it might well be that MacBrayne's evidence was 'thought then, as we think it now, of no materiality'.

Things from the appellant's point of view were now going badly.

But it was the telling to the jury by the trial judge that, in the light of his revealed ambiguous character, the presumption of innocence applied to the appellant with less effect than it would have applied to a man whose character was not open to suspicion, which finally turned the scales. In their Lordships' opinion that amounted to a clear misdirection in law.

> It is manifestly possible that, but for the prejudiced effect of denying to
> the appellant the full benefit of the presumption of innocence, and of
> allowing the point of his dependence on the immoral earnings of his
> partner to go to the jury as a point not irrelevant to his guilt of Miss
> Gilchrist's murder, the proportion of nine to five for 'guilty' and 'not
> proven' respectively might be reversed. In these circumstances we think
> that the instructions given in the charge amounted to misdirections in law,
> and that the judgment of the Court before whom the appellant was
> convicted should be set aside.

That was it. Victory.

Slater, betraying no outward signs of emotion beyond a stern-set face, but inwardly smarting with grief at the verdict's having been set aside solely on the grounds of misdirection, felt none of the victor's elation, nothing except a simmering anger and the imperative desire to leave the building which had been the stage of his ruin as quickly as possible. Restraining himself from making a demonstration, he spoke to no one. He ignored the crowd assembled in Parliament Square. He declined to be interviewed by a loitering group of hopeful reporters. He clambered into a motor-car and was driven dourly away.

In that weekend's *Empire News*, 22 July 1928, he confessed:

> I unhesitatingly say that the verdict has left me utterly displeased . . . I am only too willing to accept that I have not been a saintly man, and I have never pretended to be one, but that is an entirely different thing from accepting or leaving unchallenged the terrible things that were said about me.

Then, sadly, he recalls,

> the last letter ever written to me by my dear parents. It was posted to me on the eve of the war, and it did not reach me until the war had ended, which was two years after they had passed beyond.

It was victory – but it was a Pyrrhic victory. Oscar had won, but he was bitter. That very day of his sawdust triumph, he sat down and wrote to Doyle.

> July 22, 1928
> Dear Sir Arthur,
> Many thanks for your Congratulations and from the bottom of my heart many, many thanks for your great work.
> Sir Arthur, they went too far in throwing muck at me in an open Court, yet I don't care – but I care for my relatives and friends and I must do something for their sake.
> This cruel 5 judges, this judges, who *know the frame up* of my case, should have limited themselves a little and in not doing so, even the layman in the street know now that my character was the staff for the Crown to lean on. I will fight and expose them all. *All of them who I know have taken my confidence and have betrayed me.* I shall fight regardless of consequences.
> Yours very sincerely
> Oscar Slater.

No question had arisen in the court as to the granting to Slater of his expenses in the matter of the appeal. Neither had the subject of compensation been mentioned. Pressed by a *Daily News* reporter, Doyle admitted that he was at least a thousand pounds out of pocket over the Slater affair. Public discussion on the matter of adequate compensation began at once. There was inevitably some wrangling.

Oscar raised his voice publicly in the *Sunday Mail* of 29 July.

I see by the newspapers there has been some wrangling as to the compensation I should receive. I also read that Sir John Gilmour said in effect: 'Let him send in his bill.' . . . render some account like a tradesman might for some goods supplied. As far as I, Oscar Slater, am concerned there will never be a bill sent in. I will choose first to go to my grave rather than do such a thing . . . All the money I had was spent in defending myself from a charge which five judges in the very same court have stated was not sustained against me. And now I am asked to send in a bill as if my affair was some trifling matter like a transaction with a tailor.

In this same article Oscar writes:

When they got me to Scotland and they found they had not a leg to stand on regarding the brooch . . . they then set out on a campaign of manufacturing evidence to get me *fixed* at all costs and at all risks. The terrible allegations against me, repeated time and again by the five judges in the Court of Appeal, still crash across my mind many times a day and even in the night. These allegations of living on the immoral earnings of a woman or women. Where is the evidence? Where are the convictions that should have been secured against me with all the alleged knowledge the police had, when they caused me to be sentenced to death? The fact that I was kept out of the witness-box is not satisfactory to me now, because I claim that if I had been put in the box, and questioned about these allegations it would have been impossible for the jury to have gone away with their minds influenced by these lies. I protested at the time about being kept out of the box. I protest now and I will go to my grave protesting against it because I, better than anyone else in the world, have reason to know how much it has cost me.

In *The Sunday Times* of 29 July, Conan Doyle wrote:

And so I retire from a task which has cost me some expense, much time, considerable worry, and no satisfaction, save that the good name of Scottish jurisprudence has been restored. I would like, as a last word to say that the country owes much to William Park, of Ballantrae, who has been indefatigable and has ruined his own health in his endeavours to set the matter right. Of public men, only two – Mr Ramsay MacDonald and Mr Finburgh, MP for North Salford – have shown a real human passion for justice. Among Scottish papers of repute not one, so far as I know, save only the *Daily Record* (Glasgow), has printed one line to right an obvious wrong. The churches have helped in no way. Only certain English papers, notably the *Empire News*, the *Daily News*, the *Jewish Chronicle* and *Truth*, have really stood strongly for truth and justice.

Oscar's lofty dismissal of the question of compensation called forth a letter from Doyle.

I have read your article in the *Empire News* with interest. Of course the question is one for your decision and I can understand your feelings, but you may be sure that you will get no compensation, not a penny, if you do not apply for it. If you find this difficult I would be willing to send in a memorandum. If a sum has to be named I would suggest £10,000. You won't get it, but still it certainly is not an unjust claim. Any claim above that would alienate sympathy.

Doyle went on to say that what had to be done in any case was the paying by Oscar of his just debts.

The legal expenses . . . work out at roughly £1,200. Of this I have raised £700, in round figures, by my efforts. To the £500 which remains to be met there are certain just extra charges. Mr Park should have a fee (if he will accept it). I would suggest 100 guineas. Mr Roughead also. Perhaps 50 guineas would meet that. I will charge you nothing, but I spent 30 on seeking Helen Lambie and 20 on advertisements, which should be refunded to me. There is also a Jewish solicitor, Mr Marcus,[2] who has done some work. He probably would ask for 50 guineas. On top of this the Psychic Bookshop Publishing Company is out of pocket £250 over the publication of Park's book. We advertised it very largely and distributed it in order to get public sympathy.

Doyle went on to say that he thought that Oscar should send in a claim for expenses incurred, which might fairly be put at £1,600 less £700.

It should be clearly understood that this is quite independent of your own affair. If you are generous in refusing compensation for yourself [if you really think that is wise) you will agree that you must be just in paying what you owe to those who have worked so long and well.

On 9 August 1928, it was announced that Oscar Slater would receive what was described as an *ex gratia* payment of £6,000. Slater ought, before blithely accepting, to have consulted Conan Doyle. A spot of diplomatic threat along the lines of barratry might well have encouraged a little useful augmentation – but no, impetuous, cussed as ever, Oscar consulted only his own vision of sudden solvency, and accepted without quibble.

Tartly, the *Daily Record* commented: 'No one will suggest that the Government has erred on the side of over-generosity.'

Doyle, equally contemptuous of such scurvy ministerial miserliness, attempted one small rectification by floating the suggestion that the State might agree to bear the balance of the costs of Slater's appeal, which would amount to an additional £700 or £800.

2   Michael Marcus, BL, of 8 North St Andrew Street, Edinburgh.

The State did not agree.

The *Empire News* of 16 September announced: 'It may be taken as a fact that Oscar Slater will not pay the balance due.' This bald statement was amplified and mollified. 'His view is that as he was the injured party all costs incurred in setting right the wrong done him should be borne by the Government responsible for the error of justice resulting in his undeserved punishment.'

The last sputterings of the great compensation controversy – at least so far as the Government was concerned – were manifest in December 1928. On the 5th, Slater, installed once more at Mount Olive, in Ayr, wrote to Sir John Gilmour a last plea for payment of his costs. On the 13th, Sir John Lamb replied on the Secretary of State's behalf that His Majesty's Government was not prepared to pay out another penny.

In the months to come the very publicly aired differences between Doyle and Slater, progressing to the status of a monumental quarrel, were to write a squalid end to what had previously seemed a noble affair. A brief report in the *Daily Mail* of 20 November 1929 wrote *finis* to the whole wretched business:

> Edinburgh. Tuesday, 19 November 1929
>
> Nothing more will be heard of the action brought by Sir Arthur Conan Doyle against Mr Oscar Slater. It was announced in the Court of Sessions here today that a settlement has been arrived at. The terms were not disclosed, but I learn on reliable authority that a payment has been made by Mr Slater to Sir Arthur.[3]

Eight months later – 7 July 1930 – Conan Doyle died, aged 71. The two men had never communicated again. It was, after all that had passed between them, a crying shame. A falling-out over principal and principle.

---

3 Peter Hunt has written: 'In October a deputation of his friends called on Sir Arthur at his home, to explain that Slater was now ready to pay £250 towards the money which had been spent on his behalf. Sir Arthur accepted the explanation that misrepresentations and misunderstandings had arisen out of the patent difficulties of Slater's post-prison feelings.'

Chapter Fourteen

CODICIL
AND
CODA

The life of Oscar Slater, from the vantage point of hindsight, divides itself up very neatly into four distinct epochs or phases: the first 28 years, 1872-1900, the period of his youth and early days in Germany; the next eight years, 1901-09, encompass the date of his arrival in Britain to the time of his arrest for murder; then comes 1909-27, the terrible 18 years of his trial and incarceration in the prison by Salthouse Head; and then the fourth, and final, period, 1928-48, the last 20 years, provides a sort of codicil, a tranquil coda, to all that has gone before.

The years flicked by. Oscar was living in lodgings at No. 357 Tantallon Road, in the Shawlands district of Glasgow, whence, at Christmas 1930, he sent a seasonal greetings card to William Roughead. From Tantallon Road, he moved to a flat of his own at No. 4 James Gray Street, just round the corner, and all the while, behind the seemingly monotonous frontage of the octennial since his release, something increasingly important, increasingly exciting, had been inexorably progressing. It had started very shortly after his emergence from Peterhead. That was when, introduced by a mutual friend, he had first met Miss Lina Wilhelmina Schad.

Born on 14 April 1903, in Thistle Street, Cowdenbeath, Fife, Lina was the daughter of a butcher, Charles Schad, who had arrived in Scotland from his native Germany, en route, as he thought, for Argentina. But instead, he had met a Miss Agnes Panton Whyte, whom he had married at Cupar, and thereafter remained in Scottland.

Oscar, the mutual friend, and 24-year-old Lina, had met for a drink at the old Charing Cross Hotel, in Glasgow. Oscar and Lina had got on well together; so well that they arranged to meet again – just the two of them this time – the next evening. They went to what used to be known in Glasgow as 'the' La Scala cinema, in Sauchiehall Street. 'The film turned out to be about a murder. A son killed his father. I suddenly heard this sobbing beside me. It was Oscar. I'd never seen a man cry before,' Lina told me. She led him out of the cinema.

> As time went on, Oscar and I grew very fond of each other. It was because of him that I left Glasgow – where I had sisters, although my father and mother were dead. Actually, I left because of the Jewish connection. I wasn't Jewish, you see. Oscar was – and proud of it. I remember his saying to me that he would never change his religion to marry *anyone*. And I said that I wouldn't either. The point is that Oscar's Jewish friends thought that, if he was going to get married, he ought to marry a Jewish girl, and, incidentally, invest the compensation money in a business. I liked Oscar's Jewish friends fine, but I got fed up with all the 'Jewishness', and the sort of pressure. That's why I went off to London.
>
> When I arrived there first of all, I got a room at the YWCA and started to look round for a job. I was lucky. I got a position as cashier at the Turkish Baths at the Imperial Hotel, in Bloomsbury. I stayed at the Imperial until 1936. I used to go up to Glasgow every now and again, and stay with my sister. I didn't even see Oscar every time I went up. Sometimes I did. Sometimes I didn't. But Oscar kept in touch. He used to telephone me. We did talk of marriage from time to time, but it just stayed talk. By 1936, I was seeing someone else, and I think Oscar got afraid that if he didn't do something about it he would lose me.
>
> It was about this time that I received a box of Ferguson's chocolates from him. They arrived by post, all squashed to bits, but packed in with them was a little cupid. When I was next in Glasgow I called at Ferguson's. I knew the manager there. I told him: 'You owe me a box of

chocolates!' I explained about their arriving all squashed. And he said: 'That wasn't our fault. The gentleman who bought them wouldn't let us pack them up. He wanted to post them himself.' Oscar was shy about enclosing the cupid.

Lina told me that it was shortly after that that: 'We decided to get married.'

On 13 July 1936, seven years after their first meeting, 33-year-old Miss Lina Schad was married before the Sheriff in the County Buildings, Glasgow, to Mr Oscar Leschziner, aged 64, widower and bank bookkeeper. The honeymoon was at Ayr. On their return to Glasgow, the couple moved into Oscar's redecorated flat, No. 4 James Gray Street.

We talked it over about having children, and Oscar said that he didn't want any. He felt that the finger would always be pointed. 'That's Oscar Slater's son – daughter.' He was a very good husband. You couldn't ask for better. He did have a very quick temper, though. I remember, right at the beginning he told me: 'I flare up, but I soon calm down again. Just leave me alone and I recover.' He never hit me or showed any violence. I was more like 'an old man's darling'. Mark you, although he was thirty-one years older than me, he seemed younger than me. He was very young in his ways.

Oscar was interviewed in Glasgow in April 1939, by a newspaper correspondent named Mea Allan.

I talked yesterday with Oscar Slater – still, at 67, a powerfully-built man, tall, with a close-shaven head. He has been married now for four and a half years. His interests are in people and the small day-to-day happenings from which he was shut off for nearly 19 years.

'Lina and I are very happy,' he told me. 'I have many friends and good neighbours. But the best friend is Lina. Do you know why she married me?' His sad face crinkled into a smile. ' "Because you are not yet a hundred, Oscar," she said. But I shall live to be a hundred – yes. I want many more years of happiness, and Lina and I will always be happy.'

We were chatting in his flat, close to Bellahouston Park, where the Empire Exhibition was held. His comfortable, brown-carpeted sitting-room is a miniature museum, full of curios, among them a wastepaper-basket made from an elephant's foot, a bronze stork, and a stuffed terrier dog. Oscar Slater collects everything – 'so long as it is pretty.' He has a wonderful collection of exquisite Chinese ivories.

He told me the romantic story of his meeting with his wife, Miss Schad, a Scottish-born girl of German parentage.

'Her father interested himself in the case,' he told me. 'And from him Lina learned all the details. When I came out she was waiting for me. "Do you wish me to be friendly with you?" she asked, and I nodded gratefully. "Yes, I shall need a friend," I told her. And so we went out together, to the pictures and places like that. Then Lina got a job as a bookkeeper in a London hotel. I missed her a great deal, but we wrote to one another. Love is a funny thing, you understand. One moment you are just friends, the next moment you know that you can settle down and be happy for the rest of time. It is of no use to marry unless you are quite, quite sure. It was like that with Lina and me. When I met her again I asked her, "Will you say Yes?" And very soon we were married. I think Lina does not regret. It is very wonderful for me. But you know . . .' He leaned forward towards me, an ironical smile in his eyes. 'If I had been Lina, I would not have married Oscar Slater! No, there was too much . . . too much that went before . . . ' His voice faded out in a whisper.

Suddenly he crossed the room and brought back a wallet of photographs. 'Look at this little boy. Is he not beautiful? We would wish to adopt him, Lina and I. But he is all his mother has left. He is a refugee.' Since his release he has been in one job and another, moving from place to place. He is working as a clerk in a Glasgow hotel, his real identity is a close secret, known simply among his fellow workers as 'Oscar' – a kindly man whose face is scarred with tragedy, but who loves a joke. He has been in his present employment for nine months, and he hopes to remain for nine years. 'Because I have a wife to support now. And Lina likes pretty clothes.'

This business of being a hotel bookkeeper and, on his marriage certificate, of being a bank bookkeeper, was all nonsense. His wife told me categorically:

Oscar never worked. He made a living buying and selling things – jewellery, ivories, things like that; small antiques. He would go round the junk shops, attend auctions. He was very clever with his hands. I remember his buying a lovely little ivory figure and finding that some of its toes were missing. He borrowed some finicky little instrument from a neighbour and friend of ours who was a dentist, and Oscar carved a perfect set of replacement toes on to the ivory. He seemed to have a wonderful knowledge, a sort of instinct, where jewellery was concerned. He told me that he had been taught all about it by an uncle of his when he was a boy.

Shortly before World War II, Oscar and his wife left Glasgow and moved to Ayr, where they purchased a smart little bungalow, Oslin,[1] 25 St Phillans Avenue. It was their dream home: but the dream was to be pathetically short-lived. Even though he had recently applied

---

1   Os (car) plus Lin (a) makes Oslin!

for naturalisation, it was not long after the outbreak of war that both Oscar and Lina were interned.

With the war over, a few golden years remained to Oscar, spent quietly but extremely happily in his earthly paradise at Ayr. So happy, indeed, that sometimes, for sheer joy of life, he would stand foursquare on Rabbie Burns' Auld Brig and sing at the top of his lungs' bent, the wind carrying his weird-accented song away across the melodious waves, to the slightly puzzled, head-cocking cormorants and bobbing gulls.

Life in Ayr was lived at leisure, Oscar busying himself at his own pace about the second-hand Aladdin's caves of trinketry, and taking his collector's eye, with profit, to sundry sale-rooms.

Possessed of a good singing voice, he much enjoyed listening to music. He went frequently, too, to the theatre and the cinema. He was, always had been, a great walker. He was also a great talker. After all the years of enforced silence, he liked nothing better than a good crack. A very generous man, he was forever giving his mite to charities – in particular those concerned with the plight of sick or homeless children.

At home, when not doing a spot of wood-carving, or minute and painstaking restoration work on some small *objet de vertu*, rescued by his discriminatory taste from the rim of the scrap-heap, he would amuse himself perfecting in blueprint or working model, his latest invention. He was, too, immensely house-proud. Everything was spotless, superbly kept and in perfect working order. Oslin sparkled.

Lina told me:

We didn't quarrel. Not really. Just occasionally we might have some absolutely silly, trivial disagreement, about something like going to the pictures, perhaps. He might want to go the local cinema. I might not fancy what was on. He would look cross, put on his hat and coat and stomp off. When he came home again he wouldn't say a word. I'd know that he'd gone off to the cinema at Prestwick. He wouldn't go to the one in Ayr without me, because we were always seen around together, and he wouldn't want people to see him on his own.

Another thing with him was swimming. Oscar was a very keen swimmer. When we lived at Ayr, he did a lot of swimming. As spring came round he'd be watching the weather. 'Here comes the sun,' he'd say. And the first really nice day, off we'd go for a swim. And that was it! Once I'd been for a swim with him, I had to go every day – even if the weather-promise of that first good swimming day proved a false one. Once you'd been for a swim, you were expected to keep it up until the return of the really chill autumn days put a stop to it.

He loved the beach, he loved his modest garden at the bungalow, and longed to grow exotic flowers there. Bronzed by the sun and west-coast winds, athletic, always well-dressed, he was a familiar figure in the town, and looked considerably younger than his three score years and ten-plus.

Said his widow:

Of course everybody knew he was Oscar Slater, and I had to get used to people staring and nudging and whispering. They would go past you. Then you would hear their footsteps stop. You would look round and find that they had stopped and turned round to have a good look.

Usually, Oscar took all this in good part, but Mrs Leschziner told me:

I remember how upset he got when one day we were walking along the front at Ayr and a man came up and spoke to him. It was someone who had been in prison with him – a real rough type. Oscar said: 'I don't mind talking to him, but he shouldn't come up like that *when I'm with you*.' He used to tell me about the awful time he had in Peterhead. He hated anyone calling him Slater. I think that was because it reminded him of his time in prison when they would shout at him, 'Slater . . . do this. Slater . . . do that.'

I asked about Oscar's illness and death.

As a rule he was wonderfully fit. Never ailed. But that January of 1948, he'd been feeling a bit funny. He went to the doctor, but Oscar still felt there was something wrong. He would point to his chest and say, 'In here. It's not right.' I managed in the end to get him to stay in bed for a couple of days. What a job that was!

The day he died, 31 January 1948, I remember it was a Saturday, I'd been out doing a little bit of shopping. Oscar was in bed. I wanted to do him a little boiled fish. He wanted to go to the toilet. I told him to stay in bed, but he wouldn't. He insisted on getting up to go across to the lavatory. He got as far as the lavatory door, then fell to the floor. He was dead. It was just about four o'clock in the afternoon.

Dr Thomas Rutherford certified death as due to pulmonary embolism, phlebitis. The name of Oscar's intimate friend and next-door neighbour, William McKay, of No. 27 St Phillans Avenue, appears on the certificate as present at the death.

The funeral was at the Crematorium, the Western Necropolis, at Maryhill, Glasgow, at 3.30pm on Tuesday, 3 February 1948.

Because Oscar was not officially attached to any particular religion, Councillor J. S. Clarke, who delivered the oration, recited verses from the B*hagavad-Gita*, sacred book of the Hindus – the same as had been read over the body of Mahatma Gandhi a few days before – and read passages from the works of Krishna, the Hindu god. Only a small number of mourners, relatives of the widow, attended the funeral ceremony.

Oscar's ashes were scattered.

He left £4,917 3s. Within a year, Oscar's widow had sold the bungalow at Ayr – the little neat home in the west – and moved to a ground-floor flat at 46 Bellwood Street, back in Glasgow, within a stone's throw of James Gray Street, where it had all begun.

Why did she leave Ayr?

People used to meet me in the street and say how sorry they were about Oscar's death. It kept continually bringing it back to me. I remember the last straw was one day when I ran into a policeman who had known Oscar well, and, as he was offering his condolences, I burst into floods of tears in the street – *yet again*. I felt I must escape to somewhere where I could be more private, more anonymous.

So, rather like the way I had run away south from the living Oscar all those years before, I ran away from the dead Oscar, or, rather, from those perpetual, publicly distressing reminders of him.

Lina Leschziner was to live on, alone, in the flat in Bellwood Street, for 43 years. She died in her ninetieth year, on 21 October 1992.

To the end, she had no regrets.

To the end, she still missed Oscar.

Chapter Fifteen

IF NOT
SLATER –
WHO?

There can surely be few today who continue to nurture the notion that Oscar Slater was guilty.

But if not Slater, who? That is the question. As William Roughead, with his customary bluff clarity, put it: 'Miss Gilchrist must have been killed by somebody.'

Over the past 90 years there have been a goodly number of hazy candidates confidently sponsored as, to adapt Crashaw, 'That not impossible *he.*' And chief among these sacrificial victims-elect has been the misfortunate Dr Francis James Charteris, whose credentials we shall, in due course, make it our business critically to examine.

Although Roughead and Doyle had sown the seeds of doubt regarding Slater's guilt, and Park did most assiduously water them, the first to cast a stone – a boulder – into the deep, dark, not to say murky, waters marooning the hapless convict in Peterhead, was Detective Lieutenant Trench.

We have already, following the implied biblical adjurement,

taken a closer look at the caster of the stone. We have seen the dissolving of the aura of near-sainthood which has enhaloed the blessed name of Trench down the decades, and has perhaps rendered some purblind to the necessity to expose the allegations and accusations which Trench made to as rigorous an examination as that which they have given to the charges that were brought against Slater. To lift the burden of guilt from the back of one innocent man only to deposit it upon another's blameless shoulders does not appear to be a very satisfactory transaction.

We know that Trench was obsessed – although we do not really know *why* – with the idea that Dr Charteris was the culprit. This is truly a mystery within a mystery. A possible solution, Mr Ratcliffe, that shrewd former Assistant Chief Constable of Glasgow, suggested to me, was that it could be that Trench, who was, of course, only a detective constable at the time of his alleged conversations with Miss Birrell and Helen Lambie in 1908, might have been genuinely mistaken in thinking that Miss Birrell had said that Lambie had told her that she *recognised* Dr Charteris as the man whom she saw in the hall. Perhaps what Miss Birrell had actually said was that Lambie had told her that the man whom she had seen in the hall *looked like* Dr Charteris. If the Misses Birrell and Lambie really had confided statements to him inculpating Dr Charteris, Ratcliffe felt very strongly that Trench should have done what he must have known perfectly well that he ought to have done; namely, conveyed his misgivings to Chief Constable Stevenson, 'who was a very fair-minded and honest man'.

Ratcliffe also made the very valid observation that it is important that we should remember that there were *three* investigations into the Gilchrist murder going on simultaneously. There was that of Mr Hart, the Procurator-fiscal, and his sheriff's criminal officers, and there were two police investigations: that official one by Superintendent William Miller Douglas, of the Western Division, in whose bailiwick the crime had been committed, and that supervisory one being quietly conducted by Superintendent Ord, of Central, who was surely motivated not only by inquisitive interest, but also by the desire not to find himself excluded from so important a case.

'One should,' Ratcliffe emphasised, 'lay the blame for what went on in the continuing persecution of Slater on the Fiscal, and not just on the police.' Well spoken as an old member of the Force. One should also, perhaps, apportion some of the blame to the Crown Office and its officials.

Trench's choice of suspect was an odd one. If Miss Birrell and Helen Lambie really did tell him that Dr Charteris was the man seen in Miss Gilchrist's flat, the oddness ceases to be. But in the circumstance that they both denied – and denied vehemently – ever having told him any such thing, what are we to think?

There can be no gainsaying that, without proof positive in your hands, it was unusual, especially in that day and age, for a man in Trench's position in life to bring charges against someone so much his social superior. He must, moreover, have known how risky it was to launch an attack upon a man who was so obviously well-guarded by reputation and lawyers, even, in this case, a man whose brother was a top Glasgow solicitor. Looked at in the round, unless he was speaking total truth, Trench's conduct bordered upon the eccentric.

I believe that he was absolutely genuine in his faith in Slater's entire innocence, and blindly courageous in his determination to see him set free. He owed Slater nothing. He had not played any significant part in the investigation which had brought the unhappy man to this pass. It was not his fault that he had been wrongly incarcerated, but for some reason it came to him that *he* could be the righter of a great wrong. I suspect that when Slater did not hang, Trench felt, at least temporarily, relieved, though not permanently satisfied with the state of things. He brooded . . . and brooded . . . Then, one day in April 1912, when Shaughnessy was stirring it all up, Trench leapt out of his bath one morning determined at last, come what may, to *do* something.

The Will-o'-the-wisp figure of A.B. remained firmly unidentified down the years, the subject of ongoing speculation and rumour. But with surprising constancy the name of Dr Charteris was that pronounced in knowing, behind-the-hand whispers.

That was not, of course, the case in December 1908. Then, it was the as yet undisclosed name of Oscar Slater that was whispered from knowing lip to knowing ear. In default of anything better, anyone likelier, turning up, the police, at their wits' end, were sticking to, stuck with, their McLean-gifted prime suspect, Mr Oscar. But in the wider world a belief was gaining ground – as announced in the *Glasgow News* of 29 December – that 'the brutal murder had for its author a hardened criminal'.

It was, indeed, with the possibility of such a culprit, or culprits, in mind, that Stevenson had issued a constabular bull 'To Landladies and Others', cautioning wariness. That such folk had in consequence been put on red alert is borne witness to by an item in that same Tuesday's (29 December) *Evening Times*:

> The gay young bachelor is having a hard time in finding coast or country lodgings this Yuletide . . . Rothesay landladies are particularly nervous over the West-End murder, and lone widow women or maiden ladies absolutely refuse lone men admittance to their houses. On Wednesday last a poor soul spent the whole day in the 'Madeira'¹ in a fruitless endeavour to get lodgings for the week, and he had to return to the city in the evening to try some other place next day. He was a Glasgow minister!

Admirably, increasingly, Superintendents Douglas and Ord laboured on to attain their imperative solution. But all along one thing seemed majestically clear: Oscar Slater was their man. It was a proposition concerning which Ord, at least, never faltered. Others, as time went by, were not to be so sure. Ord went to his grave, 20 years later, still utterly convinced that he had found the killer of Miss Gilchrist.

While awaiting developments from afar, which is to say the arrest and extradition of Slater from New York, the police let it be known that they were searching for a second man in connection with the murder. This 'mysterious man', eventually traced to Belfast, where he was duly compeared on 9 January 1909, was none other than Oscar's good friend, Sam Reid. Interestingly, Reid spoke of his acquaintance with Miss Gilchrist's nephews, the Birrell brothers – James Aitken and George Gilchrist. He said that he had known them since 1903, having originally met James in Wyper's public-house, at No. 55 Sauchiehall Street.

> James Birrell used to back horses with me some years ago, but he has not put a bet on with me for the past four years, but we kept up the

1 Beautiful Bute.

acquaintance, and I last saw him in Wyper's public-house about five or six weeks ago. In fact he owes me twelve shillings which I lent him four or five years ago.

Reid's statement continued:

> I also knew George Birrell very well. He and I have had a drink together often, and about four years ago he used to back horses with me, but not since. But I have had a drink with him occasionally since, whenever I meet him. I was in his company about five or six weeks ago, but never heard either of them mention their deceased aunt, Miss Gilchrist, that she had jewellery or anything else. I never saw Cameron [Hugh Cameron, the Moudie] with either of the Birrells. I did not know Helen Lambie. On the night of Miss Gilchrist's murder, I left Glasgow about 11pm. My reason for leaving Glasgow was want of work.

The emergence of Samuel Reid must have seemed to the police to signal a very hopeful turn of events. Friend of Slater, the jewel-fancier-dealer. Friend of the Birrell brothers, nephews of the Lady of the Jewels. Friend of the Moudie. Leaves Glasgow – the country – on the *very* night of Miss Gilchrist's murder. Just *happened* to go then for want of work, did he? Was *he* the second man in West Princes Street? Or was it the Moudie? Did the police fancy that they began to scent a plot, a conspiracy? If so, who should blame them? Let him who is without the sin of occasional hasty-conclusion-jumping first cast a stone. This is, always remember, a case riven with persuasive coincidences.

The Birrell brothers had been 'shown' to Lambie, Barrowman and a number of other witnesses on 7 January 1909. None of the witnesses had identified either of them as having been seen in the vicinity on the night of the murder. Nor had they ever been seen in the company of Slater.

As a matter of routine, the police had taken statements from the Birrells.

Statement of James Aitken Birrell, aged 52, eldest son of Walter and Janet Gilchrist or Birrell:

> I am at present an advertising canvasser, but I have been out of employment for the last six months. I was at one time a marine insurance broker and underwriter, being a member of the firm Wingate, Birrell & Company, at the Royal Exchange. We also had an office at 39 St Vincent Street. We failed in the year 1888 in £100,000.

He had, he said, a faint recollection of

> being in her house and seeing her [Marion Gilchrist] when I was about five
> years old. Her father left her all his money, which caused a dryness
> between other relatives and her. I have not mentioned her name to
> anyone for many years so far as I remember. I never at any time applied to
> her for assistance for anything.

He was, it so happened, in a position to prove an alibi. He had been
drinking in Wyper's in company with a Mr Carrick, an accountant
from Bath Street. And Andrew Carrick confirmed this. He said that
he had known Birrell for about 18 months and had a distinct
recollection of being in Wyper's on the night of the murder.

> It was about 6.50 when I went there, and I found Mr Birrell there. We were
> there till 8.30pm . . . I saw him again next day about 12.30, and he had not
> heard of the murder then. I however told him what was in the newspapers.
> He seemed dumbfounded.

Statement of George Gilchrist Birrell, aged 45. He, too, had started
off in commercial life as a ship and insurance broker, but by 1894
had slipped several rungs down the ladder to the level of
mercantile clerk. Presently, though, remustering, he was more
grandly designating himself 'merchant and manufacturer's agent'.
By 1908, however, he was simply a clerk in the employ of the Tax
Office in St Vincent Street. In his precognition he said: 'I am not
aware that I ever saw my aunt, and I was never in her house.' There
is, in view of the very poor quality of the Gilchristean family
relationships, not the slightest reason to doubt this, at first sight,
rather unusual circumstance. The precognition continues:

> Three or four years ago I became acquainted with a foreigner. He was
> called Samuel Reid. He lived at one time in Kirkland Street, Glasgow. I
> cannot recall where and when I first met him, but I think that most
> probably it was in a public-house. A public-house which was a favourite
> haunt of his was the Cosy Den in Buchanan Street and Sauchiehall Street.
> Another was Loughrane's public-house at the corner of the Empire Theatre.
> He was a betting man, either made a book himself or did so for someone
> else. I knew him just from meeting him in that way, and I was two or three
> times in his house in Kirkland Street. I don't know whether he was
> German. I had no business with him unless that of betting, and once I
> called to ask him for the loan of a pound when I was hard pressed. I have
> no recollection of having mentioned to him about my having an aunt who
> was well off. I think it a thing it would be most unlikely for me to do. The
> last time I remember seeing Reid was, as I think, in November last, and I

encountered him in Peat's public-house, top of Hope Street. He was
generally alone when I saw him. About two or two and a half years ago I
remember meeting a man called Anderson. I saw him on three or four, or it
may be five or six occasions, and I think I had some bets with him. He was
about 5 feet 9, broadish shoulders, well set up, a good speaker. I cannot
say that he was a foreigner. I am not sure that I would know him if I saw
him again. I do not know a man called Oscar Slater, but it is possible the
man Anderson I have mentioned might be the same. I first got notice of
the murder about 5.30pm on Tuesday, December 22nd, from the
newspaper, otherwise I knew nothing about it.

An interesting sidelight on George Gilchrist Birrell's character is
afforded by a letter which he wrote on 16 April 1910 to William
Hodge & Company, publishers of Roughead's Notable Scottish Trials
volume on Slater. In it, he describes himself as

Hardware Factor, Agent and Importer, of 71 Vernon Street, Glasgow.
Dear Sirs –
I enclose order form – please send me one copy of The Trial of Oscar Slater
and oblige. You might also send me a few of your circulars, and say what
coms. you would allow me on the sale of this or the complete series of
volumes.* I am a nephew of the murdered lady, Miss Marion Gilchrist
having been my mother's sister, and having a large circle of friends it
occurs to me that here is an opportunity to do some business if you will
make it worth my while.
Yours truly,
Geo. Gilch. Birrell
*Or, alternatively, state the best Trade discount terms etc., you would
make for me as a direct buyer. - G.G.B.

Statement of Margaret Dawson Birrel, aged 44:

I was last in Miss Gilchrist's house on Saturday, 19th December [1908]
about three in the afternoon. I think I spent an hour with her, and we had
afternoon tea together. At that visit she pressed me strongly to come back
very soon.

Statement of Mrs Mary Greer Gilchrist or McCall, aged 42:

I am unable to state whether the general public in the immediate vicinity
of the house knew my aunt was possessed of money and jewellery, but her
friends knew of these facts and it is probable that respectable people in
the neighbourhood were also acquainted. My aunt had no banking
account, but this time last year she was carrying about £400 (in value) of
deposit receipts. She used to make her deposits at the Hope Street
Branch of the Bank of Scotland.

Mrs McCall had expressed to the Hampshire police the
considerable familiarity with her aunt's decorative treasure-trove

that she had come to have as a result of her three-week stay in West Princes Street at the beginning of 1908:

> The gold and diamond brooch I cleaned together with a pair of diamond earrings. The brooch was worn daily by my aunt, and she usually kept it on the toilet-table in her bedroom. Beside the diamond crescent brooch, she had in her possession when I last saw her a very valuable diamond necklace, single row of diamonds, some of which were nearly as large as peas; diamond earrings (single large stones); three diamond stars, could either be used as ornaments for the hair or worn as brooches. Diamond brooch shape of a bird. Two diamond bracelets. Five-stone ruby ring. Five-stone emerald ring. Four cairngorm buttons set up as a brooch. One black mourning-ring set with a single diamond. A small gold ring, either set with three diamonds and two rubies or vice versa. A very old gold keeper ring, very much worn so that only traces of the original engraving was [sic] observable. These three rings my aunt always wore, There was also a – I believe it was a George III – shilling, one side scraped flat, with a design of a ship and two initials underneath engraved thereon. The last time I saw my aunt she was in her dressing-gown and was not wearing the gold crescent brooch.'

Further questioned when she arrived in Glasgow after her aunt's death, Mrs McCall told the police that while nursing her aunt some ten months previously, she had seen very little of her jewellery. This seems to be a complete contradiction of what she had told the Hampshire police – viz. 'I saw a great deal of her jewellery.' Having had a list of Miss Gilchrist's jewellery read over to her, she commented: 'I believe I have seen most of these things. I know that she wore a watch and chain sometimes, but I do not notice it in the list.' One cannot resist the feeling that, when she invited Mrs McCall to her home, Miss Gilchrist had taken a very shrewd observer into her house – a woman whose mind held the capacity to construct all-embracing inventories.

Mrs McCall further stated that she had had no letter from her aunt since she last saw her in February [1908]. She had learned of her aunt's death when her brother had telephoned the news through to her at Bournemouth on the night of 21 December. She had then come up to Glasgow immediately, the very next day, and had attended the funeral. She had not, however, been into her dead aunt's house. She had stayed with her mother – Mrs Charteris – at No. 4 Queen Margaret Crescent.

Mary McCall spoke well of Helen Lambie.

I have every reason to believe that the girl Lambie was, in every respect, trustworthy, and was not given to gossip. I do not think she would talk outside of my aunt's affairs, and my aunt had every confidence in her . . . trusted her. I have heard her ask Nellie to go to the wardrobe and bring her dress, and I have also heard her say to Nellie, 'What do you suppose I have done with my keys? I cannot find them.' And Nellie would suggest where they might be found.

As for Miss Gilchrist's front-door security drill, Mrs McCall was a shade less pedantic, more grudging, than the version of its superlative efficiency which has been traditionally handed down: 'If she answered the door-bell, she generally put the chain on, which allowed the door to open only the length of the chain.' But not necessarily always. Security could definitely slip below the one hundred per cent mark. 'I remember one occasion when staying in my aunt's house, of Nellie Lambie going out without the key and ringing the bell. On that occasion I opened the door to her, my aunt being in bed.' Clearly though, Mary McCall was calculating an alternative scenario in which Aunt Marion was alone and someone *purporting* to be a keyless Lambie had rung at the door.

Of one thing Mrs McCall was absolutely certain, adamant: 'I have not the slightest knowledge of the man Slater.'

Since the members of the Ferguson family proved to be the main beneficiaries of Miss Gilchrist's will, it was only to be expected that the police should look with especial care at the circumstances surrounding these so fortunate legatees. They did. Nothing awry could be found with them.

The Birrells, the Fergusons, the Charterises, followed by, in descending order of likelihood, the McCalls and the Lees . . . all found blameless . . . and then there were none. It was, by police perception, a one-horse race, with Slater heavily tipped to win.

A very quiet street. That is how West Princes Street has, on considerably more than one occasion, been described. But the more you study the Slater case, the less inclined you become to go along with that description. Unless, and it is a presumption which I am most certainly not prepared to accept, *all* the witnesses are either deluded or liars, or both, West Princes Street in the dark days of December 1908 bore a closer resemblance to Piccadilly Circus.

Let us begin the justification of this latter preposterous proposition with the testimony of a sober-sided police constable, Francis Brien, sharp-eyed, 34-year-old Western District officer, who affirmed that within the four or five weeks immediately prior to the murder – so we must include the last weeks in November in our sinister equation – he had seen, some six or seven times, a man, whom he was subsequently to identify as Oscar Slater, wandering about St George's Road, near to West Princes Street. On the last occasion on which he saw him, 'He was in West Princes Street, within eight or ten yards from St George's Road. He was standing against a railing there. He appeared quite sober. From where I saw him to Miss Gilchrist's house is about 70 or 80 yards, on the same side of the street.'

Four members of the McHaffie family, living one stair up at No. 16, on the north side of West Princes Street, about 30 yards east of Miss Gilchrist's, on the opposite pavement, saw the Loitering Man. Mrs Margaret Dickson or McHaffie, 43-year-old wife of Alexander Rankin McHaffie, horse shoer, said that she saw him on at least six separate occasions, generally at about 3 or 4pm. The last time was approximately a fortnight before the murder.

> I was very suspicious of him and drew my daughter's attention to him. He would loiter for from forty to sixty minutes about the street, from the corner of St George's Road up to Miss Gilchrist's house, and then turn back, watching the windows. I used to watch him from behind my blinds. When he observed me looking at him, he put his head down and moved away.

Mrs McHaffie identified Oscar Slater as the Loitering Man.

Her daughter, 21-year-old Margaret, a clerkess, confirmed her mother's statement and added that the man generally wore a black bowler hat. Another daughter, Annie, aged 23, stated that the Loitering Man had actually called at the house at 7pm one evening some three or four weeks before the murder.

> He rang the bell and I opened the door. Our name is in large letters on a brass plate on the door. He said: 'Is there any person named Anderson lives here?'[2] I said: 'No.' He turned about and went downstairs and I closed

2 That choice of the name Anderson – as used so often by Slater – was yet another extraordinary coincidence.

the door. Within a minute, someone knocked. I opened the door and
found my cousin, Madge, at it. I asked her if she had met the man on the
stair, and she said, 'Yes'.

Twenty-year-old Madge McHaffie, describing the man, said that,
'His dress seemed peculiar. He had on a light fawn-coloured
overcoat and checked trousers.' She saw him again a few days
afterwards, between 3 and 4pm, from Mrs McHaffie's window.

He walked up and down West Princes Street and was loitering about. I
called my aunt's attention to him. He loitered for about 20 minutes or
thereby. I left shortly afterwards and I passed him in St George's Road. He
was walking leisurely in the direction of Charing Cross. He had a slouching
gait in his walk.

The two girls were later shown Slater. Said Annie: 'I believe he is a
man who called at our door.' Madge was less certain. She thought
him like the man. However, she 'could not positively say he is the
same man, but he is of the same height and build and general
appearance'. Significantly perhaps, Annie McHaffie made no
reference to the caller's having had a foreign accent. Slater, of
course, spoke in a pronouncedly guttural. German-accented voice.

THE McHAFFIES' LOITERING MAN

Age:	About 30 years
Height:	5ft 7 or 8 in
Moustache:	Dark.
Wearing:	Light overcoat, light trousers, hard felt hat.
	On another occasion, dark frock-coat.
Gait:	Had a slouching gait.

The Loitering Man – or a loitering man – was remarked upon several
occasions in December by P.C. 78 Christopher Walker, B. Division.

I was on night duty in the beginning of December 1908, and the north side
of West Princes Street formed part of my beat. On Tuesday night, I
December, as I think, I passed along it towards St George's Road about
6.45pm, and I noticed a man standing on the edge of the pavement
opposite the close at 15 Queen's Terrace. I thought he was someone I knew
and I waved my hand to him, but as he took no notice of me I found I had
made a mistake.

About three nights after that – December 3rd or 4th – about the same time [6.45pm] I saw again said man. On this occasion he was walking leisurely along the north side of West Princes Street towards Queen's Crescent.

The next occasion on which I saw him was on December 17th or 18th, at about 6.45pm. He was standing on the south side of West Princes Street at the junction of St George's Road.

PC Walker identified Slater as the loiterer.

It was Mrs Jane Mary Robertina Sim or Perry, 57-year-old wife of Dr Robert Perry, of 11 Queen's Terrace, who saw the Standing Man. During the eleven-day period, December 11-21 1908, she had seen four or five times a man standing at the corner of Queen's Crescent gardens.

He always seemed to be looking towards the houses about where Miss Gilchrist's and our houses are situated. It was generally about 10pm when I saw him. He was distant from me about the width of the street and the two pavements. I never saw his face as the light was generally behind him. I am not even sure that it was always the same man, though at the time I thought he was probably a most persistent lover. He seemed always alone.

MRS. PERRY'S STANDING MAN
Height: Medium – perhaps a shade tall.
Wearing: A greyish overcoat, perhaps tweed.

Every day, at 1pm, photographer's shop assistant 25-year-old Euphemia Cunningham, would go home to lunch via West Princes Street and Queen's Crescent. On Monday, 14 December 1908, she noticed a man standing at the corner of West Princes Street and Queen's Crescent, almost opposite Miss Gilchrist's. He was not there on her return at about 2pm, but on the following three days – 15, 16 and 17 December – there he was again, each day at one o'clock. She identified Oscar Slater, by the photograph of him that appeared in the Glasgow *Evening News*, as being the man.

EUPHEMIA CUNNINGHAM'S STANDING MAN
Age: 32 years.
Height: 5 ft. 8in.
Complexion: Dark. Clean-shaven.
Features: Rather heavy.

Hair: Very dark. Close cut.

Wearing: Dark-coloured overcoat.

                On another occasion a greenish-coloured one.

                A peaked cap.

Comment: Looked like a foreigner.

William Campbell, a 39-year-old photographer who worked at the same establishment as Euphemia Cunningham – William Fullerton's, photographer's, at 167 St George's Road – used also to go home to lunch at 1pm daily via West Princes Street and Queen's Crescent, as often as not in company with her. He, too, saw the Standing Man 'looking at Mr Adams' house from the other side of the street' on 15, 16 and 17 December at around one o'clock.

WILLIAM CAMPBELL'S STANDING MAN

Age: 25-30 years.

Height: 5ft. 7 in.

Complexion: Dark.

Hair: Dark.

Build: Ordinary.

Wearing: Dark overcoat and cap.

Campbell, looking at the *Evening News* photograph of Slater, said that although the man in it seemed familiar to him, he could not reconcile it with the Standing Man, 'but Slater resembles the man in every respect, but, as I did not pay very special attention to his features, I would not like to swear he is the same man; though in my own mind, I feel almost sure that he is'.

Both Cunningham and Campbell went home by another road at the closing of the shop at 6pm, so they were unable to say whether the Standing Man was there in the evening or not.

About the end of the week prior to the Monday of the murder, that is to say around 17 or 18 December, Alexander Gillies, 29 years old, a manufacturer by trade, who lived with his elder brother, Edgar Gillies, a stockbroker, and, as housekeeper, 52-year-old Elizabeth Donaldson, on the first floor of No. 46 West Princes Street, directly opposite Miss Gilchrist's, saw a man lurking around the foot of the stair at the back of the close of his house.

Elizabeth Donaldson stated:

> On several occasions for a week or to prior to the murder the stair gas on the landing at our door had been turned off by some person This gas-jet lights the whole stair. On the evening of the murder, I had occasion, at about 6.50pm, to be at the door and found that the stair gas had again been turned out. There is a window on the staircase leading up to our house which commands a good view of Miss Gilchrist's house and the door leading to it. Any person could easily watch Miss Gilchrist's house from our staircase window, or from behind the door at the front of the close.

She added, though: 'I saw no suspicious or strange person about the locality on the said 21st December.'

According to the statement taken by Detective Trench, Elizabeth Donaldson had then said: 'A remarkable fact about the stair gas is that it has never been turned out since the night of the murder.'

Mr Gillies, on the other hand, when being questioned on 15 March 1909, went out of his way to point out that he had 'noticed that the gas was turned off on one occasion during the last fortnight'.

MR. GILLIES' LURKING MAN
Height: 5 ft. 8 in.
Complexion: Dark and sallow. Clean-shaven.
Wearing: Fawn-coloured coat, its collar turned up,
                and a tweed cap.

Being shown Oscar Slater, Mr Gillies said: 'He resembles the man in height, build, complexion and general appearance, but I could not swear he is the same man.'

Then there was the testimony of 25-year-old Jeanetta or Jeanette Walters.

> I am a domestic servant and for six months prior to 15 February 1909, I was in the employment of John Gibson, cab driver, 122 West Graham Street. During that time I got out for an hour, from 7 to 8pm each night, and usually went along West Princes Street to Woodlands Road and back. On Wednesday, 16 December 1908, about 7.30pm, I was going along West Princes Street, and when passing Miss Gilchrist's I noticed a man standing on the pavement in front of the entrance to the house looking up at her windows. I paid particular attention to him.

The following night, 17 December I was taking my usual walk along the said street, when I saw the same man, accompanied by a man I believe to be Oscar Slater, standing at the same place, speaking together, I think in a foreign language. At that time they were both dressed alike. I stood a few yards from them till they parted, and I heard the man who I take to be Slater say to the other man, 'Goodnight, Nugent.' He then walked towards St George's Road. The other man remained at Miss Gilchrist's door.

On Sunday, 19 December between 7 and 8pm, I was again walking along West Princes Street, and when passing the residence of Miss Gilchrist I saw the man referred to come down the steps from the door of said premises. He had then the grey waterproof coat and the grey cap on. The cap was drawn well down over his eyes. He saw me and walked along the street toward Woodlands Road, I walked past him and he then turned back.

JEANETTA WALTERS' WINDOW-WATCHING MAN

Age:	About 27 years.
Height:	5 ft. 8 in.
Complexion:	Dark.
Build:	Ordinary.
Wearing:	Grey waterproof coat, grey cap.
	Dark shoes or boots.
	Gold albert across his breast and a gold ring on his finger
Comment:	Of Jewish appearance.

Detective Alexander Cameron, who took this woman's statement, expressed reservations. The witness was, in his opinion, of a low type, and not very reliable. Her former employer, John Gibson, told Cameron that Walters was 'a woman of no principle . . . She went out nightly and often hung about the close with men . . . She was a very untruthful, and certainly a dirty, useless woman'. He dismissed her for bringing men to the house.

The evidential strength of Jeanetta Walters' declaration was further vitiated by a neighbour of hers, Mrs Elizabeth Dow or Cameron, who not only said that she thought Walters was not trustworthy, but spoke of her having said that she knew Slater and the other man personally. She told of Walters going out and buying paper, writing and posting off a letter to the Chief Constable. As we shall see presently, Jeanetta Walters was not the only person to write fantasy-based letters to the authorities claiming unique and detailed knowledge of the *real* background to the West End murder.

We are on surer ground with the given in good faith testimony of Robert Brown Bryson, 45-year-old salesman. At about 7.40pm on Sunday, 20 December 1908, he and his wife were passing through Queen's Crescent and, turning the corner into West Princes Street, saw a man standing

> with his back up against the closed door of the close almost directly opposite Adams' and Gilchrist's houses. The man was looking straight across at the windows immediately above Adams' house. It was the intensity of the stare or gaze of the man at these windows that attracted my attention to him. The thought struck me at once that he intended to commit housebreaking . . . when he suddenly seemed to observe us . . . he became a bit nervous and at once held down his head a little, and then came down two or three steps from the close to the pavement, and walked past me westwards along West Princes Street. It was a clear night, but the time of night was dark. There is a lamp at the corner of Queen's Crescent, and also a lamp at Dr Adams' door, and by these, as well as by the clearness of the night I could see the man's face and appearance quite well.'

ROBERT BRYSON'S STARING MAN
Height: 5 ft. 7 in.
Complexion: Sallow.
Eyes: Small, dark, and piercing.
Moustache: Slight black moustache of a day or two's growth.
Build: Medium.
Wearing: Black jacket and vest, light-coloured trousers.
                   No overcoat.
                   Black felt hat.

Subsequently shown Slater, Bryson picked him out at once from a row of ten or twelve men – 'I had no doubt about him.'

Reliable, too, would seem to be the witness borne by Andrew Nairn. He also happened to be passing through Queen's Crescent and West Princes Street on the evening of Sunday, 20 December 1908, in his case at 9.15pm, some hour and a half after Mr Bryson. Nairn, a 38-year-old provision merchant, testified:

My wife and children were following some distance behind. On entering Queen's Crescent, I proceeded by the west side to West Princes Street. I then stood up to wait for my wife and children. I would be about 120 yards from Miss Gilchrist's house. My attention was attracted by a man standing about 12 or 13 yards off from me. He was on the north side of West Princes Street and looking in the direction of Miss Gilchrist's house. He seemed to be waiting for someone, or watching, and at the time I thought there was something suspicious about him. He kept his face away from me and I did not see it, but I took a particular look at his back.

ANDREW NAIRN'S WAITING MAN
Wearing: A light-coloured overcoat and a cap.

Nairn, being shown Slater, readily identified him as the Waiting Man – I have no doubt about him. His height, build and make of shoulders exactly correspond.'

By now, one surely has the feeling that *something* trickish was going on in and around that 'very quiet street'.

But there's more. Much more.

At about 3pm on Monday, 21 December 1908, John Mason Clunes, a 26-year-old unemployed draper's warehouseman, was

walking along West Princes Street on my way from my house – 34 Rupert Street – to the city. I was on the south side of the street, that is the same side as that on which the deceased Miss Gilchrist's house is situated. I was about 40 yards to the west of said house . . . when I noticed a man walking westward on the north side of the street. He was going in the opposite direction from me, and on the opposite side of the street. The man's face was familiar to me, and I know that I had seen him on several occasions, though I cannot remember where . . . I think, however, I had met him at Hamilton Race Meeting and at cattle shows at Cambuslang or Cathcart, probably in 1906 or 1907. I also think I had seen him previously in Argyle Street or elsewhere in Glasgow about the same time. I had never spoken to him, but I had formed the opinion that he was a person who frequented race meetings and made a living by games of chance. When I saw him in West Princes Street I was surprised, as I had not seen him in that district previously. He was walking slowly.

JOHN MASON CLUNES' PACING MAN

Age:	30-35 years.
Height:	5 ft. 9 in.
Complexion:	Dark. Clean-shaven.
Nose:	Twisted or flattened.
Hair:	Very dark.
Build:	Ordinary. Not very robust-looking.
Wearing:	Black morning-coat, dark trousers, black hat. Fairly well dressed

Next, Mrs Rowena Eliza Margaret Adams or Liddell, 48-year-old wife of George Liddell, a teacher. She said that on Monday, 21 December 1908, she had gone to visit her mother at 14 Queen's Terrace, West Princes Street.

> I came from St George's Road direction and was approaching to the steps to the door about 6.55pm when I observed a man leaning against the rail just opposite my mother's dining-room window. He was looking eastwards when I passed him, going right up to my mother's door. It flashed across my mind that he might be waiting as a loiterer, or he might be waiting on Miss Gilchrist's maid-servant, or, lastly, he might be waiting to see one of my sister's pupils home. I saw him leave and go eastwards and I passed into my mother's house.

MRS. ROWENA ADAMS OR LIDDELL'S LEANING MAN

Age:	30 years or less.
Height:	5 ft. 8 in.
Complexion:	Sallow. An unhealthy colour. Clean-shaven.
Nose:	Most peculiar. Long and tapering towards the mouth.
Wearing:	Brown mixed tweed overcoat. Tweed cap, well drawn over face. Dark clothes.

At about 7.10pm on 21 December in West Princes Street, Miss Agnes Brown, a schoolteacher, saw two running men, one of whom collided, or nearly collided, with her.

MISS AGNES BROWN'S RUNNING MAN No. 1

Age:	30 years.
Height:	5 ft 9 in
Complexion:	Clean-shaven.
Hair:	Dark.
Build:	Medium.
Wearing:	Three-quarter-length grey tweed overcoat. Dark tweed cap without flaps. Dark trousers, probably brown.

MISS AGNES BROWN'S RUNNING MAN No. 2

Age:	30 years.
Height:	5 ft. 9 in.
Hair:	Very dark, probably jet-black. Well-groomed and glossy.
Build:	Medium, but seemed 'squarer' than other man.
Wearing:	Navy-blue overcoat with velvet collar. Dark trousers. A stand-up white collar which seemed very clean. Black boots. Bare-headed.
Comment:	Carried something in his left hand; perhaps a walking stick, although it looked clumsier than that.

When, later, Slater was exhibited to her for identification, Miss Brown recognised him, she said, as Running Man No. 2, adding that he resembled 'a man whom I had seen repeatedly in Grant Street, always between 7 and 8pm'

27 year-old Miss Amelia Dewar and her sister, Elizabeth Alexandra Dewar, aged 22, were vouchsafed a glimpse of the Ordinary Walking Man at around 7.15pm on the evening of 21 December.

> My sister and I were in Great Western Road and called at a shop opposite Cromwell Street at about seven o'clock. We stood looking at some fancy boxes then for about five minutes more or less. Then we left and went along Great Western Road and up Melrose Street into Queen's Crescent. Immediately after entering Melrose Street, I observed a man coming meeting us, walking at an ordinary pace. The man was raised and excited

looking. He passed us by without remark. I did not look at him, but was struck by his face and expression. If he walked straight on, he would be in Great Western Road in less than a minute.

AMELIA DEWAR'S WALKING MAN

Age:	About 35 years.
Height:	5 ft. 9 or 10 in.
Complexion:	Clean-shaven.
Features:	Coarse and heavy.
Wearing:	Greeny-brown overcoat, either a waterproof or rainproof. A black pot hat. (That is a bowler hat.)

It was also around 7.15pm on 21 December that, according to William Grant Young , a 16-year-old apprentice pattern maker, that he and his friend James McGuire, aged 15, encountered two men walking in West Princes Street.

They were coming from the direction of St George's Road, and were on the same side of the street as Miss Gilchrist's house. They were walking at an ordinary pace. They were passing a lamp when I happened to notice them. I did not get a good look at their faces, but I might know their build and general appearance. In a minute or two after I had seen said men pass the lamp, I saw the girl Lambie come down the steps from Miss Gilchrist's house and speak to a policeman. She seemed to have a newspaper in her hand. The men were out of sight by this time. I heard the girl say, 'I wish I hadn't gone for the newspaper.' I also saw Adams with the girl.

WILLIAM GRANT YOUNG'S WALKING MEN
Man No. 1

Age:	25-28 years.
Height:	5 ft. 7 or 8 in.
Build:	Ordinary.
Wearing:	Dark overcoat.
	Dark bowler hat.

Man No. 2

Height:	5 ft. 7 or 8 in.
Wearing:	Dark overcoat.
	Dark clothes.
	Dark bowler hat.

Somewhat strange, too, was the tardily emergent witness, Mrs Minnie Lavinia Hayburn or Hamilton or Brown, aged 36. She, too, she averred, happened to be walking through that very quiet street at near enough a quarter-past seven on that crowded evening of 21 December 1908. From all accounts her reliability is not to be rated very highly. However, this is what she had to say: 'I am twenty-nine years of age[3] . . . Up to a short time ago I had a restaurant at 415 Argyle Street.' She was, she said, walking back to her restaurant after having visited a friend in Maryhill.

> After leaving Great Western Road, I went through Melrose Street, Queen's Crescent and into West Princes Street. I crossed to the opposite [south] side of the road. I was proceeding down West Princes Street when a man came running down so quickly that he knocked up against me and knocked me down. I saw him as he was coming down the steps . . . [He] ran on at full speed towards St George's Road. I did not see anyone else in the street at the time.

Indeed, the very quiet street seems on that December evening to have been positively chock-a-block with the purblind – the unseen Barrowman (apparently invisible to Adams and Lambie), who didn't see Agnes Brown, who wasn't seen by Young or McGuire, who didn't see Minnie Hayburn or Hamilton or Brown, who hadn't seen anyone!

MRS. MINNIE HAYBURN OR BROWN'S COLLIDING MAN

Height:	About medium.
Features:	Thin face.
Moustache:	Fair, heavy and pretty long at the points.
Build:	Slim.
Wearing:	A light waterproof with a wide sack back with no split in it, that came down to the top of brown leggings. A Donegal hat, pulled well over his eyes. Brown boots.

Having taken a good look at Slater's photograph in the newspaper, Mrs Brown commented: 'He is certainly not the man I saw running away that night.'

3 She was in fact born in Cardiff on 3 May 1873.

Finally, leaving West Princes Street, we must take into the reckoning Miss Annie Armour, the 19-year-old booking clerk's sighting at Kelvinbridge subway station, between 7.30 and 8pm on 21 December of the Hurrying Man, who, without speaking a word, threw down a penny for his train fare, rushed wildly through the turnstile, and plunged, stumbling and tumbling in great haste, down the stairs to the platform. He struck Miss Armour as being 'very frightened looking'. He had one hand – his left, she thought – in his coat pocket, and did not seem to be carrying anything. The view that she got of the man was all of the right-hand side of his face, his back and his head.

MISS ANNIE ARMOUR'S HURRYING MAN
Height: Medium.
Complexion: Dark. Clean-shaven.
Wearing: A light waterproof overcoat, with collar
              half turned up.
              Darkish hat or cap.
              A high collar – not sure whether single, double,
              or folding

Taken to see Slater in the line-up of a dozen, Miss Armour had no difficulty in picking him out as the Hurrying Man.

A grand total of 19 people testified to the disquieting presence in the very quiet street, or thereby. All smoke-clouds of witnesses? No fire? I cannot think that. But smoke gets in your eyes. It is practically impossible to see significance clearly.

Two things are certain. Some people *thought* to see the image of Oscar Slater in these 'apparitions' of the street. No one described anything like Dr Charteris' craggy, yet refined, Scottish features.

That some man – or men – *were* watching Miss Gilchrist's premises is surely indisputable. We shall in due course attempt to provide a likely explanation for the presence of these ghosts in the machine of abstract justice.

Chapter Sixteen

THE
LADIES
OF
LANARK

Following the central literary canon – that is: Roughead's *Trial*, 1910; Doyle's *The Case of Oscar Slater*, 1912; and Park's *The Truth About Oscar Slater*, 1927 – the first book to appear, nearly a quarter of a century later, was Peter Hunt's *Oscar Slater: The Great Suspect*, in 1951.

This book was written under Willie Roughead's close aegis, was indeed dedicated to him, and reflected, so far as the laws of libel permitted, for Dr Charteris was still very much alive and Emeritus Professor of Materia Medica in the University of St Andrews, Roughead's particular prejudices. Certainly, Hunt will have been privy to the 'open secret' that Dr Charteris did it. Indeed, on page 15 of the Introduction to the American edition of his book, published in August 1962, he writes:

> When this book first appeared some critics were tantalized because I
> hinted at the name of the man I believed to be guilty, without naming him.
> I make no apologies for that. It is one thing to believe that a man is guilty
> of murder and quite another to know that he is. If I had the necessary
> evidence I would present it to the authorities. As it is I have a name and a
> credible motive – beyond that I may not go. At the time of the murder the

police satisfied themselves that this man's alibi was in order. That is what they said.

Yet, on page 173 of the English edition, he writes, circa 1951, of A.B.: 'From what I have heard since, he had a cast-iron alibi.' But we know, from Charteris himself,[1] that his alibi was the exact opposite of cast-iron. He had, actually, no alibi at all. A canard has circulated that he was delivering a baby boy at the time of the commission of the crime. The story has its origin, so I have been told, in a scribbling which some person unknown pencilled in the margin of a copy of one of the newspapers preserved in the Mitchell Library in Glasgow.[2]

What, then, was Hunt's final conclusion? He writes[3]:

> My own studies also convince me that two men were involved. Whether they were complete strangers to Miss Gilchrist or well known to her, I am not prepared to say. Consideration of the first hypothesis . . . does not account for the box of scattered documents, the failure to pick up so many jewels which were lying about, the failure to pick the safe and Miss Gilchrist's known fear of intruders. The second hypothesis admits no consideration whatever at this stage. Perhaps fifty years hence, when all the gentlemen who may have been involved in the West Princes Street mystery are explaining themselves to a higher authority, there may then be cause for some more enterprising criminologist than I to plumb the almost unfathomable depths of the story. I can only say that, if he sets about it the right way, he will find some startling documentary evidence on which to base his case . . . There are still wise ones who say that Slater was guilty, and they are not confined to the readers of Sunday sensations. I have not come across one particle of fresh evidence which links him in any way with the case. I believe that the man who murdered Miss Gilchrist was – but that is another story.

I believe that those closing words of Peter Hunt's book are no more than a literary device. In a presentation copy of the volume which I possess he has written on the title-page:

> He was innocent.
> Peter Hunt.
> The real murderer was
> a man whose initials are R.B..

---

1 See page 255 – interview with Mowat Phillips.

2 Peter Costello provides Dr Charteris with his spurious alibi in *The Real World of Sherlock Holmes*, Page 121

3 See *Oscar Slater: The Great Suspect*, page 241

That seems to make it clear that, howsoever Roughead may have brainwashed him, Hunt did not subscribe to the belief in Charteris' blood-guilt.

But who is R.B.? B. for Birrell? Perhaps. But R.? The only person that I can call to mind connected with the case and bearing those initials was Robert Bryson, and I am confident that by no stretch of the imagination could he be transformed into Miss Gilchrist's killer. Sadly, Peter Hunt died young. I spoke with him on only one occasion and never found the chance to question him as to his true belief.

In a letter addressed to George Jacobs,[4] dated 1 April 1949, Hunt writes:

> I do not think there is any evidence for saying that A.B. was the murderer. Of course A.B. was mentioned by Lambie on the night, but I think two men were involved. One of them may have been him, but I have the clearest evidence to show, in private, that another person very close to the murderee might well have been involved. Nothing can be said along these lines at the moment, or for some years to come.

The innominate quarry of Hunt's chase remains, nearly fifty years on, mysterious, and, after as long a period of wide-ranging and in-depths research of my own, I am tempted to say apocryphal.

On the other hand, Hunt's view, which was also that of Roughead, David Cook and E Clephan Palmer, that two men were involved, I think is likely to be correct. I do not, however, share the additional gloss that it was most probably Dr Charteris who made a dignified exit through the lobby after the arrival of Lambie and Adams put an end to his foraging, and that the actual murderer made his escape by some other avenue. It was suggested that this second man might have hidden on the upper landing, outside the empty flat upstairs, or contrived to skulk inside that upper flat until the coast was clear for a rapid getaway down the main stairs. As a matter of fact, the police, alive to both these possibilities, made a thorough examination which disclosed no evidence of any such thing having happened.

Back in 1955, in his Preface to his book *Background to Murder*, my friend the late Nigel Morland wrote:

4 George Isidore Jacobs, a Glasgow businessman with a keen amateur interest in the Slater case.

Another case I have often been asked to re-present is that of Oscar Slater. I
shall oblige in my next book in this series . . . because it would not be
possible to exclude certain statements made to me some 17 or 18 years
ago by the late Ivor Back, a great surgeon and a remarkably kind man.
What he told me named by clear inference the instigator of the murder of
Miss Marion Gilchrist, a man who died some years ago in a notable odour
of sanctity.

Morland cannot, then, have had Dr Charteris in mind, for he was still
very much alive in 1955. He continues:

One further thought: the late William Roughead wrote that: 'And if as I
believe – and I am by no means singular in that persuasion – Helen
Lambie holds the key to the mystery, her refusal to "face the music" is, in
the interests of justice, the most regrettable feature of the late
proceedings.' In this I heartily concur with Roughead but not in his belief
that two men were concerned in the affair. There were three – the
instigator (who could walk in and out of Miss Gilchrist's, recognised but
unchallenged and erased from mind when questions were asked), the
'middleman', and the killer.

It was not until 11 years later that the 'next book in this series',
Pattern of Murder, came out, in 1966, but, as promised, it contained a
chapter on 'The Great Suspect'. What it did not contain was any
reference to Mr Ivor Back and his confidences.

Morland's own view, as here expressed, coincided with Edgar
Wallace's conclusion regarding the stranger in Miss Gilchrist's
apartment; namely that: 'Obviously Nellie Lambie knew him.' And,
Morland added, 'As obviously to my mind, the murderer was in the
house when she left to buy a newspaper.'

Early in 1956, Morland had received a letter, which he
subsequently passed on to me.

9 Romney Court,
Jameson Road,
Bexhill-on-Sea.
10/1/56

Dear Mr Morland
I have read *Background to Murder* with interest and am encouraged by the
Preface to pass on to you a sidelight on the Oscar Slater case.
At the time when it was clear that he would soon be released I was living
in a small country town near Glasgow where two rather flustered old ladies,
sisters, kept a confectionery shop.

Probably because I was a J.P. one of them came to me in great distress to
see if I could do anything to ensure that Slater was kept in prison. I replied
that I could not, as even if he were guilty, which I did not believe, he had
served more than the usual 'Life' sentence, and anyway my influence was
nil. She then murmured that he would be sure to kill her and her sister as
her brother was the Adams who was a witness. I assured her that the one
thing he would not do would be to risk being arrested again.

Then she said 'We never told about the man who came over the
window.' It seemed that while her brother was trying to get into Miss
Gilchrist's flat the two sisters saw a young man come down the pipe past
their sitting-room window. She said this was the son of a prominent
businessman and that he (the son) committed suicide shortly afterwards.

Oscar Slater was released shortly afterwards and did not attack the
old ladies so there was no need for me to do anything but I thought this
might be of interest to you.

Yours sincerely,

(Mrs) Agnes C. Findlay Wilson.

Research has shown that the lady who wrote this letter, Agnes
Cameron Findlay Wilson, was the daughter of Alex Findlay, the
grand old man of bridge-building, world-famous and responsible for
all the bridges on the West Highland Railway, and she was the
widow of William Scott Branks Wilson, a solicitor. She died in
February 1972, aged 87.

The 'small country town near Glasgow' was Lanark, where the
Adams family's unmarried womenfolk, having quit West Princes
Street by 1915 – although their brother continued to live in the old
home, and was found dead there in 1942 – had settled. They set up
house at Roselands, No. 16 Hyndford Road. Laura and her younger
sister, Octavia, kept a sweet shop in the High Street.

A careful search has failed to disclose either the existence or
identity of any young man of the type described by the Ladies of
Lanark who committed suicide in Glasgow around the material time.

What is of especial interest about the foregoing narrative is
that it disposes of the 'locked room' type murder, to which some
people have believed the West Princes Street crime to have
belonged. It is true that all the doors and windows of Miss Gilchrist's
apartment were found secured – *with the single exception of the kitchen
window, which was discovered open some two or three inches at the top*. That

means that someone *could* have raised the sash, clambered out of the lower part of the window, pulled the window down behind him, and descended by the adjacent rone pipe, passing over the Adams' back sitting-room window en route, as described.

Glasgow researcher, Andy Melbourne, brought to my notice the theory propounded by Archie C. A. Ogg, like George Isidore Jacobs, a Glasgow businessman, and like him one of those dedicated amateurs who have left spoor marks splaying across the archives of the Slater case. He is of the opinion that two men were involved in Miss Gilchrist's death, and that they escaped by the dunny.[5]

Ogg believes that, between Adams' two visits, Man No. 1 sent his accomplice, Man No. 2 (the killer), down to the dunny to wait. When Man No. 1 dashed down the stairs, he did *not* go out of the front-door of the close, but scampered back *up* the close, down the few steps, and out of the back, where he found the waiting Man No. 2, and the pair of them ran across the back green and scrambled over the wall, out into Down Lane, which runs between Grant Street and West Princes Street. Emerging at the end of Down Lane into West Cumberland Street, they turned right and ran to the corner of West Cumberland Street and West Princes Street, stopping momentarily to look back towards No. 49, before resuming their running in a westerly direction.

They may well have been the two men seen by the teacher, Agnes Brown, who watched them turn to the left out of West Cumberland Street, run up West Princes Street, turn right into Rupert Street, and pelt through it to Great Western Road.

The schoolmistress' report somewhat upset the police applecart, for it meant that if what she was saying was right, then their star witness, Mary Barrowman, was wrong. Thus it was that Item No. 1047 seems to have been quietly, almost surreptitiously, slipped into page 262 of the police Information Book[6] and thereafter overlooked 'by a mistake on purpose', as it were. It is the record of

5 The basement floor leading out on to the back green.
6 Lodged in the Strathclyde Regional Archives. Item SR 22/63/10 is described as 'Information Book 1908-1909'. It is inscribed upon its spine 'No. 475 Information Book Within Bounds. From 5th December, 1908: To 5th January, 1909.'

a visit paid at half-past seven on the evening of Saturday, 26 December 1908, to the Northern Police Office.

> Reported by Agnes Brown (24) a teacher residing c/o McGregor, 60 Grant Street, that about 7.10pm on Monday, 21 December 1908, while she was in West Princes Street, she saw two men running from the direction of 15 Queen's Terrace.

Miss Brown subsequently enlarged upon her experience. The first words of her first fuller statement conflict with the personal details previously recorded. She now says: 'I am thirty years of age and reside at 48 Grant Street, Glasgow.' The discrepancy is puzzling. The revised statement continues:

> At 7.08pm I left the house there to attend evening classes in Dunard Street School. I went along Grant Street and turned into West Cumberland Street. I then walked north along the east side of that street till I came to the corner of West Cumberland Street and West Princes Street. I was in the act of stepping off the foot pavement there to cross West Princes Street, at an angle towards Carrington Street (a north-westerly direction), when two men came running along from the direction of St George's Road, and passed behind me. They were going very quickly. I stood for a moment at the corner of Carrington Street to see where they went. I remember that the time at which I saw them was about ten minutes past seven. I fix this time because I should have left the house at seven to be in time for my class, and was late that evening and was hurrying. In crossing Great Western Road I saw the time on a clock in a chemist's shop – Wilson & Wood's, 147 Great Western Road – and it was then 7.12pm.
>
> The first I heard of the murder was when I returned home from my classes. I got back to the close leading to my house shortly after ten o'clock. I met my two sisters. They stated that they had heard that a murder had taken place in West Princes Street. I went round with them and saw a crowd and heard of the murder from the crowd. On the way home I mentioned to my sisters that I had seen two men running away. I also mentioned this at home. I did not at the time associate the two men with the murder, but next morning after reading a description in the *Glasgow Herald* of a man who was said to have left the deceased's house, I thought he might be one of the two referred to.

It seems odd that, despite their alleged chiming presences in West Princes Street, Miss Brown caught no glimpse or echo of Mary Barrowman's running man.

With this timetable in mind, one should recall PC Neill's statement that at 7.15pm he 'passed the house [No. 49] about 6-7 minutes before'. That would be between 7.08 to 7.09. Remember,

Neill was coming *from* west to east, and therefore had at least 250 yards to go with a clear view of the street before him at pretty well exactly the time that Adams saw him 'in the distance'. Mary Barrowman also, at this time, *ought* to have been seen running after *her* running man, who had pushed against her.

Obviously, we are entering here into territory of very considerable dubiety. Things are far from being as black and white, cut and dried, as they did at one time seem. In succeeding chapters it will be necessary, in pursuit of some measure of reasonable certainty, to call forth the witness of all the experts on the case who have materialised since the pioneers laid down their pens.

Chapter Seventeen

THE HOUSE THAT JACK BUILT

Jack House was already a Glasgow journalist of wide renown in the town when he turned to the Slater case. There had been other journalists there before him.

In 1952, a barrister who had taken up the practice of journalism, Edgar Lustgarten, had entered the Slater lists. In the September of that year he was writing a series of articles, 'Woman in the Case', in *Reynolds News*. For him, Nellie Lambie was, as Irene Adler to Sherlock Holmes, *the* woman. And her *bona fides* were made the subject of an exceptionally devastating attack – a regular slatering, you could say.

Clearly pro-Oscar, he wrote that one would not have expected a lass like her to lend herself to the furtherance of a trumped-up murder charge. She was not, in his character evaluation, either a rogue or a fool. She was not in dread of the police because of something in her past, nor had she any illusions as to the impact of her actions upon the future – Slater's future, or rather, curtailment thereof. She had defects. She seemed conceited, self-opinionated, pert at times to the point of insolence, but, equally, she had always, when it came to it, proved herself trustworthy and capable.

Lustgarten points out that,

Slater and the criminal were admittedly alike (we have Adams' word that there was 'a close resemblance') and it may be, after so much concentrated priming, Helen did *suspect* – as she put it at first – that Slater was the man. And being a vain and mulish little madam, having once plumped for a particular view, she would fight tooth and nail to get that view upheld. In her limited and egocentric vision, the real issue at the trial was not 'Is Slater guilty?' but 'Is Helen Lambie right?' And no smart lawyer was going to prove her wrong.

Lustgarten was not alone in the harbouring of unflattering thoughts about Nellie. The trial judge called her 'superficial and unreflective'. Craigie Aitchison appraised her as 'untruthful' and 'unscrupulous'. William Roughead said that she was 'ignorant and irresponsible'.

Lustgarten saw Slater as the victim of an organised conspiracy; his prosecution as the supreme example in British legal history of a manufactured case – 'a lasting monument of shame to those who manufactured'. It is his feeling that although the names of functionaries stand highest on that monument, 'inscribed there also in perpetuity is that of a young woman who, through vanity and pride and thoughtlessness, served their design more faithfully than she knew'.

I think that the defence-minded Mr Lustgarten is decidedly overstating his case here. We shall have considerably more to say in respect of Nellie Lambie's true beliefs later on.

The first footings of the positive edifice which Jack House was to raise over the next three decades were dug in shifting sand. The foundation was laid down in the autumn of 1954 in a lengthy series, 'Glasgow's Square Mile of Murder', which he contributed to the Glasgow *Evening News*, the last five parts of which, published 4-8 October, dealt with the Slater case.

'Was Oscar Slater the Scottish Dreyfus?' he asked. 'Was he an innocent man round whom the authorities bound a chain of "evidence", and whom they kept in prison in order, to put it politely, to save trouble?'

And he answered his own question.

'In my opinion he was. I believe many people in the Glasgow Police and among the Crown officials knew in their hearts that Oscar Slater was not guilty. But with a single exception, they thought it better to keep their mouths shut.'

House then presents what I can only suppose to be a deliberate false clue. He confides to his reader that 'one particular and somewhat distinguished' name has been bandied about Glasgow for years. This man he describes as 'an important official, but also a rather raffish character', and adds that there are many people who will tell you that he is the real murderer of Marion Gilchrist. 'In fact,' says House, 'he was as innocent as Slater.' So all this hope-raising verbiage swiftly cancels itself out.

But next we are given House's theory as to what *really* happened that drizzly December night.

Two men called on Miss Gilchrist. Their object neither robbery nor murder. It was merely to get possession of some document, say a will, or proof of illegitimacy, or legitimacy for that matter. They wait until Lambie goes out for the evening paper. Then ring the bell. Miss Gilchrist lets them in without hesitation. She knows them. They have been in her house before. One man hustles her into the 'parlour'. The other goes straight into the spare bedroom, lights the gas and prepares to search for the document. Miss Gilchrist faces up to the first man in the parlour. There is an angry scene. In sudden rage the man strikes her. The old lady falls back and hits her head on the fender. Though losing consciousness, she gives the signal to the Adams family below, knocking three times on the floor with her heels. Her assailant sees this signal, realises that she will be able to identify her attacker. He lifts a chair and, kneeling on her chest, uses one of the legs of the chair to smash the old lady's head. Arthur Adams comes up and rings the bell. Getting no response to his ringing, he goes back to his own house. While the coast is clear the murderer flees. House has him exit down the staircase and out of the front-door of the close into the empty street. All this time the other man is in the spare room searching for the elusive document.

He hears the stramash in the parlour, but carries on searching. Then Helen Lambie opens the door. He decides to brave it out, walks through the lobby, dashes down the stairs, out of the front-door and away into the night. Lambie does not say a word, because, like Miss Gilchrist, she knows him as a perfectly respectable visitor to the house.

This piece of pure fiction has, over the years, become the received truth.

Mr House defends it:

This theory fits every single bit of evidence in the Gilchrist murder case. The original descriptions given by witnesses were of two men, and they were described as young and gentlemanly. A private detective in Glasgow went to police headquarters with information as to the real identity of the murderer, and was told to go away and mind his own business. One thing is perfectly obvious. Helen Lambie knew the man she saw in the lobby that night.

Four years later, in December 1958, House comes back for another six bites at the cherry, and adds a further storey to the house of cards he was busily building. In a six-part series, 'Oscar Slater: The Facts at Last' – 15-20 December – contributed this time to the Glasgow *Evening Times*, poor old Paddy Nugent got it! House revealed that Slater himself had suggested that Lambie's boyfriend, Patrick Nugent, should be investigated. He had not said that Nugent had committed the murder, but he thought that Nellie might have told him about her mistress' jewels – in fact, she had – and that Nugent might have told a pal.

Next, House resuscitates the 'dead' Lambie. There is, he says, 'only one person alive who can deny what I have to say – Helen Lambie, now 71, and living in the north of England'. And yet in his previous article of 4 October 1954, House had written that Helen Lambie died without revealing a word as to the identity of A.B..

Accompanying the 1954 article there had been a picture captioned as being that of Helen Lambie 'taken in 1929, when she was 41'. It has been used many times since and in many places: it is actually a photograph of Minnie Hayburn or Hamilton or Brown.

Writing in 1958, with a new note of positivism, House tells his readers that, although *he* knows their names, because the two men involved in the murder are survived by their families in Glasgow, he is not going to reveal them –

> Even though a relative of one of them came to me not long ago and said,
> 'We know that Uncle did the murder.' Strangely enough he was wrong.
> 'Uncle' was the A.B. of the Slater case, and A.B. did not commit the murder.

House is here claiming that he was approached by one of the Charterises' nephews.

His next disclosure is that Miss Gilchrist gave birth to an illegitimate daughter, and that she kept this daughter with her as a servant for some time. The daughter then got married and had a baby girl. 'Miss Gilchrist was very fond of her daughter, and even for der of her granddaughter. She made a will leaving most of her money and estate to them. This did not make her popular with the rest of the family.'

What House writes can only refer to Mrs Ferguson and Marion Gilchrist Ferguson, but as we have already seen, no doubt exists as to Maggie Galbraith or Ferguson's Barra parentage.

House now improves upon the detail of his 1954 theory. The 'two men' who called on Miss Gilchrist become 'two young men close relatives of Miss Gilchrist'. New circumstantial details – totally devoid of any substantiating evidence – are supplied. These two young men

> discussed the position. They were in the house of the mysterious A.B.. He
> was one of the young men and we'll call the other C.. They determined to
> face Miss Gilchrist and extract from her a paper which would be valuable
> to them. It's possible, too, that they'd been watching Miss Gilchrist's flat for
> some time to find out the best moment for a private visit.'

Why then, one wonders, choose the ten minutes, if that, when the servant was out getting an evening paper, instead of the matter of hours available while Lambie was away on her afternoon or evening off?

> Some time before seven o'clock that night they left A.B.'s house [situated
> at 400 Great Western Road] by the back garden and a lane, and made their
> way to 49 West Princes Street. They waited till they saw Helen Lambie
> leave the flat, and then rang the bell. Normally, she would open the door
> to her relatives, even if she didn't like them. This explains the mysterious
> entry.

House then makes the most extraordinary statement.

> I should explain that C. suffered from epileptic fits. Not the serious kind,
> but more like the Adolf Hitler sudden-rage type. Under the influence of

> such a fit C. was capable of doing anything and not realising its
> consequence. C. lost his temper with Miss Gilchrist and struck her . . .
>
> When Lambie opened the flat door and the man walked across the
> hall, she showed no surprise.
>
> Why should she? She knew A.B. was a relative of Miss Gilchrist's
> and had seen him in the flat before that night . . . A.B. ran down the stairs,
> was joined by C., and they both ran back along West Princes Street and up
> Rupert Street to get into the lane behind A.B.'s house. They were seen just
> then by the schoolteacher, Agnes Brown – a key witness, who was not
> called. The Crown were satisfied with Mary Barrowman, the wee message
> girl. And so A.B. and C. got back to A.B.'s house and were sitting there,
> quite joco, when the police arrived to make inquiries. They could assure
> the police they had never left the house all evening.

This is utter nonsense. There was never any question of the police's
having paid a visit to Dr Charteris' house on the night of 21
December.

> But Mr House will not desist.
>
> In Victorian and Edwardian days the great thing was to be respectable. The
> Glasgow police just could not conceive that any such respectable chaps as
> A.B. and C. had anything to do with the brutal murder of Miss Marion
> Gilchrist.

In the days of Elizabeth II, the great thing was to be circumspect
regarding the perils of defamation. Thus, in the sixth and final part
of his 'Oscar Slater: The Facts at Last' series, 20 December 1958,
House declared: 'The two men I wrote of yesterday, when I
presented my reconstruction of what happened in Miss Gilchrist's
flat on the night of 21 December 1908, are dead.'

Untruth, it would seem, as well as discretion, is the better part
of valour.

In 1961 Mr House decided that his news-sheet labour was
worthy of more permanent preservation between hard covers.
Messrs W & R Chambers, apparently agreeing, issued the 253-page,
full dress, bound version of *Square Mile of Murder*. It was to become
his best-known book. Its subject was those four outstanding
Glasgow murder cases – Madeleine Smith, Jessie McLachlan, Dr
Edward William Pritchard, and Oscar Slater – of which he had
treated in his newspaper series. His accounts of the first three cases
were in the main unexceptionable. His study of the Slater affair,
titled 'The Man Who Didn't', fell, alas, a shade or two short, while, at

THE OSCAR SLATER MURDER STORY

the same time, advancing a league or two too far along a dubious route.

The account rendered in the first edition is, generally speaking, the same as that previously presented in the newspaper versions, but a few extra mistakes are introduced. Nothing really major, but worrying evidence of carelessness as to details. Miss Gilchrist's age is given as 83. Lambie is sent off to collect an *Evening News* instead of an *Evening Citizen*. Arthur Adams is said to have been a flautist in the Scottish Orchestra. (There is no mention of his name in the Scottish Orchestra records.) Oscar is said, incorrectly, to have died on 3 February, 1948, at the age of, also incorrect, 75.

But there are compensatory revelations. Many years after the trial, says House, Mary Barrowman turned up at 'a certain house in Glasgow' – sadly, we are never told *which* – wanting to confess. She had not been in West Princes Street at all on the night of the murder. Her mother, who was an alcoholic, had made her tell the story so that she could share in the reward. The one drawback to this fascinating insight is that at the time when Mary Barrowman first told her story no reward was on offer.

House's reconstruction of the crime remains much the same. A 't' is crossed here, an 'i' dotted there. The two men – A.B. and C. – are the same, but now *either* Nellie Lambie let them in before she went out, *or* they arrived soon after she left. And House supplies a reason why we know that two men were involved. If, he says, the man who lit the gas in the bedroom with the Runaway Matches had been the murderer, then his hands would inevitably have been bloodstained. Since no marks of blood were found on the casket, the matches, or anywhere in the room, he cannot have been the killer. And A.B.'s mission is here, for the first time, hailed as successful – 'In the back bedroom A.B. had found the document at last.'

Who says so? W*hat* document?

Now, C. is no longer down 'in the back green' or 'across West Princes Street', but 'waiting on the landing above'.

Again, who says so?

The second edition of *Square Mile of Murder* appeared in 1975.

By then Dr Charteris was 11 years' dead, and people could, and did, attack his *post mortem* reputation with courageous impunity.

> When this book was first published, I put forward my theory. Since then I have realised I was wrong. The difficulty with this case is the identification of A.B., the mysterious man who walked through the lobby past Nellie Lambie and Arthur Adams and was supposed to have done the murder. He has been identified over the years with a Dr Charteris, a nephew of Miss Gilchrist's.[1]
>
> When, many years after the murder, he was asked if he was A.B., he denied it completely. But, of course, what he was denying was that he had murdered Miss Gilchrist, because all through the case, AB is supposed to have been the murderer.

It is absurd for Jack House to say that Charteris denied that he was A.B.. As we have seen, the term A.B. signified Dr Charteris – nothing more, nothing less. House's equating of the term A.B. with 'the mysterious man who walked through the lobby past Nellie Lambie and Arthur Adams' betrays a dangerous confusion.

House also fails to make the crucial point that Charteris stated that, at the time that the murder was committed, he was at his own house in Great Western Road. He was not making any limited admission or confession of partial guilt. What he was saying, politely, loud and admirably clear, was that he was elsewhere at the time of the killing and had had nothing to do with it. 'But,' House continues, 'if you think it out carefully, you must realise that the man who walked through the lobby, call him by any initials you like, was not the murderer. Let me spell out the theory I have come to over many years . . .'

Then, like a cony out of a gibus, Mr House magically produced Mr Austin Birrell.

> Now, as I see it, two men called together on the night of the murder. They were, I believe, relatives – the aforesaid Dr Charteris and a man named Austin Birrell. It's not real proof of course, but I have met a nephew of Austin Birrell's, who told me that the whole family knew that Uncle Austin had done the murder.

It is to be observed that Mr House appears to have had the happy knack of meeting up with the loquacious nephews of the putative assassins of Miss Gilchrist, for had he not reported 20-odd years before that a nephew of A.B.'s had come and told him, 'We know

1   Which, as we have already noted, he was not.

that Uncle did the murder'? Austin Birrell, verily, but entirely coincidentally, bearing the initials A.B., is endowed with the epileptiform fits formerly ascribed to C., and the theory as to the shape of events on the night of the murder remains unaltered, save for the fact that now, instead of running rapidly downstairs after the murder, Austin Birrell went

> upstairs to the landing where the flat was unoccupied . . . waiting on the landing above, he saw Charteris leave, followed him, and the two ran along West Princes Street to Charteris' house. They were not seen by Mary Barrowman, because Mary Barrowman, as we know now, was never there. They were seen by Agnes Brown, the schoolteacher.

Alastair Phillips, that doughty Scots journalist and indefatigable chronicler of the Slater and Trench causes, wrote, in the course of a lively piece in the *Glasgow Herald*, on 15 February 1975, beguilingly titled 'The Case of the Dedicated Detective':

> Among the fairy tales that have been current among the local experts wanders a dingy and demented character full of remorse by the name of Austin Birrell. This is the imaginary A.B., a person of whom there is no true record, and who almost certainly never existed.

Now the man who begat Austin Birrell was Jack House, in the fifth article in his Glasgow *Evening Times* series, 'Oscar Slater: The Facts at Last', 19 December 1958. He did not, however, put a name to him until 1975, when he brought out the second edition of *Square Mile of Murder*.

I myself conducted a really deep-raking archival search for this sinister and unwholesome personage, whom I remember House telling me he had had pointed out to him as Austin Birrell, and whom thereafter he used to see from time to time on the streets of Glasgow. He described him, memorably, as having a weird stretch of dark, 'dead-looking' skin on the back of his head and neck. I could find not the flimsiest breath of evidence that – under the name of Austin Birrell – he ever existed.

I put my conclusion fairly and squarely to my friend House that Austin Birrell was a sort of Glaswegian *fata Morgana*, and he most carefully explained to me the genesis of this phantasmagoric being as having been presented to him in convincing detail by the man's own nephew.

The name of this nephew, I elicited, was Alexander

Macdonald Sommerville. He lived at No. 2 Grenville Drive, Cambuslang, Glasgow, and was chairman and managing director of Sommerville & Milne, Ltd, a Glasgow advertising agency. He had, I discovered, died in Hairmyres Hospital, East Kilbride, on 25 August 1953, aged 58. I managed, however, to track down a relative of his, Mrs Elizabeth Tulloch, who, interviewed, said that, so far as she knew, the late Mr Sommerville had never had any particular interest in the Slater case. On the other hand, yes, he had been a larger than life character, a leg-puller with a great sense of humour. He was also a notable raconteur, and the story of someone called Austin Birrell being his uncle and the killer of Miss Gilchrist was just the sort of tale he could have dreamed up.

I duly communicated this intelligence to Jack House, and from that day forward Austin Birrell was expunged from the House guest list of suspects.

Not so, unfortunately, in the case of the authors, George Forbes and Paddy Meehan, of *Such Bad Company*, issued by Paul Harris Publishing, Edinburgh, in April 1982. The book, telling the story of the 'long and bloody saga of Glasgow criminality' – the Neds and all that – paints, in the words of the *Scotsman's* critic, George Saunders, 'a very vivid picture of the Glasgow underworld'. The Slater case, however, figuring as Chapter 5, 'The Judas Goat', goes back a long, long way, and must of necessity have relied upon hearsay. By line six, Austin Birrell has been resurrected. In this incarnation he is – shades of Nigel Morland and the Misses Adams – 'the son of a prominent city businessman'. His companion, watching and waiting round Miss Gilchrist's flat at 14 [sic] Queen's Terrace, is Dr Charteris, 'a nephew of the old woman'.

As it was in the beginning, so it is the whole way through. Lambie has supplied these two relatives of 83-year-old [sic] Aunt Marion with a duplicate set of keys. Having poisoned the watchdog, they plan to steal a newly-made will which leaves their aunt's considerable fortune to her illegitimate daughter. These two quietly enter the premises, using their duplicate keys, and start searching the spare bedroom for the casket containing the will. But Miss Gilchrist, ever alert, caught them at it. Austin Birrell thereupon dragged her into the dining-room and, in an epileptic frenzy, bludgeoned her. He escaped out of the back window, shinning down a drain-pipe. More shades of Morland! Charteris, who had finally found the will, walked calmly past Lambie and Adams, met up with Birrell in the street outside, and the two of them ran off to Charteris' house nearby, to clean up, change their clothes and await, composed and prepared to act as each other's alibi, what they thought would be the imminent arrival of the police.

But to be fair, Jack House had, by 1982, following my long and earnest chat with him, jettisoned 'poor Austin'. His new view as to the 'onlie begetter' of the West Princes Street tragedy was echoed in an article, 'A Very Respectable Murder', by Maggie Allen, published in the *Scottish Field* in June 1987.

By now, Austin Birrell is away with the fairies, whence he should never have been summoned in the first place. In his stead, at Dr Charteris' side, stands the doctor's brother, Archibald (who had as much to do with the affair as John Betjeman's teddy bear, Archie!), a prominent solicitor and lecturer in law at the University of Glasgow.

The guiding hand of Miss Allen's Slaterian mentor seems plain. She had, by the way, been the script editor of a BBC 1 television programme, *The Trials of Oscar Slater*, which had been put out on 10 and 17 July 1980, as the two final parts of a series based on House's *Square Mile of Murder*. The illegitimate daughter fallacy is repeated. The Charteris brothers visit Miss Gilchrist – who would, of course, admit them – to ask for the reinstatement as heiress of their half-sister, Mrs Mary Greer Gilchrist or McCall. Charteris is now searching, not for a will or legitimacy document, but for the letter to his aunt in which he had arranged the meeting. The article, quite incorrectly, avers that Charteris 'shortly before his death, at the age of 90 in 1963 [sic], admitted that he *had* been the man in the hall seen by Lambie'.

Miss Allen's impeachment of the brothers Charteris seems very shaky, although it was not without its appeal to those who look for a class-based solution. She holds to the familiar theory – favoured by Trench among others – that there was a furious family row over Miss Gilchrist's will, and informs us that a month before the murder the old lady added a codicil cutting out Mary McCall.

Now Miss Gilchrist's will, that subject of so much ill-founded speculation, rests in Register House, Edinburgh, for all to see. A look at it instantly reveals that what Miss Allen says is wrong. Nobody was in fact disinherited by that November 1908 codicil. Mrs McCall, together with her two children, receive substantial legacies, unaffected by the provisions of the codicil.

Miss Allen claims that a police cover-up operation directed that the Charteris brothers' names be kept out of all reports. Yet I have before me a copy of Detective Inspector John Pyper's precognition. In it, he states that both brothers have been seen and that 'they do not resemble the description given of the man wanted'.

Miss Allen believes, too, that she has discovered a new cover-up for the respectable Charterises. This concerns the schoolteacher, Agnes Brown. Miss Brown positively identified Slater as one of her two men. It is virtually axiomatic that she was not called to give evidence at the trial because her testimony, showing Slater running in the wrong direction, would have cancelled out that of the prosecution star witness, Mary Barrowman. According to Miss Allen, the two fleeing men were the brothers Charteris. She also claims, absolutely wrongly, that 'No relevant report survived or was published'. Actually, Miss Brown's statement was sent to New York for Slater's extradition proceedings, and she gave further evidence at the Secret Inquiry of 1914. Her statements are preserved in official archives, and, in any case, are reproduced in Roughead's *Trial* volume.

Finally, Miss Allen sees the Charteris brothers' respective career moves – Francis to St Andrews and Archie to Australia – made more than ten years after the murder, as flights from justice!

During Heritage Week 1988, Jack House delivered, on 6 June a lunch-time talk on the Slater case at Hutchesons' Hall in John Street, Glasgow, in which he announced that the actual murderer was a man named Archibald Charteris!

That was really Jack House's swan-song. He died, on 11 April 1991, aged 84, in Glasgow's Western Infirmary, where, so many years before, the young Dr Francis Charteris had been an assistant house physician.

The wheel had somehow turned full circle.
It felt like the end of an era.

Chapter Eighteen

THE SECRETS OF LOT 631

Lot 631 was stuffed carelessly away on a shelf in the New Bond Street saleroom of the famous London auction house of Sotheby's. No wise prepossessing, it lay, a grimy white folder bulging with some 78 letters and postcards, inconspicuously there for would-be bidders to examine that sale afternoon of Wednesday, 7 December 1966.

James Laing of the *Scottish Daily Mail*, who attended the sale, wrote an 'eye-witness' piece. The bulk of the letters – holograph – were, he reported, from Sir Arthur Conan Doyle to William Park, and, of course, were concerned with the Slater case. They were written from London, Crowborough in Sussex, and Minstead in the New Forest, Hampshire, between 1925 and 1928. The correspondence was not arranged in any sort of order, and, indeed, only one letter bore a specific date; and that was a letter of no chronological significance anyway, referring to nothing more than its author's state of health – 'a little under the weather'.

Doyle's cramped, sloping handwriting and the patchily fading ink rendered the letters difficult to read. But it was worth making the effort at decipherment – if only to know what 'Sherlock Holmes' really thought about the case.

In one, Doyle wrote: 'I have never been satisfied with the Charteris situation.' This is most interesting as confirmation absolute that Doyle and Park were not only aware of the true identity of A.B., but must have discussed the subject at length.

Two further letters provide what Laing describes as 'a startling indication of Conan Doyle's confidence that Dr Charteris was involved'. He asks Park:

> Are you sure Dr C. is still alive? Don't you think some Pressman will get at him one of these days and ask his opinion? I would imagine a suicide and a written confession to be a possible end of the whole matter. He must lead a very jumpy life.

'The letters reveal the torments of indecision and the frustration of the two men,' writes Laing. Doyle tells Park: 'You will be the hero when this is cleared up' and 'I was told from spirit séances a little while ago that it was all about to be cleared up.'

Laing talks of 'a mysterious man named as the 'Bookie' [who] flits through two letters with sinister but vague reference'. This was actually Nellie Lambie's short-term boyfriend, Patrick Nugent.

'I never could see why Lambie should perjure herself up to the eyes to save Dr Charteris,' mused Doyle, 'but I see very clearly why she should do so in order to save her lover and also why she did not give him away at the door.' She, by the way, seems to Laing, from the context of one of the letters, obviously to have consented at one stage to 'confess' – although he thinks the references in the letters to this confession are vague. 'I don't know how far it will help us,' Doyle writes. 'If we could find who paid the hush money then indeed we would be on the track.'

Laing feels that 'That remark, the sinister 'Bookie', along with reference to a 'secret document', scream for speculation.' The secret document will be the one referred to by Doyle in another of the letters.

> I was looking at the sheet from the police book the other day – the one he [Trench] tore out . . . You will have observed that there is the sentence, 'The clue was first received against Slater and was not stronger than

against the other suspects.' What was originally typed was 'not nearly so strong as' . . . this was clearly thought to be a dangerous admission so it has been obliterated but it is still legible and the word 'stronger' substituted. Of course some might, and would, say that the torn leaf is in favour of the police as showing that they had honestly probed the possibility of the relatives being involved. What I can't make out is if Dr Charteris did it, then why should they shelter Dr C. and select a scapegoat? That is the one obscure point in all our case and it is a vital one.

Doyle wonders whether Lambie had herself been involved in the affair: 'If she was cognisant of contemplated crime (and her entering the drawing-room[1] last of all looked as if she was giving the fugitive time to escape) then all becomes clear.'

But things did not become clear: 'As you say, it the case against Slater] is a perfect cesspool of lies and villainy. We must be persistent and we shall get through.'

Also in the sale were two letters from Slater – to Park and Doyle respectively – both written after his release and full of thanks. Later, though, Slater was to reject Doyle and refuse to repay him out-of-pocket expenses. Doyle wrote: 'O.S. is obviously mad.'

After Slater was set free, Conan Doyle and William Park were justified in their work. But they still had no answers to the thousands of questions and doubts that arose about the case. In one letter Doyle wrote: 'There is a providence and a reason for all things. We may see it some day.'

The forthcoming sale had inspired Jack House to pen some further *prose d'occasion* – in the Glasgow *Evening Times* of 5 December 1966.

I have seen these letters and the other documents, and I'll be surprised if there is not some keen bidding on Wednesday (6 December), especially from American criminologists and collectors. The Oscar Slater case is nearly as well known in America as it is in Scotland. In the letters Doyle mentions by name a Glasgow man who was long suspected of carrying out the crime . . . He was Dr Francis James Charteris.

House proceeded then to examine the effect of these letters put up for sale as 'The Property of a Gentleman', and goes on to disclose the name of Miss Gilchrist's alleged illegitimate daughter, Mrs Ferguson, the 'former servant'. In a second article in the following

1 This should be the dining-room.

day's *Evening Times* (6 December 1966) he wrote:

> They [Doyle, Park and Roughead] thought that there were two men
> involved in the murder. I suggest that they were two men in the habit of
> calling Miss Gilchrist 'Auntie Mirren', although the doctor's [Charteris]
> relationship was a far-out one.[2]

House also says:

> In my opinion, only Nellie Lambie can tell us who A.B. was. A nephew of
> hers was a former doorman at the Citizens' Theatre in Glasgow, and he told
> me that it was common knowledge in the family that Auntie Nellie was
> going to release the truth after her death.
>
> Two London reporters [Fagence and MacNab] traced Nellie Lambie
> down, but she would not speak to them . . . If my theory is correct, and
> Charteris was one of the two men in the flat, then he was the murderer. If
> he was indeed A.B., then Nellie Lambie can tell us, and the murderer was
> the other man. And who was the other man? Well, there is a businessman
> in Glasgow who has told me that his family are convinced they know the
> murderer of Miss Gilchrist and that it was a relative of his. Where confusion
> in this already confused case arises is that this man's initials were actually
> A.B. His second name was Birrell.[3]
>
> If I had the money, I'd be bidding for Lot 631 at Sotheby's
> tomorrow. Not only for the Conan Doyle letters, but for the one which
> Oscar Slater wrote to William Park. In it Slater says that he feels it was Park
> who was the mainspring in getting him released and that he encloses a
> little gift in gratitude. The 'little gift' was £200.

'Sold! to the Man Who Doesn't Care.' That was the headline in the
Scottish Daily Mail on the morning of 8 December, bringing the news
that Lot 631 had been knocked down the previous day for £800. The
buyer, Mr Lew David Feldman, was a dealer from New York. He
bought the letters undramatically in a small series of bids made by
merely raising his eyebrows. They were to go back with him to his
rare books, manuscripts and works of art establishment – The
House of El Dief, 139 East 63rd Street, New York.

Wrote Charles Greville:

> I was rather disappointed that no veiled lady in black or tight-lipped
> Scottish gentleman from Glasgow was bidding for them to protect a long-
> dead reputation. Sir Arthur – since he was writing at a time when most of
> the people involved were still alive – was sometimes indiscreet in his
> speculations. All of this seemed of little concern to Mr Feldman. 'I am

---

2 I have found no evidence of the existence of any nephews who called Miss Gilchrist
by this name.

3 This is the coming event. Austin Birrell casting a shadow before!

possibly the world's greatest connoisseur of Arthur Conan Doyle,' he said after the sale. 'What's in the letters doesn't matter.'

Nearly a quarter of a century more was to elapse before further and, hopefully, better revelations would be forthcoming regarding the still tantalisingly mysterious Slater affair.

The year 1989 had opened up promisingly with the unsealing of the secret files, that is the scheduled release, on 1 January, under the reduction of the hundred-year closures to the 75 year rule, of a batch of Slater case papers.

'Fresh Light is Cast on Crimes of Century' ran the over-optimistic headline in the *Scotsman* of Monday, 2 January, wherein Robbie Dinwoodie reported the outcome of his press preview examination of the newly released documents. One could see now, he told readers, the Crown Office correspondence after the trial, among which was Lord Guthrie's submission agreeing that Slater's death sentence should be commuted, and defending his own handling of the trial. Other material made public for the first time included the Duke Street Prison diaries, in which the death-watch warders had recorded the hour-by-hour demeanour of the doomed man throughout his 18 agonising days in the condemned cell before the eleventh-hour news of his reprieve from the rope arrived.

Hope of discovering anything really significant in these new releases diminished as one read steadily on. That was the general feeling. However, as we shall hear presently, nestling in those freshly opened files were certain papers – anonymous letters – which have since been held in certain quarters to have been of positively revolutionary import in labelling the mystery solved.

Meanwhile, 17 June 1989 saw the seventy-fifth anniversary of the Scottish Secretary, Mr McKinnon Wood's, announcement in the House of Commons of the outcome of the Great Whitewash, the 1914 Secret Inquiry: namely, that no case had been established to justify any interference with the conviction of Oscar Slater; and in that anniversary day's *Glasgow Herald* Richard Wilson wrote an article to mark the occasion, 'The Downfall of a Man Called Trench'. He neatly evoked John Thomson Trench as a 'moustachioed square-jawed man of considerable presence who wore a bowler hat and carried a brolly' and 'looked more like a city gent than a policeman'.

Sadly, Wilson, understandably confused by Jack House's perpetually shifting position and even shiftier argumentation, perpetuated some old errors and confusions regarding the bugbear A.B., saying that House contended that A.B. was Austin Birrell. Not so. House said that Austin Birrell was *the actual killer*, and identified A.B. as 'the man in the hall'. By this time, House had totally relinquished his belief in Austin Birrell anyway, and was claiming that the man who had told him about 'Uncle Austin' had really said 'Uncle Archie' – and that was Archibald Charteris. So Jack House was now tendering two university professors as homicidal prospects – Frank and Archie Charteris!

Wilson's article drew a response from Alastair Phillips in the *Glasgow Herald*, a week later.

> Few *causes célèbres* are as durable as the Oscar Slater murder case, largely because of the histrionic challenge that it has presented these 80 years to the genius of the Glasgow story-teller. It will never go away. Now and again one little fairy tale gets itself discredited but there will always be another to take its place. The latest 'anniversary' allows one to re-examine the touchy case of Detective Lieutenant John Thomson Trench, who dedicated himself to righting a miscarriage of justice and suffered at the hands of his vindictive colleagues for his presumption. His misjudgment was to point the finger of accusation in a direction distasteful to the mores of the West End of Glasgow; not to mention to the *amour-propre* of what in its day was the most ineffectual and vindictive congregation of senior detectives on record.

Personally, I feel disinclined to go along with this overly harsh judgment. The police surely had their faults and their prejudices, but they were operating under excessively heavy public pressure in the case of the murder of Marion Gilchrist, and the path which they were endeavouring to follow was positively strewn with the most extraordinary series of misleading coincidences. One can with justification criticise such things as the absurdly mismanaged identity parades[4] which they mounted, but, on the whole, theirs were, in my opinion, errors of stupidity rather than constructive malice. They genuinely believed in the guilt of Slater.

Phillips' article goes on to say that:

4 One of which, incidentally, was supervised by Trench.

By absolving Oscar Slater, Trench indicted another innocent. This was a
mystery that we lived happily with for more than half a century during
which time Glasgow created for itself a fascinating mythology and invented
a villain who informed the conversation even of such apparent authorities
as the late Professor John Glaister, on whom we rely for the last word on
forensic medicine. On one social occasion he drew us to one side to inform
us from behind his hand of the true identity of the man who murdered
Miss Gilchrist. The confidence was couched in the established form of such
communications in these parts: 'Of course you know who really did it.' And
at that time we didn't really know but subsequent events have
demonstrated that we still don't know.

Phillips then, once again, spells it out.

The prime suspect since 1914 was the late F. J. Charteris, an emeritus
professor of materia medica at St Andrews University. Though he was
probably the last person to be aware of what surrounded him, it was
Professor Charteris that Lt. Trench put the finger on. This did nothing to
diminish the good stories and rumours that continued to decorate the Slater
saga . . . The trouble was that . . . Lt. Trench's precognition and the evidence
that he gave to the secret inquiry which was ordered by the Secretary of
State for Scotland in 1914 categorically named Professor Charteris as the
fleeing murderer whom the servant Nellie Lambie encountered in the hall of
Miss Gilchrist's flat. His guilt was formally discounted, but in an access of
fine feelings the official report of the inquiry was subedited and filled with
asterisks. The name of the professor was abbreviated to the random initial
A.B. This was generally identified as a gesture on behalf of the good name of
a Glasgow professional family of doctors, lawyers, and pillars of the church.

This provoked a most muddled and muddling letter criticising
Phillips' article from Mr Ted Ramsey, published in the *Glasgow Herald*
of 6 July 1989.

I am afraid that the light directed by Alastair Phillips on the murder of Miss
Gilchrist had all the brilliance of a Toc-H lamp. It would be interesting to
know where Alastair Phillips got the idea that immediately following the
discovery of the body, Helen Lambie was in a state of hysteria. Inspector
Pyper, Arthur Adams, Margaret Birrel [*sic*] and the gentlemen of the press
who were present all testify to her being remarkably cool and collected.

Ramsey went on to say that, to his knowledge, Trench had never
pointed the finger of accusation at anybody 'as far as the identity of
the murderer was concerned'. He denied that any evidence existed
that Helen Lambie had ever identified the man in the hall as being
like Charteris, 'for the very good reason that there was no evidence
which places Charteris at the scene of the murder at any time'. And

he finds the very idea that the police would have permitted someone who was not a close relative even to be in the flat, let alone present at the examination of an important witness, preposterous. But he allows that:

> It is, however, possible that Charteris was present in the flat and yet not identified. It might also be a part explanation as to why the finger of suspicion was later pointed at him. Miss Gilchrist was pronounced dead twice that evening. First, by a Dr Adams who lived opposite and who later set himself up as being something of an expert on the case and, secondly, by a police doctor who for some reason was never identified.

If, suggested Ramsey, the unidentified police doctor turned out to be Charteris, then that would explain a lot.

He was also extremely critical of Professor Glaister.

> The murder of Miss Gilchrist turned out not to be one of Glaister's better efforts. Although informed of the murder at around 8pm he did not bother to go to the scene of the crime until 10am the next morning. Having finally got there he then proceeded to make a whole series of mistakes for which, in the best traditions of the medical profession, someone else would have to pay. In this case it was Oscar Slater, the innocent bystander, who was lumbered with the bill. Glaister's mistakes could not have passed unnoticed by other members of the profession and his evidence at the trial must have raised a few eyebrows. I suspect that among those who voiced a critical opinion was the future professor Charteris and that in retaliation Glaister spread the word that perhaps Charteris knew a deal more about the mystery than he was prepared to admit. But this, I admit, is only speculation.

Ramsey speculates about the police, too.

> Implicit in the argument that Charteris was the stranger in the hall, and the murderer, is the rather peculiar notion that in Edwardian Glasgow the professors of the university enjoyed such power that they were able to get away with murder. With all due respect to Gilmorehill the altar before which the police quailed was that of mammon and not of scholarship. Trade, not book-learning, paid their wages.

Finally, Ramsey asks:

> Is it worth while to rake over the embers of a case which happened so long ago? I think it is. There is also the question of setting right, even posthumously, the wrongs done by society to those individuals who were the unwitting victims of the murder, it could not have been very pleasant for the son of Oscar Slater,[5] for the Charteris family, and for Alexander Birrel[6] [sic] and his family, to live out their lives under such a shadow.

5 I have no notion where Mr Ramsey got hold of the idea that Oscar ever had a son. He most certainly has not surfaced anywhere in the course of my very lengthy research.
6 See p 268

Brenda M. White, of the Department of Economic History at the University of Glasgow, and co-author with M Anne Crowther of *On Soul and Conscience: The Medical Expert and Crime* (Aberdeen University Press, 1988), took up several of Mr Ramsey's points in a letter to the *Glasgow Herald*, 20 July 1989.

> To prevent any further proliferation of red herrings in the Oscar Slater case, may I inform Ted Ramsay [*sic*] that Dr Francis Charteris was not the police surgeon called to inspect Miss Gilchrist's body. The western district police casualty surgeon was John Wright, a general practitioner. His corcise report gave a brief description of her injuries. Casualty surgeons were obliged to inspect all dead bodies found in their districts. Despite the fact that the Professor John Glaister referred to by Alastair Phillips must, I feel, be John Glaister junior, Ted Ramsay's [*sic*] remarks give the impression that John Glaister senior was solely responsible for the Crown's medical evidence in the Slater case. This is not so. Under Scots law murder cases require two doctors. Glaister senior could not, and did not, act alone. Glaister and Professor Hugh Galt, of the St Mungo Medical School, were called by the Procurator-fiscal as medico-legal examiners. They examined the body at the locus and later carried out a post-mortem.

In January 1990, a second batch of Slater case papers was released, and this included the full text of the hitherto asterisk-besmirched report of the 1914 Inquiry.

'New light to be shed on the Oscar Slater case?' queried the ubiquarian Alastair Phillips (*Glasgow Herald*, 6 January 1990). 'So far as official record is concerned,' he began, 'Oscar Slater murdered Marion Gilchrist on 21 December 1908, and was duly and properly condemned and sentenced. He was of course later released but he was never formally pardoned.'

Sheriff Gerald H. Gordon confirmed (*Glasgow Herald*, January 10th, 1990) that Phillips had been correct in saying that Slater had never been pardoned. His conviction was quashed.

Wrote Sheriff Gordon:

> It is true that the conviction was quashed on the grounds of misdirection by the trial judge, and not on the ground that the High Court was satisfied of Slater's innocence, but it was quashed, so that there was neither need nor any room for any pardon. Whatever the effect of a pardon – a matter which raised some problems in relation to the pardon granted to Patrick

Meehan[7] – there is no doubt that a conviction which has been quashed on appeal no longer stands as a conviction, but it is, as the Americans would say, stricken from the record.

Phillips continues: 'In fact, Oscar Slater simply tholed his assize and it has been left to succeeding generations of authors and journalists to take his innocence for granted and to concentrate their guesswork upon the illusive A.B.'

Alastair Phillips is the first to realise that the disclosures of the newly released documents will not much advance the quest for the ultimate truth. Made public are some of the letters which an angrily baffled Slater dashed off white-hot to the Scottish Secretary. They uniformly protest innocence and bemoan injustice – 'My Lord, believe me, I have been treated awful unfair. I can prove I have not been legal identified. Money it was. £200 reward offered by the Glasgow police to the witnesses. If I get identified and convicted, that done me all wrong.'

Phillips agrees:

Slater, a loser from the start, did not get a fair trial. Key witnesses were suborned by the police, the identification procedures were a farce, and the fact that Slater had as his living-in girlfriend an attractive Frenchwoman 'who received gentlemen' at their flat moved the Judge Lord Guthrie in his summing up to tell the jury that Slater was not entitled, as other men were, to the presumption of innocence until proved guilty.

Quite correctly, Phillips pointed out what hard luck it was on Slater that so soon after his trial he became, in effect, a mere bystander, an incidental bit-part player, in the 'more enduring drama of the tragic history of the fate of Lieutenant John Trench who had the professional indiscretion to think that Oscar Slater was innocent and to do something about it'.

---

7   Patrick Connelly Meehan was sentenced to life imprisonment for breaking into the house of 72-year-old Mrs Rachel Ross, No. 2 Blackburn Place, Ayr, with James Griffiths in the early hours of 6 July 1969, and causing her death. He was convicted of murder on 24 October 1969. On 19 May 1976, his innocence securely established, Meehan was granted a unique royal pardon.

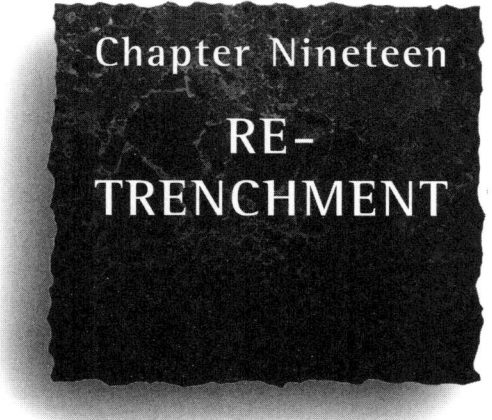

Chapter Nineteen

RE-
TRENCHMENT

There was a buzz of activity at the beginning of 1968. Its dynamic centre was that seasoned old journalistic warrior in whose company we have already much dallied, Alastair Phillips. He it was, who, writing 'An Editorial Diary – Popular Fiction and Oscar Slater' in the *Glasgow Herald* of 9 February 1968, started the Trench hare up. He wrote:

> There is no doubt that . . . the Glasgow police were inefficient; and it is not improbable that in the end, so far as Lieutenant John Thomson Trench was concerned, they were a little vindictive – not in dismissing him from the force, a penalty which he brought upon himself, but in pursuing him later with a trumped-up charge of resetting.

I feel uncomfortable about Phillips' use of the term 'trumped-up'. I think – as it seems likely that the trial judge may also have thought – that the charge against Trench was wrongly framed as reset, but I think that the fundamental dishonesty of his motivation and actions is unquestionable. Whatever, Mr Phillips proceeds to become one of the first writers to hint that there was perhaps less altruism in Trench than met the eye.

The irresistible attraction which has kept the Oscar Slater case in perennial public discussion is the fiction which it has inspired in a succession of self-appointed connoisseurs; and the correspondence which has lately been running in our columns reminds us that the originator of the tall tale was Lieutenant Trench himself. It was a critical remark about 'over-enthusiastic police work' that started the recent exchange.[1]

But the over-enthusiasm was Trench's; and it was the tactful reticence of the inquiry into the case by the Sheriff of Lanark in 1914 that gave rise to all the imaginative theories and socially intriguing identifications . . . The Procurator-fiscal knew the facts and did not think it necessary to introduce such an irrelevancy into the court.'[2]

Alastair Phillips was wildly off beam here, for all the documents go to show that James Neil Hart knew nothing of any accusations against Dr Charteris in 1908-09. Phillips continues:

Lieutenant Trench, then a detective not intimately concerned in the investigation, picked up a bit of hearsay which had already been checked out and properly assessed, and developed this into a theory with which he became so obsessed that he made it the substance of a report which he submitted in a roundabout way to the Secretary for Scotland. The essence of his allegation was contained in the first two questions which were later put to the inquiry:

Did any witness to the identification on the night of the murder name a person other than Oscar Slater?

Were the police aware that such was the case? If so, why was the evidence not forthcoming at the trial?

Alastair Phillips asserts that 'much evidence was withheld by the police, thereby placing the Fiscal in the position of not having the full facts'.

1 A letter from Dr Gerald H. Gordon, in the *Glasgow Herald* of 22 January 1968, pointed out that, while it might be true that, unlike England, Scotland 'had no record of any person being hanged for murder who was later found to have been innocent,' it should also be noted that 'one of the most notorious British examples of wrongful conviction, based in the main on over-enthusiastic police work, occurred in Scotland, in the trial of Oscar Slater.'
2 That irrelevancy being the precise identity of a respectable and innocent bystander who might be occasioned embarrassment by even marginal involvement in so notorious a context – i.e. Dr Charteris.

I think it would be as well at this point to allow Dr Charteris to speak for himself.

It was Alastair Phillips' 'wee brother', William Mowat Phillips, also a journalist, who, in September 1961, then a reporter on the *Scottish Daily Mail*, took an elementary, straightforward and momentous step. All through the years – 47 of them – Dr Charteris was there for the questioning, but it was not until now, when he was 86, that anyone had taken the trouble to ask the question.

Mowat Phillips kicks off in vintage journalese: 'Sitting by his fireside in a quiet little Scots town is an old man, white-haired, a little hard of hearing, but otherwise as spry as ever, with his pipe, his slippers and his memories . . . and his secrets.'

In the *Scottish Daily Mail*, 4 October 1961, Mowat Phillips triumphantly announces:

> I am able to reveal the true identity of A.B. He is Professor Francis James Charteris. Now, for the first time, here is the true story of A.B. himself, as he told it to me in his pleasant semi-detached house at St Andrews, where he lives alone in his retirement.[3]

This is what Charteris had to say:

> On the night of the murder the police got in touch with my mother's lawyer, in the mistaken belief that he was Miss Gilchrist's lawyer. In fact they lived next door to each other and had the same name. The lawyer communicated with me at my surgery at 400 Great Western Road and told me what had happened. He asked me to break the news gently to my mother. But instead of doing so right away, I decided to go round to Miss Gilchrist's flat. I suppose it was partly curiosity. I was a young doctor and I had never seen a murdered person. And I wanted to see for myself what had happened.
>
> When I got there the police superintendent (John Ord) was interviewing the servant-girl, Nellie Lambie. She was very excited I remember. Her eyes were practically jumping out of her head. The police were trying to get a description from her of the man she had seen leaving the flat. She was very vague, almost incoherent, and I remember remarking to myself that they could hardly rely on anything she had to say. Then quite suddenly she blurted out, 'He was like Dr Charteris there.'
>
> Of course it was nonsense and everybody knew that. After all, if I had been the man I would hardly have been stupid enough to come back to the house knowing that two people had seen me leaving, would I? Still, I am very glad everybody realised it was nonsense, because if they hadn't

3 Westlands, 2 Kennedy Gardens, St Andrews.

and Nellie had persisted in saying it was me, I would have had a very hard job proving an alibi. I was working alone all afternoon in my laboratory. I had seen no one before the lawyer called me, and my surgery was just beside the subway station – the next one to that for West Princes Street. For all that I could prove to the contrary, I might have gone to Miss Gilchrist's flat, done the deed and returned without being seen. Of course I didn't, and it wasn't until a long time afterwards that I heard from my elder brother who was a lawyer [Archibald] that Trench, the detective, still suspected I was the man.

I don't remember having seen Nellie before and I wondered how she knew me. But I found out later that after my wedding the previous year – it was a big affair and caused quite a stir in Glasgow – Nellie had come to my clinic at the Western Infirmary, no doubt out of curiosity. That is probably where she had seen me.

Who did Charteris think it was who had committed the murder?

It certainly wasn't Slater. That's obvious. How could he have got in, for one thing? Miss Gilchrist had double locks on the doors, and she was so nervous that she asked me and my wife to get her a watchdog. Unfortunately, it wasn't much good. It was too friendly. Of course it must have been one of the family or a friend of Nellie Lambie. Of course there's only Nellie Lambie's word for it that she was out for just ten minutes, or that she left the door locked. She could have been out for an hour. As a matter of fact I've always had the thought that some friend of Nellie's was involved.

Mowat Phillips intervenes to make a point. Why, he asks, did the 1914 inquiry go to such lengths to hide Dr Charteris's name?

Far be it from me to suggest that the sheriff was awed by young Dr Charteris' family connections. But these were impressive. His father had been a famous professor at Glasgow University; he was married to Annie Kedie, daughter of one of Glasgow's wealthiest and most respected merchants. Principal Archibald Charteris, head of Glasgow's divinity college, was his uncle. He married them in Hyndland Church in what had been Glasgow's 'wedding of the year' in April 1907. Everybody with any pretence to social eminence was there, including Marion Gilchrist. His brother was senior partner in one of Glasgow's leading law firms. Still, I think the sheriff's decision to conceal his identity was fully justified. It would have been grossly unfair to blight a promising career on Trench's unsupported story. However, the sheriff made an unfortunate choice of initials to hide the name. Mr X would have been much better. For it happened that A.B. fitted the most likely candidate – most of Miss Gilchrist's relatives were named Birrell – for the rôle of murderer. I mentioned the name to the professor. 'Ah, yes,' said Professor Charteris, 'I vaguely remember him. He was the black sheep of the family, as I recall.'

Given Professor Charteris' account of matters as retailed by Mowat, his brother, Alastair Phillips, referring to Lambie's comparison of Dr Charteris' appearance with that of the man whom she had seen in the hall, says:

> This alleged identification, which must have come to Trench at second hand (for he was not one of the immediate police team), and this confusion, were made clear in another connection by the judge himself in his otherwise inexcusable summing-up. It has always been obvious that the identifications by the chief witnesses in this case were utterly unreliable, and Lord Guthrie was aware of this (although it was of Slater he was speaking) when he described Helen Lambie as a superficial and unreflective girl of small mental capacity . . . 'when she says that the prisoner is the man, you may think that she only means he is like the man.'
>
> That is how it was with A.B. whom later amateurs of criminal investigation improved to the romantic public taste until he became an epileptic, subject to insane rages, the owner of three bawdy houses in Garnethill, and a middle-class ne'er do well rifling his aunt's house for a will.
>
> The call is made again for the rehabilitation of Lieutenant Trench. We are now doubtful if he is worthy of such attention.

This brought in a fluster of letters.

George Jacobs came on at the gallop. Furiously, he indicted (*Glasgow Herald*, 14 February 1968):

> Sir Arthur Conan Doyle and Mr William Park were prepared to carry on the fight for the rehabilitation of Trench. This was not to be. Trench – whom Mr Ogg[4] describes as the hero of this dreadful case – may have been guilty of a breach of police discipline, but it was not a breach to further his own ends, it was a breach to further the ends of justice, surely an extenuating circumstance that should have been considered before the Glasgow magistrates passed their vindictive decision of dismissal.
>
> I wonder if some recognition of Trench's selfless devotion to the cause of justice might now be made by, first, the Glasgow magistrates, the successors of the men who banished him. If this could be done it would be a source of comfort to his 93-year-old widow and his family. Or should we just forget what we owe Trench and his self-destroying action?

Sir Compton Mackenzie was certainly not to be numbered among those who thought so. Indeed, he had, in 1962, published a book,

4   Archibald C A Ogg, an exceedingly prominent member of the pro-Trench brigade. (See p. 227)

On Moral Courage, in which he applauded Conan Doyle's sterling defence of Lieutenant Trench. In the course of this, he wrote the doubly unfortunate sentence: 'The murderer was a nephew of Miss Gilchrist, who was going to leave her money to the daughter of an illegitimate daughter of her own.'

Marion Gilchrist Ferguson or Cresswell, the legatee of the citing, quite properly outraged at the raising again of the old illegitimacy rumour, promptly wrote a letter of protest to Mackenzie, and received in due course an arrogant reply, a disconcertingly dusty answer.

All-out warfare over Trench was to hang fire for a twelvemonth.

It was Jack House who, in April 1969, fired the first shots of the big skirmish. Between 14 and 18 April he published a five-parter, 'Trench's Last Case', in the Glasgow *Evening Times*. This was the House call to arms:

> John Trench died fifty years ago, on 13th May, 1919, and now there is a move among the Jewish community in Glasgow to make a presentation to his widow. A letter circulating in the community says, 'The Jews have long memories of the horrors of the past. It is fitting to remember where there has been honour.'

In the fourth article of the series – that of 17 April – House really goes to town on the conveniently dead Dr Charteris.

> In his inquiries into the case in 1909, Trench had interviewed Helen Lambie, and she admitted that she recognised the man who was seen in the lobby as a Dr Charteris, a far-out relative of Miss Gilchrist. The Slater case has been humbugged ever since with the idea that Dr Charteris murdered Miss Gilchrist. And Dr Charteris admitted to a newspaper man before he died that he was the man who walked through the lobby.

This is sheer Housean fantasy. In fact, Dr Charteris vigorously denied that he was the man who walked through the lobby!

House went on to state categorically that there were two men in the flat that night.

> Dr Charteris had the job of searching the contents of a wooden casket containing papers. I think that it was his partner and relative Austin Birrell, who hustled Miss Gilchrist into her dining-room and murdered her. Back in 1914 Trench was sure that Oscar Slater was innocent, but he also thought that Dr Charteris was closely connected with the murder.

Three months went by. On 16 August 1969, William Allsopp

announced in the *Scottish Daily Express*:

> Glasgow magistrates are to be asked to petition the Scottish Secretary and
> the Lord Advocate for a full inquiry into the sacking of a city detective 55
> years ago. They will also ask that reference to the detective's dismissal in
> Glasgow Corporation's minutes of the time should be amended, if
> necessary, in the light of new evidence. The men who seek 'once and for
> all' to establish whether Trench was rightfully dismissed by his superiors
> are Glasgow magistrates Bailie John Young and Police Convener Bailie
> James Anderson.

Bailie Young felt that someone or some group of people had framed
Trench. He and Anderson were seeking to clear Trench's name, if he
were innocent, in the lifetime of his 94-year-old widow, and to put
an end to a recurring slur on Glasgow, its police and administration.
He had, he said, made intensive research into the case, and:

> It might well be that a tremendous cover-up job was done at that time, and
> an innocent man was nearly hanged for murder and an equally innocent
> detective was got out of the way, sacked and ruined to support a false
> case. We are sure there are records and documents in existence which
> have never been produced, which tell the whole story. We want to see
> these.'

Bold words; but there is not a shred of evidence to support such
fearsome insinuations.

On 25 September 1969, nine of Glasgow's 20 magistrates met
together in Room 4 at the City Chambers. It took them one and a
half hours to reopen and firmly shut for ever, as they believed, the
case of John Thomson Trench. Glasgow's town clerk, James F
Falconer, informed the assembled magistrates that there was
nothing in law which could be done to set aside the earlier decision.
The man (Trench) pled guilty to the disciplinary offence on which he
was charged. They voted, five to two, with two abstentions, not to
revive the matter. Bailie John Young said that he was very
disappointed. Bailie James Anderson expressed himself disgusted.

Jack House, somewhat fatuously, objected:

> Mr Falconer says Trench 'pleaded guilty to this offence'. Trench was never
> charged in court. He appeared before the Glasgow magistrates, and
> admitted that he had made contact with another party, the lawyer David
> Cook, in connection with the information he had gained as a police officer.
> To say he 'pleaded' guilty suggests that Trench was convicted in a court,
> whereas he was dismissed by the Glasgow magistrates from the police
> force.

Whatever which way, the Trench affair was over. Well . . . for the moment.

In 'An Editorial Diary: The Interminable Saga of Slater and Trench', (*Glasgow Herald*, 27 September 1969), Alastair Phillips, somewhat wearily, summed up: 'What the Trench lobby does not know or ignores is that his moral offence was deeper and more inexcusable than a mere technical breach of police regulations. What he did by inflating his own sketchy and inaccurate second-hand knowledge of the early interrogations was to impeach a respectable Glasgow physician who patently, and to the satisfaction of the Procurator-fiscal and the very senior officers on the scene, had had nothing to do with the crime. And he did this six years after the event. Trench's intervention consisted of the quotation from memory of precognitions and statements of which no record existed and which the witnesses denied were ever made. It had the effect, aided by rumour and speculation that were rife through the town, of causing an official but secret inquiry that found his allegations to be without substance. And the only other lasting effect was to concentrate suspicion – which soon became, and remained, popular conviction – upon the innocent head of Professor F. J. Charteris.'

Phillips' conclusion, 30 years ago, is that:

> There is now no one who could offer any reliable evidence about the Slater case. There is nothing that could be said at an independent inquiry that could lead to any more definite conclusion than that the magistrates of the time maybe were a little hard on Trench, who, though he put a nasty and enduring stain on another man's reputation, was himself perhaps the victim of his assessment of his own talent for deduction.

Trench's widow, Mrs Margaret Arthur Trench, died in her one-hundred-and-first year in Berwick-upon-Tweed Infirmary, on 10 February 1975.

Trench was to lie on in his disgraced slumber a further 15 years before another campaign was mounted by posterity on his behalf.

In 1990, Tom Walsh advocated the granting of a pardon to Slater, and argued that Trench should be rehabilitated. The eightieth anniversary of Trench's ignominious dismissal –

September 1994 – saw Bailie John Young and Thomas Toughill writing to the Scottish Office pleading for his name to be cleared. And three years after that the ammunition for the new assault was lovingly assembled by a gentleman named John Scott, a retired medical administration officer, described in his brevet as 'a member of the public who had long had an interest in the rôle of Trench'.

Mr Scott, living at Burnside, Glasgow, only a short distance from Rutherglen Cemetery where Trench is buried, had for many years paid visits to the grave, and in October 1997, moved to action, he wrote a simple letter to Donald Dewar, the Scottish Secretary of State, asking him to consider a pardon, or some such form of rehabilitation, to correct a 'great injustice to a redoubtable and renowned police officer'.

The Police Division of the Scottish Office Home Department was asked to look into the matter. A report was requested from Strathclyde Police, and Inspector Alistair Finlay, staff officer to the Deputy Chief Constable, was detailed to undertake the necessary inquiries. He subsequently forwarded his findings to the Scottish Office.

The first public salvo marking the opening of this latest offensive was fired by John Linklater in the *Herald* of 29 June 1998. He wrote in a news story: 'Eight decades after his dismissal with ignominy . . . the case of Detective Lieutenant John Thomson Trench is being reviewed,' and quoted Inspector Finlay:

> Mr Trench comes over as a person fighting for some degree of truth. Whether or not the disciplinary action was right on technical grounds, and whether it was right on moral grounds, is a difficult question. I am not sure where we go from here. The other difficulty is that Mr Trench never took any steps to appeal the decision against him. He, as the principal, chose never to pursue it. He had the opportunity, but whether he had any faith in it is another matter. There looks as though there was something of a cover-up, extending as far as the Secretary of State.

Writing in the same issue of the *Herald* an impressive 'Newsview' article, 'Destroyed by a Sense of Duty', Linklater says of what he described as the first serious reappraisal of Trench since 1969, that 'A difficult decision confronts Scottish Secretary of State Donald Dewar. It is one which must address the questions of professional codes of duty against personal ethics, and inflexible law against the interests of justice.' Mr Scott, Linklater told us,

> is modest about his rôle in reopening the Trench files. 'I'm not important in this, just the catalyst. Everything should be done to keep the name of Trench in the view of the public. Obviously, he made powerful enemies. It was a pyramid structure of society and anyone who bucked the system was hammered.'

Linklater observed that:

> Previous attempts foundered through a lack of an appropriate mechanism, and because the dismissal of Trench had been generally interpreted as correct on technical grounds, if grossly unfair given Trench's honourable motive and his exemplary record after 21 years' service in the police.

John Linklater's research (*Herald*, 30 June 1998) confirmed discoveries of my own regarding Trench and his true demeanour. I quote:

> It has always been supposed that his [Trench's] police record was unblemished, but this was not the case. I present the details here because, paradoxically, they may endorse rather than undermine his reputation. I was directed to the information by Joe Craig, a former inspector with 31 years' service in Strathclyde Police. [He] learned from his grandfather [who joined the City of Glasgow Police in August 1908] that at grassroots level it was almost universally believed that Trench was victim of a great injustice, but there was also a feeling that he had broken ranks. Craig discovered that this was not the first time.
>
> [Trench] was following in his older brother's footsteps by joining the City of Glasgow Police from the same regiment, the Black Watch. Robert Trench had completed six years' service and gained several commendations for housebreaking arrests when John was appointed a probationary constable on 31 May 1893. The brothers both served in C. Division, but their brief partnership ended abruptly. On 25 September 1894, Robert was dismissed for allegedly misrepresenting his rôle in a housebreaking arrest. He had received a reward for the arrest. It was his first black mark, and his last. This was a prophetic episode. It must have lead [sic] to difficulties for Trench. His name may have become marked in C.Division.
>
> Two years later he was in trouble of his own. He was fined by the Chief Constable for disorderly conduct on 23 September 1896. The service record does not go into details, but there is a ledger of Complaints Against Police Officers, C. Division[5] . . .
>
> This reveals that John Trench was quarrelling and fighting with a fellow constable, William Cordner, in Dalmarnock Road while both were on duty and in uniform. Eight police witnesses observed the affray.

5 Preserved in the City Archives in the Mitchell Library, Glasgow.

Archivist Rob Urquhart at the Mitchell [Library] has been
conducting statistical research on police service records from 1832 to 1932,
and he has noted that it was quite common for successful and high-ranking
officers to have picked up disciplinary action early in their careers.

However, there may have been more to this particular incident. Joe
Craig speculates that it might have been an early instance of Trench
refusing to bow to peer pressure and declining to involve himself in
petty graft that was routine between local beat men and the publicans.
The presence of eight police witnesses appears to support this. Craig's
theory is: 'If Trench got into a dispute about this kind of thing with
another officer, maybe words turned to blows. He was his own man and,
undoubtedly, this could have caused him problems within the force.'

Knowing what I know of him, though, I find it difficult to think
of Trench as the one man out of step within a coven of dishonest
policemen!

Linklater, on the other hand, thought that,

The implications are intriguing. In C. Division of the City of Glasgow Police,
it is clear that the name of Trench was equated with Trouble. There may
have been many gunning for Trench long before he ever stuck his neck out
for Slater. The harshness of the treatment he received has never been easy
to comprehend, unless Trench's enemies had found the pretext to
terminate the rising success of his career.

A letter from Councillor John H Young, one of the two main sponsors of
the 1969 onslaught, printed in the Herald of 16 July 1998, is of interest.

When I put forward a motion in Glasgow Corporation on 19 August 1969, to
the effect that the magistrates ask the Secretary of State and the Lord
Advocate to institute an independent inquiry into Trench's dismissal from
the Glasgow Police Force, this failed for one precise reason.

Basically, 'the crux of the matter was, did the magistrates in 1914 act
harshly? . . . In the light of subsequent events perhaps they did.

On the other hand, as Trench had frankly admitted his guilt, it
was their unanimous decision that he be dismissed.

The magistrates of 1969 decided there was nothing they could
do legally to reopen the case'.[6]

The last living links of the gaslight era of the early years of this
century in Glasgow had made contact with us. There was the likes of
a retired police officer who was almost 100 years of age who had

6 These paragraphs are quoted by Councillor Young from Douglas Grant's *The Thin Blue
Line: The Story of the City of Glasgow Police*, p58.

served with John Trench and indicated that he found him always to be a man of honesty and fine character.

There was a communication from another man, well into his nineties, who claimed to have driven a cab and horse from near West Princes Street in Great Western Road on the night of the murder down to St Enoch Square and his passenger was a male whose clothes was [sic] covered in blood. In addition, there was a woman who was 87 or thereabouts who as a girl had been sent out by her mother for a message that night and passed a man on the stair where the murder took place, and she indicated that the police were not interested at the time.'

Young went on to say that he had been advised by the then town clerk, James Falconer, that the 1866 Police Act had been used in 1914, and that he had been repeatedly told that no mechanism whatsoever existed with which he could try to clear the late Inspector Trench's name. And attempts to see the minutes of the meeting of July 1914 had also met with little or no success. Finally, they had been shown a photocopy of roughly two handwritten sentences which indicated that the magistrates of the time had deliberated on the case of John Trench and decided to dismiss him from the force. There were no other details whatsoever and yet the meeting must have lasted a considerable length of time.

Young's letter continued:

> An offer was made from a source that suggested there were what are termed Police Minutes in existence, and these might be shown to us providing we gave an undertaking that we would not make use of their contents. This assurance could not be given. I felt I was being blocked almost at every turn.

It seemed that the only success of that campaign was the establishing of the John Thomson Trench Prize at Glasgow University for 'distinctive and original contributions in the field of social sciences, to the welfare of the university, or of the wider community'.

In a consequent letter to the Glasgow *Herald*, Lewis MacDonald queried what exactly Trench's supporters really aimed to achieve:

> If they wish to win an admission from present-day officialdom that Trench was treated harshly by Chief Constable Stevenson and the Glasgow

magistrates in 1914, then so be it: that is one thing. If, however, they are seeking an implicit endorsement of Trench's wide-ranging accusations, which were aired in front of the sheriff's inquiry in that year, then that is quite another matter.

That 1914 Inquiry 'was a bizarre business, held behind closed doors, at which neither Slater – nor for that matter Charteris – was represented, although it became virtually the trial of Charteris'.

What must be emphasised is that at that shrieval inquiry Trench utterly failed to substantiate, let alone prove, his claim that Dr Charteris was the man seen escaping from Miss Gilchrist's flat on the night of the murder. What was in Trench's mind, what drove him to make his preposterous charges against Charteris, is as big a mystery as that of the identity of the murderer. The one thing that can be said is that the uncensored report of the 1914 Inquiry, which was released to the public in 1990, makes the entire innocence of Dr Charteris plain for all to see.

It was on 12 January 1999, as a new millennium loomed that the welkin rang with the glad tidings; Strathclyde's Chief Constable John Orr, James Verdier Stevenson's official lineal descendant, was all set to honour Lieutenant John Thomson Trench's – 85-years-disgraced, now suddenly honourable – memory, at a special ceremony to be held in the Police Museum at Strathclyde Police Headquarters, in Pitt Street, Glasgow.

By late June 1998, Alistair Finlay's report to the Scottish Secretary was almost complete. In it he was to comment: 'The charge [against Trench] appears to have been technically correct, but it raises a moral question. It is not a case of black and white. There is a balance between the morality of an action and the legality of an action.'

Mr Dewar heard, but found that he lacked the statutory authority to grant pardon or posthumous rehabilitation; there was simply no mechanism, no official way of overturning the determination of the magistrates of 1914.

However . . . thundering in to fill the unfortunate redress-gap came Orr at the full charge, taking the view that,

> while Detective Lieutenant Trench's conduct in the strictest sense was
> illegal, in hindsight it may be considered that his actions were both well,
> and most honourably intentioned, and that he probably struggled with the
> dilemma between the illegality and the morality of his decisions.

Orr was diplomatically careful to add: 'I am certain the Magistrates in dismissing also acted in what they believed were the best interests of the City.'

So it came to pass that at tea-time on the afternoon of Wednesday, 13 January 1999, in the presence of Lieutenant Trench's daughter, 87-year-old Mrs Nancy Stark, brought for the occasion from a nursing home in the Borders, and his grandson, Ian Stark, aged 61, who brought with him to witness this triumphant, emotional vindication Trench's two great-granddaughters, Chief Constable Orr unveiled a commemorative plaque or panel which has been placed in the Force Museum – an enduring gesture of reconciliation with the Trench family. Present, too, was the hero of the hour, John Scott.

The panel bears these words:

> There are now appeal processes for both criminal cases in the courts and
> police discipline hearings, which neither Mr Trench nor Mr Slater had the
> benefit of at that time. The fact that these safeguards are now in place and
> have been for many years, is perhaps a fitting legacy to the hardship that
> these individuals endured in the spirit of truth and justice.

I don't know about that, but it is without doubt a pious sentiment and graceful admission.

In the midst of all the triumph no one seems to have paused to consider how Trench's canonisation was the implicit damnation of Trench's 'victim' – the innocent Dr Francis Charteris.

Chapter Twenty

EIGHTY
YEARS
ON

Fitfully, like a fire that will not go out, the interwoven Slater and Trench cases keep flaring up. The news broke on 7 March 1989, via Jack Webster's column in the Glasgow Herald, that a former Glasgow shop steward, Ted Ramsey, who had been made redundant from Lanarkshire steelworks, where he was a plant engineer, had that day published under his own aegis a book about the Slater case. It was the first for 37 years and was titled *Stranger in the Hall*.

Mr Ramsey had unquestionably shouldered an enormous work load of research, but, unfortunately, his version of events does not seem to lie easy with received reality. The act of murder, he decides, was performed by Nellie Lambie, in cahoots with her lover, Patrick Nugent. The killing did not take place, as generally believed, in the dining-room. Nor did it occur at around 7pm. No. It was about five o'clock when Miss Lambie lured her mistress into the kitchen, and there struck her down with a cosh supplied by Paddy, with whom she was having a passionate affair. Miss Gilchrist's body was then dragged into the dining-room.

Patrick Nugent was the stranger in the hall, seen by Adams and an unsurprised Lambie.

The motive for the killing was that Lambie had been found out fiddling Miss Gilchrist's household accounts. She was also in the habit of borrowing her mistress' jewellery, wherewith to adorn herself on her nights out. This had not as yet been discovered, but since she had recently had the misfortune to lose Miss Gilchrist's celebrated diamond crescent brooch, it was only a matter of time before her perfidy was revealed.

Ramsey tells us – but neglects to indicate the source of his information – that Archibald Robertson, whom he describes as Miss Gilchrist's stockbroker, 'who called every Saturday afternoon', had interceded on the young maid-servant's behalf to prevent Miss Gilchrist from sacking her, as he privately considered that Marion Gilchrist was too tight with her money. It was, says Ramsey, a combination of these factors which pushed Nellie into a conspiracy to murder with Nugent. But Nugent, as we know, was thoroughly investigated – and exonerated – by Trench; and despite the most careful searching I have found no precognitions by the said Archibald Robertson, who was not anyway Miss Gilchrist's stockbroker. That was John Stewart.

Ramsey's other main assertion is that A.B. was not Dr Charteris, but one Alexander Birrell.[1] This man was, he claims, a nephew of Miss Gilchrist's, and also a cousin of the Glasgow millionaire shipping magnate Sir William Burrell (1861-1958), the man behind the world-famous Burrell art collection. Lambie is said to have deliberately put the finger of suspicion on this Alexander Birrell, and William Burrell[2] used his influence to expunge any mention of his cousin from the police records of the case, in order to protect the Burrell family name.

What, in essence, Ramsey does, is, first, to confuse Margaret Dawson Birrell, Miss Gilchrist's niece proper, who lived at 19 Blythswood Drive and later at 61 Rupert Street, Glasgow, with quite

1   The Alexander Birrel (of Chapter 18, page 250) has now acquired an additional terminal 'L'.
2   He was not of course Sir William then. He was knighted in 1927, when he was 66 years old, for his services to art.

another Margaret Birrell, who lived at No. 6 Kelvinside Terrace North, alternatively designated No. 275 Wilton Street, and who had a brother, Alexander.[3] This family of Birrells was not in any way related to Marion Gilchrist.

Secondly, confusion worse confounded, Ramsey insists that this Margaret and Alexander Birrell were cousins of William Burrell This, again, is not correct. According to Ramsey, the person who supplied the vital link between the Birrells and the Burrells was one Alexander Burrell, an uncle of Sir William Burrell's.

Sir William's grandfather, George Burrell, and grandmother, Janet Houston or Burrell, had three sons – William, George and Alexander. Ramsey informs us that Alexander was born in 1837, in the Parish of Old Kilpatrick, Dunbartonshire, and that his family moved to Glasgow when he was a child.

Wrong. Alexander Houston Burrell, Sir William Burrell's uncle, was born in Glasgow, not in 1837, but in 1856, and died, aged 51, on 4 April 1908. It is Ramsey's assertion that, 'for some unfathomable reason', this Alexander changed his name to Birrell, and married Miss Marion Gilchrist's sister, Margaret, with whom he lived at 6 Kelvinside Terrace North.

As a matter of historic fact, Alexander Burrell did not change his surname to Birrell; he did not marry at all. His supposed wife, Margaret Gilchrist, died, aged eight, on 23 January 1844, more than twelve years before he himself was born, on May 4th, 1856 He was not the Alexander Birrell who lived in Kelvinside Terrace North.

And what of the Birrells who *did* live at that address? There *was* an Alexander Birrell there. And he *did* have a wife named Margaret, and a daughter, Margaret, and sons, Samuel and Alexander. It is *this* son Alexander who is Ramsey's candidate for A.B., and he died, aged 66, on 21 May 1929. His sister, Margaret Birrell, never married, and she continued to occupy the old family house at 6 Kelvinside Terrace North – which had been bought by her father, Alexander Birrell, in 1874 – until shortly before her death, also at the age of 66, on 3 October 1912. It is obvious, then, that this Margaret Birrell could not have been the one who was a witness at the 1914 Inquiry.

Mr Ramsey is also, as the Christian Scientists say, in error, in

3 The same mistake, indeed, as Trench made in his 1914 pre-Inquiry statement.

his belief that Helen Lambie had previously been Miss Margaret Burrell's servant. *Which* Miss Birrell, one is tempted to wonder. The answer is very definitely neither's. Nellie's first job was, as we have seen, with a Mr Levi Newman, whose employ she entered around February 1901, a short time before her fourteenth birthday and with whom she remained for about two and a half years. Then, *circa* August 1903, she went to work for Mrs Agnes Martin Scott or Guthrie, before going into Miss Gilchrist's service.

Interviewed by George Forbes, Ted Ramsey was reported in the Glasgow *Evening Times* (20 February 1993) as saying:

> I found that in those Edwardian days the Police Committee had the power to hire and fire members of the force at will, with no appeal. They could promote or ruin a career in the force. And the man who chaired the committee at the relevant time was Sir William Burrell. He was in a position to influence events in any police investigation. The chief suspect was an Ayrshire businessman called Austin Birrell.[4]
>
> It was the name which probably threw most researchers off the scent because to all intents and purposes he was a nonentity with no influence at all. I found by digging into the family tree that the Birrells were in fact a branch of the Burrell family, whose name had been slightly changed in the distant past.

On the well-established principle that it never rains but it pours, also in 1989, actually within a mere four months of Ted Ramsey's 37-year-silence-breaking volume, another Glaswegian, Frank Kuppner, who had hitherto practised mainly as poet and playwright, produced, on 26 June, a book, *A Very Quiet Street*. Herein, based upon the circumstance that he had, in 1951, been born in, and subsequently brought up in, the house next door to Miss Gilchrist's – 'virtually through the wall from the scene of a classic murder' – he took an oblique look at Slater and his times through his 1980s' eyes.

The result is a curious and curiously fascinating hybrid work, part novel, part journal, part factual, part faction, in which, somewhat in A J A Symons' Corvine quest style, he acquaints himself and his reader simultaneously with random-seeming pickings-over of the Slater-Trench story. Kuppner states: 'I don't

---

4   Mr Forbes' pen, or word processor, appears to have slipped a ratchet here, unless it was the interviewee's memory that slipped, for Mr Ramsey's A.B. was Alexander Birrell – not Austin Birrell.

start this book with a definite opinion telling what is what. I take it step by step, changing my mind where I learn new facts.' A later Kuppner opinion: 'It is clear the murderer was known to Miss Gilchrist and must have been one of these (youngish) male relatives.' He adds: 'I have heard that another of these ambiguous gentlemen had a criminal record, but I could find out nothing more about him.'

Mr Kuppner pursues the trail and trial through the Mitchell Library, the second-hand bookshops and chance meetings with sundry others making collections of rescued facts. He finds the murder accounts 'brimming with social history of a kind you seldom meet in text books; what people ate, how much they drank, at what time they rose in the morning'.

He lived and wrote in a room overlooking Wilton Street – where the wrong Margaret Birrell had lived – picking his way along pathways through mountains of books he buys from the city's old book dealers. He does not read much fiction. 'I agree with Emerson: why go for imitation, ersatz, when the real thing is out there around you, always fascinating.' And, Slaterwise by candlelight, he sums up: 'Despite pressures throughout the years, the authorities remained steadfast. If the police were not just plain inefficient, then something very murky indeed was going on.'

But looking for an answer is like asking the wrong person for street directions, or opening an infinite series of diminishing Russian dolls. What does the dumbstruck nucleal figurine say? That the man in the hall was Charteris? That Charteris had been told by the police of the murder? That it was most interesting to discover that Miss Gilchrist's niece, Margaret Birrell, had been Helen Lambie's previous employer? Not a lot. And all wrong.

A *Very Quiet Street* is a captivating book written *around* the Slater case, but it does not add, does not pretend to add, anything of any real factual or interpretative importance to the enduring mystery. It is a daring *jeu d'esprit* on a dark stage.

It was in the December of the year following the Slaterian

resurgence promoted by Messrs Ramsey and Kuppner, that Mr Tom Walsh, a former dominie taken in his retirement to television script and song writing, took also to the Slater case, and proceeded to set up his stall for yet another attempt at the redemption of the late John Trench.

The tidings of this newest venture were brought to the readers of the *Glasgow Herald* on the morning of 22 December, 1990.

> Eighty-two years ago yesterday the murder of Glasgow spinster Marion Gilchrist set in train a series of events which shamed British justice . . .
> Now the case of Detective Trench has been taken up by Tom Walsh, who wants Slater cleared by posthumous pardon and Trench rehabilitated.

Then comes the claim. The needle slips into the well-worn groove. 'Walsh has unearthed startling records which support the theory that Slater was the victim of an elaborate and scandalous cover-up.' Murray Ritchie, in an article, 'Following the Loot in the Trench Case', explained: 'Now Tom Walsh, retired teacher, has taken up the cause of clearing Trench . . . His inspiration in examining this case was Simon Jenkins, editor of *The Times*, who wrote recently that the iron rule of investigative journalism was to "follow the loot".'

Suiting the action to the tag, Mr Walsh hared off for a look at Miss Gilchrist's will, 'which produced some absorbing theories'.

One stroke of beginner's luck for Mr Walsh was that the onset of his research happily happened to coincide with written evidence, which had recently been made available by the Scottish Records Office, officially and unequivocally identifying A.B. 'Following the loot', Tom Walsh suggests that Dr Charteris stood to gain handsomely by finding favour with Miss Gilchrist. 'The old woman, who could be disagreeable, had made a will seven months earlier. And a month before she was murdered she had added a codicil. If Charteris had been cultivating her for a bequest he had failed.'

Walsh arrived at the conclusion that the actual killer was Dr Charteris' brother, Archibald – in accord, that is, with Jack House's last testament. But, says Walsh, his task is not to apportion guilt, but to remove injustice. What, above all, the papers which he has unearthed show is 'the lengths to which the Scottish legal establishment was prepared to go in suppressing any mention of Dr Charteris'.

One of the newly-released documents which he saw had been

written by an aide to the Lord Advocate, who pointed out that, in his view, the mere suppression of Charteris's name in the publication of the 1914 report would be insufficient to ensure anonymity; it would still be possible for a number of people to identify him from the context, unless that, too, were excised. The writer of this note added:

> There is one question on which I confess I should have liked a little light and perhaps the Secretary for Scotland would also, if his attention were drawn to it. What led the police to make inquiries regarding Dr C. at all, why did they think it necessary to satisfy themselves that he had nothing to do with it? His arrival at the house after the murder and his explanation to Superintendent Douglas as to how he came to be there, would not have aroused any suspicions. What made the police think inquiries as to his movements necessary?

'In other words,' says Tom Walsh, 'even before the suppressed paper was issued, the suppressor was expressing the gravest disquiet about the whole business.'

Pointing out that when Trench gave his evidence to the Secret Inquiry everyone contradicted him – Margaret Birrell changed her story, saying that Nellie Lambie never mentioned Charteris; Nellie said that her alleged statement about Charteris was false; police witnesses professed no knowledge of Trench's talking about Charteris – Walsh asks: 'How was this done? And, more important, why was this done?'

Replying to his own question, Walsh hazards: 'The answer, of course, is that the police fell over themselves to believe in Slater's guilt. In their hurry to pin the murder on Slater they were prepared to ignore evidence from other sources: and that was good news for the Charteris family.'

Still on the trail of the loot, Walsh noted – and accepted – that the murdered spinster had an illegitimate child. He also noted that Miss Gilchrist's will showed her principal beneficiaries to be Marion Gilchrist Ferguson, whom he named as her granddaughter, and Maggie Galbraith Ferguson, who, according to Walsh, was Miss Gilchrist's daughter.

> 'All other beneficiaries in a trust she set up were female [writes Murray Ritchie], with the exception of a grand-nephew and, curiously, a James Johnstone in Shanghai, to whom she left a generous bequest. 'I wonder,'

says Tom Walsh, 'if that might be the father of Marion Gilchrist's illegitimate child?' Miss Gilchrist was determined to cut out the men in her family. Her will excluded men gaining from their wives' interests and exempted the women's bequests from debts incurred by their menfolk.

Tom Walsh expands:

Here is a rich old lady, alienated from her nearest relatives and with few visitors, the most frequent being her illegitimate daughter and her much-loved granddaughter. The Charteris family was only indirectly related to Miss Gilchrist, the mother being the widow of one of Miss Gilchrist's brothers. Yet Dr Francis Charteris began to cultivate socially this unpleasant old lady. He visited her, and more important, he invited her to his wedding, along with her servant, Nellie, and her favourite grandchild, Marion Gilchrist Ferguson. Why, one asks? The answer must surely be to curry favour in the hope of benefiting from the old woman's wealth.'

If so, it certainly did not work. Walsh states that the last item in Miss Gilchrist's will stipulates that the residue of her estate shall go to Marion Gilchrist Ferguson, or, if she died before Miss Gilchrist, to Marion's brothers and sisters. That will was signed on 28 May 1908, but on 20 November following, a codicil was added cutting out her male grandchildren in favour of her two Ferguson granddaughters. Any hope that the Charteris brothers may have cherished of gaining from her death was thus removed.

Walsh then takes a gigantic step into the surmisal business.

Getting wind of this, Francis and his brother, Archie, visited her [Miss Gilchrist] when Nellie popped out for an evening paper. When tempers were lost Archie struck her, fatally, as Francis searched for her will in another room. The neighbours arrived to investigate the noise . . .

Recipe: the mixture as before.

The Charteris brothers were taken to the police station, dismissed and discounted as suspects. Why, remains a mystery. But they must have had friends in high places.

Walsh goes along with the popular theory among Oscar Slater investigators that Nellie simply yielded to police pressure to change her statement and Margaret Birrell's retraction was made to save the Charteris family from scandal.

Walsh's final say:

Whoever was the murderer, however fascinating, is now irrelevant because all the participants are dead and the guilty cannot be brought to justice. But justice can still be sought on two other counts. Slater's innocence has never been formally declared. His conviction was quashed on grounds of misdirection of the jury. He deserves a posthumous pardon.

The bait dangled by Murray Ritchie's article and Tom Walsh's punditry was smartly seized by Ted Ramsey. Letter. Glasgow *Herald*, 4 January 1991:

> Walsh quite clearly believes that he is the first person to have 'followed the loot' by his reading of Miss Gilchrist's will . . . on the morning after the murder detectives called on the lady's solicitor where they examined the will. It was, however, a wasted morning for the will contained nothing that might point to the identity of the murderer.
>
> It would seem that Walsh did not read the will too closely. Contrary to what he suggests there are four men named as beneficiaries – Robertson, Stewart, McColl [*sic*], and Johnston.[5] The fact that one beneficiary was to enjoy the income from a small trust with the capital going to certain charities on death is not extraordinary.
>
> Walsh 'notes' that Miss Gilchrist had an illegitimate daughter, an allegation common at the time of her death and without a scrap of proof to support. It was also alleged that she was, variously, a notorious fence, the chief of a gang of criminals, and the procuress of young women for wealthy men. There was also, for some reason, a rumour that she buried a cache of diamonds under a flagstone in the street as well as leaving more diamonds littering the floor of her flat.
>
> In one of the original stories concerning the illegitimate child, Marion Ferguson, the 17-year-old daughter of Margaret Ferguson, a former maid, is identified as the daughter. This would have made Miss Gilchrist 67 at the time of the birth. A variant of this story says that Margaret Ferguson is the daughter, which would have made Miss Gilchrist about 42 at the time of the birth. Scarcely more credible.

But, if nothing else, Walsh is, Ramsey is prepared to allow, clearly a trier.

> On the strength of his having been left £500 in the will he identifies John [*sic*] Johnston of Singapore as being the possible father of these elusive children. And yet at the same time he admits to not having the slightest idea who Johnston was. He could have been a small boy for all he knew.
>
> Trench, admirable detective that he undoubtedly was, was never involved directly in the investigation of the Gilchrist murder. As he himself said the nearest he ever got to the scene of the crime was the landing outside the flat. Nor is there any evidence to suggest that he was an unswerving believer in the innocence of Oscar Slater. Although he would later appear to criticise the series of farces that passed for identification parades, it must not be forgotten that he was the man who set up the parades.

In Ted Ramsey's opinion, what seems to have been more likely is that

> Trench was made angry when, in the wake of the conviction of Slater, he

5 The beneficiary referred to is actually James Johnston of Shanghai. Walsh calls him James Johnstone of Shanghai. Ramsey refers to him as John Johnston of Singapore.

saw lesser men being promoted ahead of him. It would seem that this was in part his motive for beginning his unofficial investigation into the murder. What this investigation quickly turned up was undoubted proof of the deliberate destruction by senior officers of part of the file and the wholesale suborning of witnesses. This was seemingly the burden of his submission to the Secretary of State. As a successful outcome for Trench would have meant the establishing of the guilt of these officers, then Trench simply had to be crushed.

Tom Walsh replied – on 9 January:

The reason for my studying the will was not only to see where the money went, but also where it did not go. Mr Ted Ramsey opines that it seems I did not read the will too closely. Closely enough. Two of the men he lists were mentioned in Murray Ritchie's article (Johnston and McCall, the grand-nephew); the other two were her executors.

If Miss Gilchrist's illegitimate daughter was the 17-year-old Marion Gilchrist Ferguson's mother, Margaret Galbraith Ferguson, Miss Gilchrist would have been, according to Mr Ramsey, about 42 at the time. 'Scarcely more credible', he says. On the contrary it is most conceivable, as many women aged about 42 will attest.

Mr Ramsey, some time ago, produced a book, *Stranger in the Hall*, suggesting to his own satisfaction that the mysterious A.B. was a certain Alexander Birrell . . . Documentary evidence is now available for scrutiny, and was reproduced in Murray Ritchie's article, that proves beyond all doubt that A.B. was simply a code name for Dr Francis Charteris.

The sixty-third anniversary of the quashing of the conviction of Oscar Slater by the newly-created Scottish Court of Criminal Appeal was marked by the publication, on 20 July 1991, in the Glasgow *Herald*, of an article by Robert Dickson, Sheriff of South Strathclyde, Dumfries and Galloway at Airdrie, 'Murder Story That Awaits a Final Twist'. In it, Sheriff Dickson remarked: 'Perhaps the most interesting point to come to light recently is the fact that despite his eloquent plea on behalf of Oscar Slater and his triumph of 63 years ago Craigie Aitchison did not share Sir Arthur Conan Doyle's faith in Slater's innocence,' and, Dickson comments,

If Oscar Slater did not do it, who did, and why were there no clues found that gave any indication of the presence of such a third party? Despite all that has been written and said about the matter, and about its principal character, the question as to whether the mysterious German Jew was responsible for the brutal murder and robbery remains a mystery.

Out of the thus drawn covert popped Ted Ramsey, for a spot of kettle calling pot. *Glasgow Herald*, 1 August 1991.

I am surprised that Sheriff Dickson should have made so many mistakes in his article. He would have done well to have first referred to my book on the case . . . There is no doubt in my mind that the person who murdered Miss Gilchrist was her maid, Helen Lambie. During her evidence at the extradition trial in New York, Gordon Miller, Slater's American attorney, forced Helen Lambie to admit that there was only one set of keys to the Gilchrist flat. This was confirmed by police records. When Helen Lambie went to buy the paper that night she locked the door behind her and took the keys with her. Thus the whole time she was out of the flat no one could get in or out. In the commission of the murder Helen Lambie was assisted by Paddy Nugent, her married lover, a bookmaker from Motherwell. According to a friend of mine who knew Nugent all his life, the description of the man seen by Rowena Adams at the door to the Gilchrist close shortly before Helen Lambie left the house fitted Nugent.

I have also a copy of an anonymous letter written by someone claiming to be a maid in a house in West Princes Street and a friend of Helen Lambie. This girl claims that Nugent was in the Gilchrist flat that evening at 6.30. I suspect that the author of this letter was the girl who was known to have spent most of the afternoon with Helen Lambie in the Gilchrist flat just before the murder. Who killed Miss Gilchrist should never have been a mystery to anyone who approached the case with an open mind. Helen Lambie only got away with it, in my opinion, simply because being a maid she was generally accepted to be stupid. After hours of the most detailed examination in the witness-box at the hearing in New York, she still had her wits about her sufficiently to stop Gordon Miller dead in his tracks. Miller never had any doubt about the fact that Helen Lambie was guilty nor that she was very clever.

Whence Mr Ramsey derives his 'facts' is a puzzlement. All that can be said is that the greater part of them do not square with those presented by the majority of students of the case, and my own very extended research has failed to find any confirmation as to their correctness.

Replying to a swift interlocutory from the pen of Lewis MacDonald – published in the Glasgow *Herald* of 14 August 1991 – Ramsey writes:

Trench says that while he went alone to interview Margaret Gilchrist [he means Birrell], Pyper and Douglas, the two senior officers in the case, were away interviewing A.B. But all he appeared to have known with certainty was that the two officers went by taxi to A.B.'s house. Dr Frank Charteris was at that time living at 400 Great Western Road. His widowed mother and solicitor brother were living nearby in Queen Margaret Crescent. It is difficult to see, then, how the two senior officers could justify the expense of a taxi to visit a suspect who lived on a main road well serviced with tram cars and about fifteen minutes' walk away.

Ramsey now descends into realms where it is impossible to follow him: 'Superintendent Douglas told the secret inquiry that, as usual in murder cases, all of Miss Gilchrist's male relatives were interviewed.' So far, so good. But then we are told:

> Alexander Birrell, Margaret's brother, had recently married and had bought himself a house just outside Prestwick. As he seems to have been the only relative living out of town then he would seem to be the likeliest candidate for a visit by taxi. Certainly the police had every reason to question him for a week before her death, Alexander had visited his aunt to try and borrow money. According to Helen Lambie this meeting ended in a row. Helen Lambie knew both Charteris and Alexander and in turn she pointed the finger of suspicion at both men.

This brought a new war correspondent, Thomas Toughill, hastening into the bloodied field.

Herald. October 1st, 1991: Toughill expressed amazement that Mr Ramsey should be ignoring one of the basic facts of the Slater case; to wit, that Dr Francis Charteris was A.B. It should always be remembered that, as Toughill is careful to distinguish, A.B. is *not* synonymous with the stranger in the hall. Neither is the stranger in the hall necessarily synonymous with the murderer of Miss Gilchrist. They are three separate entities.

Nor was Toughill at all happy about the slur which he considered to have been cast on Trench, whom he regarded as a man of the highest integrity, who sincerely believed that Slater had been wrongfully convicted. He thought the suggestion that Trench had brought about the Inquiry simply because some of his colleagues had been promoted above him preposterous.

Stung, as though by an ichneumon, Ramsey reacted angrily, hazarding in the *Herald* of 9 October:

> I would guess that the reason why Mr Toughill dislikes my book is that it destroys many of the myths in which he so obviously believes. Toughill accuses me of ignoring one of the basic facts in the Slater case, Dr Charteris. This, of course, is nonsense, for Charteris can in no way be described as being a basic fact unless it is being suggested that he was the murderer. As Toughill admits he is making no such claim, then the doctor's rôle in the affair is reduced to that of being one of the unfortunates upon whom suspicion fell for a brief moment. As I say in my book, Charteris was at that time nothing more than a red herring, and it

would seem that he is still playing that unwanted rôle today.

One of the principal myths still surrounding the case is that of John Trench selflessly sacrificing his career as a police officer in an attempt to prove Slater's innocence. In truth this claim, widely believed, has even less going for it than the claim that Charteris was the stranger in the hall. We now know that, with one exception apart from Trench, all the witnesses who appeared before the 1914 inquiry were lying. The mystery, then, has to be why Trench ever imagined that they would tell the truth. Trench made a mess of his case by moving before he had collected all the evidence and had it tied up tightly. It is this that suggests to me that he was acting out of personal anger.

The mystery for me, is how Ted Ramsey came to reach the bizarre conclusions in which, with such obvious sincerity, he has come to believe.

Chapter Twenty-One

THE
MYSTERY
SOLVED?

It was Bruce McKain, Law Correspondent of the Glasgow Herald, who broke the news therein, on 7 October 1992, that Thomas Toughill, 'a former history teacher and Hong Kong policeman has written a book, confidently entitled *Oscar Slater: The Mystery Solved*, revealing in print for the first time the name of the man the author is convinced is the real killer'.

That man was Wingate Birrell.

What, in a nutshell, were Thomas Toughill's contentions and conclusions?

In the wake of the Kennedy assassination, conspiracy theories have become the currency of the self-styled mystery-solvers at what Frederic Lindsay,[1] with every justification, calls 'this disillusioned end of the century'. And Toughill alleges that Slater was the victim, not of a simple miscarriage of justice, but of a conspiracy which extended to the topmost levels of the Scottish legal establishment. He firmly believes that early on in the history

1 Reviewing Toughill's book in *Scotland on Sunday*, 5 December 1993.

of the case it was agreed to settle the blame on Oscar Slater for the murder which had been committed by Wingate Birrell, and in which crime the Charteris brothers were crucially involved. He subscribes to the well-whiskered theory that the murder came about as the ultimate result of a family squabble over Miss Gilchrist's will. He contends that, months before her death, the old lady had determined to bequeath the bulk of her estate to her illegitimate daughter.[2] Prior to this, the heir presumptive had been Mrs Mary Greer Gilchrist or McCall, the daughter of Mrs Elizabeth Charteris by her first marriage to Miss Gilchrist's brother, James Gilchrist. Hearing of this change of will, the Charteris family were up in arms. They determined to seize the offensive document, either to destroy or challenge it. Cannily anticipating such a reaction, Miss Gilchrist virtually barricaded herself in her flat, and went to considerable pains to keep unwanted visitors out.

Toughill tells us that the old lady was known to be dying of kidney disease, which meant that time was of the essence, and, against the clock, entrance had somehow to be effected to Fort Gilchrist. I am not aware of any evidence that Miss Gilchrist's kidneys were in a condition that was putting her life at risk, let alone threatening a close-looming terminal illness. As we have already seen, the post-mortem report stated merely that both kidneys were granular from chronic kidney infection, but that she was, overall, in very good health for a woman of her years.

We are, then, presented by Mr Toughill with the following scenario: the Charteris brothers – Francis the doctor and Archibald the lawyer – decide to exploit Miss Gilchrist's mentally unbalanced nephew, Wingate Birrell, in a bid to lay hands on the old lady's will.

As it happens, I had at one time myself harboured very serious suspicions about Wingate Birrell and, consequently, taken a very

---

2   Actually, it was not to Mrs Maggie Galbraith or Ferguson (whom Toughill identifies as Miss Gilchrist's illegitimate daughter) who was named as Miss Gilchrist's main beneficiary. Her residual fortune was, as we have already recorded, willed to Mrs Ferguson's daughters, Marion and Margaret.

close-focus look to see what I could discover about this hitherto
somewhat shadowy figure.

Wingate Birrell was the sixth child and fifth son of Walter and
Janet Gilchrist or Birrell, born at 9 pm on Monday, 28 September
1868, at Rockbank House, Helensburgh. In 1892, the 24-year-old
Wingate was in business, with a partner – J F Aitken, of 3 Hayburn
Crescent, Partick – trading as Messrs Aitken & Birrell, general
agents, at 93 Hope Street, Glasgow, and was probably living at
home with his parents, his 29-year-old brother, George Gilchrist
Birrell, and his 28-year-old sister, Margaret Dawson Birrell, at
Middlefield, Partickhill, Glasgow. Their elder brother, James Aitken
Birrell, aged 36, long fled the parental nest and married, was living
with his wife elsewhere in Glasgow.

By 1893, the firm of Aitken & Birrell had vanished from the
Glasgow Post Office Directory, never to reappear. The next sure point I
was able to establish was Wingate's enlistment in the 10th Hussars,
on 17 June 1895, at Glasgow. His regimental number was 4011. He
is described in his military record as: Height: 5 ft 8½ in.
Complexion: Fresh. Hair: Brown. Eyes: Grey. Scar upper lip.
Indistinct tattoo mark on left forearm. Trade: Clerk. His age is given
as 26½.

Three years later, he was posted as a deserter, having
disappeared from Canterbury on 31 December, 1898. It was after
this desertion, some time between 1899 and 1909, that, calling
himself, for what are now obvious reasons, William Gilchrist, he
served in the merchant navy. My researches have for the first time
disclosed that it was on 19 January 1909 that he was admitted to the
Dreadnought Seaman's Hospital, Greenwich. His private address at
the time of his admission was given as 31 Albert Road, North
Woolwich, and his occupation as hawker and seaman. The occupant
of No. 31 is listed in a contemporary Kelly's Directory as George
Sayers, builder. The likelihood is that the place was a rooming-
house.

Since Wingate is described as a 'hawker and seaman', we may
reasonably suppose that he had not been functioning solely as a
seaman for quite a while. A hawker's life, travelling from door to
door in all weathers, offering, often unwanted, goods for sale, is a

hard enough life for anyone. For a man with tuberculosis draining away his vitality it must have been appalling. He had never married, so now, in his hour of absolute need, there was no wife to look after him, no in-laws to stand by him. His situation would be dire. Did he somehow contrive to scrape the shillings together to buy himself a someway decent second-hand suit and overcoat? Did he make the supreme effort to clean and tidy himself up to the old respectability? Did he, by heaven alone knows what shifts and devices, raise the money for a third-class one-way ticket to Glasgow? Did he set off, a rare ray of hope illuminating the dark places of his soul, to see his well-heeled Aunt Marion and beg her for a little help in this his truly bleakest moment?

Suppose, just suppose, that he did manage to summon up from his rapidly waning health the strength to do all these things. It would not be the first time a Birrell had come cap-in-hand, pride-in-pocket, to Aunt Marion seeking help, and been flea-in-ear despatched[3]. Suppose that he knocked at Aunt Marion's door, and that, flesh of her flesh, she let him in. Suppose that he made his request – humbly, desperately – for a little late charity, and suppose that he received the same sort of response as Mary Birrell, his sister-in-law, had received. Or, indeed, rougher, as befitted a male 'scrounger'.

Miss Gilchrist was said to have a nasty tongue on her. Perhaps she used it once too often. It may be that, goaded, his poverty mocked, his terrible ill-health set at a contemptuous, uncaring discount, Wingate, beside himself, hit out at Aunt Marion. She fell. Cracked her skull against the sharp edge of the coal-scuttle. Blood. Everywhere. Panic. Horrified by what he had done, frantic, afraid of the consequences, Wingate seized a chair, began to beat . . . and beat . . . and beat . . . at the supine figure on the hearth-rug. Seeing her there, now become a grotesquely transformed, injured, blood-covered *object*, he hit, and hit, and hit again, in the sort of paroxysmal terror one has of a half-mangled, half-alive creature coming at one, the overwhelming need to prevent that at all costs, as, barefoot, one hammers and hammers at a scuttling cockroach with the heel of a

3   Remember the approach made by Mrs Mary Nimmo or Birrell in 1901, and its abortive result, p. 69.

shoe, long after reason tells you that it is quite, quite dead. Then, somehow, Wingate manages to pull himself together, begins a search for money in the bedroom, is disturbed by the advent of Lambie and Adams, picks up a diamond crescent brooch *en passant*, so as not to depart this disaster totally empty-handed, and, made rig d and ultra-calm by the sheer fear of necessity, disciplines his ravaged body and ragged nerves to an automatory casual exit through the lobby, past the stuffed pink flamingo that stands sentinel in the hall, past the transfixed Lambie and Adams. The chair had shielded him from the ambuscades of spurting blood and soft flying pellets of brain tissue. That very night he takes a train back to London and a shabby room in Woolwich.

Such is the Wingate scenario. I did not believe in it for one minute. I am now in a position to dismiss it absolutely, for the following documentation has come to light:

> Copying Book No. 45. Page 33. Typewritten.
> Copy of telegram received from the London
> Metropolitan Police.
> Office stamp.
> Glasgow, Dec 31, 08.
> Limehouse, 36/1/24.   Received 1-49 p.m.
> To Chief Supt. City Police, Glasgow.
> Re. your letter and telegram re. Gilchrist:
> it has been ascertained that William Gilchrist alias Birrell was at home at
> North Woolwich on night of 21st inst.
> Supt. Cameron, Limehouse, London.
> John Ord, Supt.

This telegram refers to Wingate Birrell. He died, six weeks later, on Thursday, 4 March 1909, of pulmonary tuberculosis – at that time a very common disease among seamen – certified by A S Burgess, MRCS, and the informant of his death being J W Garnier, Steward at the Seaman's Hospital.

I have been told that Wingate was at one time in trouble with the police – allegedly for housebreaking. If that is so, it would mean that after his desertion from the Army the general trend of Wingate's progress was downhill. He may even have landed up for a time in prison. But that does not make him a murderer.

My friend, the late Andrew Melbourne, who had spent many decades studying the Slater case, sent me a copy of a letter which he had received from a Mr Alex Thomson, of 38 Preston Street, Glasgow. It was dated 15 July 1961.

> I am 76 years old and remember relatives of old Miss Gilchrist I lived, in those days far-away, with my father and mother, plus two brothers who are now dead, in Woodlands Road. My memory serves me reasonably. It was known to some that Mr Slater didn't do the murder of the old spinster, but it was a relative W. Birrell, who done the awful murder. William [sic] Birrell was a bad lot and was convicted for shopbreaking at least once, around the time of 1905, in Glasgow. He drank heavily and was barred from Miss Gilchrist's house by her. In the twenties I wrote to Mr Conan Doyle and got no answer to my letter. Oscar Slater was innocent, that I'm sure of. W. Birrell I am sure had something to do with her death. Birrell had a slight squint. My father drank with him in Harvey's public-house and some of the clubs of the day in Glasgow.

Melbourne told me:

> When I pressed the old fellow for more concrete information as to his allegations and the source of these important revelations, he told me that he was reared in the Woodside district of Glasgow [which embraces West Princes Street] and that his own father knew Miss Gilchrist and most of her Glasgow relations, and that it was well known that Miss Gilchrist had discouraged the male members of the family from visiting her, and that the reason for this bar was that the Birrell males were constantly tapping Miss Gilchrist for money. I, personally, when interviewing Mr Thomson, felt he was genuine and very sincere.

It is tempting, especially with suspicion at least buttressed by the anonymous letters seen by Toughill and myself in official files opened up in recent years, to go nap on Wingate Birrell as the murderer. Toughill does. I do not.

Toughill suggests that Wingate, so that he might when the necessary time came be smuggled into Aunt Marion's flat, wooed Nellie Lambie, promising her marriage, and an easeful, as well as a happy, ever after. He and the Charteris brothers then set a watch on No. 49 West Princes Street. They also poisoned Miss Gilchrist's watchdog. On the evening of the murder Wingate was in the flat with

Lambie's innocent connivance. After she had gone off to get an evening paper, he let Dr Charteris in. Then we are back to the old, old story . . . the search for the will. Charteris began to hunt for it in the bedroom. Suddenly, something went wrong. There was a fierce flare-up between Wingate and his aunt. He lost his temper and battered her to death, then fled in panic, escaping via the kitchen window and climbing down the drain-pipe at the back of the house.

Dr Charteris was still rummaging in the bedroom when Adams and Lambie arrived on the scene. He walked calmly past them and hurtled down the stairs. Archibald Charteris was waiting in the street, and the pair ran off to Francis' nearby home, where Wingate presently joined them. Having heard his account of what had happened, the Charteris brothers told him that he would have to get out of Glasgow. Wingate rushed off to Kelvinbridge subway station, where his erratic and panicky behaviour drew the attention of Miss Annie Armour, the booking clerk at the turnstile. Dr Charteris returned to Miss Gilchrist's flat. He was exercised that Lambie's recognition of him should not be put on record by the police. He was also anxious to supply senior police officers with an account of what had really taken place, coupled, perhaps, with a timely reminder of this family's personal friendship with Alexander Ure.

So, within hours of the murder, the upper echelons of the Glasgow detective force knew the identity of the murderer, exactly how the murder had come about, and that two influential Glasgow families – the Charterises and the Birrells – were guiltily involved, although, of course, such junior officers as Trench then was would not have been informed of the true situation.

It was, says Toughill, in the due process of their inquiries into Lambie's background that Oscar Slater first came to the attention of the officers investigating the killing of Marion Gilchrist. Those inquiries led them to Hugh Cameron, who, calling himself Patrick Nugent, was paying assiduous court to Helen Lambie. He was found to be in possession of a pawn-ticket for a diamond brooch. This, he quickly explained, was the property of a German Jew named Oscar Slater, a professional gambler, who was on the verge of departing for America. Slater proved to have a minor criminal record and was known to the police as a man suspected of living off the proceeds of prostitution. In fact, his flat was currently under active surveillance for evidence of its being used as a brothel.[4] The watch was now stepped up and Cameron was told that he must inform the police the moment that he knew when Slater was going to leave the country.

Toughill states that a physical resemblance between Slater and the Charteris brothers was noted by senior police officers and the Procurator-fiscal quite early on. I must frankly confess that my eye cannot be as good as theirs. I fail to see the resemblance. Particularly registered, Toughill points out, was the curious dip at the bridge of the nose which all three shared. This clue, he adds, may well have been provided by Lambie, who, according to him, knew Slater by sight. Something, incidentally, that she expressly denied – and something for which I have failed to find any confirmatory evidence.

If the authorities had taken a deliberate decision to set Slater up as the murderer, why, it may be wondered, was he not arrested there and then? Toughill provides the simple answer: the authorities *wanted* Slater to get away to America. What is more, they did not want the extradition proceedings to succeed. They would normally have feigned outrage, made great show of their dissatisfaction at the lack of co-operation by the United States authorities, but the resultant *impasse* would in reality have suited them extremely well. Wingate Birrell, Doctor Charteris and Lawyer Charteris would be well clear of danger of prosecution. Slater would have come to no harm, and the Gilchrist murder would, in the fullness of time, have been written off as an attempted burglary that went tragically wrong. It even seems possible, Toughill thinks, to detect the hand of Archibald Charteris, expert on international law, collector of comic anecdotes,[5] in this well-woven web.

It was Slater himself who scuppered the master-plan by, most unexpectedly, electing to return to Scotland to clear his muddied name. And the consequence was: that what had started out merely as an attempt to pervert the course of justice escalated to an official conspiracy to the judicial murder of Oscar Slater.

Toughill confides: in the moment of her crisis, Mrs Elizabeth

4 Which it was not: a brothel being a premises where more than one woman is engaged in the trade.

5 He published in 1932 *When the Scot Smiles in Literature and in Life*. (Alexander Maclehose, London).

Charteris turned to her trusted family friend, Ure, the Solicitor-General and Lord-Advocate-to-be, to protect her sons, Frank and Archie. Nor did he let her down. It was his influence which induced the Procurator-fiscal, James Hart, as well as William Douglas, John Ord, and other top-brass CID officers of Glasgow, to pursue Slater; to make the Jewish pimp the scapegoat. To be fair to them, though, it was not just friends that Ure, Hart, Douglas and Ord were shielding; like good Scots, they were intent upon preserving the order and well-being of the Scottish Establishment. It did not bear thinking of that the sons of a professor and nephews of a leading light of the Church of Scotland should even be involved in so sordid a case, never mind being actually put on trial for murder.

Professor Glaister was surely another friend to whom the Charterises could have turned. And did he not give it as his expert medical opinion that Slater's little tin-tack hammer could have wrought such savage lethal havoc? Did he not also choose to dismiss the auger, with its adherent cargo of iron-grey strands of what appeared to be the victim's hair?

It is likely, Toughill believes, that Ure and Hart were hoping for a Not Proven verdict from the Slater jury, but Ure, for the prosecution, went too hard. Clearly, Lord Pentland was not happy with the death sentence, and Lord Guthrie, consulted, thought that life imprisonment would more suitably meet the case. But Pentland's deputy, Dodds, was strong for the prescribed penalty to be carried out. It was the day before making his final decision to reprieve that Pentland received an anonymous letter from 'an unknown lady', who felt herself under compulsion by 'divine command' to tell to him the truth.

Toughill's theoretical solution founds heavily upon two anonymous letters – never the safest of foundations. Both were probably from the same hand, although that is not, nor claimed to be, certain. Toughill concludes only that the writing of both was in a female hand. Both were addressed to the Secretary for Scotland, and received while Slater lay under sentence of death in Duke Street Prison. One of them is no more than a surviving fragment of the original. The second, however, is an intact, full-length letter.

The two of them had, for 80 years, remained hidden from prying eyes in the fastness of the closed official files, but in January 1989, File HH16/109 was released for public inspection, and herein Thomas Toughill made what he considered to be the grand find.

Now I, too, had examined the letters which so excited Toughill, but reached a somewhat different conclusion. I think it best to begin by providing the reader with the full texts of the documents, so that he or she may, in due season, make his or her own value judgment.

The fragment of the letter received at the office of the Secretary for Scotland on 18 May 1909, reads:

> . . . the letter that was sent to Duke Street – was to put off scent of real Murderer, who was a relation of Miss Gilchrist and left Glasgow between 21 and 23rd of Dec – He also was a Member of Ally Sloper and Moter Club – He often said he would do for the 'Aunty' yet. Hugh Cameron courted Nelly Lambie – as a single man, to get information. He is (Nugent seen with her aft . . .

Someone, clearly an official, has written at the top of the fragment a remark which would seem to relate to the content of the Duke Street letter referred to in the said fragment: ' . . . Glasgow says "Adams did Murder and his sisters screamed . . . (indecipherable) No. No." '

James Miller Dodds, Under Secretary for Scotland, has written on the cover of the file containing this fragment: 'The L[ord] A[dvocate] informs me that these suggestions were familiar to the prosecution and the defence, and were regarded as without foundation.'

The second anonymous letter contained a great deal of material which claimed to shed a new and true light on the murder.

West Princes Street,
Glasgow
May 20, 1909
To the Secretary for Scotland

My Noble Lord!
I am so frightened you are going to hang Oscar Slater – He *never committed*

the Murder – Nelly Lambie was engaged to Birrell, Miss Gilchrist's Nephew – he was a very wild chap – and none of his people would have anything to do with him as he was always borrowing money from them & kicking up rows – But Nelly said she did not care as she would be far grander than anybody in the Street some day – her Mistress was a bad woman – and had two weans – when she was young so she walked out with Cameron the Bookie – who said he was Nugent – to hear all about Birrell on the night of the Murder she had a man in the kitchen – at 6.30 when she went out or was expecting anyone she put a piece of coal between the doorstep & door, then a slight *push opened it.* She told *all the servants to do that – although we never did –* she said the old Lady once found a bit of coal in the lobby & she said it fell of the shovel – she is fly well after the Murder the man went over the Kitchen window *crossed* the Street into the *Crescent* saw the crowd around the close – and walked away – he left that night for London sold the *brooch to a Dealer in Little College St and left for New Zealand before anyone knew,* after Slater is hanged Nelly Lambie is going to join him – Cameron and *Nelly – know who did the Murder –* Nelly never knew Slater – she had heard of him – only – as the Toff – who gambled and kept a lovely Girl for his self. The Gilchrists gave out in March that Birrell had died in London, big lie – lift coffen & see – they say. Disgusted with old woman – [indecipherable] all the servants in the street were warned by *their masters not to tell the police* anything *or the world would say they were harlots,* & Slater deserved to be hanged – Cameron is afraid to return the Boys are going to give him a killing [kicking?] I *cried when my* Mistress said it was a pity for Slater's old folks at Germany. I *don't know Slater* even by sight but I know Cameron and Lambie – *don't tell anyone* I told you (God told me to tell you) or I will get notice to leave my place. Please forgive me It is all true

So far as the alleged plot on high to inculpate Slater is concerned, Toughill does not seem able to supply any convincing reason as to why these lofty officials – the Lord Advocate of Scotland, the Procurator-fiscal of Lanarkshire, senior police officers of Glasgow and eminent pathologists – should expose themselves to the possibility of total professional ruin just to protect the Charterises and the Birrells from the consequences of their own avarice and folly. Furthermore, the image of them which he purveys as two 'distinguished' Glasgow families is overblown. To be sure, the Charterises were well settled in the ranks of the solid middle class, but the Birrells were in no wise a well-connected or influential clan. They were, to be truthful, thoroughly down-at-heel by 1908. The brothers James and George, living distinctly threadbare lives, could by no stretch of charitable imagination be regarded as constituents of one of Glasgow's more illustrious houses.

In the world of conspiracy, the miniaturisation enthusiasts' slogan, 'small is beautiful', sings a very true note. Mr Ure's conspiracy, as punted by Toughill, would plainly have involved just too many people in too many spheres for the comfort, not to say the safety, of the individual conspirators. It is central to Toughill's thesis that the powerful Alexander Ure should be prime mover in the plot. But where is the *proof* of motivation? Why *should* he have laid his professional life, his whole peaking career, on the line for the albeit respectable Charterises and the far from illustrious Birrells?

Ted Ramsey was not going to stand by mute. He had poked his head above the parapet very smartly after Bruce McKain's article extolling Toughill's enterprise appeared. His response in the Herald[6] (14 October 1992) to the preliminary trumpeting of Toughill's achievement had been, as one would expect, forthright – 'Thomas Toughill will have to come up with some better evidence if he wants to convince the public that he has solved the mystery of the murder of Marion Gilchrist.' He then takes aim and snipes at a couple of Toughill's reported points: 'Toughill claims that Miss Gilchrist was suffering from chronic kidney failure . . . I find this remarkable . . . Glaister made the specific point that the internal organs were all healthy and functioning normally.' Mr Ramsey also remarks that it 'would be interesting to know on what ground Toughill bases his claim that the Crown Office quite deliberately attempted to fail in the extradition of Slater from America'.

A fortnight later, ignoring the second question Toughill replied in the Herald (28 October 1992): 'I do suggest in my book that Miss Gilchrist was dying from kidney failure and quote as evidence the post-mortem report.' But that report says that, other than the presence of small tumours in the womb and its appendages, all the organs of Miss Gilchrist's body were healthy. Both kidneys were described as being 'granular from chronic kidney affection,' but there was no expressed, or indeed justifiable, view that she had

6 It had become the Herald, shedding Glasgow from its masthead with effect from 6 February 1992

been menaced by any imminent life-threatening kidney failure. Granulated contracted kidney, otherwise nephrosclerosis, is a frequently encountered senile change. It is of little importance clinically or pathologically, as sufficient kidney tissue remains unaffected and kidney function is not seriously impaired. It most certainly does not amount to a death sentence.

Relying upon the anonymous letter's assertion of Miss Gilchrist's having delivered forth two illegitimate weans, Toughill cites, first, Maggie Galbraith, and secondly – signposting this with large-letter warnings of 'Speculation Only' – Wingate Birrell, as her offside offspring. And this becomes one of his pivotal concepts.

Toughill had not, apparently, yet learned that one should always exercise a benign caution when any discussion arises relative to the quantum of a lady's years. His polite mistake was to take a woman's word as to her age! Unfortunately, misled by Maggie Galbraith's own statement as to her quotient of years he selected the wrong Galbraith. Failing to widen his search sufficiently, he could find recorded only, for the year 1863, the birth, on Barra, on 11 February of a child – christened not Margaret but Mary – whose parents' christian names, John and Isabella, were, confoundingly, the same as those of the parents of Maggie Galbraith. He should, however, have held his hand when he saw that this John Galbraith was not a 'shoemaker master', as Maggie described her father on her marriage certificate, but a crofter. Nonetheless, Toughill, while admitting his failure to find available documentary evidence to support his contention that Miss Gilchrist was Maggie Galbraith's mother, finds, notwithstanding, strong reasons for crediting the story. Barra, isolated and remote, strikes him as providing an ideal *locus* for a pregnant Victorian spinster's discreet confinement and parturition. And a poor crofter could surely have been, without too much difficulty, induced by the great universal persuader – money – to have accepted the infant as his own.

Wingate Birrell's birth certificate seems deceptively all in order. It shows Walter Birrell, ship-broker, and Janet Gilchrist or Birrell as his parents. Toughill concedes that a major objection to the illegitimacy theory is that Walter Birrell duly signed Wingate's birth certificate. Even so, he thinks that Walter, who appears to have been on terms of close and sympathetic affection with his wife's family, might well have felt sorry for his sister-in-law Marion's plight if once again she had become an unmarried mother. Toughill sharply notes that, whereas the other three Birrell children were all born in Glasgow, the circumstance that Wingate was born in Helensburgh might be significant. Toughill writes of Helensburgh that it was 'a small resort town on the banks of the Clyde about fifteen miles to the west of the city. Did Marion Gilchrist go there to have her second child, away from prying eyes and wagging tongues?' It seems to me very wrong, smacking indeed of the sort of wrong about which he complains in the case of Oscar Slater, that Toughill should cast this veridically unsupported slur upon the good name and pious memory of a God-fearing, completely respectable spinster lady.

It is Toughill's serious belief that it was after reading the second, that is to say the full-length and circumstantially detailed-seeming, anonymous letter, that Lord Pentland could not have permitted Slater's execution to take place. It is my view that the Secretary for Scotland would be unlikely to feel obliged to interfere with the law's taking its course upon the basis of a last-minute letter containing immediately unverifiable material written by a correspondent who declines to reveal his or her identity. In practically every major legal cause letters of varying tone, from sheer crankiness to alarmingly persuasive plausibility, come toppling in to the authorities, and the general, unwritten, rule has self-protectively evolved to discount any documents to which the sender refuses, or omits, to append his or her authentic, or authenticating, signature.

In this case, viewing the internal evidence, it has been thought that the anonymous correspondent may have been one of the female servants employed in West Princes Street or its vicinity. Elizabeth McIntosh, the 19-year-old maid who worked for Dr John Adams at No. 1 Queen's Crescent, and who had as it happens spent part of the afternoon of the day of the murder in Miss Gilchrist's flat with her close friend Nellie Lambie, has been put forward as the possible author of the letter, or rather letters, for it is thought that both communications were penned by the same person. Looking at them, Toughill asks, with a very proper caution, if it is all true or if, indeed, any of it is true. He confesses to being impressed by the tone and detail of the letters, and by the sincerity of the writer – God told her to write. More than that, she becomes, with Trench, the decicatee of his book: ' . . . and to an anonymous lady who obeyed God's commands'.

It is from these letters that Toughill derives the story of Hugh Cameron, the Moudie, setting out, posing as a single man and using the name Patrick Nugent, to court Lambie, so as to hear all about Birrell.

Frankly, this does not seem to me to hold water. We know for a fact that Nellie had been introduced to the *real* Nugent at a dance at Craigneuk way back at the end of 1907 or beginning of 1908, by a man named Charles Findlay. They had subsequently met on a great many occasions, even contemplating marriage at one time. It is unlikely that this man was Cameron. Incidentally, both Lambie and Cameron stoutly denied in their respective precognitions that they had known each other prior to the murder. And, the anonymous letter apart, there is no reason to doubt this. Toughill's response to their denial is of the Mandy Rice-Davies brand – 'Well, they would, wouldn't they?' In his scenario the Moudie becomes an exceedingly busy character. He is impersonating Nugent. He is courting Lambie. He is trying to sell Slater's pawn-ticket. He is working for the police.

But it is what the anonymous letters have to say regarding Wingate Birrell that is supremely important. Having made that gentleman's more intimate acquaintance for the first time in these letters, Toughill, accepting, it is to be presumed, the writer's evicentially unsupported testimony that Wingate, whom we did already know to be a wild character and not on good terms with his family, was a member of the Sloper and Motor Clubs, and engaged to Nellie Lambie, apparently accepts him as the killer of Aunt Marion. Interpreting somewhat widely the adjective 'wild', Toughill seems to graft on to Wingate the characteristics previously ascribed to the fictitious Austin Birrell – violent, epileptic, mentally unbalanced, not quite right in the head – without the smallest piece of properly attested evidence. He uncritically accepts, or at any rate does not question, the letter-writer's claim that Wingate left for

London later on the night of 21 December; that he sold Miss Gilchrist's diamond crescent brooch to a dealer in Little College Street, Westminster, (incidentally, *was* there a jewellery dealer's premises in Little College Street in December 1908? Did Toughill check?); and that he subsequently left for New Zealand.

Toughill 'hears' that Wingate's death is not what it seems. A false death certificate has been issued. Noting that the certificate bears two names for the deceased – Wingate Birrell and William Gilchrist – Toughill asks why would a man use his mother's name? Did he find it necessary because he could not use the name of his real father? One is left to suppose that the Dreadnought Seaman's Hospital, where he was *said* to have died of tuberculosis on 4 March 1909, was also in on Alexander Ure's plot.

And, taking on board the anonymous writer's assertion that the official story of Wingate's demise was a 'big lie', Toughill indicates that he would certainly wish to 'lift the coffin and see' . . . Would it be empty? Would it contain some other person's body? Or, if it really was Wingate's corpse, would it display the suicide's broken neck or strategic bullet hole? Or would it, perhaps, contain tell-tale traces of poison? Then he would not have died of TB. And if not . . . Once again, Toughill stands by the ever-open door of unlimited speculation.

One such speculation gangs a-gley. Thinking to catch the Glasgow force out in dubious conduct, Toughill observes that Ord stated in a precognition dated 2 March 1909, that the manner in which Miss Gilchrist was killed suggested that the murder had been committed by someone 'acquainted with deeds of violence in America', rather than by a Scotsman, and that this information had led the police to inquire about foreigners in the city. Comments Toughill:

> One is surely justified in suspecting that Ord invented these details and included them in order to point the finger of accusation towards a foreigner like Slater, who had spent time in America. . . . It need hardly be said that none of this is supported by contemporary evidence.

Oh, but it is! The reader will recall the letter received from the sea-captain, J Lumsdane.[7] And how does the world and his wife's favourite suspect, Dr Francis Charteris, come out of all this? Toughill definitely exonerates him, so far as the wielding of the bludgeon or being the lethal 'chairman': that is, he unequivocally did not kill Miss Gilchrist. But, in Toughill's book, he was present when the bludgeoning was done. And he was the man who walked past Lambie and Adams.

Here, Toughill echoes the view taken by Peter Costello, who, in his book, *The Real World of Sherlock Holmes*, published in 1991,[8] devoted a couple of chapters to 'The Case of Oscar Slater' and 'Why Miss Gilchrist Died'. Costello subscribed to the 'Dr Charteris was the man in the hall' school of thought. He also accepted the somewhat threadbare motive of the unpopular Gilchrist will. He embraced, too, the now well-exploded fallacy of the illegitimate daughter, and made the mistake of saying that the residue of Miss Gilchrist's £12,259 1s 4d estate went to Mrs Galbraith or Ferguson, instead of to her daughters.[9]

Toughill claims that Margaret Dawson Birrell was 'the woman who orchestrated the accusation against Dr Charteris' (that is, of course, if one accepts Trench's story), and he reminds us that she was the sister of the man named in the anonymous letter as the murderer. Interestingly, Toughill's apparent discovery that Margaret Birrell made not one but two statements to Trench or his supporters is completely at variance with the evidence given by Trench himself.

Another argument advanced by Toughill is that although Charteris may have been tall and thin as a young man, whereas Slater was unquestionably stocky, 'facially the two men had a general likeness. The shape of Charteris' nose is particularly important'. Toughill is thoroughly satisfied – displays photographs to prove it – that both Francis and Archibald Charteris bore a strong resemblance to Slater. I absolutely dispute it. Obviously, resemblance must, like beauty, lie in the eye of the beholder. Everyone who ever beheld Slater observed that he *looked* Jewish and *looked* foreign. The Charterises certainly did not.

7 See p. 31

8 Robinson Publishing, London.

9 After the disbursement of legacies totalling £5,820 (including a bequest of £1,000 to Mrs Ferguson), the remainder amounted to £6,439. Costello gives the residual figure as £6,280.

Most puzzling is Toughill's declaration that what lay behind the accusations against Francis Charteris was 'the hatred which the Birrells felt towards the Charteris family'. I have discovered no hint of there being any such animosity between the two houses. Toughill, who has frequent resort to Shakespeare, seems to have elected to cast the twain as the Montagues and Capulets of Glasgow.

It will be recalled that Charteris, in his interview with Mowat Phillips in 1961 – more than half a century after the murder – had given the same explanation as to how he had learned of the murder as he had given to Superintendent Douglas at the time, namely, that the police had contacted Mrs Charteris' lawyer in the mistaken belief that he was Miss Gilchrist's lawyer. And the lawyer, in turn, had telephoned Dr Charteris with the bad news. Toughill repeats the mistake perpetuated by Costello – that Charteris had said that it was *the police themselves* who had got in touch with him. Triumphantly, he cites this apparent change of story as a palmary example of a man condemning himself out of his own mouth. He maintains that in his relating of a story which does not stand up to the smallest scrutiny, Charteris, at one fell swoop, swept away any faint doubts which might have remained that he was the stranger in the hall, the man who walked past Lambie and Adams on the night of the murder. And Toughill espies confirmation of his suspicions in the circumstance that the police themselves do not corroborate having asked the doctor to break the news of Miss Gilchrist's murder to his mother. On the contrary, he points out, Superintendent Douglas actually quotes Charteris' statement that he came to Miss Gilchrist's house because he had been informed of her death by a lawyer.[10]

Precisely.

I think that Mr Toughill and Mr Costello must both have suffered a *lapsus oculi* when reading – as I trust they did – Mowat Phillips' account of his interview with Professor Charteris in the *Scottish Daily Mail* of 5 October1961.[11]

An interesting item which I had not seen recorded elsewhere appears in Costello's book. The prison chaplain at Peterhead during part of the time that Slater was there was John Lamond, friend, and

---

10 Miss Gilchrist's solicitor, James Macdonald, lived some distance away from the scene of the murder, at 2 Buckingham Terrace, off Great Western Road. Mrs Elizabeth Charteris' solicitor, the other James Macdonald, lived at 8 Queen's Crescent, about 100 yards from Miss Gilchrist's flat. Documents in Register House, Edinburgh, confirm that this James Macdonald was Mrs Charteris' agent.

later biographer, of Conan Doyle. He heard Slater's insistent claims to innocence without a qualm. Never for a moment did it occur to him that Slater might *be* innocent.

11 See page 255.

Chapter Twenty-Two

IN THE EYE OF TIME

Not everyone accepted that Oscar Slater was innocent. Indeed, the only two people who actually saw the man in the hall did not dismiss Oscar. To the end of her life Helen Lambie continued to believe that he had murdered her old mistress.

I am able to publish here for the first time extracts from letters of the utmost importance written absolutely spontaneously by Helen Lambie to her mother. They incontrovertibly prove that all the newspaper reports of her retraction of her evidence were false, and that the *Empire News* article of 23 October 1927, alleged to have been written by her, was completely bogus.

Here is the authentic voice of Helen Lambie, speaking from beyond the grave.

From Peoria, she writes to her mother:

> *November 13th, 1927.*
> . . . no one has come here yet and we are keeping all the pieces of
> newspaper . . . So we will see how far they will go, as I can see plainly all is

a frame-up, and Conan Doyle has no statement from me in my handwriting. He says he has a copy, so Conan Doyle knows he is working on a false statement. The Government will not allow themselves to be fooled by falseness, and if I come forward on my own accord no one will pay our expenses. So I know to watch myself here. In 1914 at the private inquiry it was a false statement they used then. So Conan Doyle may give up, falseness will never clear or get Slater free. He should have got hanged years ago. They should hang him yet; as he is the man and no other man. Conan Doyle is only aggravating and causing an agitating [sic] in the papers to get the public on his side. If the public uses their brains they will see plainly it is a frame-up, all false . . . So, Mother, don't let any of these Editors in your house, as they are liable to tell lies on you. I have had my experience with them all.

November 20th, 1927.
I had a letter with two pieces of Old Country newspapers from my Auntie Leezie. It was the *Empire News*. My Auntie Leezie says she feels very angry at the lies they have in the papers about me and she hopes Rabbie[1] makes them stump up for it. There has never been anyone called at [sic] me yet, so this may be a move to try and find me out. Rabbie says if anyone calls on me when he is at work they have to be told to call back after six o'clock. He is going to tell them he is not going to allow me to say any more. That is all past. Mother, this is the reason why they are lying and agitating so much in the papers – so as to get me to come forward to [sic] my own expense. And I won't do that. Nor even at their expense, whoever they are. I have already told them that Slater is the man. No one has ever come near me, and I never sent any statement – so that is all false. I still would say Slater is the man and no other.

November 27th, 1927.
Your papers received, and I also got another piece of paper of [sic] my Auntie Leezie last Monday, the 21st November, letting me know that Slater got out of jail on the 15th.[2] But Slater is no innocent man. What [sic] I account for Mary Barrowman changing her story, they Editors has used a sweet tongue and fooled her, as I see by the papers there are words, and far more, added to her statement than she really told.

November 29th, 1927.
We are all amused at the papers you sent, especially Maisie.[3] Rabbie says

1   Robert, her husband.
2   In fact, Slater had been released on Monday, 14 November 1927.
3   Her elder daughter, Margaret Balfour Gillon. Generally known as Maisie. She would be 16 then.

that is a thing they can't do as put me in the pictures.[4]

Rabbie says we can't make a case, and I don't see the Crown Head saying anything or doing anything, or even Miss Gilchrist's friends trying to stop all this, and I have no wealth to start on [sic]. If I paid my passage home I would have nothing left. So Slater is lucky to have such a smart, wealthy body at his back, and being treated so kindly and given flowers on his return to Glasgow. Slater's lawyers might be the means of him being a very wealthy man yet, if they can go on as they are doing and gets him compensation. I am thinking the Crown Head is waiting and watching to get a chance at Conan Doyle and the other agitators. I see by your letter you are angry. We are too over it all. There are [sic] no offer to back us. So that helps to keep us where we are. It's enough to cause the public to raise trouble at a murderer being set free. Innocent – if he would tell the truth that would find him out, and he is no innocent man. He knows that, too, the coward. He is a fly man and it is these other smarties that is doing all for him.

December 6th, 1927.

Slater's lawyer said I was telling lies when I was in New York. Slater sent for this lawyer. His name is Goodhart. He belongs to Baltimore. So if Slater says he is a poor Jew and pretends he can't speak good English, he has a smart lot to speak for him, and if he proves his innocence it will be by telling lies, as I know perfectly well Slater is the man that passed me out of Miss Gilchrist's house. Slater is a coward for not telling the truth . . . A mob should form up and blow Slater to pieces. Give him what he gave the old lady. Batter him to pieces.

December 12th, 1927.

Mother, I feel sorry to hear of those agents worrying you. Mother, Rabbie says I have to give no written statement with my name on it to the news agents, and if any of the Government officials calls say nothing to them either unless one of the Holytown policemen are with them so as you are sure of them. And then tell them I am still as I was at the trial.

December 18th, 1927. [With this letter to her mother Lambie enclosed a statement which she had written.]

December 18th, 1927
By Helen Lambie
or Mrs Gillon

I wish to put a denial to the statement recantly [sic] published in Newspapers. There is no truth in that statement. Connan [sic] Doyle used a

4 This must refer to the rumour that Slater was to appear in a film about the case.

false statement. I would not blame another man. Slater is the man that I saw coming out of the house of Miss Gilchrist. I am as strong and of the same mind as I was at the trial. If Slater would tell the truth he is not an inocent [*sic*] man.
From Helen Lambie
now in the U.S.A.

Mother . . . I think the best one to give this statement to is the police, as they can read it in court and it will be more valuable at that time. If an inquiry is held in Edinburgh, speak to the Holytown police. See the advice they give you.

Arthur Adams, too, has been reliably reported as secretly believing that it really was Slater whom he saw walking towards him across Miss Gilchrist's lobby.

Adams' fellow-musician, John Hardie Ratcliffe[5], has amusingly recounted how on one occasion when it was suggested to Adams, physically a very small and rather delicate person, that he might at least have had a go at stopping the man from escaping, he held out his little arms expressively to indicate his size and weakness of physique, as if to say, 'How could you expect me to be able to stop him?'

Ratcliffe, who was to become general secretary of the Musicians' Union, knew Adams personally, and once actually asked him: 'Was the man you saw in the hall Dr Charteris?'

The answer was a simple, unqualified 'No'.
And in 1993, Mr Harry Gardner came forward to bear a kind of witness-at-a-remove testimony.

At a small dinner party in the winter of 1940-41, I met the late Horace Fellowes, a professional violinist with the Scottish Orchestra. He was a good friend of Arthur Adams'. He told us that Arthur had no doubt that Slater was the man who brushed against him. When asked why he had not then identified him in court, Adams replied that it was because he knew that if he, as well as Helen Lambie, had done so, Slater would have hanged, and that he [Adams] did not believe in capital punishment.

We have it also, it will be recalled, on the eminently sound authority of Sheriff Robert Dickson – *Glasgow Herald*, 20 July 1991 – that Craigie

5 The brother of the former Assistant Chief Constable of Glasgow, William Ratcliffe.

Aitchison was by no means convinced as to his client's innocence.[6]

There are, unarguably, some points which go unfavourably for Slater. For instance: his inability to produce what, from a legal point of view, could be regarded as a firm, acceptably-witnessed alibi for the precise period of the commission of the murder. And, arguably, there is the massive consensus of identification evidence marshalled against him, albeit, when broken down, this did tend to evaporate.

Permit me to state unequivocally my personal conclusions and beliefs.

I believe that Oscar Slater was innocent. I do not for one moment suggest that he was a lovable or an admirable character. I am sure that his basic honesty was widely open to question, and there seems to me no doubt that he acted as a pander and significantly supported himself and his gambling upon the immoral earnings of women. But that is irrelevant. What is a crucial point is that despite, we may be sure, the most dedicated efforts, no one at any time was ever able to show there to have been any connection whatsoever between Oscar Slater and Marion Gilchrist.

I believe that, generally speaking, the Glasgow police did their honest best by their lights – even if they were moonbeams or penny candles lit in jars! – to catch the killer of Miss Gilchrist, but mesmerised themselves into the conviction that the German Jew pimp was the murderer.

I believe that no member of either the Birrell or Charteris families had anything at all to do with the brutal death of Marion Gilchrist. I have examined without prejudice every one of the relatives of Miss Gilchrist, as well as the non-blood-related candidates, and have been unable to find a jot or tittle of real evidence to indicate guilt against any one of them. Neither, frankly, can I find valid motive.

I believe that rumours, many of them started up by newspaper speculation and subsequently bedecked with spurious detail in pub, club, kitchen and drawing-room, became invested with the trappings of apparent truth, and increased and multiplied without let or hindrance down the decades.

6 See p. 276

I would put, against the widely sponsored view, disseminated in so many previous books and articles on the case, that the murder was an internecine domestic affair, the suggestion that the circumstances of a robbery that went wrong is a very persuasive scenario which could satisfactorily account for virtually all of the conflicting factors which have successfully bedevilled every effort to find a rational answer to questions which, for 93 years now, have buzzed like indestructible bluebottles about the unquiet grave of the old lady of West Princes Street.

Let us empty our minds of all the adherences with which the ingenuity – and ingenuousness – of the years has adorned the bare surfaces of the murder. What is the most outstanding feature of the tragedy at No. 49 West Princes Street? What stands out like a pricking thumb – or itchy palm?

Draw back without prejudice, and look.

It is the familiar criminal allurement: a rich old woman, living virtually alone, unprotected – the presence of a frail, 21-year-old girl can hardly rate as an adequate shield – surrounded by portable goodies. The enticing set-up focuses the gaze as irresistibly as one of those 'pop-up' pages in an old-fashioned, Victorian children's book. And these things *do* get known; *always* get around. Who cleans? Who paints and decorates? Who sweeps the chimneys, washes the windows? Who services the gas? All, like G K Chesterton's postman, are possessed of the quality of 'invisibility' – and an 'Open, Sesame!'

There is, of course, the inevitable temptation to flirt with all those Agatha Christie-like complexities, permutations of plot and plotting: murder most maze-like. The plain truth, though, is that the more one sounds out, and rings the changes on, the fanciful familial-involvement theory, the more hollow the response becomes, especially since the purloining of the altered will as motive proves, when you pause to think about it, to be pure rubbish.

I believe, too, that over the years the received image of Miss Gilchrist's absolutely invincible determination *never* to open her own front-door has become exaggerated. After all, we know for a solidly reported fact that she did so to the calling carpet-sellers at the time of the Great Glasgow Exhibition of 1901. It must be allowed also that, for all the talk of locks and bars, no home is really a fortress, however stout its bolts.

The 'solving' of the Oscar Slater Murder Case seems to have got somewhat out of hand – rather like what has happened in the case of Jack the Ripper.[7]

There is, I repeat, no target like a rich, elderly woman living on her own. But it is also a dangerous one. Things can, for the smallest unforeseen reasons, go drastically wrong. The elderly are fragile. In the 1990s, the aged *femme sole*, killed without specific intent in the course of a burglary, was an only too horrifyingly familiar figure.

We are not, I think, looking for Birrells or Charterises. The police did that, without profit. Nor, for that matter, are we looking for common or garden sneak thieves. We are, I am strongly inclined to think, looking for a pair – or possibly a trio or quartet, a gang – of heavy professional criminals after serious jewellery. They will have planned fastidiously. They will have been the watchers in the quiet street, seen by some of the witnesses. Criminals of this type actually prefer to carry out stop-watch robberies under pressure. They would have considered the maid's ten-minute absence ample for their adrenalin-hyped purpose.

Rumours of good booty at No. 49 had got out. Miss Gilchrist, attracting by her extraordinary way of life, with, as it were, jewelled butterflies pinned to the curtains, inviting the fate that befell her, had the eminently predictable misfortune to be targeted by such prowling predators.

The joint-enterprise was robbery. We may be sure that one of the pair of entrants would boast all the skills of the con man, bringing with him the smooth-working key of a well-oiled tongue. One of the two, probably both, would have dressed, as Adams was to observe, in gentlemanly fashion. He would have been the one who went off to the bedroom to ransack for plunder, leaving his fellow-villain to take care of Miss Gilchrist, held hostage in the dining-room. They would have expected an 82-year-old, intimidated, to present no problem.

But this old lady, true to her known character, proved very

7   See *The Quest for Jack the Ripper*, by the author, Patterson Smith, New Jersey, 2001.

unintimidated, very unco-operative, not to say downright difficult. She was, perhaps, delivered a sharp, admonitory tap, fell, hit her head on the coal-scuttle, and started to knock on the floor and kick up a rumpus, which ended, and was ended, only when, panicked, her assailant – who had no weapon with him as no violence had been intended as any part of the plan – picked up a heavy dining-chair and perpetrated a frenzied, silencing overkill. He then slithered out of the inches-open kitchen window, pushing it down again behind him in order to disguise his route of departure. His transit was, however, observed by the Adams sisters as he passed over their window on his way down the rone pipe.

The smooth one, searching in the spare room, was then disturbed; first, by Adams' ringing, and after that by the arrival of Lambie and Adams. However experienced a criminal may be, he is still liable to panic when a crime goes wrong. The searcher would have abandoned all thoughts of theft, even leaving, as surprised robbers have been known to do in such circumstances, obvious and easy pickings untouched. Anyway, the plan having misfired, he would not have wanted, if the worst had come to the worst and he had been captured, to be found with swag on him. Albeit he might perhaps, almost absent-mindedly, as of habit, have pocketed the diamond crescent brooch – or, indeed, he might have picked it up before the alarm – and equally absent-mindedly, left his box of Runaway Matches behind. All thoughts other than the achievement of a safe getaway would, of necessity, have been driven out of his head.

Having glided towards Lambie and Adams on a snail-track of mimed insouciance, he would either have joined his fled companion on the back green and the pair of them gone over the wall into Down Lane, turned right along West Cumberland Street, and out into West Princes Street; or he might otherwise have rushed out of the close-door, hared up West Princes Street on his own and, higher up that street, been joined by his partner. A third, less likely, possibility is that both met at the front of No. 49 and rushed across West Princes Street to exit, via Queen's Crescent and Melrose Street, into the swirling anonymity of Great Western Road. It seems likely that the pair were the well-dressed running men encountered by Agnes Brown as they sped out of the closeting, claustrophobic peril of the tight, dark plexus of sequestered streets, up Rupert Street towards the bright-lit, populous haven of Great Western Road.

The probability is that the two had worked together before. The near-certainty is that they never would again. After that terminal fiasco they would have split up for good and all.

Respectability of aspect would have been the best disguise, as most of the Scottish criminals of that era would have been thought of both by the police and, indeed, Miss Gilchrist, as being of the lower and rougher classes. Bill Sikes in kilts. This pair would have been distinctly out of the common run. The police should have been looking for a dark-featured con man who resembled Slater. Even if he had never been caught – although it is unlikely that he would not at some time in his criminous career have been arrested – there would surely have been previous incidents which conveyed a description.

Unfortunately, inter-regional police investigations were rudimentary in 1908. The ironic thing is that the police, following their instincts, were most probably right in the first place, when they regarded the Gilchrist murder as a robbery turned sour. Then they were taken in by the false clue of the pawned brooch and, although made very early aware of its falsity, never looked back from that Priestleyean dangerous corner . . . but went chasing off across the Atlantic after the aforesaid moonbeams.

The Imaginative Liftman. That was what, in his old-fashioned way, the late Jack House, writing in the Glasgow *Evening News* of 15 October 1954, called him. He wrote:

> Next in my revelations comes a 'confession' about the West Princes Street murder. It's an anonymous letter written in an illiterate hand. Though he doesn't sign his name, I know it comes from a liftman employed in a Glasgow building.[8] He sold his story to a Sunday newspaper a few years ago and it was published in a somewhat different form.

8 In Renfield Street, Jack House told me.

The previous story to which Jack House is referring appeared on 29 February 1948, four weeks after Oscar died, in the *Sunday Express*. Written by Brendon Kemmet, it claimed that, moved by the death of Slater, a man had come to him in the Glasgow office of the *Scottish Sunday Express*, and told him: 'I know who committed the murder. I wish to tell the story that would have saved Slater and sent two men to the gallows.'

Kemmet's informant, who was 59 – born in 1889, and therefore 19 in 1908 – had spent most of his life in prison. He said that at the time of the Slater case he was one of a gang of thieves in Glasgow.

There were four of us. The other three were: J., always well dressed. His appearance and general build much resembled Slater. But he was clean-shaven, whereas Slater had a moustache. At the time he was aged about 22-25. W. was not so much like Slater in build, but he had a broken nose (like Slater) and a moustache. At the time he was aged about forty. G., a barman, the only married man of the four, at one time fairly prosperous.

J. was the man who struck Miss Gilchrist down.

A fifth man whom I never met comes into the story. He was the brains behind our robberies. He used to supply us, through W., with information about the contents of houses, gleaned from charwomen and daily helps.

Before the Gilchrist murder a charwoman had told 'The Brain' that in West Princes Street was an old woman who lived alone with a large sum of money and a large quantity of jewellery in the house. W. brought us that news. But the address he gave us was that of a Miss Crosbie, another old lady who lived alone near Miss Gilchrist, but who, I have since found reason to believe, was poorly off. 'The Brain', I think, had got the addresses of Miss Gilchrist and Miss Crosbie mixed up.

For weeks we kept a watch on the house of Miss Crosbie. Never once were we lucky enough to catch her leaving the house unattended. Each of us took turns of visiting, on one pretext or another, but on each occasion Miss Crosbie answered the door. I posed as a window cleaner; J. and G. as insurance agents. During those weeks of watching the name of Miss Gilchrist was never mentioned. I did not know of her existence until she had ceased to exist.

A few months before the murder, G. and I were arrested on a charge of reset. He got 6 months, I got 12. After our arrest 'The Brain' seems either to have discovered his error or for some reason suggested switching to Miss Gilchrist's house. The murder was committed while I was in prison. The first I heard of it was when a Glasgow detective named Gordon came to see me in Barlinnie Prison. Gordon, had he but known it, was on the right track. He had information, he said, that I 'and others unknown', had been watching and planning a robbery in the vicinity of the crime. 'Who were the others?' he demanded. I not only refused information, but I stoutly denied all knowledge of the affair.

Some months after my release, Gordon pounced on me for housebreaking, and brought several other charges against me. I was sent to a High Court, and received a five years' sentence. I was 21 years old. A sentence of that type on a man of my age was rare. So for the greater part of the next 20 years I toiled and suffered in the granite quarries of Peterhead Prison – alongside Slater, the man I should have saved.

In 1921 I had six weeks of liberty, and for the first time in 13 years met W. We met in a public house in Crown Street, Glasgow. W. was more alarmed than pleased to see me. He was agitated throughout all the brief time we spent together. But he did tell me what had happened on the night of the Gilchrist murder.

W said he kept watch. J. went with his jemmy to the house. He rang the bell. Miss Gilchrist, thinking it was the maid coming back, opened the door and then returned to the dining-room. J. struck at Miss Gilchrist, but did not knock her out as he expected. So he followed her, striking again and again with his jemmy, until she collapsed. By this time the people underneath had become alarmed, and were making for Miss Gilchrist. J. had no time to hunt for money or jewellery. He may have snatched a piece or two hurriedly before he was disturbed, but to the best of my knowledge the two men gained nothing by the murder.

Miss Agnes Brown, a schoolteacher, told the police that two men rushed past her in West Princes Street. One, she said, had his arm pressed close to his side. That was J., supporting the jemmy under his jacket. The jemmy was thrown into the River Kelvin. J. who lived in Partick, went home by subway.

From the day of that meeting with W. I have never seen any of the old gang. If W. is alive today he is over 80. But Oscar Slater I did see, again and again. We became good friends in Peterhead. We never discussed the murder, for I was terrified to tell of what I knew.

Jack House's rendering of the story contained a few additional bits and pieces –

The man who struck Miss Gilchrist down was a fully qualified chemist. He was a native of Partick . . . W., the outside man, cut through the park and home. He resided in Berkeley Street . . . Then our Imaginative Liftman goes on to traduce Detective Lieutenant Trench and David Cook, the lawyer, in a most despicable way.

And House opines: 'I have seldom read such a farrago of nonsense . . . the Imaginitive Liftman's tale is sheer tripe.'

That was not, however, the conclusion reached by ex-Detective Chief Superintendent Robert Colquhoun, who, in 1962, brought out, with the ghostly assistance of the well-known Scottish journalist, the late Bill Knox, his memoirs, *Life Begins at Midnight* (John Long, London), and in a final chapter, 'Postscript to a Crime', supplied a rather fuller account of the story first told by Brendon Kemmet.

Superintendent Colquhoun's informant told a story which fundamentally agreed with those told by Kemmet's anonymous visitor and House's anonymous correspondent. Neither Kemmet nor House gave any *nom de guerre* to the man. Colquhoun designated him 'Andy'.

The late Brendon Kemmet did, however, confide to Superintendent Colquhoun that the man who told him the story which he published in the *Sunday Express* was one James Inglis, a notorious Glasgow housebreaker, who died on June 29 1960, at the age of 71.

As a result of careful investigation of internal clues, I am able to reveal that Colquhoun's informant, the man he calls 'Andy', was one Richard Craig. Glasgow born – in 1890 – and bred, Craig had been a reprehensively active member of the Caulfield-Craig gang, credited with much mischief during the first decade and a half of the twentieth century. He and Caulfield were found guilty of breaking into a public-house, at 60 Eglinton Street, Glasgow, and stealing £3, and £28 from a lockfast safe. Tried at the High Court before Lord Salvesen, Caulfield, aged 36, was sentenced, on 25 February 1915, to ten years' penal servitude. Craig's record was much less weighty than that of his older criminous confederate, and Lord Salvesen, staying the full power of his elbow, gave him a serious warning, reinforced by a three-year spell of penal servitude in which to ponder the proposition that the game of burglary did not pay.

The tale which Craig had to tell is as follows.

In the year 1909, a 19-year-old at the outset of a career of safe-blowing, Craig found himself the unwilling recipient of a confidence, a confession really, of a friend, James Inglis, whom he had got to know when they were both doing time in Barlinnie Prison. Jimmy told Craig that there had been three men involved in the West

Princes Street murder – himself, Wilson, an engineer who was periodically crippled with rheumatism, and Jamieson, a man about the same height and build as Slater, who had something to do with a chemist's shop.

There was a woman who worked as a cleaner in various places around West Princes Street, and it was she who told her man that there was a Miss Crosbie who kept money in her house and that Miss Gilchrist had a box of jewellery which she kept hidden behind the grate in her room. And the cleaner's man told Inglis and his friends about the old lady. They decided to get this box of jewellery, and kept loitering about Miss Gilchrist's house, watching to see if they could find an opportunity to slip in.

It was just then that Jimmy Inglis was lifted by the police, and jailed for 12 months. It was while he was in custody that Miss Gilchrist was murdered. The next thing he knew was a detective whom the boys called Black Gordon (Detective Alexander Gordon from the Central Police Office) coming to interview him in Barlinnie. Gordon said that Inglis and two men had been seen loitering near Miss Gilchrist's house, and asked Jimmy who the two men were. He just denied all knowledge. He had never been there. He knew nothing of any two men.

I consider it most unlikely that Inglis would invent such a story to tell Andy, who was his respected and genuine benefactor – and who I knew was always regarded by Inglis as his most intimate friend. I am convinced that Andy believes his account of the murder of Marion Gilchrist to be the truth. There are differences between the story published in 1948 and that told to me by Andy, but these are mostly trivial and both accounts obviously emanated from the same source.

Inglis, in his published account, refers to a man J. – the murderer – as being very like Slater in build, but clean-shaven. The man with him, W., was not so much like Slater in build but had a broken nose, like Slater, and a moustache. It seems quite possible that the man seen by Mary Barrowman could well have been Wilson flying from the scene. Jamieson would not be likely to emerge until a few minutes later, and could have done so after the girl had passed. Wilson could have waited nearby, until joined by Jamieson, and the teacher, Miss Brown, did speak of seeing two men running along West Princes Street from the direction of Miss Gilchrist's house. Miss Brown also spoke of one of the men carrying a heavy article about the size of a walking stick, and Inglis speaks of the jemmy having been thrown into the River Kelvin. Andy agrees that this was never mentioned to him, but Miss Brown in her evidence said she saw the two men turn into Rupert Street towards Great Western Road. A bridge in that street crosses over the Kelvin.[9]

'I believe,' says Colquhoun, 'that James Inglis' story may well be the final solution.'

Whether it is, in fact, truth or fiction, may never be proved in terms of law. But Andy's account should, I feel, be known.

Ex-Detective Chief Superintendent Colquhoun died on 22 September 1969.

I am very much persuaded – although I must, and do, emphasise that it is no more than a personal opinion, based upon a long study of the circumstances surrounding the case – that the true cause of the murder of Marion Gilchrist was a jewel theft that went wrong. It was the late Detective Lieutenant John Trench alone, who, with his almost universally contradicted testimony, brought the red herring of Dr Charteris into it, and all ensuing complications date from that.

9 Miss Brown did not describe it as 'a heavy article about the size of a walking stick'. Her actual words were: 'It might have been a walking stick, but I thought it looked clumsier than a walking stick.'

Chapter
Twenty-Three

ODDS
AND
ENDINGS

It is always fascinating to know what happened to the actors and actresses after the footlights and the limes went out. Endings are not, alas, necessarily as neat and tidy as one would wish. Sometimes they straggle away to nowhere; they become, and remain, hidden. But here, to satisfy, as far as I am able, the reader's very proper curiosity, are accounts of what the Fates held in store for such of the principals and bit-players in our long-drawn-out drama as we have not previously followed to their destinations.

At the time of the Slater trial, Archibald Hamilton Charteris was 35, was a lecturer on Public and Private International Law at the University of Glasgow, and a partner in the firm of Charteris & Hill, writers, of 19 St Vincent Place, Glasgow. He was joint-author with James Bone, under the twin-headed pseudonym, 'James Hamilton Muir', of a very well thought of book, *Glasgow in* 1901, published by William Hodge & Company[1] to coincide with the Great Glasgow Exhibition of that year. He also wrote a very nicely fashioned study

---

1 Publishers subsequently of the *Notable Scottish* and *Notable British Trials* series.

of Scottish literary humour, When the Scot Smiles, which displayed his wide reading of Scots literature. He had, in fact, quit Scotland in 1920, taking up the chair of the Challis Professorship of International Law at the University of Sydney. Before leaving his native shores, he had married Margaret, daughter of Mr H B Rossiter, of Paignton, Devon. She bore him a son, John Hamilton Charteris, who was still a schoolboy when, on 4 October 1940, Archibald died, aged sixty-six, at Turramurra, near Sydney, New South Wales.

Archibald and Francis' mother, Elizabeth Greer Gilchrist or Charteris, died on 29 September 1921, in her eightieth year. Some time before her death she had left No. 4 Queen Margaret Crescent, at Hillhead, in Glasgow, to reside for a time at Edgecumbe, Sydney Road, Guildford, Surrey, but latterly she had moved into the home of her daughter, Mary Greer Gilchrist or McCall, at 33 Christchurch Road, Bournemouth, where she died, leaving estate valued at £459 4s.

Margaret Dawson Birrell, spinster, of 61 Rupert Street, Glasgow, married, on 7 November 1916, at St Aloysius' Roman Catholic Church, Glasgow, at the age of 52, Henry Kerr, 61-year-old widower, a wine merchant, of 24 Blythswood Drive, Glasgow. The marriage was sadly short-lived. He died, aged 67, at Hunter's Quay, Dunoon, on 13 August 1922, away from his usual Glasgow residence, at 51 Rupert Street. His widow survived him by a quarter of a century, dying, aged 82, on 16 May 1947, at Cubrieshaw Hall Nursing Home, West Kilbride. She is remembered as a very nice old lady, about 5 ft 6 in tall, rather wizened, who spoke with an attractive, educated accent, and displayed precision in thought behind all that she said. She left £13,697 19s 5d. She was especially fond of her grand-nephew, James Wingate Sellars Birrell, the son of George Gilchrist Birrell, junior. A sergeant in the Royal Air Force, he was killed, aged only 20, on 30 May 1943, in the course of air operations at Ennepe Dam, near Breckerfeld, Germany.

It was just over 33 years after the murder of Miss Gilchrist upstairs, that Arthur Montague Adams, still living at 51 West Princes Street, was, on 3 January 1942, found dead in his home. He was 73. He had last been seen alive at Hogmanay. His death was from natural causes: influenza and heart failure. Another of the celebrated Slater case coincidences: Arthur Adams' death certificate was signed by Dr John Smith McLaren Ord – none other than the late Superintendent John Ord's son. Adams had married, on February 11th, 1922, Annie Amelia Martin, the 40-year-old daughter of Sir William Martin, a shipping agent. She was employed as a health visitor. Although there was 13 years' difference between them, she died only two months after Arthur, of rheumatoid arthritis and acute and chronic nephritis. Arthur Adams left estate amounting to £4,293 12s 5d.

He was survived by his sisters, Laura and Octavia, who kept the sweetshop in Lanark. Laura died on 26 March 1943, in St Mary's Hospital, Lanark, of cardiovascular degeneration and fracture of the neck of the femur. She was 76. Octavia also reached the age of 76, dying, on 6 May 1948, in Lockhart Hospital, Lanark, of carcinoma of the large intestine.

Rowena Eliza Margaret Adams or Liddell had died back in 1915, only weeks after the death of her 83-year-old mother, Mrs Rowena Sophia Gambrill or Adams, who succumbed to cardiac disease while living at Roselands, in Lanark, on 31 October 1915. Rowena Adams or Liddell also passed away at Roselands, on 13 December 1915. She was 55. Her death was certified due to *morbus cordis* and syncope.

And what became of the Fergusons – Miss Gilchrist's heirs? Maggie Galbraith or Ferguson lived until 1927, dying on 2 December of that year, at 27 Ballantine Drive, Ayr. Miss Gilchrist's main joint-beneficiaries, Marion Gilchrist Ferguson and Margaret Galbraith Ferguson, are both dead.

Marion married, when she was 25, on 17 July 1918, at the Parish Church, Kilmarnock. Her husband was Hubert Frank Cresswell, also 25, described on his marriage certificate as an organist. He was a keen musician all his life, although he earned his living as an income tax inspector, working in Ayr until his retirement in 1958.

Margaret, who had a job as a clerkess, married when she was twenty-three. Her groom was a 25-year-old nurseryman, John G Gledhill, of Elmscott, St David's Road, Llandudno. Their wedding took place at St John's United Free Church, Kilmarnock, on 28 April 1920.

Such was the persuasive power of rumour that Margaret's daughter, Mrs Margaret Land, and her brother truly believed that their grandmother (Mrs Maggie Galbraith or Ferguson) was Miss Gilchrist's daughter. Mrs Land says:

> Miss Gilchrist was in the habit of visiting my grandparents in Kilmarnock quite often, sometimes not saying when, just getting on the train by herself and finding her way to our house, usually with all her jewellery in a bag, much to their horror. But that was her way. The family spent a lot of time with her, both in Glasgow and in Kilmarnock, and they all went on holiday together every year, sometimes to Girvan or Oban, and very often to the Isle of Arran. My mother used to talk about those holidays a lot and would say how much they had enjoyed them. Unfortunately, the last one, in Girvan the summer before Miss Gilchrist died, was a sad one. It was during that holiday that my mother's brother, David, died from peritonitis, and from then on my grandmother was not well, which was why the doctor was called in to see her during her stay with Miss Gilchrist later in the year. Then, after the murder which followed so quickly on the death of David, my mother said that my grandmother never really recovered from so much sorrow.
>
> As regards the question as to why Miss Gilchrist changed her will so as to make equal provision for both Marion and me, I can only tell you what my mother used to tell me. Seemingly, it was one particular occasion in Kilmarnock, not long before Miss Gilchrist's death. My Aunt Marion [that is Marion Gilchrist Ferguson, later Mrs Cresswell] didn't want to stay and keep her company. She preferred to go out. So my mother [that is Margaret Galbraith Ferguson, later Mrs Gledhill] stayed in and looked after her, which was typical of Mum. And it was after that that Miss Gilchrist altered her will.'

Mary Barrowman died young. She was only 40 when, on 14 April 1934, carcinoma of the cervix and cachexia brought her life to a close in Stobhill Hospital, in Glasgow. Her career had been a chequered one. On 11 July 1914, Mary Sword or Barrowman, spinster, aged 20, stationer's assistant, of 19 Windsor Street, Glasgow, married, after United Free banns, 22-year-old James Laurie, silversmith (journeyman), of 669 Garscube Road, Glasgow. On 1 March 1924, declaring herself a spinster, Mary Sword, charwoman, aged 30, of 21 Robb Street, Glasgow, married 33-year-old William Collins, steam crane driver. Mary had previously given birth to two children – Andrew Pollock Laurie, born 1 September 1914, and Margaret Laurie, born 17 February 1916. She is said to have proved an unsatisfactory mother, both of her children being removed from her into care. She is also said to have become an alcoholic and to have been sent to prison.

That other important witness in West Princes Street, the schoolteacher, Miss Agnes Brown, became Mrs Black on 13 July 1921, when she, age 44, married 47-year-old manufacturer's agent, Peter Morris Black. She died, aged 87, at Collisdene, an old folk's home at Strathaven.

Over the years the police who had been concerned in the Slater case gradually died off. One of the first to go, Detective Lieutenant William Gordon, died, aged 65, on 10 March 1915.

The year 1921 saw two deaths. On 1 September John Orr, who, with the rank of Assistant Chief Constable, had retired in 1917 to his home town, Ayr, died there at the age of 68. On 18 December, Superintendent William Miller Douglas, still in harness but having been off work for about two months, died, aged 58, of cancer.

Oscar's old arch-enemy, Superintendent John Ord, died at his home, No. 2 Monteith Row, Glasgow, on 9 April 1928, nine days after his sixty-sixth birthday. He had retired on pension just under three years before. His granddaughter, Mrs Gertrude McLaren Ord or Stewart, said that Slater, after his release in 1927, would stand in the gaslight outside the house in Monteith Row, a haunting, accusatory figure. On his very deathbed, Ord continued to maintain that Slater was the murderer.

Detective Inspector John Pyper, who retired in 1920, lived on until 1932, when, on 17 May he died at the age of 77, at West Kilbride, Ayrshire. He had been promoted Detective Lieutenant in 1912, the style of which rank had, in 1913, been changed to Chief Detective Inspector.

Detective Sergeant James Dornan, feeling that he had been passed over for promotion, convinced that if he had had his rights he should have been Chief Constable, took early retirement with the rank of Detective Lieutenant. He was only 56 when he died of heart failure on 17 May 1932, at Torhouse, Wigtownshire. His granddaughter, Mrs Margaret Button, remembers him with bitterness. He was, she says, very harsh with his wife, very tough, and what he said went. Mrs Button's mother had been 'an unpaid slave' at Dornan's Torhouse farm. According to Mrs Button, Dornan was convinced that Slater was guilty, and after his release became obsessed with the idea that Oscar would track him down – presumably to take revenge.

The demises of what may for this purpose be generally referred to as the 'legal personnel' started off in 1909, with, as we have already recorded, the sudden death of Ewing Speirs.

Slater's leading defence counsel, Alexander Logan McClure, KC, was 72 when he died at his home, 16 Heriot Row, Edinburgh, on 29 July 1932.

Thomas Brash Morison of the prosecution team had gone from strength to strength – Solicitor-General for Scotland, Lord Advocate, elevated to the Bench – and died aged 76, on 28 July 1945.

The trial judge, Lord Charles John Guthrie, was seventy-one when he died of cancer at his home, 13 Royal Circus, Edinburgh, on 20 April 1920.

Craigie Aitchison became Lord Advocate in 1929, and four years later was appointed Lord Justice-Clerk. He died on 2 May 1941, at the early age of 59.

Lord Pentland, Secretary for Scotland 1905-12, died on 11 January 1925. The Rt. Hon. Thomas McKinnon Wood, Secretary for Scotland 1912-16, died on 26 March 1927.

The Reverend Eleazer Philip Phillips, Oscar's unfailing champion, died in 1943.

Helen Lambie – as we have already seen – died in 1960. Her elder daughter, Margaret Balfour Gillon (Maisie) died, unmarried, on 17 December 1980, at 3 Lascelles Mount, Leeds. She left her house to her married sister, Marion (Mrs Jack Cook). She was living there when, in December 1982, I went to see her. Marion Cook – named, surely, after old Miss Gilchrist – was then 64. She looked remarkably like Helen Lambie and still spoke with a Scottish accent. She told me: 'Mother never talked of the murder.'

Two of the longest lived players in the Slater drama were ladies. Lieutenant Trench's widow, who died aged one hundred years, on 10 February 1975, and Oscar's widow, who died half-way through her ninetieth year, peacefully, in that same Stobhill

Hospital wherein, 58 years before, Mary Barrowman had died.

There is no one left now to mourn the spoilt life of the prisoner of Peterhead's weeping granite.

BIBLIOGRAPHY

Anonymous, The Flat Mystery! Life and Trial of Oscar Slater,
      J & D R Burnside, Glasgow, c. 1914

Bailey, Brian, The Guinness Book of Crime, Guinness Publishing, 1988

Birmingham, George A. Murder Most Foul, Chatto & Windus, 1929

Bland, James, True Crime Diary, Volume I. Macdonald, 1987

Block, Eugene, The Vindicators, Alvin Redman, 1964

Blundell, Nigel., Strange But True, Blitz Editions, 1992

Blundell, Nigel, & Boar, Robert, The World's Greatest Unsolved Crimes,
      Octopus Books, 1984

Booth, Martin, The Doctor, the Detective and Arthur Conan Doyle,
      Hodder & Stoughton, 1997

Borchard, Edwin Montefiore, Convicting the Innocent,
      Yale University Press, 1932

Bresler, Fenton, An Almanac of Murder, Severn House, 1987

Brome, Vincent, Reverse Your Verdict, Hamish Hamilton, 1971

Brown, Ivor, Conan Doyle: A Biography of the Creator of Sherlock Holmes,
      Hamish Hamilton, 1972

Browne, Douglas G & Brock, Alan, Fingerprints, Harrap, 1953

Bunson, Matthew E, The Sherlock Holmes Encyclopedia, Pavilion Books,
      1995

Burrowes, John, Great Glasgow Stories, Mainstream, 1998

Campbell, Margaret, Strange Stories of Glasgow and the Clyde,
      Lang Syne Publishers, Glasgow, 1989

Carr, John Dickson, The Life of Arthur Conan Doyle, John Murray, 1949

Cohen, Daniel, The Encyclopedia of Unsolved Crimes, Dorset Press,
      New York, 1989

Cole, Margaret, in Great Unsolved Crimes, Hutchinson, 1935

Collins, Dr. Kenneth E, Second City Jewry, Scottish Jewish Archives,
      1990

Colquhoun, Robert, Life Begins at Midnight, John Long, 1962

Coren, Michael, *Conan Doyle*, Bloomsbury, 1995

Costello, Peter, *The Real World of Sherlock Holmes*,
Robinson Publishing, 1991

Crowther, M Anne & White, Brenda, *On Soul and Conscience: The
Medical Expert and Crime*, Aberdeen University Press, 1988

Cuthbert, C R M, *Science and the Detection of Crime*, Hutchinson, 1958

Cyriax, Oliver, *Crime: An Encyclopedia*. André Deutsch, 1993

Dilnot, George, *Rogues' March*, Geoffrey Bles, 1934

Doyle, Arthur Conan, *The Case of Oscar Slater*, Hodder & Stoughton,
1912

Doyle, Arthur Conan, *Memories and Adventures*, Hodder & Stoughton,
1924

Doyle, Arthur Conan, *Memories and Adventures*, 2nd, revised.
edition, Hodder & Stoughton, 1930

Doyle, Arthur Conan, *Letters to the Press*, Edited by John Michael
Gibson and Richard Lancelyn Green, Secker & Warburg, 1986

Du Cann, C G L, *Miscarriages of Justice*, Frederick Muller, 1960

Edwards, Owen Dudley, *The Quest for Sherlock Holmes*, Mainstream,
1983

Fido, Martin, *The Chronicle of Crime*, Little, Brown, 1993

Fido, Martin, *The World of Sherlock Holmes: The Facts and Fiction Behind
the World's Greatest Detective*, Carlton Books, 1998

Fisher, Joe, *The Glasgow Encyclopedia*, Mainstream, 1994

Forbes, George A & Meehan, Paddy, *Such Bad Company*,
Paul Harris Publishing, 1982

Furneaux, Rupert, *Great Clashes of the Twentieth Century*, Odhams
Books, 1970

Gaute, J H H & Odell, Robin, *The Murderers' Who's Who*, Harrap, 1979

Gaute, J H H & Odell, Robin, *Murder 'Whatdunit': An Illustrated Account
of the Methods of Murder*, Harrap, 1982

Goodman, Jonathan, (Editor), *The Christmas Murders*,
Allison & Busby, 1986

Grant, Douglas, *The Thin Blue Line*, John Long, 1973

Gribble, Leonard, *Stories of Famous Modern Trials*, Arthur Barker, 1970

Hale, Leslie, *Hanged in Error*, Penguin Books (Special) 1961

Hall, Trevor H, *Sherlock Holmes and His Creator*, Duckworth, 1978

Hardwick, Michael & Mollie, *The Man Who Was Sherlock Holmes*, John Murray, 1964

Haste, Steve, *Criminal Sentences: True Crime in Fiction and Drama*, Cygnus Arts, 1997

Higham, Charles, *The Adventures of Conan Doyle*, Hamish Hamilton, 1976

Hill, C W, *Edwardian Scotland*, Scottish Academic Press, 1976

House, Jack. *Square Mile of Murder*. Chambers, 1961, revised edition, The Molendinar Press, Glasgow 1975

Hunt, Peter, *Oscar Slater: The Great Suspect*, Carroll & Nicholson, 1951

Keating, H R F, *Great Crimes*, St. Michael, N. D

Kenna, Rudolph & Sutherland, Ian, *In Custody – A Companion to the Strathclyde Police Museum*, Strathclyde Police in association with Clutha Books, 1998

Kingston, Charles A, *Dramatic Days at the Old Bailey*, Stanley Paul, 1923

Kingston, Charles A, *A Gallery of Rogues*, Stanley Paul, 1924

Kuppner, Frank, *A Very Quiet Street*, Polygon, 1989

Lamond, John, *Arthur Conan Doyle: A Memoir*, John Murray, 1931

Lane, Brian, *Chronicle of 20th Century Murder*, Virgin Publishing, 1993

Lane Brian, *The Murder Book of Days*, Headline, 1995

Lellenberg, Jon L, *The Quest For Sir Arthur Conan Doyle*, Southern Illinois University Press, 1987

Lindsay, Maurice, *Portrait of Glasgow*, Robert Hale, 1972

Livingstone, Sheila, *Confess and be Hanged*, Birlinn, 2000

Lustgarten, Edgar, *The Woman in the Case*, André Deutsch, 1955

Lustgarten, Edgar, *The Judges and the Judged*, Odhams Press, 1961

Mackenzie, Compton, *On Moral Courage*, Collins, 1962

Marriner, Brian, *Forensic Clues to Murder*, Arrow Books, 1991

Merrilees, William, *The Short Arm of the Law*, John Long, 1966

Minto, G A, *The Thin Blue Line*, Hodder & Stoughton, 1965

Morland, Nigel, In *Criminology*, January 1964 – 'My Search for Helen Lambie'

Morland, Nigel, *Pattern of Murder*, Elek, 1966

Morton, James, *The Who's Who of Unsolved Murders*, Kyle Cathie, 1994

Murder Casebook, (Partwork), Part 67, 1991

Murder in Mind, (Partwork), Part 35. 1998

Nash, Jay Robert, *Compendium of World Crime*, Harrap, 1983

Nash, Jay Robert. *Crime Chronology: A Worldwide Record* 1900-1983. Facts on File Publications, 1984.

Nash, Jay Robert, *Encyclopedia of World Crime*, Crime Books, Inc, Wilmette, Illinois, 1989

Nordon, Pierre, *Conan Doyle*, John Murray, 1966

Oakley, C A, *The Second City*, Blackie, 1946

Odell, Robin, *Landmarks in 20th Century Murder*, Headline, 1995

Orel, Harold, *Sir Arthur Conan Doyle: Interviews and Recollections*, Macmillan, 1991

Park, William, *The Truth About Oscar Slater*, The Psychic Press, 1927

Pearsall, Ronald, *Conan Doyle: A Biographical Solution*, Weidenfeld & Nicolson, 1977

Pearson, Hesketh, *Conan Doyle: His Life and Art*, Methuen, 1943

Pemberton, Max (Editor), *Great Stories of Real Life*, Volume I, Newnes, N D

Ramsey, Ted, *Stranger in the Hall*, Ramshorn Publications, Glasgow, 1988

Roughead, William, *Trial of Oscar Slater*, Notable Scottish Trials series, William Hodge, 1910.

Roughead, William, *Trial of Oscar Slater*, 2nd edition (revised), Notable British Trials series, William Hodge, 1915

Roughead, William, *Trial of Oscar Slater*, 3rd edition (revised), Notable British Trials series, William Hodge, 1929

Roughead, William, *Knave's Looking-Glass*, Cassell, 1935

Roughead, William, *Classic Crimes*, Cassell, 1951

Search, Pamela, *Great True Crime Stories. Volume I – Men*, Arco Publications, 1957

Shew, E. Spencer, *A Second Companion to Murder*, Cassell, 1961

Stone, Harry, *The Casebook of Sherlock Doyle*, Ian Henry Publications, 1991

Symons, Julian, *Crime and Detection: An Illustrated History from* 1840, Studio Vista, 1966

Symons, Julian, *Portrait of an Artist: Conan Doyle*, André Deutsch, 1979

Thomas, Donald, *The Victorian Underworld*. John Murray, 1998

Toughill, Thomas, *Oscar Slater: The Mystery Solved*, Canongate Press,

1993

Vandome, Nick, *Crimes and Criminals*, Chambers, 1992

Whittington-Egan, Richard, *William Roughead's Chronicles of Murder*,
Lochar Publishing, 1991

Whittington-Egan, Richard & Molly, *The Murder Almanac*,
Neil Wilson, 1992

Wilson, Colin, *Written in Blood: A History of Forensic Detection*,
Equation, 1989

Wilson, Colin & Pitman, Pat, *Encyclopaedia of Murder*,
Arthur Barker, 1961

Wilson, Richard, *Scotland's Unsolved Mysteries*, Robert Hale, 1989

Wilton, George Wilton, *Fingerprints*, William Hodge, 1938

INDEX

21 *Years at 'The Central'*, (Trench's Memoirs) 126

A

'A.B.' 114, 115, 118, 119, 161, 202, 223, 224, 233-8, 244, 246, 248, 249, 252, 255-7, 268, 269, 270n, 272, 276-8

'A.E.' (Russell, George William) 1

Aberdeen 167, 251
  University of Aberdeen Press 251

Aberdeenshire 92

Acrobat, The 57

Adams, Adela Florence 7

Adams, Alice Maud 7

Adams, Arthur Montague 7, 11, 12, 13, 14, 15, 16, 17, 24, 25, 27, 28, 33-5, 38, 68, 71-3, 80, 81, 98, 149, 171, 185, 186, 212, 215, 219, 220, 224, 226, 227, 229, 231, 232, 240, 249, 268, 284, 286, 289, 296, 297, 302, 305, 306, 314, 315

Adams, Dr John 17, 18, 171, 174, 182, 183, 185, 187, 215, 250, 293

Adams, Laura Emma 7, 11, 12, 29, 30, 226, 239, 315

Adams, Mrs Annie Amelia Martin *or* 315

Adams, Mrs Jane 174, 182

Adams, Mrs Rowena Sophia Gambrill *or* 7, 315

Adams, Octavia Emily 7, 226, 239, 315

Adams, Rowena Elizabeth Margaret (*see* Mrs Rowena Elizabeth Margaret Liddell)

Adams, Selina Lucy Jane 7

Adler, Irene 230

Advocates' Library, Edinburgh 79

Aitchison, KC Craigie M 2, 170, 172-4, 183-7, 231, 276, 302, 303, 318

Aitken & Birrell, Messrs 282

Aitken, J F 282

Allan, Mea 195

Allan's School, Stirling 126

Allen, Maggie 240, 241

Allsopp, William 258, 259

Alness, Lord (*see* Munro, Robert)

Ambrose Channel Lightship 46

America 86, 111, 151, 154, 156, 163, 245, 286, 287, 291, 295
  Austin, Texas ix
  Baltimore, Maryland 301
  New York 31, 45, 46, 50, 54, 55, 68, 71, 84, 149, 164, 173, 174, 184, 186, 188, 203, 241, 246, 277, 301
    Battery, the New York 46
    City Hall Park, 66
    District Court of the United States for the Southern District of New York 66
    East 63rd Street 246
    El Dief, the House of 246
    Federal Building 47, 183
    Fulton Street 71
    Harbour 47
    Manhattan 55
    New York Police Detective Bureau 46
    Post Office Building 66
    Sixth Avenue 46, 55
    Smith & McNell's Hotel 71
    Tombs Prison, the 66, 75, 77
    Washington Street 71
    West 26th Street 54, 55
  Peoria, Illinois ix, 175, 177, 178, 299
    Bradley University 177
    Caterpillar Tractor Company 177
    Commercial Solvent Corporation 178
    Corn Stock Summer Theatre 177
    Garden Street 175-6, 178-9
    Groveland Mine 178
    Haag Bros, Washing Machine Manufacturers 178
    Ideal Troy Cleaners 178
    Kew Laundry Company 178
    Public Library ix 178

Peoria Star, the 176
South Adams Street 178
San Francisco 42, 45, 50, 60
   Broadway 45
   Caesar Café, 544
   St Louis 50
   Washington 74, 75
Anderson, Adolf 40-4, 46, 55, 59, 163
Anderson, Bailie James 259
Anderson, mysterious man 209, 209n
Andy (*see* Craig, Richard)
Antoine, Andrée Hilary Junio *or*
   Kerbrow 43, 45-7, 54-7, 75, 78, 83,
   84, 86-8, 99, 111
Antoine, Malone James 47
Armour, Annie 68, 221, 286
Arran Isle of 316
Atlantic Ocean 45, 71, 76, 82, 307
Aumann, Josef 57, 83, 86
Australia 41, 50, 241
   Sydney, New South Wales 19, 34,
   314
   Turamurra, New South Wales 314
   University of Sydney, 19, 314
Ayr 33, 34, 168, 171, 172, 175, 192, 195-
   9, 315, 317
   Auld Brig 197
   Ballantine Drive 315
   Blackburn Place 252n
   Blackburn Road 168
   Mount Olive (boarding-house),
   Blackburn Road 168, 192
   Oslin, St Phillans Avenue 196-7, 199
   St Phillans Avenue 196, 198
Ayrshire 270

B
Back, vor 225
Background to Murder (Nigel Morland)
   224, 225
Ballantrae 147, 154, 190
   Mains House, Ballantrae 147
Baltic, White Star Liner, 8, 71, 73n
Band of Hope 107
Bank of Scotland 206
Barbour, William Roxburgh 107
Barlinnie Prison 308, 310
Barney, the Irish Terrier 19, 28, 29, 97,
109, 157, 184, 239, 256, 285
Barra 63, 234, 292
   Borve, near Castlebay, Barra 63

Barrowman, Barbara 31
Barrowman, Mrs Barbara 31, 236
Barrowman, Mary Sword or 1-3, 38, 43,
   68, 71-3, 81, 82, 98, 106-8, 155, 161,
   164, 165, 171, 184, 186, 188, 204, 220,
   227-9, 235, 236, 238, 241, 270, 300,
   311, 316, 319
Barrowman, Robert 31
Beck, Adolf 87
Belfast 84, 203
Bell, Glasgow gang member 130, 131
Bernstein, Bertha 40
Berwick-upon-Tweed Infirmary 260
Beuthen, Upper Silesia 48-50
Beveridge, Robert Scott 59
Bhagavad Gita 199
Birrell, Alexander 256
Birrell, Alexander 268, 269
Birrell, Alexander, junior 269, 276, 278
Birrell, Austin 237-40, 246, 248, 258,
   294
Birrell, Dawson 33, 110
Birrell, George Gilchrist 34, 64, 68, 69,
   203-6, 282, 290
Birrell, George Gilchrist, junior 314
Birrell, James Aitken 34, 64, 68, 69, 203,
   204, 282, 290
Birrell, James Wingate Sellars 314
Birrell, Mrs Jane (*née* Gilchrist) 33, 61,
   110
Birrell, Janet (*née* Gilchrist) 33, 62, 204,
   205, 282, 292
Birrell, Margaret 269, 278
Birrell, Margaret Dawson 16, 18, 33, 62,
   64, 66, 68-70, 96, 96n, 104-6, 108,
   110, 111, 122-4, 148, 154, 161, 201,
   202, 206, 249, 268, 271, 273, 274, 277,
   282, 296, 314
Birrell, Margaret May 69
Birrell, Mrs Margaret 269
Birrell, Mrs Mary Nimmo *or* 69, 70, 283,
   283n
Birrell, Samuel 269
Birrell, Walter 33, 204, 282, 292
Birrell, Wingate viii, ix, 34, 68, 280-7,
   289, 290, 292-6
Black, Mrs Agnes Brown *or* (*see* Brown,
Agnes)
Black, Peter Morris 317
Blackburn, Lord 173
Black Watch, the 101, 125, 133, 262

Bone, James 313

Bournemouth 34, 70, 104, 109, 207, 314

Boys' Brigade, 78

Brash, Herr 52

Brien, Police Constable Francis 17, 26, 209

British Government 66

Brooch, gold and diamond crescent 23, 25-7, 69, 81, 97, 207, 268, 284, 290, 295, 306

Brooks, Max 57

Broughty Ferry Murder, the 119, 120

Brown, Agnes 107, 108, 217, 218, 220, 227, 228, 235, 238, 241, 307, 309, 312n, 317

Brown, Archibald 180

Brussels 50

Bryce, Pawnbroker James 59

Bryson, Robert Brown 84, 215, 224

Buchanan, John of Messrs Robert McTear & Co 143

Buchanan, John of the Guardian Assurance Company 128-30, 232, 134, 135, 143

Buglass, William Bedlington 90

Burgess, MRCS, A S 284

Burns, Robert 197

Burrell, Alexander Houston 269

Burrell, George 269

Burrell Junior, George 269

Burrell, Mrs Janet Houston or 269

Burrell, Sir William 268, 268n, 269, 270

Burrell, William 269

Bute 203n

Button, Mrs Margaret 317, 318

C

'Case of the Dedicated Detective, The' article by Alastair Phillips 238

Cameron, Detective Alexander 110, 214

Cameron, Mrs Elizabeth Dow *or* 214

Cameron, Hugh (the Moudie) 39, 41, 45, 55, 57, 58, 82, 83, 85, 87, 185, 204, 286, 287, 290, 294

Cameron, Superintendent, Limehouse, London 284

Campania, the Cunard Line Liner 75

Campbell, Chief Detective Inspector Allan 43, 132-4

Campbell, William 212

Canada 143

Canterbury, Kent 282

Carfin 67

Carrick, Andrew 205

Carroll, The Reverend Dr John 34

Case of Oscar Slater (White Paper) 114-7, 251, 273

Case of Oscar Slater, The (Sir Arthur Conan Doyle) 98, 100, 153, 222

Caulfield Gang 130, 310

Caulfield, Robert 130, 131, 310

Challis Professorship of International Law 314

Chambers, Messrs W & R 235

Chapman, James 130

Charteris & Hill, Writers, Messrs 313

Charteris, Mrs Annie Fraser (*née* Kedie) 19, 256

Charteris, Archibald Hamilton ix, 18, 19, 33, 123, 240, 241, 248, 256, 272, 274, 277, 281, 286-8, 296, 313, 314

Charteris, D D, The Very Reverend Archibald Hamilton 20, 256

Charteris, Mrs Elizabeth (*née* Greer) ix, 18, 33, 64, 109, 207, 277, 281, 287, 297n, 314

Charteris, Dr Francis James vii, viii, ix, 18, 19, 20, 28, 33, 62, 104-6, 108-14, 122, 123, 147-9, 154, 161, 200-2, 221-5, 235-41, 244-6, 248-51, 254, 254n, 255-8, 260, 265, 266, 268, 271-4, 276-9, 281, 285-8, 296-7, 302, 312

Charteris, John 18, 19, 33

Charteris, John Hamilton 314

Charteris, Professor Mathew 18, 256

Charteris, Mrs Rossiter Margaret 314

Cherbourg 54

Chesterton, G K 304

Christie, Agatha 304

Clarke, Councillor J S 199

Classic Crimes (William Roughead) 120

Clunes, John Mason 216

Clyde, Lord. The Lord Justice General 172, 173, 175, 186, 187

Collins, William 316

Collisdene, Strathaven 317

Colquhoun, Detective Chief Superintendent, Robert 310, 312

Columbia, the Anchor Lines Liner 75-7

Compensation 166-7, 171, 189-92, 194, 301

Concitional Pardon 91, 92
Cook, David 2, 102-4, 115-7, 122-4, 127, 129, 131-44, 146, 156n, 224, 259, 309
Cook, Jack 179, 318
Cook, Mrs Marion (*née* Gillon) (*see* Gillon, Marion)
Cordner, Police Constable William 262
Costello, Peter 223n, 296-7
Court of Criminal Appeal 99, 187
Court of Criminal Appeal, Scotland 159, 169, 170, 190, 276
Cowan, Charles Frederic 106
Cowdenbeath, Fife 194
Craig, Former Inspector Strathclyde Police, Joe 262, 263
Craig, Richard 130-1, 310, 312
Craigneuk 294
Crashaw, Richard 200
Cresswell, Hubert Frank 315
Cresswell, Mrs Marion Gilchrist Ferguson *or* (*see* Ferguson, Marion Gilchrist)
Criminal Appeal (Scotland) Act 1926 169
Crosbie, Miss 308, 311
Crowborough, Sussex 95, 243
Crowther, M, Anne 251
Cunard Line 41
Cunningham, Euphemia 211, 212
Cupar 194

D

Daily Express 151, 171
Daily Mail 192
Daily News 152, 154, 160, 164, 166, 189, 190
Daily Record 28, 122, 179, 190, 191
Dardanelles, the 126
Day, Colonel Harry 169
De Silvestri, Peter 54
Devon, Dr James 90, 102, 116, 117
Devoto, John 60
Dewar, Amelia 218, 219
Dewar, The Right Honourable Donald 261, 265
Dewar, Elizabeth Alexandra 218, 219
Diamond Merchant, the 57
Dick, David 37
Dickson, Lord Justice-Clerk Charles Scott 139, 140, 253
Dickson, Sheriff Robert 276, 277, 302

Dinornis Maximus 95
Dinwoodie, Robbie 247
Dodds, Sir James Miller 92, 288, 289
Donaldson, Elizabeth 212, 213
Donegal Hat 32
Dornan, Detective Sergeant James 105, 109, 110, 162-4, 317, 318
Douglas, Superintendent William Miller 22, 23, 25, 33, 37, 44, 105, 108-11, 123, 162-4, 201, 203, 273, 277, 228, 288, 297, 317
Dow & Son, Messrs David 128, 133, 134, 135n, 137, 138, 143
'Downfall Of A Man Called Trench, The' 247, 248
Doyle, Sir Arthur Conan 2, 93-100, 104, 115, 140, 145-8, 152, 153, 155-61, 163, 170, 173, 175, 176, 183, 187, 189-92, 200, 243-7, 257, 258, 276, 285, 298, 300-1
Dreyfus, the Scottish (Alfred) 231
Duff, Jane *or* Jeanie Hay 64
Dundee 120
Dundee Police 120
Dunoon 314

E

Edalji, George 93, 94
Edinburgh 50, 51, 79, 302
   Belgrave Crescent 152
   Calton Gaol 77
   Cheyne Street 51
   Court Number Three, High Court of Justiciary 79, 127, 172, 173, 187
   Court of Session, the 192
   Crown Agent 95-6, 100, 133, 136, 138, 179
   Crown Office, the viii, 96, 109, 125, 176, 202, 247, 291
   Edinburgh City Police 51
   George Street 117
   Heriot Row 318
   High Court of Justiciary, the 79, 127, 136, 172, 173
   High Street 79
   Hill Street 170
   Houston's Temperance Hotel, Lothian Road 78
   India Street 172

New Club, the 154
New Register House viii, 63
Parliament House 79, 172, 182
Parliament Square 182, 188
Register House 241, 398n
Royal Circus 318
Signet Library, the viii
Sheriff Court 121
Thistle Street 52
University of Edinburgh 20
Waverley Bridge 52
West Register House viii
Edward VII, King 91
Ellis Island 47, 50
Elmgrove Affair, *or* Broughty Ferry
Murder, the (*see* Broughty Ferry
Murder, the)
Empire News 151-6, 158, 172, 189, 190,
192, 299, 300
Empire News statement, alleged 152
Evening Citizen, the Glasgow 6, 12, 90, 236
Edinburgh Evening Dispatch 29
Evening Standard 146
Evening Times, the Glasgow 67, 154, 203,
238, 245-6, 258, 270
Express, the Anchor Line Tender 76-7
Extradition proceedings 81, 241, 287

F
Fagence, Maurice 246
Falconer, James F 259, 264
Feldman, Lew David 246, 247
Fellowes, Horace 302
Ferdinand, Mr 54
Ferguson (*née* Galbraith), Mrs Maggie
63-5, 70, 234, 245, 273, 275, 276, 281n,
292, 296, 315, 316
Ferguson, David 63
Ferguson, David, junior 63
Ferguson, Maggie Galbraith 63, 281n,
315, 316
Ferguson, Marion Gilchrist 63, 106,
234, 258, 273-6, 281n, 315-6
Finburgh, M P, Mr 190
Findlay, Alex 226
Findlay, Charles 294
Finlay, Christina (see Gilchrist, Mrs
Christina)
Finlay, Inspector Alistair 261, 265
Fleming, Lord 173
Forbes, George 239, 270

Fox, Charles 66, 71-4
France 144
Fraser, Lovat 151
Freedman, Mrs Luise 42, 43, 45
Fullerton, William 212
Furnessia, SS 31

G
Galbraith, Isabella McKinnon *or* 63
Galbraith, James 58
Galbraith, John 63
Galbraith, Maggie (*see* Ferguson, Mrs
Maggie)
Gall's Public House, Alexander 58
Galt, Dr Hugh 30, 82, 251
Gandhi, Mahatma 199
Gardner, Harry 302
Garnier, J W 284
George V, King 114, 169
German Ocean 93
Germany 163, 193, 194
Berlin 50, 51
Breckerfeld 314
Ennepe Dam 314
Eppendorft, Hamburg 50
Hamburg 50, 51
Hamburg Municipal Hospital, at
Eppendorf 50
Thale, Prussian Saxony 43
Gibb, Adam 86
Gibson, John 213, 214
Giffnock, Renfrewshire 156, 157
Gilchrist, Christina (*see* Lee, Mrs
Christina)
Gilchrist, Elizabeth (*see* Lawrie, Mrs
Elizabeth)
Gilchrist, James 18, 33, 62, 104, 109, 281
Gilchrist, James Taylor 27, 28, 61, 62
Gilchrist, Jane (*see* Birrell, Mrs Jane)
Gilchrist, Janet (*see* Birrell, Mrs Janet)
Gilchrist, Marion vii, ix, 2, 5, 6, 7, 8, 9,
10, 11, 12, 13, 14, 15, 16, 17, 18, 19, 20,
23, 26-30, 33, 34, 37, 45-7 61-74, 79,
80, 82, 83, 85, 94, 95, 97, 98, 104-7, 109,
110, 112, 115, 119, 120, 122, 149, 150,
152, 157, 161, 162, 174, 177, 182, 184-6,
188, 200-9, 211-16, 219, 221, 223,
225-7, 232-7, 239-41, 245, 246, 248-51,
255-8, 265, 267-72, 274-8, 281, 281n,
283, 285-6, 289-97, 301-9, 311,312, 314,
316, 318

Gilchrist, Marshall 62
Gilchrist, Mary Greer (*see* McCall Mrs Mary Greer)
Gilchrist, Mrs Christina 61
Gilchrist, William (*see* Birrell, Wingate)
Giles, Procurator-Fiscal Depute, Mr 135, 137, 138
Gillies, Alexander 212, 213
Gillies, Edgar 212
Gillon, Margaret Balfour (Maisie) 177, 178, 300, 300n, 318
Gillon, Marion 177, 179, 318
Gillon, Mrs Helen (*see* Lambie, Helen)
Gillon, Robert Miller 151, 175-9, 300, 301
Gillon, Ronald (*see* Gillon, Robert Miller)
Gilmour, Sir John 146, 153-9, 166, 169, 171, 172, 190, 192
Girvan, Ayrshire 28, 316
Glaister Secundus, Professor John 251
Glaister, Professor John 30, 82, 249-51, 288, 291
Glasgow 19, 34, 43, 45, 47, 52, 53, 66, 68, 111, 120, 160, 161, 164, 167, 170, 175, 194, 204, 207, 238, 239, 249, 282, 283, 308
Arnfield Place, Dennistoun 129, 135
Argyle Street 42, 128, 135, 216, 220
Ashley Street 16
Ashton Terrace, Partickhill 33
Bath Street 35, 102, 129, 205
Bellahouston Park 195
Bellwood Street 199
Belmont Street 128, 135
Berkeley Street 34, 35, 309
Blythswood Drive (now Woodlands Drive) 16, 18, 33, 104, 268, 314
Buchanan Street 205
Buchanan Street Railway Station 167
Buckingham Terrace 297n
Cambridge Street 41, 58
Carrington Street 228
Cathedral Street 35, 36
Central District, Glasgow Police 22, 38, 76, 105, 111, 118, 124, 125, 129, 132, 141, 179, 201, 262, 263, 311
Central Police Court 180
Central Station 55, 56

Central Station Hotel 55
Charing Cross 3, 39, 56, 210
Charing Cross Hotel 194
Citizens' Theatre 246
City Archives 262n
City Chambers 259
Cleveland Street 32, 107n
Clyde, the River 29, 75, 76, 293
Glasgow Corporation 259, 263
Cosy Den, Buchanan Street, the 205
County Buildings 67, 103, 137, 163, 195
Cowcaddens Street 58
Cromwell Street 218
Crown Hall Billiard Rooms 55, 58
Crown Street, Gorbals 33, 309
Detective Department, Glasgow 22, 96, 124, 134, 286
Dowanhill 144
Down Lane 227, 306
Duke Street Prison 77, 89, 90, 102, 247, 288, 289
Dunard Street School 228
Eglinton Street 310
Elmbank Street 11, 129
Empire Exhibition 195
Empire Palace Theatre, Sauchiehall Street 57, 205
Galloway's Spirit Shop, Hope Street 58
Gallowgate 125
Garnethill 257
Garscube Road 316
George Street 28
Grant Street 218, 227, 228
Glasgow Evening News 148, 149, 211, 212, 231, 233, 236, 307
Glasgow, Great Exhibition of 1901 53, 70, 304, 313
Glasgow, Hebrew Community in 77, 159
Glasgow Herald 86, 98, 143, 144, 179, 228, 238, 247-9, 251, 253, 254, 257, 260-4, 267, 272, 275-8, 280, 291, 291n, 302
Glasgow in 1901 (James Hamilton Muir) 313
Glasgow News 71, 203
Glasgow Weekly Herald 154

Great Western Road 19, 32, 108, 109, 218-20, 227, 228, 234, 237, 255, 264, 277, 306, 307, 312

Hayburn Crescent, Partick 282

High Court 143

High Street 35

Hillhead 109, 128, 135, 314

Hope Street 58, 133, 206, 282

Hutchesons' Hall 241

Hyndland Church 256

India Street 38, 58, 163

Ingram Street 67, 103

Jamaica Street 41

James Gray Street 193, 195, 199

John Street 241

Johnston's Billiard Rooms, Renfield Street 58, 84, 86

Kelvinbridge Subway Station, 68, 221, 286

Kelvingrove Park 53

Kelvingrove Street 168

Kelvinhaugh Street 53

Kelvinside 177

Kelvinside Terrace 104, 269

Kelvinside Terrace North 104, 269

King's Arms, the, Public House 129

King's Theatre 129

Kirkland Street 205

Lansdowne Mission Hall, Walker Street 107

Maryhill 144, 198, 220

Melrose Street 218, 220, 306

Mitchell Library, the 223, 262n, 263, 271

Mitchell Street 58

Monteith Row 317

Necrópolis 35

Newark Drive, Pollokshields 68

Park Road 16, 177

Partick 144, 309

Partickhill 282

Pavilion Theatre, Renfield Street 58

Peat's Public House, Hope St 58, 206

Police, Glasgow 2, 56n, 67, 101, 115-7, 120, 149, 232, 253, 295, 303

Police, Glasgow, Northern District 31,131, 228

Police Act, Glasgow 1866 119, 264

Police Committee, Glasgow 270

Police Headquarters, St

Andrew's Square , Glasgow 38

Police Minutes, Glasgow 264

Police, Western District 18, 22, 29, 33, 42, 105, 118, 124, 162, 163, 201, 209, 251

Post Office Directory, Glasgow 282

Post Office, the General 116

Princes Gardens, Dowanhill, 144

Publicans' Annual Licensing Court 123

Queen Margaret Crescent 109, 207, 277, 314

Queen Street Station 76

Queen's Crescent 16, 27, 211, 212, 215, 216, 218, 220, 290, 293, 297n, 306

Queen's Crescent Gardens 211

Queen's Terrace 3, 7, 25, 27, 29, 31, 1 32, 68, 69, 82, 210, 211,217, 228, 239

Register Office, Shamrock Street 53

Renfield Street 35, 58, 85, 86, 307

Renfrew Street 56, 58

Robb Street 316

Robertson Street 180

Rolland Street 68

Roller-Skating Rink, Victoria Road 58

Royal Exchange 204

Rupert Street 106, 107, 216, 227, 235, 268, 307, 312, 314

Rutherglen Cemetery 261

Royal Infirmary 30, 34

Sauchiehall Street 1, 3, 39, 41, 44, 55, 57, 58, 133, 194, 203, 205

Seamore Street 31

Shakespeare Red Cross Military Hospital, Maryhill 144

Shamrock Street 53

Sheriff Court 180

South Kinning Place 25, 105

Spring Gardens, Kelvinside 177

St Aloysius Roman Catholic Church 314

St Andrew's Square 38, 40, 76

St Enoch Square 264

St George's Road Mansions 40, 42, 44, 56, 83

St George's Road 3, 6, 16, 32, 39, 40, 42, 44, 56, 58, 59, 84, 209-12, 214, 217, 219, 220, 228

St John's United Free Church, George Street 28, 35

St Mungo Medical School 251

St Vincent Place 313
St Vincent Street 32, 204, 205
Stobhill Hospital 316, 318-9
Strathclyde Police Museum, Pitt
Street 265
Tantallon Road, Shawlands 93
Tax Office, St Vincent Street 205
University of Glasgow 8, 240, 251,
254, 313
Vernon Street 206
Victoria Road 58
Walker Street 107
West Campbell Street 62
West Cumberland Street
(Now Ashley Street) 16, 32, 227, 228,
306
West George Street 65, 97
West Graham Street 213
West Princes Street 3, 5, 7, 9, 16, 21,
22, 25, 32, 34, 62, 67, 69, 73, 81, 84, 98,
107, 148, 150, 161, 164, 204, 207, 208,
209, 210, 211-7, 219-21, 223, 226-8,
234-6, 238, 240, 256, 264, 277, 285, 289,
290, 293, 297, 298n, 304, 306-12, 314,
317
Western Infirmary 241, 256
Western Necropolis Crematorium,
Maryhill 198
Wilton Street 104, 269, 271
Windsor Street 316
Woodlands Road 40, 213, 214, 285
'Glasgow's Square Mile of Murder',
series of articles by Jack House 231
Gledhill, John G 315
Goodhart, William A 66, 174, 301
Gordon, Detective Alexander Black
308, 309, 311
Gordon, Detective Lieutenant William
22, 23, 25, 26, 42, 109, 110, 317
Gordon, Sheriff Gerald H 251, 252, 254
Gordon, William 146n
Grant, Douglas 263n
Graves, Karl 126
Great Wyrley, Staffordshire 94
Greenock 63, 76
Greer, Elizabeth (see Charteris, Mrs
Elizabeth)
Greville, Charles 246
Griffiths, James 252n
Guardian Assurance Company, the
128, 134

Guildford, Surrey 314
Guthrie, Lord Charles John 78, 80, 85,
87-90, 92, 148, 150, 156n, 159, 171,173,
187, 188, 231, 247, 252, 257, 288, 318
Guthrie, Mrs Agnes Martin Scott 156,
174, 177, 270

H
H M *Advocate v Browne, Burns & Williams*,
22nd October 1903 138
Haldane, Sir William, The Crown Agent
100, 133, 136, 138
Hall, Sir Edward Marshall 87, 100, 183
Hamburger, the 58
Hampshire Police 70, 206, 207
Hansen, Annie 52, 55
Harrison, Police Constable John 12
Hart, James Neil, Procurator-Fiscal 21,
67, 68, 70, 96, 103, 106, 111, 122, 129,
132-4, 136-8, 143, 149, 156n, 162-4,
201, 202, 254, 288
Hart, William 67
Harvey's Public House 285
Hawick 19
Hayburn, *or* Hamilton *or* Brown, Mrs
Minnie Lavinia 150, 171n, 174n, 179,
180, 181, 220, 233
Helensburgh 186, 282, 293
Rockbank House, Helensburgh 282
Henderson, Gordon 163, 164
Hepburn & Marshall, Hardware
Merchants, Messrs 58, 59
Hitler, Adolf 235
Hodder and Stoughton, Messrs 98
Hodge & Company, William 93, 206, 313
Holmes, Sherlock 97, 99, 158, 230, 244
Holytown, Lanarkshire 67, 152, 177,
179, 301, 302
Neilson's Land 177
Sunnyside Avenue 179
Sunnyside Road 177
Thankerton Colliery 175, 177
Home Office, the 68
Hong Kong 280
Hoppe, Mrs Elsa 42, 43
House of Commons, the 169
House, Jack 230-41, 245, 246, 248, 258,
259, 272, 307, 307n, 308-10
Howat, James 107
Howitt, James (*see* Howat, James)
Hudson, the 46

Hunt, Peter 102, 146, 151, 192, 222-4
Hunter, Lord 143, 144
Hunter's Quay, Dunoon 314

I

Imperial Billiard Conservatory 58
India 34
Inglis, James 310-2

J

Jack the Ripper 305
Jackson, Jacob 81
Jacobs, George Isidore 224, 224n, 227, 257
Jamieson, Glasgow gang member 311
Jenkins, Simon 272
Jewish Chronicle 159, 190
John Thomson Trench Prize 264
Johnston, James 273, 275, 276
Johnston, Peter 86
'Judas Goat', the 239
Junio, Madame (*see* Antoine, Andrée Hilary Junio *or* Keilbrow)
Junio, Mr O (*see* Slater, Oscar) 55

K

Kedie, Annie Fraser (*see* Charteris, Mrs Annie Fraser)
Kedie, Robert 19
Keibrow, Madame (*see* Antoine, Andrée Hilary Junio)
Keith, Detective Inspector Andrew Nisbet 105, 106, 108, 125, 130
Kelly's Directory 282
Kelvin, the River 309, 312
Kemmet, Brendon 308, 310
Kerr, Henry 314
Kilmarnock 63, 133, 315, 316
St John's United Free Church, Kilmarnock 315
King's Police Medal 113, 314
Knox, Bill 310
Krishna 199
Kuppner, Frank 270, 271

L

La Scala Cinema, Sauchiehall Street, Glasgow 194
Ladywell, Glasgow 35
Laing, James 243, 244
Lamb, Sir John 100, 155, 159, 192

Lambie, Helen (Nellie) *or* Gillon ix, 3, 5, 12, 13, 14, 15, 16, 18, 23-6, 28-30, 33, 38, 64, 65, 67, 68, 70-2, 73n, 80-2, 95-8, 104-6, 108-12, 122-4, 148, 149, 151-8, 161, 171-9, 183, 184, 186, 188, 191, 201, 202, 204, 208, 219, 220, 224, 225, 230-, 23, 233-7, 239, 240, 244-6, 249, 255-8, 267, 268, 270, 271, 273, 274, 277, 278, 284-7, 289, 290, 293, 294, 296, 297, 299-302, 304, 306, 318
Lamond, The Reverend Mr John 298
Lanark 225, 226, 315
High Street 226
Hyndford Road 226, 315
Lockhart Hospital 315
Roselands, Hyndford Road 226, 315
Lanarkshire 152, 176, 177
Land, Mrs Margaret 316
Laurie, Andrew Pollock 316
Laurie, James 316
Laurie, Margaret 316
Lawrie, Mrs Elizabeth (*née* Gilchrist) 33, 61, 62
Lee, Mrs Christina (*née* Gilchrist) 33, 61
Leeds 179
Lascelles Mount, Harehills, 179, 318
St James' Hospital, Burmantofts 179
Leeson, Detective Lieutenant George T 46
Leipzig, University of 19
Leschnik's *Peoria City Directory* 178
Leschziner, Adolf, Oscar's Father 48, 49
Leschziner, Mrs Lina (*see* Slater, Mrs Oscar)
Leschziner, Oscar Joseph (*see* Slater, Oscar)
Leschziner, Paula, Oscar's Mother 49
Letters, anonymous 288-90
Liberton, Lasswade 101
Liddell, George 11, 217
Liddell, Mrs Rowena Elizabeth Margaret (*née* Adams) 11, 217, 277, 315
Liddell's Pawnshop 41-3, 59
Life Begins at Midnight (Robert Colquhoun) 310

Lindsay, Frederic 280
Lindsay, John 115, 116
Lindsay, Superintendent Andrew Gow
124, 125, 129, 132, 138
Linklater, John 261-3
Little Wrestler 57
Littlejohn, Professor Harvey 82
Liverpool 34, 45, 47, 68, 73n, 75, 84,
111, 185, 187
Lime Street Railway Station, 45, 111
North Western Hotel, Lime Street
45, 111, 187
Liverpool Bar 68
Llandudno 315
Lloyds, Messrs 143n
London 42-5, 50, 51, 53-6, 68, 75, 112,
175, 185, 194, 243, 284, 290
Albemarle Street 53, 55
Albert Road, North Woolwich 282
Athenaeum 170
Bloomsbury 51, 194
Bouverie Street 160n
Buckingham Palace 114
Charing Cross Road 56
Denmark Street 56
Dover House, Whitehall 136
Dreadnought Seaman's
Hospital, Greenwich 282, 284, 295
Empire, Leicester Square, the
Promenade of 54
Fitzrovia 51
Greenwich 282
Hatton Garden 53
Imperial Hotel, Bloomsbury 194
Kings Cross 51
Limehouse 284
Little College Street,
Westminster, SW1 290, 295
Lord Advocate's Chambers 136
New Bond Street 243
Newman Street 55
Oxford Street 55
Soho 51
Sotheby's 243
Travellers Society Club, the,
Denmark Street 56
Victoria Street 147
Westminster Abbey 147
Whitehall 136, 154
Woolwich 34, 282, 284
Y.W.C.A. 194

Loreburn, Lord 92
Loughrane's Public House 205
Lucania, the 54
Lumsdane, Captain J 31, 295
Lusitania, the 45, 46, 86, 111
Lustgarten, Edgar 230, 231
Lyon, Detective Sergeant David 40, 41
Lyon, William, Advocate Depute 79

M

MacBrayne, Duncan 44, 108, 173, 184,
185, 188
Maccallum, Colin Gillies 107
Maccallum & Son, Boot & Shoe Makers,
Malcolm 32
Maccallum, Mary B 107
Macdonald, James, Miss Gilchrist's
solicitor of 2 Buckingham Terrace 33,
35, 65, 110, 297n
Macdonald, James, Dr Charteris's
solicitor of 8 Queens Crescent
109, 297n
MacDonald, Sir John Haye Athole, Lord
Kingsburgh 91n
MacDonald, Lewis 264, 265, 277
MacDonald, Ramsay 153, 159, 160, 190
MacKenna, P Fraser 143
Mackenzie, Kennethina 41
MacKenzie, Sir Compton 257, 258
Maclehose, Alexander 287n
MacMillan, Hugh Patison (Later Lord
MacMillan) 159
MacNab, John 241
MacNaghten, Sir Melville Leslie viii
Macpherson & Dunlop, SSC, Messrs
Norman 170, 172, 179
Macready's, Newsagent 6, 12
'Madeira', the 203
Magistrates, the Glasgow 118, 119,
257, 259, 265, 266
Magistrates' Committee, Glasgow 115,
118
Maidenhead 34
Mair, John 79
'Man Who Didn't, The', Jack House 236
Manchester 170
Marcus, B L, Michael 191n
Martein, Paul Jules 126
Martin, Annie Amelia (see Adams, Mrs
Annie Amelia)
Martin, Sir William 315

Mascot Club, the 58
McArthur, John 127-38, 140-4
McArthur, Mrs Maggie 141, 142
McCall, Dr Anthony 34
McCall, Mary Greer (née Gilchrist) 18,
    33, 34, 62, 64, 70, 104, 109, 206-8, 240,
    241, 275, 276, 281, 314
McClure, KC, Alexander Logan 79, 81-7,
    318
McColl, Mary Gilchrist (see McCall, Mary
    Greer)
McDonald, Alexander 130, 131
McGimpsey, Detective John 31, 33
McGuire, James 219, 220
McHaffie, Alexander Rankin 209
McHaffie, Annie 209, 210
McHaffie, Madge 210
McHaffie, Margaret 209
McHaffie, Mrs Margaret Dickson or
    209-10
McIntosh, Detective Constable Arthur
    133
McIntosh, Elizabeth (Lizzie) 16, 293
McKain, Bruce 280, 291
McKay, William 198
McKellar, Detective Sergeant John 124,
    130, 131
McLachlan, Jessie 235
McLaren, Peter Crawford 42, 43
McLean, Allan 38-40, 111, 148, 203
McLelland, James 65
McLelland, Mrs James 65
McLelland, Thomson & Towers Clerk,
    Writers, Messrs 65
McLeod, Warden D 90
McTear & Co, Messrs Robert 148n
McVicar, Detective Constable Duncan
    22
Meehan, Patrick (Paddy) Connelly 239,
    251, 252
Melbourne, Andrew 227, 285
Melvin, Detective Sergeant Charles 131
Merchant Navy 282
Metropolitan Police 44, 284
Midwives Institution, Oppeln 49
Millar, KC James Gardner 103, 104,
    106-9, 111, 112, 116, 121, 122, 149,
    154, 155, 156n, 254, 256
Miller, Hugh Gordon 66, 72-4, 149, 174,
    277
Miller's in Cambridge Street, Andrew
    58

Millican, Detective Constable John 40-1
Milne, Miss Jean 119-20
Minstead, Hampshire 243
Mitchell, William, Advocate Depute 134
Moffat 144
Monte Carlo 43, 44, 50, 54
Montgomery, Detective Sergeant John
    124, 125, 131
Morison, KC, Thomas Brash, Advocate
    Depute 79, 318
Morland, Nigel 224, 225, 239, 240
Morton, George, Advocate Depute
    137-38
MOSC Club (see Sloper Club)
Moss Empire Palace Theatre 57n
Motherwell 67, 277
Motor Club, the 58, 163, 289, 294
Moudie, the (see Cameron, Hugh)
Mr Oscar (see Oscar, Mr)
Muir, James Hamilton 313
Munro, Robert, Lord Advocate (later
    Lord Alness) 134, 136-8, 173, 184
Murray, Chief Detective Inspector
    George 130-4
Musicians' Union, the 302

N
Nairn, Andrew 84, 215, 216
Neill, Police Constable William 12, 16,
    17, 228, 229
New Zealand 290, 295
Newman, Levi 177, 270
News Chronicle 160
Nice 50, 54
Notable British Trials Series 313n
Notable Scottish Trials Series 93 160,
    182, 206, 313n
Nugent, Patrick 67, 96, 97, 214, 233,
    244, 267, 268, 277, 286, 290, 294

O
Oban 316
Ocean Chambers 97
Oder, Upper Silesia, the River 48
Ogg, Archie C A 227, 257
On Moral Courage (Compton MacKenzie)
    258
On Soul and Conscience: The Medical
    Expert and Crime (Brenda M White &
    M Anne Crowther) 251
Opole, Katowice 49n
Ord, Dr John Smith McLaren 315

Ord, Superintendent John 21,
24-6, 31-3, 37-9, 44, 105, 108, 111,
121-4, 162, 163, 201, 203, 255, 284, 288,
295, 315, 317
Orr, Chief Constable John 265, 266
Orr, Chief Superintendent John 104,
105, 108, 113, 114, 123, 124, 132, 133, 317
Oscar, Mr 38-41, 148, 203
'Oscar Slater: The Facts at Last' series
of articles by Jack House 233-5, 238
Oscar Slater: The Great Suspect by Peter
Hunt 139, 146n, 222, 223n
Oscar Slater: The Mystery Solved by
Thomas Toughill 280
Owen, Professor Sir Richard 95

P
Paignton, Devon 314
Palmer, Ernest Charles Clephan 160-2,
164, 168, 224
Paradise, Isaac 56n
Paris 47, 50, 55, 75
Park, Helen 147, 156
Park, William 2, 146-51, 154, 156, 160,
166, 168, 170, 172, 175, 176, 190, 191,
200, 243-7
Parliament, the English 100, 159, 169
Pattern of Murder (Nigel Morland) 225
Paul Harris Publishing, Edinburgh 239
Pentland, Secretary for Scotland, Lord,
90, 91, 94, 100, 252, 288, 293, 318
Perry, Dr Robert 18, 28, 211
Perry, Mrs Jane Mary Robertina Sim or
27, 211
Peterhead Convict Prison 92, 93, 119,
144, 145, 167, 193, 194, 198, 200, 297,
309, 319
Peterhead Railway Station 167
Phillips, Alastair 238, 248, 249, 251-5,
257, 260
Phillips, Amy (Rabbi Phillips'
daughter) 168, 173
Phillips, Mrs (Rabbi Phillips' wife)
168, 173, 187
Phillips, Rabbi, The Reverend Mr
Eleazer Philip 77, 89, 99, 167, 173,
187, 318
Phillips, William Mowat 223n, 255, 256,
257, 297
Pierrepoint, Henry 90
Pilgrim, The (see Palmer, Ernest
Charles Clephan)

Pinckley, Deputy United States
Marshall John William M 174, 182,
188
Pittsburgh Press, 152,
Pittsburgh, Pennsylvania 151, 155, 157
Police Information Book 227, 227n, 244
Polks Peoria City Directory 178
Post Office Savings Bank 59
Powell, Detective Inspector William
39, 40, 42
Practical Treatise on the Criminal Law of
Scotland, A (Sir J H A MacDonald
[Lord Justice Clerk]) 91n
Prestwick 197, 278
Pritchard, Dr Edward William 235
Psychic Bookshop, 147, 191
Pyper, Detective Inspector John 22, 25,
26, 29, 45, 65, 68, 71, 75, 77, 81, 105,
109, 110, 162-4, 241, 249, 277, 317

Q
Quest for Jack the Ripper, The by Richard
Whittington-Egan 305n

R
R.B. 223, 224
Ramsey, Ted 249-51, 267-71, 275-9, 291
Rankin, Inspector Alexander 29
Ratcliffe, John Hardie 302
Ratcliffe, William A 121, 131, 201, 202,
302n
Rattmann, Max aka Schmidt, George
45, 56, 57, 83, 86
Real World of Sherlock Holmes, The (Peter
Costello) 223n, 296, 298
Reid, Percy 84
Reid, Samuel 84, 168, 203-5
Reis & Co, Messrs Charles L 128, 130-
6, 138, 142, 143
Reynolds News 230
Rice-Davies, Mandy 294
Ritchie, Murray 272-4, 276
Robertson, Archibald 268, 275
Robertson, Mrs Helen 25, 105, 106
Robertson, Dr William George
Aitchison 84
Rogers, Robert 53, 55, 60
Rose, P J 153, 154
Ross, Mrs Rachel 252n
Rossiter, H B 314
Rothesay 203
Robertson, Mrs Helen 25, 105, 106

Roughhead W S, William 2, 80, 86, 93, 94, 96, 97, 100, 102, 104, 115, 120, 152, 154, 160, 161, 170, 172, 174, 175, 182, 187, 191, 193, 200, 206, 222, 224, 225, 231, 246

Royal Highlanders 101

Royal Scots Fusiliers 125

Rue des Trois-Fréres, Montmartre 75n

Runaway Match, the, Bryant & May 23, 26, 236, 306

Russell, George William 1

Russell, Ruby 40

Rutherford, Dr Thomas 198

S

Sabin, George 41, 59

Salter, Mrs (see Antoine, Andrée)

Salthouse Head 193

Salvesen, Lord 310

Sandilands, Andrew 103, 112

Sando, Anna (see Antoine, Andrée)

Sando, Mrs Anna 46, 47

Sando, Otto (see Slater, Oscar)

Sands, Lord 173

Sandy Hook 46

Saunders, George 239

Sayers, George 282

Scarborough, Yorkshire 54

Schad, Charles 194

Schad, Miss Lina Wilhemina (see Slater, Mrs Oscar)

Schmalz, Katharina 40, 42-4, 55, 56, 83, 86, 99

Schmidt, George, aka Rattmann, Max (See Rattmann, Max)

Schuttenberg, Herr 49

Scotland on Sunday 280n

Scotland Yard 123, 154, 155

Scotsman, the 98, 239, 247

Scott, John M 261, 262, 266

Scottish Court of Criminal Appeal 159, 169

Scottish Daily Express 259

Scottish Daily Mail 243, 246, 255, 297

Scottish Field, 240

Scottish Office, the 100, 153, 154, 156, 159, 261

Scottish Orchestra 236, 302

Scottish Records Office 272

Scottish Sunday Express 308

Secret Inquiry, the 103, 116, 119, 241, 247, 254, 265, 273

Shakespeare, William 297

Shanghai 273

Shaughnessy & Sons, Writers, Messrs Joseph 77

Shaughnessy, Alexander 2, 93-7, 101, 102, 111, 115, 150, 202

Shaughnessy, John 96n

Shaw, S S C Mr 117

Shields, Commissioner John A 66, 71-4, 174

Shotts, Lanarkshire 178

Sikes, Bill 307

Sitwell, Sacheverell 3

Slater, Oscar Joseph, (Leschziner) vii, ix, 2, 40, 41, 43-8, 60, 66, 68, 71-96, 98-100, 103, 105, 106, 108, 111, 115, 116, 118-120, 122, 124, 126, 127, 140, 142, 144-53, 155, 156, 159, 160-77, 180, 182-204, 206, 208-16, 218, 220-3, 225-7, 230-2, 235, 236, 238, 239, 241, 243-54, 256-8, 260, 263, 265-7, 270-81, 285-91, 293-6, 298-301, 301n 302, 303, 305, 307-9, 311, 313, 315, 317, 318

Slater, Oscar, Son of 250

Slater, the first Mrs Oscar (Mary Marie or May Curtis Pryor) 53-5, 86

Slater, the second Mrs Oscar ix, 194-9, 318

Sloper Club, the 38, 41, 45, 58, 289, 294

Sloper, Ally 58

Smith, Jewellers, Messrs James 133-5, 138, 143

Smith, Madeleine 67, 235

Soldier, the 57

Sommerville & Milne, Ltd. Glasgow 239

Sommerville, Alexander Macdonald 239

Sorley, Councillor William 35, 43

Sorley's Pawnbrokers Shop 43

Speirs, Ewing 2, 77, 90, 93, 111, 318

Spilsbury, Sir Bernard 174

Square Mile of Murder (Jack House) 235, 236, 238, 240

St Andrews, Fife 241, 255

Kennedy Gardens 255n

University of St Andrews 19, 222, 249

Stark, Ian 266

Stark, Mrs Nancy 266
Stashower, Daniel 146n
Stationery Office, the 114
Stephen, Sir Herbert 146
Stevenson, James Verdier, Chief
 Constable of Glasgow 31, 38, 46,
 115-20, 122, 124, 129, 132, 135-8, 142,
 143, 201, 203, 214, 264, 265
Stewart & McDonald, Messrs 19
Stewart, John 65, 268, 275
Stewart, Mrs Gertrude McLaren Ord *or*
 317
Stirling 126
 Stirling Police 126
Stirton, Detective Lieutenant George
 Christie 179, 180
Stobcross Quay 76
Stranger in the Hall (Ted Ramsey) 267,
 276
Strathclyde Police 261
Strathclyde Regional Archives 65, 227n
Strathclyde, Lord (*see* Ure, Alexander)
Strathern, John Drummond 179
Struthers & Stewart, Stockbrokers,
 Messrs 65
Stuart & Stuart, House Furnishers,
 Messrs 56
Such Bad Company by George Forbes &
Sunday Express, the 308, 310
Sunday Mail, the 175, 176, 189
Sunday Pictorial, the 151
Sunday Times, the 190
Sword, Mary (*see* Barrowman, Mary)
Symons, A J A 270
Symons, Arthur

T

Tail o' the Bank, off Greenock 76
*Teller of Tales: The Life of Arthur Conan
 Doyle* (Stashower) 146n
Tenth Hussars 282
*The Thin Blue Line: The Story of the City of
 Glasgow Police* (Douglas Grant) 263n
Thomson & McLelland, Writers, Messrs
 65
Thomson, Alex 285
Times, the 99, 272
Torhouse, Wigtownshire 162, 317, 318
Toughill, Thomas 91, 261, 278, 280,
 281n, 285-97
Trench, Detective Lieutenant John

Thomson vii, 2, 67, 101-44, 146, 156n,
 161-3, 200-2, 213, 238, 240, 244, 247,
 248, 248n, 249, 252-68, 269n, 270,
 272-9, 286, 294, 296, 309, 312
Trench, Mrs Margaret Arthur 260, 318
Trench, Mrs Margaret Thomson *or* 121
Trench, Robert 262
'Trench's Last Case', series of articles
 by Jack House 258
Trial of Oscar Slater (*Notable British Trials*
 series) 80
Trial of Oscar Slater (*Notable Scottish Trials*
 series) 93, 206, 222, 241
Trials of Oscar Slater, BBC Television
 Programme 240
Truth 190
Truth About Oscar Slater, The (William
 Park) 47, 148, 151, 156, 157n, 159,
 191, 222
Tulloch, Elizabeth 239

U

Ure, KC, MP Alexander, Lord Advocate
 (later Lord Strathclyde) vii, 78-87,
 98, 147, 148, 150, 161, 162, 164, 171,
 183-6, 286-91, 295
Urquhart, Rob 263

V

Valentine, Police Constable David 51
Veitch, Dr Alexander 84
Very Quiet Street, A (Frank Kuppner)
 270, 271
'Very Respectable Murder, A', article by
 Maggie Allen 240

W

Waldie, John 88
Walker, Police Constable Christopher
 210, 211
Wallace, Edgar 225
Walsh, Tom 260, 271-6
Walters, Jeanetta or Jeanette 213-5
Warner, Charles 119, 120
Warnock, Chief Sheriff Criminal Officer,
 William 68, 75, 77, 163, 173
Watson, William KC, MP (Lord
 Advocate) 153-5, 162, 174, 187
Webster, Jack 267
Weekly Mail, the 78, 92
Weekly News, the 126, 140, 142

Weekly Record, the 165n
Weir, Chief Detective Inspector Duncan 126, 133, 137, 143
West Kilbride 314, 317
   Cubrieshaw Hall Nursing Home, West Kilbride 314
Westminster Gazette, the 99
When the Scot Smiles in Literature and in Life (Archibald Charteris) 287n, 314
White Paper, the Parliamentary 114-7
White, Brenda M 251
White, Catherine 41
Whyte, Agnes Panton 194
Wigan, Lancashire 178
Willy the Artist 57
Wilson & Wood, Chemists, Messrs 228
Wilson, Agnes Cameron Findlay 225, 226
Wilson, Glasgow gang member 311
Wilson, Richard 247
Wilson, William Scott Branks 226
Wilson's, the Sauchiehall Street Grocer, John 44
Wingate, Birrell & Company 204
'Woman In the Case', series of articles by Edgar Lustgarten 230
Wood, Thomas McKinnon 100, 102, 103, 111, 116-9, 146, 247, 249, 254, 318
Wright, Dr John 18, 250, 251
Wylie & Lochhead, Undertakers, Messrs 34
Wyper's Public House 203-5

Y
Yorkhill 76
Young, Bailie John H 259, 261, 263, 264
Young, William Grant 219, 220

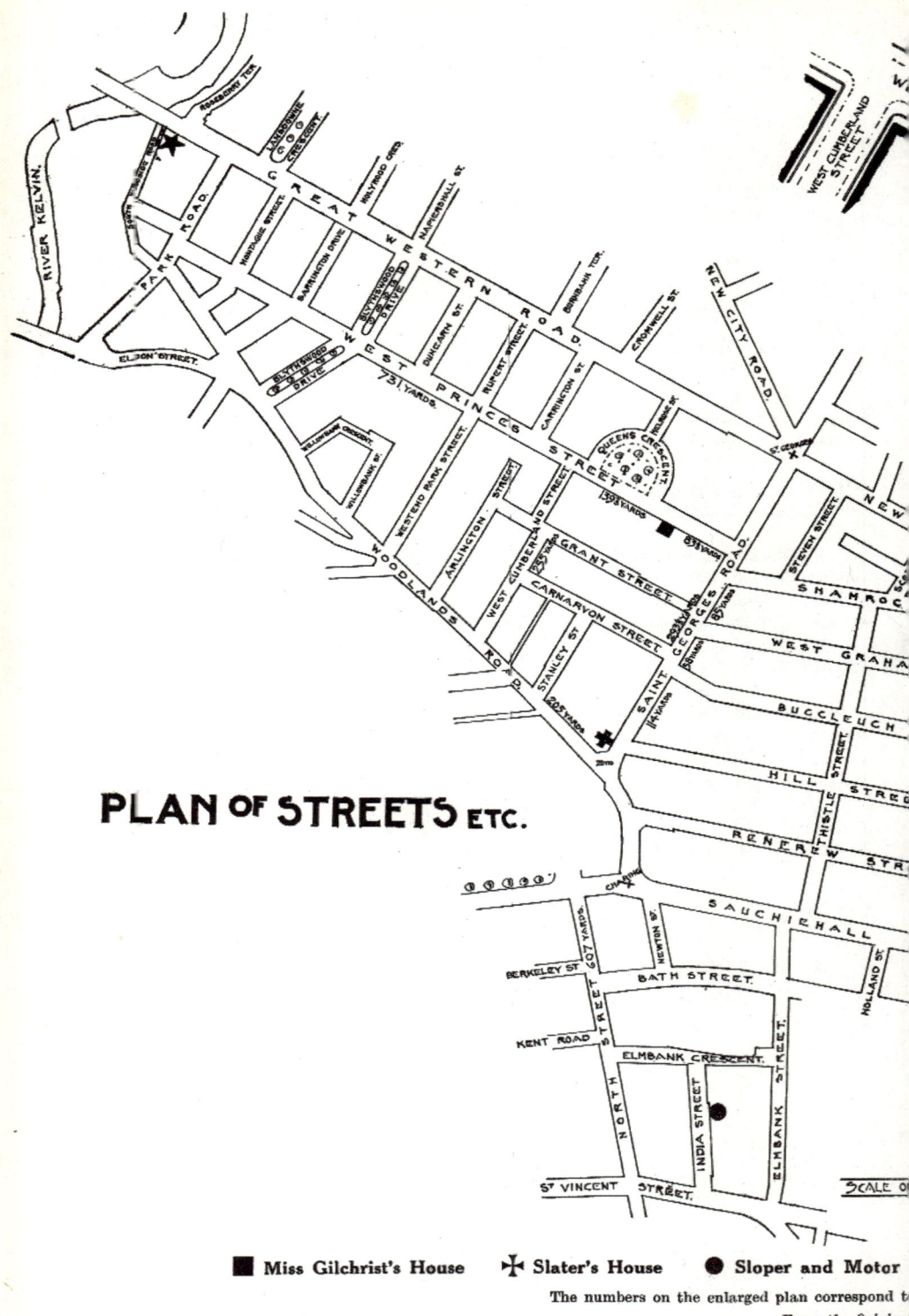

PLAN OF STREETS ETC.

RIVER KELVIN

WEST CUMBERLAND STREET

GREAT WESTERN ROAD

ROSEBERRY TER.

LANSDOWNE CRESCENT

HAMILTON STREET

WILTROAD CRES.

NAPIERHILL ST.

SOUTH WOODSIDE ROAD

PARK ROAD

BARRINGTON DRIVE

BLYTHSWOOD HOLDING HOUSE

BURNBANK TER.

CROMWELL ST.

NEW CITY ROAD

ELDON STREET

BLYTHSWOOD DRIVE W.

WEST PRINCES STREET

DUNEARN ST.

RUPERT STREET

CARRINGTON ST.

MELROSE ST.

QUEENS CRESCENT

ST. GEORGES

KELVINBANK CRESCENT

WEST END PARK STREET

ARLINGTON STREET

WEST CUMBERLAND STREET

GRANT STREET

GEORGES ROAD

STEVEN STREET

NEW

SHAMROC

WOODLANDS ROAD

CARNARVON STREET

WEST GRAHA

STANLEY ST

SAINT

BUCCLEUCH

HILL STRE

THISTLE STREET

RENFREW STR

SAUCHIEHALL

BERKELEY ST

NEWTON ST

NORTH STREET

BATH STREET

HOLLAND ST

KENT ROAD

ELMBANK CRESCENT

INDIA STREET

ELMBANK STREET

ST VINCENT STREET

SCALE O

731 YARDS

■ **Miss Gilchrist's House**   ✝ **Slater's House**   ● **Sloper and Motor**

The numbers on the enlarged plan correspond t

From the Origina